개정판

Essence of English Grammar

성 은 경

에센스영문법

한국외국어대학교 출판부

머리말

흔히 영어를 공부하는 데 있어서 말하기와 듣기의 중요성을 강조하면서 영문법에 대해서는 소홀히 여기는 경향이 있습니다. 그러나 영문법을 제대로 익히지 못하면 말하기, 읽기, 듣기, 쓰기 모두를 제대로 하기가 어렵습니다. 영어 문장을 문법에 맞게 제대로 쓸 수 있어야 비로소 자신의 뜻을 누구에게나 정확하고 명료하게 전달할 수가 있습니다. 영문법을 정확히 아는 것만큼, 짧은 시간 내에 영어구사 능력을 일정 수준 이상으로 올려 놓는 효과적인 방법도 없습니다.

이 책은 2006년에 출간된 '에센스 영문법'의 개정판입니다. 영어를 배우는 한국 학생들 입장에서, 영문법 가운데 '이것만은 확실하게 알고 가자'는 진수(essence)들을 익히는데 중점을 두었습니다. 초판에 없는 Warm-up, Reading, Word challenge, Reveiw test 부분 등을 새로 넣었고, 예문들을 좀 더 보강하였습니다. 딱딱하기 쉬운 영문법의 특성을 고려하여, 재미있는 이야기, 실용적인 예문, 다양한 task들을 많이 포함시키고자 힘썼습니다. 부록인 MP3 CD에는 이 책에 나오는 모든 문장이 원어민의 음성 파일 형태로 들어 있습니다. Listening과 발음 연습을 위한 자료로 활용되길 기대합니다.

전체 13개로 된 chapter들은 각각 Warm-up, Grammar, Reading, Word challenge, Practice, Review test, Supplementary reading 등으로 구성되어 있습니다. Warm-up에서는 미드보다 더 흥미진진한 Brett, Aaron & Camille의 이야기를 통하여 다양한 표현과 문법을 익힐 수 있도록 꾸몄습니다. Grammar 부분에서는 핵심적인 문법 사항을 Focus 1, 2 & 3으로 나누어 공부하게 됩니다. Reading에서는 재미있는 주제의 글을 읽으면서 독해, 어휘, 문법을 동시에 익히게 됩니다. Word challenge에서는 우리가 흔히 접하면서도 쉽게 혼동하는 단어들의 정확한 쓰임을 배우게 됩니다. Practice에서는 각 주차에서 나온 문법사항들을 문제를 통해 총 정리하게 됩니다. 각 주차의 마지막에는 Review test를 넣었습니다. 나아가 관련 내용을 더 공부하고 싶은 학생들을 위해서 Supplementary reading을 소개하였습니다. 또한 영어권 문화를 엿볼 수 있는 Culture corner를 각 과마다 수록하였습니다.

모쪼록 이 책이 영어의 기본 골격을 가장 탄탄하게 익히는데 도움이 되기를 바랍니다. 끝으로 이 책이 나오기까지 많은 도움을 준 Joseph Branca, 교정을 맡아 수고해 준 김수민 조교, 그리고 한국외국어대학교 출판부 여러분에게 감사를 드립니다.

2010년 3월

성 은 경

CONTENTS

Tenses 01 Unit

Introduction

Topic: An unexpected call (뜻밖의 전화)

Lesson objectives:

To understand verb tenses (동사 시제 이해하기)

- simple present/past/future (단순 현재, 과거, 미래)
- present/past/future progressive (현재, 과거, 미래 진행)
- present/past/future perfect (현재, 과거, 미래 완료)

WARM-UP

(On the telephone, Brett and Aaron talk for the first time in months. At first, there is some awkwardness. But after the initial surprise, they fall into a more comfortable conversation.)

Brett : Hi. Aaron?

Aaron : Yes. This is him.

Brett : Hey, it's Brett (simple present).

Aaron : Oh, hi. I didn't recognize your voice. (simple past)

Brett : Well, it's been a while since we've talked. (present perfect) How are you?

Aaron : I'm good. Are you still living in Los Angeles?

Brett : Only until next week. My company is transferring me back to the home office. (present progressive) Sometimes it's hard to believe I will have been here for over a year this week.

Aaron : Well, it will be good to have you back. But I'm sure you're going to miss the sunny California weather. It's getting cold here in New York (present progressive).

Brett : I'm so busy; I don't have much time to enjoy it anyway.

Aaron : Well, it's all the same then.

Brett : Have you seen any of the other guys recently? It's been a while since I've talked to anyone back home. (present perfect)

Aaron : I saw Dan a few weeks ago; we were wondering about you (past progressive).

Brett : Oh, really? How's he doing?

Aaron : He's good, I guess. He had been unemployed for a long time (past perfect). But now he's got a part in a local theater production. He's still dreaming about becoming a famous actor. (present progressive)

Brett : Well, I guess everyone has grown apart.

Aaron : Yeah. It's hard to find the time these days.

Brett : Listen, I have to get back to work. But I wanted to see if you have time to get dinner one night next week.

Aaron : Sure, for you, I will find some time. (simple future)

Brett : All right, well, I'll give you a call when I get settled in.

Aaron : Oh, and I almost forgot, there's someone I really want you to meet.

Brett : Ah, it sounds like you have a new girlfriend.

Aaron : We only met a few weeks ago. (simple past) But I'll tell you more about that later on.

Brett : I'll talk to you next week then.

Aaron : Okay, talk to you then.

Brett : Bye.

Aaron : Bye.

Translation

(Brett와 Aaron은 몇 달 만에 처음으로 전화상으로 대화를 한다. 처음에는 약간의 어색함이 있다. 처음에는 약간 놀라지만 그들은 점점 더 편안한 대화를 나누게 된다.)

Brett : 안녕 Aaron?
Aaron : 네. 접니다.
Brett : 야, 나 Brett이야.
Aaron : 어, 안녕. 네 목소리인 줄 몰랐어.
Brett : 뭐, 우리가 얘기 한지가 오래 됐으니까. 잘 있었니?
Aaron : 응 잘 있었어. 넌 여전히 Los Angeles에 살고 있니?
Brett : 다음 주까지만 있을 거야. 회사에서 나를 다시 본사로 발령 내고 있는 중이야. 이번 주가 되면 이 곳에 내가 온 지도 일 년이 된다는 것이 믿기지가 않다.
Aaron : 그래, 돌아온다니 잘 되었구나. 그래도 분명히 California의 맑은 날씨를 그리워할 것 같은데. 여기 New York은 점점 추워지고 있거든.
Brett : 나는 너무 바빠. 어차피 그런 날씨를 즐길 시간도 없어.
Aaron : 그럼 뭐 마찬가지겠구나.
Brett : 최근에 다른 애들은 좀 만나봤니? 고향에 있는 애들이랑 얘기해 본지가 오래 됐거든.
Aaron : 몇 주전에 Dan을 봤어 우리는 네가 어떻게 지내는지 궁금해 했었지.
Brett : 정말? 그는 어떻게 지내니?
Aaron : 잘 지내는 것 같아. 그는 오랫동안 취직이 안 되었었지. 그러나 지금은 지방 영화제작사에서 일자리를 얻었어. 그는 여전히 유명한 배우가 되기를 꿈꾸고 있어.
Brett : 그래, 모두들 각자의 일 때문에 바쁘구나.
Aaron : 응. 요즘에는 시간 잡기가 힘들지.
Brett : 나 자리로 가서 일해야겠다. 다음주에 한 번 너와 저녁식사를 같이 하고 싶은데 시간이 시간 되는지 모르겠다.
Aaron : 물론이지, 난 시간 낼 수 있을거야.
Brett : 좋아, 그럼 내가 정리가 좀 되면 전화할께.
Aaron : 아, 그리고 잊어버릴 뻔했는데 너한테 꼭 보여주고 싶은 사람이 있어.
Brett : 여자친구가 생겼나보구나.
Aaron : 몇 주전에 만나게 됐어. 자세한 얘기는 나중에 할께.
Brett : 그럼 다음주에 얘기하자.
Aaron : 그래, 그때 얘기하자.
Brett : 안녕.
Aaron : 안녕.

Comprehension Check

1. Why is Brett going back to New York?
   (a) to visit a friend
   (b) to visit his girlfriend
   (c) his company is transferring him to an office there
   (d) for a short business trip

2. Brett and Aaron are most likely:

(a) old friends

(b) business acquaintances

(c) complete strangers

(d) on a sports team together

3. The purpose of this call is:

(a) to make dinner plans

(b) to create a sales lead

(c) to catch up with an old friend

(d) both (a) and (c)

4. From the dialogue, we can guess that Dan is probably a(n):

(a) adversary

(b) celebrity

(c) mutual friend

(d) Aaron's brother

Useful Expressions

In this dialogue	Explanation
1. It's been a while since we've talked.	1. At the beginning of the dialogue, Aaron doesn't recognize Brett's voice. And Brett responds casually that it has been a while since they've talked. This expression is most often used between friends when some time has passed and there has been little contact between them. Its meaning is the same as the expression, "It's been a while since we talked," but only slightly more colloquial.

In this dialogue	Explanation
2. It's hard to believe I will have been here for a year this week.	2. "Hard to believe," is used to mean thata situation or fact seems untrue. This expression can be used in both a positive, as in the dialogue, and negative context. In both, it is a means to express doubt. An example of its usage in a negative context might be a mother questioning her son. "It's hard to believe you didn't eat the cookies, since there are none left and no one else was home,"she could say if she suspected he was lying.
3. I guess everyone has grown apart.	3. The expression "grown apart" can be used to convey that some distance, figuratively speaking, has come between people. "We've grown apart," is simply another way to say "we're not that close anymore." In this case, we might also say that the guys have gone separate ways.
4. I'll give you a call when I get settled in.	4. The expression "settled in" refers to making oneself comfortable after some travels or ordeals. In the process of settling in, one might wash up, unpack, have a rest, or even catch up on emails. Brett might have also said, "I'll give you a call when I get back into town." But he's not planning to call immediately; he'd like some personal time first.

Grammar

Focus 1 Simple tense (단순시제)

01 simple present (단순현재)

일반적인 일, 언제나 일어나는 일, 사실 등에 대해서 말할 때 단순 현재 시제를 씁니다. 어떠한 행위가 말하는 그 순간에 일어나는지 하는 것은 중요하지 않습니다.

(1) 현재의 사실

- I'm so busy; I don't have enough time to enjoy it.

(나는 너무 바빠서 여유를 즐길 시간도 없습니다.)

- I have to get back to work.
  (일하러 돌아가야 합니다.)
- She lives in Thailand.
  (그녀는 태국에 삽니다.)
- The house is empty.
  (집이 비어있습니다.)
- He articulates himself well.
  (그는 자신을 명료하게 잘 표현합니다.)

(2) 현재의 습관, 직업, 성격

- Daniel goes to work five days a week.
  (Daniel은 주 5일 근무를 합니다.)
- He teaches English at an academy.
  (.그는 학원에서 영어를 가르칩니다.)
- She never takes cream in her coffee.
  (그녀는 커피에 절대로 크림을 넣지 않습니다.)

cf) always, usually, often, never 등의 빈도 부사는 주동사 (main verb) 앞에 옵니다.

- She always makes too many promises.
  (그녀는 항상 너무 많은 약속을 만듭니다.)

(3) 불변의 진리

- Water freezes at 32° F (32 degrees Fahrenheit).
  (물은 화씨 32도에서 업니다.)
- Honesty is the best policy.
  (정직이 최고의 정책입니다.)
- One lie often breeds another.
  (거짓말은 또 다른 거짓말을 낳습니다.)
- The current crisis stems from an old problem.
  (현재의 위기는 과거의 문제로부터 시작된 것입니다.)

(4) 과거 대용

역사적 사실이나 옛사람의 말을 인용할 때 현재 시제를 써서 생동감 있는 표현이 되도록 합니다.

- Now Caesar leaves Gaul, crosses the Rubicon and enters Italy.
  (Caesar는 이제 Gaul을 떠나 Rubicon강을 건너서 이탈리아로 들어섭니다.)
- Dryden says that none but the brave deserve the fair.
  (Dryden은 용감한 자만이 미인을 차지할 자격이 있다고 말합니다.)

(5) 미래 대용

왕래발착을 나타내는 동사(go, come, start, leave, arrive, depart, return, ride)나 시간, 조건을 나타내는 부사절에서 현재 시제를 씁니다.

- He leaves for Japan next week.
  (그는 다음 주에 일본으로 떠납니다.)
- We are having a party this Saturday.
  (우리는 이번 토요일에 파티를 할 계획입니다.)
- I'll give you a call when I get settled in.
  (내가 정리가 좀 되면 전화를 하겠습니다.)
- We will not go hiking if it rains tomorrow.
  (내일 비가 오면 우리는 하이킹을 가지 않을 것입니다.)

cf) I want to know if it will rain tomorrow.
(내일 비가 올 것인지 알고 싶습니다.)

02 simple past (단순과거)

(1) 과거의 동작, 상태, 습관

- I didn't recognize your voice.
  (당신 목소리인줄 몰랐습니다.)
- We only met a few weeks ago.
  (우리는 불과 몇 주전에 만났습니다.)
- The company grew rapidly during the 1990s.
  (그 회사는 1990년대에 급속히 성장했습니다.)
- John and Sandra were sick last week.
  (John과 Sandra는 지난 주에 아팠습니다.)
- We used to visit our grandparents every summer.
  (우리는 매 여름마다 조부모님을 방문하곤 했습니다.)
- Math always came easy to her.
  (그녀에게 수학은 항상 쉬웠습니다.)

(2) 역사적 사실

- He said that World War II broke out in 1939.
  (그는 2차 세계대전이 1939년에 일어났다고 말했습니다.)

(3) 가정법 과거

현재 사실을 가정할 때 과거시제를 씁니다.

- If I were you, I would not accept the offer.
  (내가 당신이라면, 나는 그 제안을 받아들이지 않을 것입니다.)
- What would you do if you had a million dollars?
  (당신이 100만 달러를 갖게 된다면 무엇을 하겠습니까?)

03 simple future (단순미래)

- I'll find some time for you.
  (내가 당신을 위해 시간을 한번 내보겠습니다.)
- We're going to get a new car soon.
  (우리는 곧 새 차를 살 것입니다.)
- The weather will be warm and sunny tomorrow.
  (내일은 따뜻하고 맑은 날씨가 될 것입니다.)
- The candidate will accept his nomination at a London hotel.
  (지원자는 London호텔에서 그의 임명 수락을 할 것입니다.)

cf) 미래를 나타낼 때 will대신에 be going to를 쓸 수도 있습니다. 대개의 경우, 뜻의 차이 없이 바꾸어 씁니다. 그러나, 곧 일어날 일을 예측하거나 미리 계획한 일을 말할 때는 be going to를 많이 쓰고, 즉석에서 결정한 일에 대해 얘기할 때는 will을 사용하는 것이 더 자연스럽습니다.

- We're going to spend the month of August in Europe.
  (우리는 8월을 유럽에서 보낼 것입니다.)
- A: I think somebody is knocking on the door.
  (누군가 문을 두드리는 것 같습니다.)
  B: I'll go and check.
  (내가 가서 살펴 보겠습니다.)

Task 1

Choose the best word from the box to complete each sentence. Some words can be used more than one time.

sing	sang	sung	will	sing	sings

1. I _______ at the school fair two days ago.
2. Katie usually ________ for me when I feel down.
3. I didn't ____ today but I _____ at the music festival next week.

Focus 2 Progressive (진행형)

'be + ~ing'로 표현되는 진행형은 be동사의 현재 및 과거형으로 현재진행과 과거진행을 만들고, 미래를 나타내는 will/shall과 결합하여 미래진행형을 만듭니다.

01 present progressive (현재진행)

말하고 있는 그 순간에 진행되고 있는 일이나 일시적인 상황을 표현할 때 현재 진행형을 씁니다.

(1) 현재 동작의 진행이나 일시적 상황

- My company is transferring me back to the home office.
  (회사에서 나를 다시 본사로 발령 내고 있습니다.)
- It's getting cold here in New York.
  (여기 New York은 점점 추워지고 있습니다.)
- They are talking in the room.
  (그들은 방에서 이야기하고 있습니다.)
- We are staying at a wonderful hotel.
  (우리는 훌륭한 호텔에 머물고 있습니다.)
- They are currently debating next year's budget.
  (그들은 지금 내년도 예산을 논의하고 있습니다.)

cf) 말하는 그 순간에 일어나고 있는 것은 아니지만, 그 즈음에 진행되는 일을 표현할 때도 진행형을 쓸 수 있습니다.
Jenny wants to work in Spain, so she is studying Spanish.
(Jenny는 스페인에서 일하고 싶어 합니다. 그래서 스페인어를 공부하고 있습니다.)

(2) 습관적인 행위

always, forever, continually, constantly 등의 부사와 함께 쓰이며, 화자의 불만을 나타내기도 합니다. 즉, 화자가 생각할 때 지나칠 정도로 자주 일어나는 일을 표현하는 것입니다.

- You are always interrupting me.
  (당신은 항상 나를 방해합니다.)
- He is continually making poor excuses.
  (그는 항상 서투른 핑계를 냅니다.)
- Politics in this country are constantly becoming more corrupt.
  (이 나라의 정치는 계속 부패해가고 있습니다.)
- She is forever listening to the same song.
  (그녀는 계속 같은 노래를 듣고 있습니다.)

cf) I always go to work by car. (O)
I'm always going to work by car. (X)

(3) 미래 대용

이미 예정하고 있는 일에 대해서 말할 때 현재 진행형으로 미래를 표현합니다.

- Jack is having a party next Saturday.
  (Jack은 다음 토요일에 파티를 열 것입니다.)
- We're getting married.
  (우리는 결혼할 것입니다.)
- He's filing the paperwork tomorrow morning.
  (그는 내일 아침에 서류를 제출할 것이다.)
- We're announcing the merger at a news conference this afternoon.
  (우리는 오후 기자회견에서 합병을 알릴 것이다.)

02 past progressive (과거진행)

(1) 과거 동작의 진행

어떤 일을 하는 중에 다른 일이 일어난 것을 표현하기 위해서 과거형과 과거진행형을 함께 사용하기도 합니다.

- I saw Dan a few weeks ago. We were wondering about you.
  (나는 몇 주전에 Dan을 봤습니다. 우리는 당신에 대해서 궁금해했습니다.)
- We were watching TV when the doorbell rang.
  (초인종이 울렸을 때 우리는 TV를 보고 있었습니다.)
- At 4:30 he was still waiting for the bus.
  (그는 4:30에 여전히 버스를 기다리고 있었습니다.)
- He was getting better at the violin, but stopped practicing.
  (그의 바이올린 연주 실력은 계속 향상되고 있었으나 연습을 그만두게 되었습니다.)

(2) 과거 시점에서 반복되거나 변화되는 것

- The boy was coughing all night long.
  (소년은 밤새 기침을 했습니다.)
- The children were growing quickly.
  (아이들은 빠르게 성장하고 있었습니다.)
- The story was getting interesting.
  (그 이야기는 점점 재미있어 졌습니다.)

03 future progressive (미래진행)

미래 시점에서 진행되는 것

- She will be waiting for you when you get home tonight.
  (오늘 밤 집에 도착하면 그녀가 당신을 기다리고 있을 것입니다.)
- We will be hosting a fundraiser for cancer awareness.
  (우리는 암 예방을 위한 모금행사를 개최할 것입니다.)

cf) 진행형으로 잘 쓰이지 않는 동사

- 느낌(feeling) 이나 감정(emotion)을 나타내는 동사
  ⇒ love, like, hate, prefer, appreciate, want, dislike
  ⇒ 그러나 love, hate, like 등은 구어체에서 진행형으로 쓰이기도 함
  ex) I'm loving this chocolate cake. / I'm hating my job these days.
- 감각(sense)을 표현하는 동사
  ⇒ see, hear, taste, smell
  ⇒ 그러나 see, hear, taste 등은 구어체에서 진행형으로 쓰이기도 함
  ex) I'm seeing the manager soon. / He was not hearing what I was saying.
- 지식, 의견, 믿음을 나타내는 동사
  ⇒ think, understand, believe, know
  ⇒ 그러나 think, understand 등은 구어체에서 진행형으로 쓰이기도 함
  ex) What are you thinking about? / I'm not understanding you very well.
- 소유(possession)를 표시하는 동사
  ⇒ have, own, belong, possess
  ⇒ 그러나 have, own 등은 구어체에서 진행형으로 쓰이기도 함
  ex) We're having a great time. / The Doosan Bears are owning this game.
- 그 외 동사
  ⇒ owe, exist, need, appear

Task 2

Check if each sentence is correct (O) or incorrect (X).

	O	X
1. My shoulders are really hurting from working out too hard.	( )	( )
2. She is leaving school last year.	( )	( )
3. At 3:30 tomorrow, I will playing football with my friends.	( )	( )
4. Their baby is waking up very early these days.	( )	( )

Focus 3 Perfect (완료형)

완료형은 have/has + 과거분사 (현재완료), had + 과거분사(과거완료), will have + 과거분사(미래완료)로 표현됩니다.

01 present perfect (현재완료)

현재와 관련이 있는 것을 표현합니다. 부사 just, already, yet 등이 자주 쓰입니다.

(1) 행위의 완료

- Sue has just passed her exams.

  (Sue는 방금 그녀의 시험을 통과했습니다.)

- I have not finished my report yet.

  (나는 보고서를 아직 끝내지 못했습니다.)

Cf) 완료형은 과거 시간을 표현하는 부사 (two years ago, yesterday, last night) 와 쓰이지 않는다.

- They've finished the work ten minutes ago. (X)
- They finished the work ten minutes ago. (O)

  (그들은 10분 전에 일을 끝냈습니다.)

(2) 경험

- Have you seen any of the other guys recently?

  (최근에 다른 친구들을 본적이 있습니까?)

- Have you heard of Tom Brady?

  (당신은 Tom Brady에 대해 들어본 적이 있습니까?)

- I've been to England twice.

  (나는 영국에 두 번 가봤습니다.)

(3) 계속

- It's been a while since we've talked.

  (우리가 이야기를 나눈 지도 꽤 되었습니다.)

- He has known her since they were children.

  (그는 그녀를 어릴 때부터 알았습니다.)

- How long have you worked at that company?

  (당신은 이 회사에서 얼마 동안 일하였습니까?)

- They have become good friends over the years.

  (그들은 수년간 좋은 친구로 지내오고 있습니다.)

(4) 결과

- He has been given a camera. (= He has a camera now.)
  (그에게 카메라가 주어졌습니다. (그는 지금 카메라를 가지고 있습니다.))
- I've broken my arm. (= My arm is broken now.)
  (나는 팔을 부러뜨렸습니다.)

cf) A: Have you broken your arm? (당신은 팔이 부러진 적이 있습니까?)
B: Yes, I've broken my arm one time. (= I broke my arm in the past, but it might not be broken now.) (네. 한번 부러진 적이 있습니다.)

02 past perfect (과거완료)

(1) 과거 특정 시점까지의 완료, 경험, 계속, 결과

- He had been unemployed for a long time.
  (그는 오랜 기간 동안 실직상태였습니다.)
- She wanted to borrow my book, but I hadn't finished it.
  (그녀는 내 책을 빌리길 원했지만 나는 다 읽지 않았었습니다.)
- Had they been to China before?
  (그들은 전에 중국에 간 적이 있었습니까?)
- The house had been empty for a long time.
  (그 집은 오랫동안 비어 있었습니다.)
- The soccer player had injured his leg and couldn't run.
  (그 축구 선수는 다리를 부상 당해서 뛸 수가 없었습니다.)

(2) 과거보다 앞선 시제

- John lost the watch that he had bought at the mall.
  (존은 상점에서 샀던 시계를 잃어버렸습니다.)

03 future perfect (미래완료)

미래 특정 시점까지의 완료, 경험, 계속

- I will have finished the work by six o'clock tomorrow.
  (나는 내일 6시 까지 일을 끝낼 것입니다.)
- She will have seen the movie three times if she sees it again.
  (그녀는 이번에 또 보면 그 영화를 세 번 보는 것입니다.)

- If you don't hurry, all of the scholarships will have been given out by the time your application is complete.
  (서두르지 않으면, 당신이 지원서 작성을 마칠 때쯤 모든 장학금 지급이 끝났을 것입니다.)

Task 3

Write sentences in the perfect tense using the words in parentheses.

1. How long have you known Carol?
   (know, many years) ______________________________.
2. Is Peter the owner of this house?
   (own, since 1998) Yes, ______________________________.
3. Have you ever been to Scotland?
   (twice) Yes, ______________________________.
4. Did you get in the room?
   (forget my keys) No, I couldn't because ____________________.

Reading Google's Unique Corporate Culture

Walking around Google's corporate campus in Mountain View, California, you might find amenities normally reserved for vacation resorts or upscale apartment buildings. But in a world where technology companies often find themselves competing for the same candidates, it is important to offer top recruits something special.

Even on a Saturday afternoon, Google employees can be seen shuffling around the premises, attending programming competitions or socializing at cocktail parties. These are just a few of the things that make the corporate culture at Google unlike anywhere else. There are numerous surprises at Google, but the company's policy toward napping might be most shocking. Employees aren't scolded for sleeping on the job, but encouraged to take short rests, and even provided with leather reclining chairs.

Some employees joke that the company is trying to distract them and keep them at work as long as possible. But Google has long believed that employees who are happy and comfortable will also be the most productive employees.

Translation Google의 독특한 기업문화

California, Mountain View에 있는 Google 기업 구내를 둘러보면 당신은 휴양지에서나 고급스러운 아파트 빌딩들에서 볼 수 있는 편의시설들을 볼 수 있을 것입니다. 그러나 첨단기술 기업들은 같은 후보자들을 유치하기 위해 종종 경쟁을 해야 되고, 이러한 세계에서 최고의 신입들에게 뭔가 특별한 것을 제공하는 일은 중요한 것입니다.

토요일 오후라 하더라도 Google 직원들이 구내를 돌아다니거나, 프로그래밍 시합에 참석하거나, 칵테일 파티에서 사교를 즐기는 모습이 눈에 뜨입니다. 이것은 다른 곳에서는 볼 수 없는 Google이 창조해낸 기업문화 중 일부일 뿐입니다. Google에는 매우 놀라운 것들이 많이 있지만 그 중에서도 낮잠에 대한 회사의 규칙은 매우 놀랍습니다. 직원들은 일과 중에 낮잠을 잔다고 질책 받지 않으며, 오히려 짧은 휴식을 취하는 것을 권장 받고 있습니다. 심지어 가죽 안락 의자가 제공되기도 합니다.

일부 직원들은 회사가 그들의 주의를 분산시키고 가능한 오랫동안 일을 하게 만든다고 농담을 합니다. 그러나 Google은 행복하고 편안하게 느끼는 직원이 가장 능률적인 직원이 될 것이라고 오래 전부터 믿어왔습니다.

Comprehension Check-up

True/False

1. These days, technology companies face competition for top employees. (T / F)
2. Employees at Google are offered company sponsored cars. (T / F)
3. Google employees cannot be found on the weekends. (T / F)

Vocabulary Matching

1. amenity
2. upscale
3. recruits
4. corporate culture

a. the traditions and values of a company
b. a new member of an organization
c. luxurious, elegant
d. facilities that are provided for people's convenience, enjoyment, or comfort.

Word Challenge

Quiz

Use the words from today's vocabulary challenge to complete each of the following sentences.

see	watch	look

1. During a job interview, it's important to __________ confident.
2. I'm going away for a few days, but I'll __________ you when I get back.
3. It's therapeutic to sit on the beach and __________ a sunset.

Word Challenge

see	usage: The uses of "see" are quite varied. It can be used to mean "view." Or, it can be used in place of "meet," "visit," or the expression "make sure." examples: 1. Tonight, we're all going to see a French film. (view) (오늘밤 우리 모두는 프랑스 영화를 보러 갈 것입니다.) 2. I'm going to see her later. (visit/meet) (나는 나중에 그녀를 보려고 합니다.) 3. I'd like you to see that this project is completed properly. (make sure) (나는 이번 계획이 제대로 완성된 것을 당신이 확신하기를 바랍니다.) 4. Oh, I see. (understand) (아, 알겠습니다.)

watch	usage: Use "watch" to express observation, anticipation, or expectation of a result. examples: 1. I'll probably just stay home tonight and watch a movie. (observation) (나는 아마 오늘밤 집에 있으면서 영화를 볼 것 같습니다.) 2. It was a bad day on Wall Street and everyone was watching the markets closely (anticipation/expectation). (Wall Street는 불황이었고 모두들 시장을 주의 깊게 살펴보고 있었습니다.)
look	usage: Use "look" when talking about appearance or to express the act of examining or gazing at an object. examples: 1. She looks savvy and confident in front of crowds. (appearance) (그녀는 대중 앞에서 재치 있고 자신감 있게 보입니다.) 2. I'm going to look again for any potential errors. (examining) (나는 발생할 수 있는 문제들을 다시 살펴볼 것입니다.) 3. Don't look directly at the sun. (gazing at an object) (태양을 직접 보지 마세요.)

Practice

Task 4

Use the appropriate tense of the verb provided to complete the sentence. You can add auxiliaries such as "will", "be" or "have" if necessary.

1. 몇몇 나무가 죽어가고 있었고, 나는 새 소리도 들을 수 없었습니다.
   ⇒ Some trees were _______(die), and I couldn't hear any birds.

2. 많은 사람들은 오랜 동안 영어 알파벳을 사용해 오고 있습니다.
   ⇒ Many people ________(use) the English alphabet for a long time.

3. 편지가 도착할 때쯤 나는 다른 아파트로 이사를 했을 것입니다.
   ⇒ By the time the letter gets here, I ________(move) to another apartment.

Task 5

Check if each sentence is correct or incorrect. If the sentence is incorrect, correct it.

correct incorrect

1. Andrew was damaging his knee while he was playing football. ( ) ( )

____

2. Who was the person standing beside you when I was seeing you yesterday?

____ ( ) ( )

3. I have had a good day today. ( ) ( )

____

Culture Corner

John & Jane

우리나라에서 가장 대표적인 남자와 여자의 이름은 무엇이 있을까요? "철수"와 "영희", "갑돌이"와 "갑순이". 이러한 이름들은 교과서에도 자주 등장하는 이름들이죠. 또 서류를 작성할 때 예시로써 많이 쓰이는 이름이 "홍 길동"인데요, 영어에도 이와 같은 표현들이 있습니다.

먼저 우리나라의 "철수와 영희" 정도에 해당하는 이름을 영어에서 살펴보면 John과 Jane이 있습니다. 예를 들어 신원 미상의 남자를 가리킬 때는 John Doe, 신원 미상의 여자를 가리킬 때는 Jane Doe라는 표현을 씁니다. 이러한 예는 영화 『Seven』에서도 볼 수가 있는데요, 등장인물 중 John Doe라는 사람이 나오는데 연쇄 살인범의 신분이 정확하지 않기 때문에 그렇게 표현한 것이고 실제이름이 John Doe는 아닙니다.

또한 John Hancock이라는 표현은 미국 Massachusetts주지사였던 John Hancock이 미국 독립 선언문에 맨 처음 서명을 한 것이 유래가 되어 현재는 "서명"이라는 의미로 쓰이고 있습니다. 따라서 "Put your John Hancock on my guest book."이라고 하면 "방명록에 이름을 남겨주세요."라는 뜻입니다. Jones도 일반적인 사람을 지칭할 때 쓰입니다. 예를 들어, "Keep up with the Joneses."라는 말은 "남들 사는 대로 살다."라는 뜻으로 여기서 Joneses는 일반적인 People을 의미하는 것으로 보시면 됩니다.

여성의 대표적인 이름인 Jane과 관련된 표현도 살펴보면 Plain Jane은 "일반적인 여성"을 뜻하며 "She is just plain Jane."이라고 하면 "그녀는 평범한 여성이다."라는 표현입니다. Demi Moore의 강인한 여군연기가 인상적이었던 영화『G.I. Jane』. 영화 제목인 G.I. Jane은 여자군인을 뜻한다는 거 알고 계셨나요? 참고로 남자군인은 G.I. Joe라고 합니다. Joe도 영어권에서 흔히 쓰이는 이름으로 "Joe Blow" 역시 보통 사람을 가리키는 말이고 Honest Joe라고 하면 "성실한 사람"을 의미합니다.

속담에서 자주 볼 수 있는 Jack도 널리 알려진 이름인데요, 관련된 속담들을 몇 가지 살펴보겠습니다. "Every Jack has his Jill."은 "짚신도 제 짝이 있다." 라는 뜻이고요, "All work and no play makes Jack a dull boy." 는 "일만하고 놀 줄 모르면 사람이 둔해진다."라는 미국의 유명한 속담입니다. 또한 a Jack of all trades 라고 하면 모든 trades를 다 하는 사람으로 "팔방미인"을 칭할 때 쓰이는 표현입니다. "Jack of all trades, and master of none."는 "팔방미인은 뛰어난 재주는 없다" 라는 뜻입니다. 이와 같은 표현들을 익혀둔다면 관련된 속담을 들었을 때 혼동하는 일은 없겠죠?

- Keep up with the Joneses.
- Put your John Hancock on my guest book.
- She is just plain Jane.
- Every Jack has his Jill.
- Jack of all trades, and master of none.

Wrap-up

Key sentences

(Simple tense)

I'm so busy; I don't have enough time to enjoy it.

We only met a few weeks ago.

I'll give you a call when I settled in.

(Progressive)

It's getting cold here in New York.

I saw Dan a few weeks ago; we were wondering about you.

(Perfect)

It's been a while since we've talked.

He had been unemployed for a long time.

REVIEW TEST

Choose the correct answers. (1-5)

1. We ______ collecting empty bottles for many years.

1) will be　2) have　3) are going to　4) have been

2. These days she usually __________ tennis three times a week.

1) played　2) plays　3) will play　4) has played

3. He _______ his father.

1) is resembling　2) is resembled　3) resembles with　4) resembles

4. When the police caught the thief, he _______ the money.

1) has already spent　2) already has spent

3) had already spent　4) already had spent

5. At 4:00 tomorrow afternoon, I _______ soccer with my friends.

1) will be playing　2) will playing

3) play　4) played

Change the verb in the parentheses into the correct form. (6-10)

6. We _______ to the mountain last year. (go)

7. They will not start the meeting until the president _______. (arrive)

8. If she _______ any questions, she'll let you know. (have)

9. She recognized Mr. Brown at once, for she had _______ him several times before. (see)

10. How many times have you _______ to Lotte World? (be)

Supplementary Reading (보충 독해)

다음 글을 읽고 문제를 풀어 보세요.

The Korean Wave

The Korean Wave, Hallyu, refers to the rush of local cultural products that has hit neighboring countries in recent years. There has been a sudden surge of interest in all things Korean. This cultural phenomenon began when the popular Korean TV drama "What is Love" was aired on China's CCTV in 1997. Its huge success paved the way for other TV series. In Japan, the Korean wave reached its peak with the success of the Korean TV drama, "Winter Sonata". Many Korean singers including Baby Vox, NRG, Shinhwa and SES also made entries into the neighboring countries spurred by a successful Beijing concert by H.O.T (High Five of Teenagers) in 2000. When the blockbuster movie "Taegugki" hit the international market early a few years ago, it drew a lot of interest from people all over the world.

Korean cuisine, accessories, garments, and language are also becoming popular worldwide. More and more foreigners are volunteering to learn more about Korean culture. The number of foreigners learning Korean is constantly increasing. "There are many Japanese learning Korean because they want to talk to Bae Yong-joon," said a Japanese who is studying Korean in Korea. However, experts say that Koreans are not making enough effort to carry on the Korean wave. "Different ideas need to be produced in order to make the Korean wave last. Otherwise, foreigners' interest in Korea will fade away," say experts.

Translation 한국 열풍

한국 열풍, 즉 한류는 최근 주변 국가들을 강타한 한국 문화 상품의 돌풍을 가리킵니다. 갑작스레 한국과 관련된 것에 대한 관심의 파도가 일었습니다. 이 문화 현상은 1997년 한국의 인기 텔레비전 드라마 "사랑이 뭐길래"가 중국에서 방영되었을 때부터 시작되었습니다. 이의 큰 성공은 다른 텔레비전 시리즈의 앞길을 열어주었습니다. 일본에서는 한류열풍이 한국 텔레비전 드라마 "겨울 연가"의 성공과 함께 극에 달했습니다. 2000년도 HOT의 성공적인 베이징 콘서트에 자극을 받아 베이비 복스, NRG, 신화, SES도 주변 국가들로 진출을 하였습니다. 초대형 영화 "태극기를 휘날리며"는 몇 해전 국제 시장에 진입하였을 때 전 세계적으로 많은 관심을 불러 모았습니다.
한국음식, 액세서리, 옷 그리고 언어 또한 세계적으로 인기를 얻어가고 있습니다. 갈수록 많은 외국인들이 한국의 문화에 대해 배우려 하고 있으며, 한국어를 배우는 외국인의 수도 끊임없이 늘고 있습니다. "배 용준 과 대화하기 위해 한국어를 배우는 일본인들이 많습니다."라며 한국에서 한국어를 배우는 한 일본인이 말했습니다. 그러나 전문가들은 한류 열풍을 이끌어가는데 한국인들이 충분한 노력을 하지 않는다고 합니다. 전문가들은 "한류 열풍을 지속하기 위해서는 여러 가지 아이디어가 개발되어야 합니다. 그렇지 않으면 한국에 대한 외국인들의 관심은 사라질 것입니다."라고 말합니다.

Explanation

1. The Korean Wave or Hallyu, refers to the rush of local cultural products that has hit neighboring countries in recent years.

refer to는 '지칭하다, 가리키다'라는 뜻입니다.

Ex) The figures refer to pages. (그 숫자는 페이지를 나타냅니다.)

has hit은 현재완료(have+p.p)를 나타내며 과거의 어느 시점에서 시작된 행동이 지금까지 영향을 미치고 있음을 나타냅니다.

Ex) I have known him since I came here.
(나는 여기 온 이래로 그를 알고 지냅니다.)

2. There has been a sudden surge of interest in all things Korean.

이 문장의 시제는 현재완료이며, a surge of something은 '(감정의) 동요, 격동'을 의미합니다.

Ex) A surge of anger swept over him.
(그는 발끈 성을 냈습니다.)

3. This cultural phenomenon began when the popular Korean TV drama "What is Love" was aired on China's CCTV in 1997.

종속절의 was aired는 수동태(be+p.p) 표현으로 '방송되었다, 방영되었다'의 뜻입니다.

Ex) The game will be aired live on KBS at 7:00 tonight.
(그 경기는 오늘밤 7시 에 KBS에서 생방송으로 방송될 것입니다.)

4. Its huge success paved the way for other TV series.

pave the way for는 숙어로, '~에 대해서 길을 열다, ~을 용이하게 하다, ~을 촉진하다.'의 의미입니다.

Ex) This project will pave the way for a lasting development.
(이번 프로젝트는 지속적인 발전을 가져다 줄 것입니다.)

5. Many Korean singers including Baby Vox, NRG, Shinhwa and SES also made entries into the neighboring countries spurred by a successful Beijing concert by H.O.T in 2000.

make an entry into는 '~에 입장하다, ~로 들어가다.'의 의미입니다.
spur는 '자극하다, 격려하다, 박차를 가하다'의 의미로, 이 문장에서는 수동태로, '~의 자극을 받아서'라고 해석할 수 있습니다.

Ex) Our research made an entry into the last phase. (우리의 연구는 마지막 단계로 들어섰습니다.)

Ex) What spurred him (on) to join the meeting? (왜 그는 그 회의에 참석할 마음이 생겼을까?)

6. Koreans are not making enough effort to carry on the Korean wave.

make enough effort는 '충분한 노력을 하다.' carry on은 '~을 계속하다.'의 의미입니다.

Ex) She made enough effort to pass the exam. (그녀는 그 시험을 통과하기 위해 충분한 노력을 했습니다.)

Ex) Let's carry on this discussion at some other time. (다음에 이 토론을 계속합시다.)

7. Different ideas need to be produced in order to make the Korean wave last.

need to는 '~할 필요가 있다.' be produced는 수동태로서 '생산되다.'의 의미입니다. in order to는 '~을 하기 위해서'라는 뜻으로 목적, 의도의 의미를 가지고 있습니다.

Ex) The factory produces various items in order to suit all tastes.
(그 공장은 모든 사람의 기호에 맞도록 다양한 품목을 생산합니다.)

make(have, let)+목적어+동사원형은 '목적어로 하여금 ~하도록 시키다, 만들다' 의 의미입니다.

Ex) You can't make him go if he doesn't want to.
(그가 원치 않는다면 당신은 그를 가게 할 수 없습니다.)

8. Otherwise, foreigners' interest in Korea will fade away.

otherwise는 '그렇지 않다면, 다른 경우라면'의 뜻이며, fade away는 '사라져 버리다'의 의미입니다. away는 소실, 제거의 의미를 강조합니다.

Ex) Go away! Otherwise, I'll call the police. (가버려! 그렇지 않으면 경찰을 부를거야.)

Q.1 Choose the definition on the right that matches the word on the left.

1. surge	a) to make progress or development easier
2. pave the way	b) continually occurring; persistent
3. spur (on)	c) a heavy billowing or swelling motion like that of a great wave

4. constantly — d) to broadcast on television or radio

5. phenomenon — e) to incite or stimulate

6. air — f) something that is observed to happen or exist

Q.2 Mark True (T) or False (F).

1. Korean cultural products have been very popular for more than ten years. ( )
2. This cultural phenomenon started when the popular Korean TV drama "Winter Sonata" was aired on TV in Japan. ( )
3. Korean singers such as Baby VOX and NRG have performed all over the world. ( )
4. A growing number of foreigners want to learn the Korean language. ( )

Sentence Structure 02 Unit

Introduction

Topic: First Day, Worst Day (최악의 첫날)

Lesson objectives:

To understand sentence structure (문장 구조 이해하기)

- kinds of verbs (동사의 종류)
- sentence patterns (문장 형식)

WARM-UP

This week, Brett arrives in New York for an early morning meeting with his new boss. Before he even finds out where his new office will be, he's overwhelmed by the demands made of him. However, he's eager to make a good impression and has a hard time saying, "no".

Brett : Hi. I'm Brett Davishere to see Mr. Daniels.

Jane : He'll be able to see you in about 10 minutes. (S + V + O) He's on an important call right now. Please sit down.

Brett : Thanks. I'll stand. (S + V)

Jane : Okay. Mr. Daniels will see you now.

Mr. Daniels : Good morning, Brett. How was your trip?

Brett : It was good. (S + V + C) I'm glad to be back in New York.

Mr. Daniels : I'm sure you are. I hear you can't find a decent bagel anywhere in LA.

Brett : That's very true.

Mr. Daniels : So, let's talk about your new assignment.

Brett : Okay.

Mr. Daniels	: You're going to head our East Coast marketing team. It's a big responsibility; I hope you're up for it. You'll be in charge of a team of 12 people and you'll report your progress to me on Monday of every week.
Brett	: What should I do first?
Mr. Daniels	: Well, I'm glad you asked that. This week you're going to be doing interviews to fill the spaces on your team.
Brett	: Okay. I'll make some calls today.
Mr. Daniels	: Well, that's not all. We're competing for a big contract to market a new energy drink. I'm going to need to see some ideas from you by next week.
Brett	: Okay. I'll make that a priority. (S + V + O + OC)
Mr. Daniels	: The firm needs this contract badly. So, don't let us down. And you'll need to sort through these other proposals before the weekend.
Brett	: But it's Wednesday and there must be 200 of them here…
Mr. Daniels	: I've heard good things about you. I'm sure it's not going to be a problem.
Brett	: Um, well, I'll do my best.
Mr. Daniels	: I know you will. And don't make any plans for dinner tomorrow night. We're meeting with an important client.
Brett	: Um, well, actually…
Mr. Daniels	: Okay. So, my secretary will show you your new office. (S + V + IO + DO)
Brett	: Okay. It was, um, a pleasure to meet with you.
Mr. Daniels	: The same. Keep up the good work. Jane, come in here and show Mr. Davis his office. Oh, and bring me an iced latte; no ice, soy milk, and two sugars. (S + V + IO + DO)
Jane	: Yes, sir. Just a moment.

Translation

이번 주에 Brett은 새로운 상사와 이른 아침에 미팅을 하기 위해 New York에 도착한다. 그는 그가 일할 새로운 사무실에 가기도 전에 그에게 주어진 요구사항에 당황한다. 그러나 그는 좋은 인상을 남기고 싶기 때문에 거절하지를 못한다.

Brett : 안녕하세요. Brett Davis입니다. Daniels씨를 만나러 왔습니다.

Jane : 그분은 10분쯤 후에 당신을 만나실 수 있습니다. 지금은 중요한 통화를 하고 계십니다. 앉아서 기다려 주세요.

Brett : 감사합니다. 서 있을게요.

Jane : 그러세요. 지금 Daniels씨가 당신을 만나러 오실 거에요.

Mr. Daniels : 안녕하세요, Brett씨. 오시는 길은 어떠셨어요?

Brett : 좋았습니다. New York으로 돌아오게 되어서 기쁩니다.

Mr. Daniels : 그러실 거에요. 제가 듣기론 LA에서는 괜찮은 베이글을 찾아볼 수 없다고 하던데요.

Brett : 예, 맞습니다.

Mr. Daniels : 자 그럼 당신의 새로운 업무에 대해 얘기해보죠.

Brett : 네.

Mr. Daniels : 당신은 이제 동쪽 해안 지역 마케팅 부서를 맡게 될 거에요. 중대한 업무지요. 당신이 잘 해나가기를 기대합니다. 당신은 12명의 구성원들을 관리하게 될 것이고 매주 월요일에 진행과정을 저에게 보고해야 합니다.

Brett : 우선 제가 뭘 해야 하죠?

Mr. Daniels : 좋은 질문입니다. 이번 주에 당신 부서의 공석을 채우기 위해 면접을 실시할 거에요.

Brett : 네, 오늘 전화를 하겠습니다.

Mr. Daniels : 이게 다가 아닙니다. 우리는 지금 새로운 에너지 음료수 시판을 위한 큰 계약 건에 대해 경쟁하고 있습니다. 다음 주까지 좋은 아이디어를 주셔야 합니다.

Brett : 네. 그것을 우선적으로 하겠습니다.

Mr. Daniels : 회사에게 이 계약은 매우 중요합니다. 그러니까 실망시키지 말아 주세요. 그리고 당신은 주말 전까지 이 다른 안건들을 잘 정리해 두어야 합니다.

Brett : 하지만 지금은 수요일이고, 여기 분명 200개는 되는 것 같은데….

Mr. Daniels : 당신에 대해 좋은 얘기들을 많이 들었어요. 잘 해낼 거라 믿습니다.

Brett : 흠, 최선을 다 해보겠습니다.

Mr. Daniels : 잘 해낼 겁니다. 그리고 내일 저녁에는 다른 약속 잡지 마세요. 중요한 손님과 회의가 있을 거에요.

Brett : 음, 사실은...

Mr. Daniels : 좋아요, 자 그럼 내 비서가 당신에게 새로운 사무실을 보여줄 거에요.

Brett : 네, 그럼 음, 만나서 반가웠습니다.

Mr. Daniels : 저도요. 열심히 하세요. Jane, 들어와서 Davis씨에게 사무실을 보여줘요. 아, 그리고 아이스 라떼 한 잔 부탁해요: 얼음 빼고 두유랑 설탕 2개 넣어서.

Jane : 네, 잠시만 기다려 주세요.

Comprehension Check

1. As part of Brett's new position, he will be:
   (a) a secretary
   (b) a salesperson
   (c) one of twelve people on a marketing team
   (d) in charge of a marketing team of twelve people

2. In this conversation, Brett is likely speaking with:
   (a) his secretary
   (b) a friend
   (c) his boss
   (d) a colleague

3. Which of the following adjectives would you probably NOT use to describe Brett's boss?
   (a) direct
   (b) forceful
   (c) overbearing
   (d) easy-going

Useful Expressions

In this dialogue	Explanation
1. I hear you can't find a decent bagel anywhere in LA.	1. Many people think that food is somewhat standard throughout the United States, but, just like here in Korea, certain regionspride themselves on the quality of various cuisines. For example, clam chowder and other sea fare is a source of fame for the New England area, just as New Orleans is well known for Jambalaya, a spicy rice dish of Spanish and French influence. Bagels, a common American breakfast food,are among those that New Yorkers will likely tell you they do better than anyone else in the country.

In this dialogue	Explanation
2. We're competing fora big contract to market a new energy drink.	2. In this dialogue, Brett's new boss says that their firm is competing for a big contract. In other words, the firm is striving to attain an advantage over other firms and win the contract. A few other phrases we might use to express this idea are: "to struggle for," "to be in the running for," or "to jockey for."The first, however, implies some disadvantage with respect to the competition.
3. You'll need to sort throughthese other proposals before the weekend.	3. If you have to sort through a number of items, you're probably arranging them according to type or quality. The goal might simply be to put things into their proper categories, or it might be to select against some items in favor of others. The expression "to sift through" is close in meaning. And some other useful verbs might be "assort," "classify," or "evaluate."
4. The firm needs this contract badly.	4. In this instance, "badly" doesn't mean the contract is undesirable. Here, it is used to say the contract is important or essential to the firm. An alternative way to express this thought might be, "The firm really needs this contract," or "It's imperative that the firm get this contract."
5. Bring me an iced latte; no ice, soy milk, and two sugars.	5. There's a good chance you learned to quantify-words like sugar by specifying precise measurements, such as tablespoons, cups, or grams. But if you were to ask a barista for two sugars, or even two coffees, it's implied that you want two of whatever the standard quantity. Recently, the coffee order has become another way for people to express their individuality. Hang out in a coffee shop long enough and you'll probably hear some interesting requests. Perhaps Mr. Daniels wishes to show that he is particular and someone who knows exactly what he wants.

Grammar

Focus 1 Kinds of verbs (동사의 종류)

01 자동사 (Intransitive Verb)와 타동사 (Transitive Verb)

(1) 목적어가 필요 없는 자동사(vi)와 목적어를 필요로 하는 타동사(vt)로 나눌 수 있습니다.

- She usually sleeps late.
  (그녀는 보통 늦잠을 잡니다.)
- She sleeps the baby. (X)
  (그녀는 아이를 재웁니다.)
- Let's invite Sally and her cousin.
  (Sally와 그녀의 사촌을 초대합시다.)
- Let's invite. (X)
  (초대합시다.)

(2) 자동사 (Intransitive verbs)

- I'll stand.
  (서 있겠습니다.)
- The train is approaching.
  (기차가 오고 있습니다.)
- Spring has arrived.
  (봄이 왔습니다.)
- Please be quiet; I'm speaking.
  (조용히 해주세요, 제가 말하고 있습니다.)
- He acted in a strange manner.
  (그는 이상하게 행동했습니다.)

(3) 타동사 (Transitive verbs)

- He'll be able to see you in about 10 minutes.
  (그는 당신을 만나러 10분쯤 후에 오실 수 있습니다.)
- The judge sentenced him more harshly than we expected.
  (판사는 우리가 기대했던 것보다 훨씬 더 가혹하게 그에게 선고를 내렸습니다.)

- Anne lifted the bag onto her back and started to hike up the mountain.
  (Anne은 그녀의 가방을 등에 메고 산을 오르기 시작했습니다.)
- The university provides laptop computers to all freshmen students.
  (그 대학은 모든 신입생에게 노트북을 제공합니다.)
- We divided the profits equally among the investors.
  (우리는 투자자들에게 똑같이 이익을 배당했습니다.)

(4) 많은 동사는 문맥에 따라 타동사가 되기도 하고 자동사가 되기도 합니다.

- The boy eats well.
  (그 소년은 잘 먹습니다.)
  Why don't you eat something hot?
  (뜨거운 것을 드시지 그래요?)
- He runs around the block daily.
  (그는 매일 동네를 한 바퀴 돕니다.)
  He runs a large corporation.
  (그는 대규모의 회사를 운영합니다.)
- The door opened.
  (문이 열렸습니다.)
  Please open the window.
  (창문을 열어주세요.)
- We celebrated all night.
  (우리는 밤새 축제 분위기였습니다.)
  We celebrated the victory.
  (우리는 승리를 축하했습니다.).

(5) 타동사 중에서 두 개의 목적어를 갖는 동사가 있는 데, 항상 누구에게 무엇인가를 주는 (수여하는) 동사라고 하여 수여동사라고 합니다. 수여동사는 간접목적어(indirect object)와 직접목적어(direct object)를 취하며 간접목적어는 '~에게'라는 뜻을 나타내고, 직접목적어는 '~을'이라는 뜻을 나타냅니다.

- My secretary will show you your new office.
  (내 비서가 당신에게 새로운 사무실을 보여줄 것입니다.)
- Bring me an iced latte.
  (나에게 아이스 라떼 한잔 가져다 주세요.)
- He gave his wife a diamond ring.
  (그는 아내에게 다이아몬드 반지를 주었습니다.)

- Mother bought me the ice cream.
  (어머니는 저에게 아이스크림을 사주셨습니다.)

02 완전 동사 (Complete Verb)와 불완전 동사 (Incomplete Verb)

보어의 유무에 따라 완전 동사(complete verb) 불완전 동사(incomplete verb)로 나뉘는데 보어가 필요 없는 것을 완전 동사, 보어가 따르는 것을 불완전 동사라고 합니다.

- The bell is ringing. (완전 자동사)
  (초인종이 울리고 있습니다.)
- The wine tastes sweet. (불완전 자동사)
  (와인이 달군요.)
- We enjoyed the movie. (완전 타동사)
  (우리는 영화를 재미있게 봤습니다.)
- We elected him president. (불완전 타동사)
  (우리는 그를 대통령으로 선출했습니다.)

Task 1

Choose the best word from the box to complete each sentence.

makes	feels	runs	exists	brings

1. The cloth _____ soft.
2. Jane _____ it a rule to get up at six every morning.
3. Your question ______ me to the delicate matter I'd like to raise.
4. The bus _____ between New York and Washington D.C.
5. Some people assume that life _____ on Mars.

Focus 2 Confusing verbs (혼동하기 쉬운 동사)

다음 몇 가지 동사들은 형태는 비슷하지만, 자동사와 타동사로 용법이 구분됩니다.

01

lie: ~에 놓여있다, 눕다 (vi) lie – lay – lain
lie: 거짓말하다 (vi) lie – lied – lied
lay: ~을 놓다 (vt) lay – laid – laid

- He lay on his back.
  (그는 등을 대고 누웠습니다.)
- You're lying to me.
  (당신은 나에게 거짓말을 하고 있습니다.)
- Lay these bricks and they must lie evenly.
  (이 벽돌들을 놓으세요. 평평하게 놓여져야 합니다.)

02

sit: 앉다 (vi) sit – sat – sat
seat: 앉히다 (vt) seat – seated – seated
set: ~을 놓다, 두다 (vt) set – set – set

- They sat around the table.
  (그들은 식탁 둘레에 앉았습니다.)
- Please seat yourself in a chair.
  (의자에 앉으세요.)
- He set the glass on the table.
  (그는 유리잔을 식탁 위에 놓았습니다.)

03

rise: 오르다, (해가) 뜨다 (vi) rise – rose – risen
raise: 들어올리다, 일으키다 (vt) raise – raised – raised

- The moon is rising above the horizon.
  (달이 수평선 위로 떠오르고 있습니다.)
- She raises her voice when she's angry.
  (그녀는 화가 날 때 목소리가 높아집니다.)

cf) lay는 '알을 낳다'라는 뜻의 자동사/타동사, sit은 '앉히다'의 뜻으로 타동사, set은 '(해가) 기울다'의 뜻의 자동사로 도 쓰입니다.

cf) 자동사와 타동사로 모두 쓰이지만 의미에 따라 과거형과 과거분사형이 달라지는 동사도 있습니다.
hang: (물건을) 걸다 hang – hung – hung

hang: 교수형에 처하다 hang - hanged - hanged
- I've hung three paintings already, but I still have two more to hang.
  (나는 이미 세 개의 그림을 걸었지만 아직 두 개 더 걸어야 합니다.)
- He was sentenced to be hanged tomorrow at noon.
  (그는 내일 정오 에 교수형에 처해지는 것으로 선고를 받았습니다.)

Task 2

Check if each sentence is correct (O) or incorrect (X).

		O	X
1.	They have risen corn in Gangwondo for many years.	( )	( )
2.	The king laid the foundation of the country.	( )	( )
3.	The price of stocks rises and falls.	( )	( )
4.	Every spring the woodcock lies four multicolored eggs.	( )	( )
5.	She seats on her knees in front of her grandparents.	( )	( )

Focus 3 Sentence patterns (문장 형식)

01 S+V

문장의 주요소가 주어와 동사만으로 구성된 1형식 문형입니다. 이때 동사를 완전자동사라고 하며 보어나 목적어를 필요로 하지 않습니다.

- Please sit down.
  (좀 앉으시지요.)
- I'll stand.
  (서 있을게요.)
- My watch doesn't work.
  (내 시계는 작동하지 않습니다.)
- She arrived at the station.
  (그녀는 역에 도착했습니다.)

02 S+V+C

문장의 주요소가 주어, 동사, 보어로 구성된 2형식 문형입니다. 이때 동사를 불완전자동사라고 합니다. 또한 2형식에서 보어를 주격보어라고합니다. 상태(be, seem, appear, remain), 상태의 변화(come, grow, go, turn, become), 감각(feel, look, taste, sound, smell) 등을 나타내는 동사가 이에 속합니다.

- I will be a doctor.
  (나는 의사가 될 것입니다.)
- It was good.
  (좋았습니다.)
- The idea was impressive.
  (그 아이디어는 인상적 이였습니다.)
- Your plan appears flawed.
  (당신의 계획은 문제가 있는듯 합니다.)
- She became a ballet dancer.
  (그녀는 발레리나가 되었습니다.)
- He looked depressed.
  (그는 우울해 보였습니다.)
- This wine tastes somewhat bitter.
  (이 와인은 좀 쓴맛이 납니다.)

03 S+V+O

문장의 주요소가 주어, 동사, 목적어로 구성된 3형식 문형입니다. 이러한 문장에서의 동사를 완전타동사라고 합니다.

- He'll be able to see you in about 10 minutes.
  (그는 10분쯤 후에 당신을 만날 수 있습니다.)
- My husband spent too much money last month.
  (내 남편은 지난 달 너무 많은 돈을 썼습니다.)
- The official resigned his position.
  (그 관리는 사임했습니다.)
- She raised a valid point.
  (그녀는 중요한 점을 지적했습니다.)
- He couldn't answer the final question.
  (그는 마지막 질문에 대답할 수 없었습니다.)

- They said that she had been shouting.

(그들은 그녀가 소리치고 있었다고 말했습니다.)

cf) 주의하여야 할 타동사

resemble, discuss, attend, marry, enter, reach, greet, mention 등은 타동사로 전치사와 함께 쓰지 않습니다.

– The brothers resemble one another. (그 형제들은 서로 닮았습니다.)
  The brothers resemble with one another. (x)
– We discussed the problem. (우리는 그 문제에 대해 토론하였습니다.)
  We discussed about the problem. (x)
– He didn't attend the meeting. (그는 미팅에 참석하지 않았습니다.)
  He didn't attend to the meeting. (x)
– Mary married the man. (Mary는 그 남자와 결혼하였습니다.)
  Mary married with the man. (x)

04 S+V+IO+DO

문장의 주요소가 주어, 동사, 목적어 2개 (간접목적어, 직접목적어)로 구성된 4형식 문형입니다. 4형식 문형의 동사는 수여동사라고도 합니다. 4형식 문장을 3형식으로 고칠 때는 직접 목적어를 간접목적어 앞에 쓰며, 간접 목적어 앞에 to, for와 같은 전치사를 써서 부사구를 만듭니다.

- She gave the boy a book. (= She gave a book to the boy.)

(그녀는 그 소년에게 책을 한 권 주었습니다.)

- She made her daughter a new dress. (= She made a new dress for her daughter.)

(그녀는 딸에게 새 옷을 만들어 주었습니다.)

- My secretary will show you your new office.

(내 비서가 당신에게 새로운 사무실을 보여줄 겁니다.)

- Bring me an iced latte.

(나에게 아이스 라떼 한잔 가져다 주세요.)

- My boss offered me a promotion.

(나의 상사는 나를 승진시켰습니다.)

- The delivery driver handed me the letter.

(그 택배기사는 나에게 편지를 전달했습니다.)

cf) 간접목적어를 부사구로 만들 때, 사용하는 전치사

to 사용: give, bring, teach, offer, lend, send, promise, show, write, owe, hand
for 사용: make, buy, find, build, get, choose
of 사용: ask, beg, require

cf) 주의하여야 할 동사

explain, suggest, introduce, propose, mention, say 등은 수여동사가 아니므로, 사람 앞에 전치사 to를 써야 합니다.

– He explained the rule to us. (그는 우리에게 그 규칙을 설명했습니다.)
  He explained us the rule. (x)

05 S+V+O+OC

문장의 주요소가 주어, 동사, 목적어, 목적격 보어로 구성된 5형식 문형입니다. 5형식에서 보어는 목적어를 보충해 주는 목적격 보어입니다. 목적격 보어의 형태로는 (대)명사, 형용사, to부정사, 현재분사, 과거분사 등이 있습니다.

- John made all his five sons pastors.

(John은 그의 다섯 아들 모두를 목사로 만들었다.)

- I'll make that a priority.

(그것을 우선적으로 하겠습니다.)

- You make me nervous.

(당신은 나를 신경 쓰이게 합니다.)

- I consider the matter important.

(나는 그 문제를 중요하게 여깁니다.)

- They don't allow people to smoke indoors.

(그들은 사람들이 실내에서 담배를 피우는 것을 허락하지 않습니다.)

- She saw them dancing on the stage.

(그녀는 그들이 무대에서 춤추는 것을 보았습니다.)

- I got my shoes cleaned.

(나는 구두를 닦게 하였습니다.)

Task 3

Choose the correct word(s) in the blank.

1. The story sounds __________ (false, falsely).
2. We __________ (discussed, discussed about) the matter.
3. I __________ (suggested, suggested to) him that he should go there.
4. She made coffee __________ (to, for) all of us.

Reading Savantism

How long would it take you to work out the number of seconds a seventy year old man has lived without using a calculator? In 1751, Jerediah Buxton, one of the earliest documented cases of savantism, provided the correct answer to an even more complicated problem in about a minute and a half. The term "savantism," an abbreviation for savant syndrome, refers to a rare condition in which a person exhibits a remarkable ability, and, at the same time, is handicapped in other ways. Often savants' abilities are limited to a narrow area such as music, mathematics, or art.

The 1988 film Rain Man made the case of Kim Peek famous worldwide. From an early age, Peek could finish large texts in record times remembering 98 percent of what he had read. But, like many savants, he has trouble with tasks as simple as tying his shoes.

There are thought to be fewer than 100 people in the entire world that possess abilities like Peek's, and scientists have struggled to explain the phenomenon. Recently, however, Australian scientists claim to have made some progress in understanding what causes these abilities to develop. They say that because a specific area of the brain doesn't work very well, other abilities may be unlocked. While it's a long way off, this research might just mean that each of us has these extraordinary abilities locked somewhere inside of us.

Translation 서번티즘(savantism)

당신은 70세 노인이 현재까지 몇 초를 살았는지 계산기를 사용하지 않고 계산해 내는데 얼마나 걸리십니까? 1751년, 서번티즘으로 최초로 증명된 사람 중 하나인 Jerediah Buxton은 1분 30초 만에 훨씬 더 복잡한 문제에 대해서도 정확한 답을 제시하였습니다. 서번트 신드롬의 약어인 서번티즘이라는 용어는 한 인간이 놀라운 능력, 그리고 동시에 다른 방면으로는 장애를 갖고 있는 경우를 의미합니다. 종종 서번트의 능력은 음악, 수학 또는 예술과 같은 좁은 영역으로 제한됩니다.

1988년 영화 Rain Man으로 인해 Kim Peek의 이야기는 세계적으로 유명해 졌습니다. Peek은 어린 시절부터 방대한 양의 글을 기록적인 시간에 읽고, 그가 읽은 것의 98%를 기억해 낼 수 있었습니다. 그러나 많은 서번트들처럼 그는 신발끈을 묶는 것과 같은 간단한 일에 어려움을 겪고 있습니다.
Peek과 같은 능력을 가진 사람은 전 세계에서 100명도 채 안 되는 것으로 알려져 있고, 과학자들은 이 현상을 설명하기 위해 애를 많이 썼습니다. 그러나 최근 호주 과학자들은 이러한 능력을 발달시키는 원인을 이해하는데 약간의 진전을 이루었다고 주장합니다. 그들에 따르면 두뇌의 특정한 부분이 제대로 기능을 하지 못하기 때문에 다른 쪽의 능력들이 열려있다고 합니다. 아직 해결해야 할 것이 많기는 하지만, 이러한 연구는 우리 개개인이 이러한 특출 난 능력을 우리 내면에 가둬두고 있다는 것을 의미하는지도 모릅니다.

Comprehension Check-up

True/False

1. The term "savant syndrome" refers to a "stroke of genius" present in normal, healthy people. (T/F)
2. There are more than 12,000 people worldwide that are deemed savants. (T/F)
3. The genius many savants exhibit is often accompanied by severe disabilities. (T/F)

Vocabulary Matching

1. handicap	a. a shortened version of a word or phrase
2. phenomenon	b. overpowering or enormous
3. abbreviation	c. something impressive or extraordinary
4. overwhelming	d. a disadvantage

Word Challenge

Quiz

Check Your Understanding: Choose the best word from the box to complete each sentence.

see talk speak

1. Don't _____ in class.
2. If you don't __________ up, he'll never know how you feel.
3. I __________ leaving early in the morning is our best option.

Word Challenge

speak	usage: The verb "speak"broadly means to utter language, but can be used to express a variety of ideas when used as part of a verbal phrase. examples: 1. He was so surprised he could hardly speak. (to utter language) (그는너무 놀라서 말을 할 수 없었습니다.) 2. The prettiest girl at the dance is already spoken for. (to be taken; unavailable) (무도회에서 가장 예쁜 소녀는 이미 임자가 있습니다.) 3. This injustice will continue to occur unless we speak out. (express an opinion) (우리가 용기를 내어 말하지 않으면 이런 부당한 조치는 계속 일어날 것입니다.)
talk	usage: When used as a verb, "talk" generally implies communication or the exchange of ideas with another person though the range of uses is quite varied. We can also use the verb "talk" to mean: to deliver information, to consult, to speak about, or to perform the act of speech. examples: 1. I talked to him this morning before first period. (to communicate) (나는 오늘 아침 첫 시간 전에 그와 얘기했습니다.) 2. Jane talked with her professor about the lackluster grade she received. (to consult) (Jane은 그녀가 받은 형편없는 점수에 대해 그녀의 교수와 상의 했습니다.) 3. He talked of travels throughout the French countryside. (to deliver information) (그는 프랑스 시골지역 여행에 대해 알려주었습니다.)
say	usage: Maybe the most versatile of the verbs we'll look at in this unit, "say" can be used when you want to denote an expressions in words, make a report or allegation, indicate or show something, or provide an estimation.It can also simply mean: to produce language. 1. I should have said it another way. (to express in words) (나는 그것을 다른 식으로 말했어야 했습니다.) 2. What does it say on the company's web site? (to indicate or show) (회사 웹사이트에 뭐라고 공지되어 있습니까?) 3. What did she say? I couldn't hear. (to utter or pronounce) (그녀가 뭐라고 말했나요? 나는 들을 수가 없었습니다.)

	4. Let's say it costs $200; that's still more than we can afford. (to make an estimation) ($200정도 비용이 든다고 추측해봅시다. 그래도 여전히 우리가 감당할 수 있는 정도를 넘어섭니다.)

Practice

Task 4

Choose the best word to complete each sentence.

1. They _____ London two weeks ago.
   (a) arrived (b) left (c) went (d) came

2. He _____ me about the wonderful experiences he had in Asia.
   (a) explained (b) said (c) talked (d) told

3. I found her _____.
   (a) dozed (b) dozing (c) doze (d) dozes

4. The boy doesn't _____ his father at all.
   (a) appear (b) look (c) resemble (d) seem

5. The company will _____ children with books.
   (a) supply (b) give (c) send (d) mail

Task 5

Find the sentences that are incorrect, and correct them.

		correct	incorrect
1.	I don't want you to show this document for anyone.	( )	( )
	____________________		
2.	Tony introduced the girl us at the party.	( )	( )
	____________________		
3.	The food looked awful but it tasted well.	( )	( )
	____________________		
4.	Please let us know if you will attend the meeting or not.	( )	( )
	____________________		

Culture Corner

Matchmaker (중매인)

미국에서도 우리나라처럼 중매인이 존재한다. 우리 나라에서는 이렇게 데이트 또는 결혼 상대자를 중매 해 주는 사람을 흔히 커플 매니저(couple manager) 라고 하는데 사실은 match-maker란 용어가 정확하며 cupid라는 속칭을 쓰기도 한다. 예전에 미국에서는 우리나라만큼 matchmaker란 직업을 가진 이도, 그러한 중매인을 통한 만남도 그렇게 많이 이루어지지 않았지만 최근에는 사람들이 이들을 많이 찾고 있다. 미국에서는 특히 Online Dating Service라고 하여 온라인 상으로 데이트 상대를 찾을 수 있는 중매 싸이트가 폭발적인 인기를 끌고 있는데 eHarmony.com 그리고 Match.com등이 그 대표적인 싸이트이다. 이러한 싸이트에 회원으로 등록하여 사진, 이력 등 자기 소개서를 올리고 회원비를 지불하면 자신과 어울리는 상대를 소개받을 수 있으며 자신이 직접 싸이트에서 상대를 골라 연락을 할 수도 있다.

이러한 중매업체의 인기에 힘입어 미국에서는 Matchmaking Institute가 문을 열었다. 이 중매 기관은 예비 중매인들에게 certificate(자격증)을 부여하는 교육과정을 제공하는 기관이다. 중매인을 cupid 라고 부르기도 하는 것처럼 이 기관을 Cupid Academy 라고 비공식적으로 부르기도 한다. 아직 미국에서는 온라인 상의 중매업체가 더 많이 사용되고 있지만 우리나라의 듀오처럼 Great Expectations(대단한 기대), It's Just Lunch(그저 점심 한끼 - 점심 식사를 통해 편하게 만나보라는 뜻에서) 라는 실제 중매 업체들이 속속 생겨나고 있다. 우리 나라와 차이점이 있다면, 우리나라는 결혼을 전제한 만남이 이루어지는 반면 미국에서는 가볍게 데이트 할 상대를 구할 때에도 이러한 업체에 의뢰하는 경우가 많으며 연령층도 우리나라는 20대 중반에서 30대 중반 정도로 제한되어있는 반면 미국에서는 40대까지도 이러한 중매업체를 사용한다. 또한 우리나라만큼 조건위주의 만남보다는 성격과 취미에 맞춰 소개를 하는 경향이 있다.

이러한 소개를 통해 만난 커플 중 잘 어울리는 커플을 well-matched couple, 반대는 ill-matched couple 이라고 한다. 또한 천생배필이라는 표현은 a match made in heaven 이라고 한다. 미국에서는 이성과의 만남을 원하나 matchmaker의 도움은 받고 싶지 않을 땐 신문, 잡지 등에 아주 짧은 광고를 싣기도 하는데 그것을 'personal ad'라고 한다. 누군가를 만나서 첫 눈에 반하게 되는 것을 love at first sight 라고 하고, 생의 반려자가 되는 사람을 찾는다는 표현은 to find the love of your life 라고 한다.

- They are match made in heaven.
- Do you believe in love at first sight?
- It sometimes takes years to find that special someone, the love of your life.

Wrap-up

Key sentences

1. I'll stand. (S+V)
2. It was good. (S+V+C)
3. He'll be able to see you in about 10 minutes. (S+V+O)
4. My secretary will show you your new office. (S+V+IO+DO)
5. I'll make that a priority. (S+V+O+OC)

REVIEW TEST

Find the correct answers in the blanks. (1-5)

1. By the time we left, the young man made us ________ the product.
   (1) buy (2) to buy (3) buying (4) bought

2. If I ________ him tomorrow, I'll tell him the truth.
   (1) see (2) will see (3) would see (4) saw

3. They _______ the children to say away.
   (1) speak (2) said (3) let (4) told

4. Would you get a beer ________?
   (1) to me (2) for me (3) of me (4) me

5. As we ________ the market, I could smell something sweet.
   (1) entered to (2) came
   (3) entered (4) came back

Change the verb in the parentheses into the correct form. (6-10)

6. Susie was ________ between two handsome guys. (seat)

7. I can't allow my children _______ like that. (behave)

8. The result of the election left many people ________. (dissatisfy)

9. She heard her name ________. (call)

10. Robert _______ his brothers in many respects. (resemble)

Supplementary Reading (보충 독해)

다음 글을 읽고 문제를 풀어 보세요.

Why apples?

An apple a day keeps the doctor away. Modern research has provided scientific evidence that supports this age-old advice. Apples and all other members of the fruit family possess properties that actually help you reduce the risk of developing cancer. In addition, men who eat five or more apples a week appear to have better lung function than men who do not eat this fruit. Researchers have also reported that fresh apples have the highest levels of substances that fight cell damage when compared to other fruits and vegetables.

While no one knows exactly how long apples have existed, there is proof that people have enjoyed apples for at least 750,000 years. Apples were a favorite of the ancient Romans and Greeks. The first settlers to the United States brought apple seeds with them. According to legend, Johnny Appleseed was born in 1774 and spent 49 years of his life in the American wilderness planting apple seeds. His dream was for a land where blossoming apple trees were everywhere and no one was hungry. He might have eaten quite a few apples. The only time Johnny Appleseed got sick was at the time of his death!

Translation 왜 사과를?

하루에 사과 한 개는 의사를 멀리할 수 있도록 해줍니다. 현대 연구는 옛날부터 내려온 이 충고를 지지하는 과학적 증거를 제공해 왔습니다. 사과를 비롯한 모든 다른 과일은 실제로 당신이 암을 키울 위험을 줄이도록 도와주는 성분을 가지고 있습니다. 게다가 일주일에 5개 이상의 사과를 먹는 사람들은 이 과일을 먹지 않는 사람들 보다 더 나은 폐 기능을 가진 것으로 보입니다. 연구자들은 또한 신선한 사과가 다른 과일이나 야채와 비교할 때 세포 손상을 억제하는 물질을 가장 많이 보유하고 있다고 보고했습니다.
아무도 사과가 얼마나 오랫동안 존재해 왔는지 정확히 알지 못하나 적어도 750,000년 동안 사람들이 사과를 즐겨 먹었다는 증거가 있습니다. 사과는 고대 로마인과 그리스인들이 가장 좋아했던 것이기도 합니다. 미국의 첫 번째 정착민들은 사과씨를 가지고 오기도 하였습니다. 전설에 따르면, Johnny Appleseed는 1774년에 태어나 미국 황무지에서 사과 씨앗을 심으며 49년을 보냈습니다. 그는 꽃이 피는 사과 나무가 나라 전역에 있고 아무도 배고프지 않는 땅을 꿈꿨습니다. 그는 꽤 많은 사과를 먹었을 것입니다. Johnny Appleseed는 죽을 때를 제외하고는 아파 본 적이 없습니다.

Explanation

1. An apple a day keeps the doctor away.

keep away 는 '멀리하다, 거리를 유지하다' 라는 뜻입니다. keep A away from B (A를 B로부터 멀어지게 하다)의 표현으로 자주 쓰입니다.

Ex) You should keep your computer away from liquids.

(당신의 컴퓨터를 액체로부터 멀리해야 합니다.)

2. Modern research has provided scientific evidence that supports this age-old advice.

주격 관계대명사that이 이끄는 관계사절이 scientific evidence를 설명하고 있습니다.

Ex) There is research that proves exactly what I'm saying.

(제가 말하는 것을 완벽히 증명해주는 연구가 있습니다.)

3. Men who eat five or more apples a week appear to have better lung function than men who do not eat the fruit.

주격 관계대명사 who가 이끄는 관계사절이 주어를 수식합니다. 본 동사는 appear로서 appear to be는 '~처럼 보이다, ~인 것 같다' 라는 뜻을 갖고 있습니다. appear 다음에 that절이 오기도 합니다.

Ex) He appears to be in good condition. = It appears that he is in good condition.

(그는 상태가 좋아 보인다.)

4. Researchers have also reported that fresh apples have the highest levels of substances that fight cell damage when compared to other fruits and vegetables.

동사 report 다음에 접속사 that이 쓰이고 있으며 이때 that절이 목적어의 역할을 하는 명사절이 됩니다. substances 다음에 나오는 that은 주격 관계대명사입니다. compared to는 '~와 비교하여, ~와 비교했을 때' 라는 뜻입니다. compared to 앞에는 주어와 동사인 they are가 생략되어 있습니다.

Ex) I agree that it was a great mistake. - 접속사 that

(그것이 큰 잘못이었다는 데에 동의합니다.)

Ex) Shipments were up only 14.1 percent in the second quarter of this year, compared to 21.1 percent in the first quarter.

(금년도 2/4 분기의 수출량 증가는, 1/4 분기의 21.1%에 비해, 겨우 14.1%에 그치고 있다.)

5. While no one knows exactly how long apples have existed, there is proof that people have enjoyed apples for at least 750,000 years.

while은 부사절을 이끄는 접속사로 '~하는 한편, ~하지만'의 뜻으로 쓰이고 있습니다. 또한 이 문장에서 쓰인 that은 접속사로 that이 이끄는 절이 proof와 동격으로 쓰이고 있습니다.

Ex) She is rather homely while her sister is very pretty.

(그녀의 여동생은 매우 예쁜 반면 그녀는 좀 못 생겼습니다.)

Ex) I admire your belief that you are always right.

(나는 네가 언제나 옳다는 너의 믿음에 감탄하지 않을 수 없다.)

6. Johnny Appleseed was born in 1774, and spent 49 years of his life in the American wilderness planting apple seeds.

본명은 John Chapman으로 미대륙의 광야에서 일생의 49년간 사과 씨를 심었다 해서 Johnny Appleseed라는 이름으로 불리게 되었습니다. 이 문장에서 planting은 분사구문으로 '~하면서' 라고 해석을 할 수 있습니다.

Ex) Saying "good-bye", he went out of the house.

(그는 안녕이라고 말하면서 그 집을 나갔습니다.)

7. He might have eaten quite a few apples.

may/might + have + p.p.는 과거에 대한 추측을 나타내고 있습니다.

quite a few는 '적지 않은, 많은' 의 뜻입니다.

Ex) I might have lost the book.

(저는 그 책을 잃어버린 것 같습니다.)

Q.1 Choose the definition on the right that matches the word on the left.

1. property	a) to diminish in amount or degree
2. reduce	b) a material of a particular kind
3. function	c) to come into flower, to develop
4. substance	d) the danger or possibility of loss
5. legend	e) something owned
6. blossom	f) an unproved story handed down from earlier times
7. risk	g) a specific occupation or role

Q.2 Mark True (T) or False (F).

1. Apples are the only fruit that possess properties that help reduce the risk of developing cancer. ( )
2. Men who do not eat apples tend to have worse lung function than men who eat an apple a day. ( )
3. There are reports that show fresh apples have the higher levels of cell-damage fighting substances than stale apples. ( )
4. How long apples have existed is unsure, but it is likely to have existed for more than 750,000 years. ( )
5. Johnny Appleseed was the first settler to bring apple seeds with him to the United States. ( )

Infinitive and Gerund 03 Unit

Introduction

Topic: Nice to Meet You, Again (다시 만나 반가워.)

Lesson objectives:

Infinitives and Gerunds (부정사와 동명사)

- the usage of to-infinitives (to부정사 용법)
- the usage of gerunds (동명사 용법)
- verb + to-infinitives / verb + ~ing (to부정사와 ~ing형을 목적어로 취하는 동사들)

WARM-UP

After a hard day at work, Brett arrives at a familiar restaurant to meet Aaron. The two haven't seen each other in quite some time and plan to catch up over dinner. However, Aaron's guest turns out to be the topic of conversation.

Brett : Hi. I apologize for being so late; I came right from work. (gerund)

Aaron : It's no problem. You look like you've had a long day.

Brett : Yeah, having more responsibility is nice, but I'm struggling to keep up. (gerund / to-infinitive)

Aaron : I'm sure you'll be fine. You were always the ambitious one in our group of friends.

Brett : Well, it seems my new boss' goal is to test my mettle right away. All I do is work, work, work. (infinitive)

Aaron : I guess that's the life of a busy executive: documents to file, reports to read, memos to write, clients to meet. (to-infinitive)

Brett : Anyway, it's really good to see you. (to-infinitive)

Aaron : You, too. It's nice knowing you're back in town. (gerund)

Brett : So, where is this special guest that you started to tell me about? (to-infinitive)

Aaron : She's in the washroom. I think she must check her makeup every 15 minutes; and she's always worried about her hair not being perfect.

Brett : How did you two meet?

Aaron : My newspaper sent me to take some photographs of Fashion Week, she was working as a sales representative for an up-and-coming designer, and we ran into each other at one of the events. (to-infinitive)

Brett : Hm. Interesting.

Aaron : Here she comes now.

Brett : Who? Her?

Aaron : Yes. Brett, I'd like you to meet Camille.

Brett : Hi, Camille. I'm surprised to see you here. (to-infinitive)

Camille : Hi, Brett. How have you been?

Aaron : Wait. Do you two know each other?

Camille : Yes. We do.

Aaron : Um, well, do you mind if I ask how?

Brett : Um, well, I think you left to go on an assignment in South America for a few months. (to-infinitive)

Aaron : And…

Camille : We dated for a while.

Aaron : And…

Brett : Well, I got transferred to Los Angeles and things ended there.

Aaron : This turned out to be quite a reunion.

Camille : I'm considering ordering the salmon. (gerund)

Translation

힘든 하루 일과를 마친 후, Brett은 자주 가는 레스토랑에 Aaron을 만나러 왔습니다. 둘은 꽤 오랫동안 보지 못했기 때문에 회포를 풀기 위해 저녁식사를 합니다. 하지만 Aaron의 손님이 결국 대화의 중심이 됩니다.

Brett : 안녕. 늦어서 미안하다. 일 끝나고 바로 왔어.
Aaron : 괜찮아. 오늘 굉장히 힘든 하루를 보낸 것 같구나.
Brett : 응, 더 많은 책임을 지게 된다는 것은 좋지만 버텨내기가 힘드네.
Aaron : 넌 잘 해낼거야. 너는 항상 우리 친구들 사이에서 야심만만한 아이였잖아.
Brett : 근데 내 새로운 상사의 목표는 내 근성을 당장 시험해보는 것인 것 같아. 내가 하는 것은 모두 일, 일, 일뿐이야.
Aaron : 그게 바쁜 관리자의 생활인 것 같아: 정리해야 할 서류들, 읽어야 하는 보고서들, 써야 하는 메모들, 만나야 할 고객들.
Brett : 어쨌든 만나서 정말 반갑다.
Aaron : 나도 그래. 네가 돌아온다는 소식 듣고 반가웠어.
Brett : 근데 네가 말하기 시작했던 특별한 손님은 어디에 있어?
Aaron : 화장실에 갔어. 내 생각에 그녀는 15분마다 화장을 고쳐야 하는 것 같아. 그리고 항상 머리가 완벽하지 않은지 신경 쓰지.
Brett : 두 사람은 어떻게 만났니?
Aaron : 신문사에서 Fashion Week에 낼 사진을 찍어오라고 나를 보냈는데 그녀가 유명 디자이너의 영업사원으로 일하고 있었거든. 그리고 우리는 한 이벤트에서 우연히 만났어.
Brett : 음. 재밌네.
Aaron : 그녀가 오네.
Brett : 누구? 저 여자?
Aaron : 응, Brett. Camille이야.
Brett : 안녕, Camille. 여기서 만나게 되다니 놀랍네.
Camille : 안녕, Brett. 어떻게 지냈어?
Aaron : 잠깐. 둘이 아는 사이야?
Camille : 응. 알고 있어.
Aaron : 음, 그럼, 어떻게 아는 사이인지 물어봐도 될까?
Brett : 네가 몇 달 동안 일하러 남미로 갔을 때인 것 같다.
Aaron : 그리고…
Camille : 잠시 데이트를 했었어.
Aaron : 그리고…
Brett : 그런데 내가 LA로 발령이 났고 그때 끝났지.
Aaron : 여기서 재회하게 된거구나.
Camille : 연어를 주문할까 생각중인데요.

Comprehension Check

1. Which of the following best describes Camille?
   (a) Brett's ex-girlfriend
   (b) Aaron's date
   (c) the waitress
   (d) Brett's ex-girlfriend and Aaron's date

2. From this dialogue, we know that Aaron is most likely:
   (a) a journalist
   (b) a marketing executive
   (c) a photographer
   (d) a travel agent

3. Why did Camille and Brett end their prior relationship?
   (a) Camille moved away.
   (b) Aaron moved to South America.
   (c) Brett moved to California.
   (d) Camille was busy with Fashion Week events.

Useful Expressions

In this dialogue	Explanation
1. You look like you've had a long day.	1. It's not as impolite to say to someone, "You look like you've had a long day," as it might be to tell them they look tired, sick, grouchy, or just plain awful. In fact, it may even show you are concerned. But you should probably only use this expression in personal, not professional, situations.

In this dialogue	Explanation
2. I'm struggling to keep up.	2. If you're struggling, you're having a difficult time. In this dialogue, Brett tells his friend that he has hit a rough patch at work and that it's not easy meeting the demands of his boss. He could have also said he's "working hard," "having a rough time," or "bending over backwards" trying to keep up with his workload.
3. Well, it seems my new boss' goal is to test my mettle right away.	3. The expression "a test of mettle" refers to a trial of character; a challenge of fortitude and strength. Let's take a look at another example in use, "The task of restoring the economy will test the young leader's mettle early in his term."In this case, the failed economy is a problem that will require ingenuity and determination to overcome. The situation will allow us to see whether the leader possesses these skills.
4. We ran into each other at one of the events.	4. When cars run into each other, it's often a disastrous event. However, when we use this same verb phrase with reference to people, it implies an unexpected, yet casual,meeting. For example, you might run into an old friend at the mall or a coworker at the supermarket. And remember that you can also use this phrase to say you've encountered an unanticipated problem, like traffic, for example.
5. Do you mind if I ask how?	5. If you prideyourself on good manners, you might want to preface requests with, "Do you mind if…". This construction serves to make your inquiries a little less direct. Some other examples include "Do you mind if I sit here?", "Do you mind if I have a sip of your cola?", or "Do you mind if I bring a friend?"
6. This turned out to be quite a reunion.	6. Here, the phrase "turn out" is used to indicate the outcome of a particular situation. For example, let's take a look at the sentence, "It turned out to be a beautiful day."This means that up until this point, we didn't know what to expect, but now that the day has arrived, we can see that the weather is just fine.

Grammar

Focus 1 to-Infinitive (to부정사)

to부정사는 동사의 성질을 가지고 문장에서 명사, 형용사, 부사의 역할을 합니다.

01 명사적 용법

문장에서 주어, 목적어, 보어, 동격어로 쓰입니다.

- To learn a foreign language is not easy. (주어)
  (외국어를 배우는 것은 쉽지 않습니다.)
- I want to see the manager. (목적어)
  (나는 지배인을 보기 원합니다.)
- My new boss' goal is to test my mettle right away. (보어)
  (내 새로운 상사의 목표는 내 근성을 당장 시험해보는 것입니다.)
- It is natural for children to follow their parents' example. (it: 가주어, to부정사: 진주어)
  (자녀들이 부모의 전철을 밟는 것은 자연스러운 것입니다.)
- We found it difficult to come to an agreement. (it:가목적어, to부정사:진목적어)
  (우리는 합의에 이르는 것이 어렵다는 것을 발견했습니다.)
- To err is to be human.
  (과오는 인간의 일상적인 일입니다.)
- My goal is to finish this project before the vacation begins.
  (제 목표는 방학이 시작하기 전에 이번 프로젝트를 끝내는 것입니다.)
- I want to make her feel welcome here.
  (나는 그녀가 여기서 환영 받기를 원합니다.)
- It's hard to imagine such a thing.
  (그런 것은 상상하기 힘듭니다.)
- It was difficult to concentrate during class today.
  (오늘은 수업시간에 집중을 하기 어려웠습니다.)

cf) All I do is work, work, work.
(내가 하는 것은 일뿐입니다.)
All you have to do is clean your own room.
(당신이 해야 할 것은 당신 방을 깨끗이 치우는 것입니다.)
주어가 all, the best, what, the only thing 등으로 시작하는 문장에서는 주격보어로 원형 부정사를 쓸 수 있습니다.

02 형용사적 용법

문장에서 명사, 대명사를 수식합니다.

- I guess that's the life of a busy executive: documents to file, reports to read, memos to write, clients to meet.
  (그게 바쁜 관리자의 생활인 것 같습니다: 정리해야 할 서류들, 읽어야 하는 메모들, 만나야 할 고객들.)
- Everybody needs somebody to love.
  (모든 사람들은 사랑할 누군가가 필요합니다.)
- I've got work to do.
  (나는 해야 할 일이 있습니다.)
- Give the boy a toy to play with.
  (그 소년에게 가지고 놀 장난감을 주세요.)
- We're all looking for something to do on Friday.
  (우리 모두 금요일에 할 일을 찾고 있습니다.)
- After finishing the exam, you'll probably want some time to relax.
  (시험이 끝난 후에 당신은 아마도 휴식을 취하고 싶을 것입니다.)
- I need another minute to think.
  (저는 좀 더 생각할 시간이 잠깐 필요합니다.)

03 부사적 용법

문장에서 형용사, 동사, 다른 부사를 수식하며, 목적, 원인, 이유, 조건, 결과, 정도의 의미입니다.

- I'm surprised to see you here. (원인)
  (당신을 여기서 만나서 놀랐습니다.)
- I'm struggling to get through this semester. (목적)
  (이번 학기를 마치기 위해 열심히 노력 중입니다.)
- She must be a genius to solve that math problem. (이유, 판단의 근거)
  (그 수학 문제를 풀다니 그녀는 천재임이 분명합니다.)
- The boy grew up to be a millionaire. (결과)
  (그 소년은 자라서 백만장자가 되었습니다.)
- He is old enough to live alone. (~할 정도로 ~하다)
  (그는 독립할 수 있을 만큼 자랐습니다.)

- This box is too heavy to lift. (너무 ~해서 ~할 수 없다)
  (그 상자는 너무 무거워서 들 수가 없습니다.)
- His parents must be proud to have a son that has accomplished so much at such an early age.
  (꽤 어린 나이에 그렇게 많은 일을 해낸 아들을 두어서 그의 부모님은 자랑스러울 것입니다.)
- The defendant is not competent to testify at trial.
  (피고는 재판에서 증언할만한 능력이 없습니다.)

04 be + to 부정사 용법

의무, 예정, 의도, 운명 등의 의미를 갖습니다.

- We are to obey the law. (의무)
  (우리는 법을 준수해야 합니다.)
- They're to be married next month. (예정)
  (그들은 다음 달에 결혼하기로 되어 있습니다.)
- If you are to please her, you must listen to her. (의도)
  (당신이 그녀를 기쁘게 해주고 싶다면, 그녀의 말에 귀를 기울여야 합니다.)
- He was never to see his children again. (운명)
  (그는 다시는 아이들을 보지 못할 운명이었습니다.)
- You are to be home before eleven!
  (11시 전에는 집에 있어야 합니다.)
- If she is to win an Olympic medal, she needs to work harder.
  (올림픽 메달을 따고 싶다면 그녀는 더 열심히 노력해야 합니다.)

Task 1

Fill in the blanks using the expressions from the box.

to spend   to lose   to be   to give   to turn down   to buy   to vote

1. I have no money __________ clothes.
2. It is unfair __________ her another chance to play that piece.
3. Mark isn't old enough __________.

4. She was too busy __________ time with her family.
5. You must be a fool ___________ the offer.

Focus 2 Gerund (동명사)

V+~ing 의 형태로, 동사의 성질을 가지며, 문장에서 명사의 역할을 합니다.
즉, 동명사는 뒤에 목적어를 취할 수 있고, 문장 내에서 주어, 목적어로 쓰입니다.

01 명사의 용법

- Having more responsibility is nice, but I'm struggling to keep up. (주어)
  (더 많은 책임을 지게 된다는 것은 좋지만 버텨내려고 안간힘을 쓰고 있습니다)
- I like watching action movies. (목적어)
  (나는 액션 영화를 보는 것을 좋아합니다.)
- I am fond of talking with foreigners. (전치사의 목적어)
  (나는 외국인과 이야기하는 것을 좋아합니다.)
- Waking up early is not my idea of a vacation.
  (일찍 일어나는 것이 나의 방학계획은 아닙니다.)
- The next president should concentrate on fixing the economy.
  (차기 대통령은 경제를 재정비하는데 초점을 맞춰야 합니다.)

02 동사적 성질

(1) 시제

- I apologize for being so late. (단순형)
  (늦어서 죄송합니다.)
- I am sorry for having wasted your time. (완료형)
  (당신의 시간을 낭비하게 해서 미안합니다.)
- She is proud of his winning the prize.
  (그녀는 그가 상을 수상한 것에 대해 자랑스럽게 여깁니다.)

- Thank you for choosing us for your banking needs.
  (당신의 은행 업무를 우리에게 맡겨주신 것에 대해 감사합니다.)
- Local officials deserve credit for having managed the crisis effectively.
  (지점들은 위기를 효과적으로 처리한 것에 대해 높게 평가 받을만합니다.)

(2) 부정

- She is ashamed of not being honest.
  (그녀는 정직하지 못한 것에 대해 부끄럽게 여깁니다.)
- He has considered not going to college.
  (그는 대학에 가지 않는 것을 고려했습니다.)

(3) 수동태

- I was ashamed of being scolded.
  (나는 꾸중을 들은 것이 부끄러웠습니다.)
- The boy admitted having been hit.
  (소년은 맞은 것을 인정했습니다.)

03 관용적 표현

- It's no use making such an excuse. (~해도 소용없다)
  (그러한 변명을 해도 소용없습니다.)
- There's no use crying over spilled milk.
  (우유를 쏟은 후에는 울어봐야 소용없습니다.)
- I couldn't help laughing. (~하지 않을 수 없다)
  (나는 웃지 않을 수 없습니다.) (= I couldn't help but laugh.)
- There's no telling what he will choose. (~할 수 없다)
  (그가 무엇을 선택할지 말할 수 없습니다.)
- I don't feel like eating out. (~하고 싶다)
  (외식하고 싶지 않습니다.)
- She likes to go shopping on Sundays. (~하러 가다)
  (그녀는 일요일에 쇼핑하러 가는 것을 좋아합니다.)

cf) go hiking/swimming/fishing/skating/skiing/hunting

- What do you say to having a coffee? (~이 어때요?)
  (커피 한잔 어때요?)
- We look forward to hearing from you. (~을 고대하다)
  (우리는 당신으로부터 소식을 듣기를 고대하고 있습니다.)

- They are used/accustomed to getting up early. (~에 익숙하다)
  (그들은 일찍 일어나는 것에 익숙합니다.)
- Do you object to changing the plan? (~을 반대하다)
  (당신은 계획을 변경하는 것에 대해 반대합니까?)
- On coming into the room, he turned on the light. (~하자마자)
  (그는 방에 들어오자 마자, 전등을 켰습니다.)
- His brother is far from being handsome. (결코 ~하지 않은)
  (그의 형은 결코 잘 생기지 않았습니다.)
- I had difficulty (in) solving the problem. (~하기 힘들다)
  (문제를 풀기가 힘들었습니다.)

Task 2

Read each sentence carefully and check if the gerund is used correctly(O) or incorrectly(X).

	O	X
1. It's no use taking a taxi to the appointment because you are already late.	( )	( )
2. She is fond of baking cakes for her friends.	( )	( )
3. He is able to doing it.	( )	( )
4. We really hope meeting you again.	( )	( )
5. Mel didn't buy anything because she wanted saving money.	( )	( )

Focus 3 Verb + to-infinitive / verb + ~ing

01 to부정사를 목적어로 취하는 동사

소망, 기대: wish, hope, desire, expect, want, seek, need, offer, plan, choose, prefer, try, prepare, aim
결정, 동의, 거절: determine, decide, agree, consent, promise, refuse
외양: appear, seem, tend, pretend
기타: deserve, manage, fail, afford, care

- I expect to receive a full refund.
  (나는 완전한 환불을 받을 것이라고 예상합니다.)
- I do not want to bother you.
  (나는 당신을 방해하고 싶지 않습니다.)
- She prefers to sleep late on the weekends.
  (그녀는 주말에는 늦잠 자기를 좋아합니다.)
- She refused to take the money.
  (그녀는 돈을 받기를 거절했습니다.)
- You deserve to win the scholarship.
  (당신은 그 장학금을 탈 자격이 있습니다.)

02 동명사를 목적어로 취하는 동사

완료, 진행: finish, stop, quit, abandon, give up, go on, keep on

회피: avoid, evade, miss, escape, mind

연기: postpone, put off, delay

언급, 추천: mention, suggest, consider, understand

허락, 부인: permit, admit, excuse, forgive, favor, resist, resent, deny, prevent, prohibit
감정, 기타: anticipate, appreciate, enjoy, dislike, miss, fancy, imagine, practice

- He finished writing the letter.
  (그는 편지 쓰는 것을 끝마쳤습니다.)
- I'm considering changing my major.
  (나는 전공을 바꿀 것을 고려하고 있습니다.)
- I don't mind staying late.
  (나는 늦게까지 머무는 것에 개의치 않습니다.)
- We anticipate falling prices over the next year or two.
  (우리는 내년이나 후년에 가격이 떨어질 것을 기대합니다.)
- Busy parents often miss spending time with their children.
  (바쁜 부모님들은 종종 아이들과 함께 할 시간을 놓쳐 버립니다.)
- I thoroughly enjoy perusing the morning newspaper.
  (나는 조간신문을 정독 하는 것을 정말 즐깁니다.)

03 동명사, to부정사 모두를 목적어로 취하는 동사

(1) 의미 차이가 별로 없는 동사: begin, start, continue, cease, attempt
(2) 의미 차이가 있는 동사: stop, forget, remember, regret
목적어가 동명사인 경우: 과거사실, ~한 것, ~하는 것
목적어가 부정사인 경우: 미래사실, ~할 것, ~하기 위해

- She stopped to help when she saw the accident.
  (그녀는 그 사고를 목격하고 돕기 위해 하던 일을 멈추었습니다.)
- She stopped walking when she saw the accident.
  (그녀는 그 사고를 보고 가던 길을 멈추었습니다.)
- I regret to tell you that Alice left.
  (나는 당신에게 Alice가 떠났다고 이야기하게 되어 유감으로 생각합니다.)
- I regret telling you that Alice left.
  (나는 당신에게 Alice가 떠났다고 이야기 한 사실을 후회합니다.)
- I forgot to buy the magazine.
  (나는 그 잡지를 사는 것을 잊었습니다.)
- I'll never forget meeting the king.
  (나는 그 왕을 만난 것을 결코 잊지 못할 것입니다.)

Task 3

Choose the correct word(s) in the blank.

1. We should not postpone ________ (to clean, cleaning) up the oil spill. That work is urgent.
2. Bob forgot ________ (to post, posting) Nancy's birthday card, which disappointed her.
3. Can you imagine ________ (to live, living) without a cell phone?
4. I can't afford ________ (to buy, buying) a new bicycle.
5. I have to practice ________ (to drive, driving) so that I can pass my driving test.

Reading Wonder Drug

Wouldn't it be nice if a single drug could prevent cancer, reduce the risk of Parkinson's disease, relieve headaches, and improve your memory? Or, perhaps, it already exists. Every once in a while this ancient remedy makes its way into newspaper headlines as the latest, greatest treatment for a modern malady. Most recently, it was championed as a means to prevent the onset of type 2 diabetes. Still not sure what we're talking about? Maybe you start your day with a hot frothy mug of it: coffee.

Thousands of studies have been done over the years to gauge the benefits of coffee consumption and the findings have long been a matter of dispute among health experts. However, most recent studies, including one at Harvard spanning 18 years and 126,000 participants, indicate that the benefits of drinking coffee far outweigh any of its detriments. What's more, it appears that these benefits increase along with the quantity you consume.

Of course, this doesn't mean that you can get away with drinking six sugary lattes every day. And you should also consider the health costs associated with sleep deprivation: an unintended side-effect linked to caffeine consumption. For now, anyway, the general rule may be "the more, the better," especially when it comes to preventing disease.

Translation 신비한 약

약 하나로 암을 예방할 수 있고, 파킨슨 병의 위험을 감소시킬 수 있으며, 두통을 완화시킬 수 있다면, 그리고 당신의 기억력을 높일 수 있다면 좋지 않겠습니까? 아니 아마도 그것은 이미 존재합니다. 때때로 이 고대 치료법은 현대 만성병을 위한 가장 최근의 그리고 최고의 약으로써 뉴스의 머리글을 장식하기도 합니다. 최근에, 이것은 제2형 당뇨병의 발병을 예방하는 수단으로써 등극했습니다. 아직도 우리가 무엇에 대해 이야기하고 있는지 모르시겠습니까? 아마도 당신은 하루를 뜨거운 거품이 가득한 이 한 잔과 함께 시작할 것입니다: **커피.**

수 천 가지의 연구들은 다년간 커피섭취의 적절량을 연구해왔으며 조사결과들은 건강 전문가들 사이에서 논쟁의 핵심이 되어왔습니다. 그러나 18년에 걸쳐 126,000명의 참가자들을 대상으로 Harvard에서 진행된 최근 연구들은 커피섭취의 이로운 점이 이것의 유해성을 압도할 정도로 훨씬 많다는 것을 밝혀냈습니다. 게다가, 이 이로움은 당신의 섭취량에 따라 늘어나는 것으로 보입니다.

물론, 이것이 매일 설탕을 넣은 여섯 잔의 라떼를 마실 수 있다는 것을 의미하지는 않습니다. 그리고 카페인 섭취와 연관된 뜻하지 않은 부작용인 수면부족으로 인하여 건강에 해가 될 수 있다는 것을 고려해야 합니다. 어쨌든 현재에는 커피는 많이 마실수록 더 좋다는 것이 일반적인 생각입니다. 특히 질병을 예방한다는 측면에 있어서는 말입니다.

Comprehension Check-up

True/False

1. The findings of studies on coffee consumption have always been widely agreed upon. (T/F)
2. According to many recent studies, the more coffee you consume, the greater benefit you'll derive. (T/F)
3. There are no negative effects associated with excess coffee consumption. (T/F)

Vocabulary Matching

1. remedy	a. disagreement
2. detriment	b. healing medicine or treatment
3. dispute	c. disadvantage
4. malady	d. a disorder or disease

Word Challenge

Quiz

Check Your Understanding: Choose the best word from the box to complete each sentence.

hear	listen

1. Those students who refuse to __________ will be punished.
2. I can't __________ the television. Can you turn up the volume?
3. I __________ to talk radio every morning in the car on the way to work.

Word Challenge

hear	Usage: In general, the verb "hear" means to perceive or receive sound. However, it has several other, maybe less often seen, uses. Among them are "to listen or give attention," and "to give attention for the purpose of rendering an official judgment." examples: 1. I always sit in the front row so I can hear the teacher. (to perceive sound) (나는 항상 맨 앞줄에 앉아서 선생님 말씀을 잘 들을 수 있습니다.) 2. I'd like to hear what you think.(to give attention) (나는 당신의 생각을 듣고 싶습니다.) 3. The judge heard both sides of the case before deciding in favor of the defendant. (to give attention for the purpose of rendering an official judgment) (판사는 피고의 편을 들어주기 전에 양측 의견을 들어보았습니다.) 4. Have you heard whether the deal was successful?(to be informed) (그 거래가 성사되었는지 들었습니까?)
listen	Usage: The uses of "listen", as compared to "hear", are far narrower. We use listen to indicate attention or the act of heeding a request. examples: 1. Listen closely now, or you're likely going to have questions later. (to pay attention) (지금 잘 들어두지 않으면 당신은 나중에 궁금증을 갖기 쉽습니다.) 2. It's always a pleasure to listen to Dr. West's lectures. (to hear, to pay attention) (West박사의 강의를 듣는 것은 항상 기쁜 일입니다.) 3. Children rarely listen to their parents. (to heed a request) (아이들은 부모님의 말씀을 잘 듣지 않습니다.)

Practice

Task 4

Change the verb in the parenthesis into the appropriate form to complete the sentence. You can add either "~ing" or "to."

1. My parents managed __________ there in time. (get)
2. He is not accustomed to __________ in public. (speak)
3. We haven't seen Mary for a long time, but we expect __________ from her soon. (hear)
4. No matter how hard I tried, my friend wouldn't stop __________. (cry)
5. It was stupid of you __________ such a mistake. (make)

Task 5

Find the sentences that are incorrect and correct them.

	correct	incorrect
1. Mary seems knowing the answer. ______________________________	( )	( )
2. They enjoy reading novels. ______________________________	( )	( )
3. Would you mind to open the window? ______________________________	( )	( )
4. My parents persuaded me going on a blind date. ______________________________	( )	( )

5. Have you found somebody to help you this Saturday? ( ) ( )

____

Culture Corner

Cheers

술은 어색한 인간관계를 좀더 친숙하게 만들어 주기도 하고 속마음을 터놓을 때 유용하게 쓰이기도 하지만 자칫 잘못하면 오히려 독이 될 수도 있습니다. 특히 음주문화는나라마다 조금씩 다르기 때문에 외국인 친구를 사귈 때 상대방의 문화를 미리 알아두면 실수하는 일도 없고 좀 더 발전된 인간관계를만들어 갈 수 있을 것입니다.

우선 미국에서는 술에 관한 규정이 매우 까다롭습니다. 그래서 술집마다 문 앞에 Door man이라는 사람이 신분증을 검사하는데요, "I need to ID(identify) you.", "I need to card you." 또는 "ID, please."라고 하면 신분증을 제시해야 합니다. 또한 만 21세 이상이어야 술집출입이나 주류구입이 가능합니다.

술에 관한 규정이 까다로운 만큼 음주운전에 대한 규제도 강화되어있는데요, 음주운전을 체크하는 검문소는 술 깬(sober) 정도를 점검한다고 "Sobriety checkpoint"라고 하며 음주여부를 테스트하는 경우 입김(breath)을 불어넣는다고 "Breathalyzer test"라고 합니다. 우리나라에서는 음주자들을 위한 대리운전이 보편화 되어있는데요, 미국에서는 친구들 사이에서 "A designated driver"를 선정해서 그 사람은 그날 무알콜 음료를 마시고 친구들을 위해 운전을 해줘야 합니다. 또한 음주운전을반대하는 어머니들의 모임(Mothers Against Drunk Driving)이 결성되어 활발한 활동을 벌이기도 합니다.

이제 술과 관련된 용어를 살펴보겠습니다. 미국에서는 "Happy hour"라고 해서 무료로 또는 저렴한 가격으로 술을 마실 수 있는 시간이 있습니다. 무료로 안주를 주는 경우에는 "service"라고 하지 않고 "It's on the house."라는 표현을 쓴다는 것도 기억해두시기 바랍니다. 그리고 우리말로 흔히 "한턱 낼께."라는 표현은 "This round's on me." 또는 "Drinks are on me."라고 합니다. 또한 술을 너무 마신 친구에게는 "You are cut off!"라는 표현을 사용해서 귀가를 종용하기도합니다.

- Bottoms up! / Cheers! / To John! / To the New Year! / To John's new job!
- I need to ID you. / I need to card you. / ID, please.
- This round's on me. / Drink's are on me.
- You are cut off (= We won't let you drink anymore.)

Wrap-up

Key sentences

1. To-infinitive
   (1) It seems my new boss' goal is to test my mettle right away.
   (2) I guess that's the life of a busy executive: documents to file, reports to read, memos to write, clients to meet.
   (3) I'm surprised to see you here.
   (4) I think you left to go on an assignment in South America for a few months.
   (5) We are to obey the law.

2. Gerund
   (1) Having more responsibility is nice, but I'm struggling to keep up.
   (2) I apologize for being so late.
   (3) It's no use making such an excuse.
   (4) I'm considering ordering the salmon.

REVIEW TEST

Find the correct answers in the blanks. (1-5)

1. I can't afford ____________ a vacation this summer.
   (1) take (2) taking (3) to take (4) to taking

2. Linda was disappointed ____________ that she didn't get the job.
   (1) learn (2) learned (3) learning (4) to learn

3. The boss gave up ____________ the company.
   (1) to manage (2) manage (3) managing (4) managed

4. I'm not used to ______________ speeches in front of a lot of people. I always get nervous.

(1) make (2) making (3) be making (4) have made

5. What are you doing this afternoon? What do you say to ______________ with me?

(1) go shopping (2) go to shop (3) going shopping (4) going for shop

Change the verb in parentheses into the correct form. (6-10)

6. We hope you have enjoyed _________ with us. (travel)

7. Are you tall enough __________ that box for me? The one on the top shelf. (reach)

8. On my way home from work, I stopped at the store __________ some beer. (buy)

9. He finally decided ___________ for the job. (apply)

10. I could not help __________ about her condition. (worry)

Supplementary Reading (보충 독해)

다음 글을 읽고 문제를 풀어 보세요.

What's your blood type?

There is a widespread belief in Korea and Japan that blood type determines, or corresponds to, personality. People in these countries tend to fit others into blood group stereotypes, and blood types are discussed as commonly as horoscopes and zodiac signs are in the West. Career and partner choices may also be influenced by blood type.

It is generally said that type O people are confident, strong-willed, idealistic, and in control of their emotions. They want to be leaders, and when they see something they want, they keep striving until they achieve their goal. Type A people are sensitive, reserved, responsible and indecisive. They like harmony, peace, and organization. Type B people are cheerful, straightforward, creative, and emotional. They are not good at following rules set by others and they like to get their own way. Type AB people are efficient, critical, and controlled. They can read a situation and discern the character of others very well, but they always keep everybody at a distance.

However, it's not surprising that science does not support any of these beliefs. An individual's personality is affected by a complex mixture of genetic and environmental factors such as parents, education, and relationships with others. While blood type is genetically determined, any influence on personality must be very small, if it exists at all.

Translation 당신의 혈액형은 무엇입니까?

한국과 일본에는 혈액형이 성격을 결정 짓거나 그에 상응한다는 믿음이 널리 퍼져있습니다. 이 두 나라사람들은 다른 이들을 혈액형에 따른 고정관념 속에 끼워 맞추는 경향이 있습니다. 그리고 혈액형은 서양의 별점과 별자리만큼 흔히 거론됩니다. 직업과 파트너 선택 또한 혈액형의 영향을 받을 수 있습니다.
일반적으로 O형의 사람들은 자신만만하고 의지가 강하며 이상주의적이고 자신의 감정을 잘 다룹니다. 그들은 지도자가 되고 싶어하고 자신이 원하는 것을 발견하면 그 목표점에 도달하기까지 계속 노력합니다. A형의 사람들은 감수성이 강하고 내성적이며 책임감이 강하고 우유부단합니다. 그들은 조화, 평화와 질서를 좋아합니다. B형의 사람들은 쾌활하고 직선적이며 창조적이고 감정적입니다. 그들은 다른 사람이 세워놓은 규칙을 잘 따르지 못하며 자신의 방식을 고집하기 좋아합니다. AB형의 사람들은 효율적이고 비판적이며 조심스럽습니다. 그들은 상황을 읽을 줄 알고 다른 이들의 성격을 잘 분별하지만 모든 사람들에게 항상 일정한 거리를 둡니다.
그러나 과학이 이러한 믿음을 하나도 뒷받침하지 않고 있다는 것은 놀라운 일이 아닙니다. 개인의 성격은 부모, 교육과 인간관계 등 유전적이고 환경적인 요인의 복잡한 구조에 의해 영향을 받습니다. 혈액형이 유전적으로 결정되긴 하지만, 성격에 미치는 영향은 반드시 아주 적을 것입니다. 그런 것이 존재한다면 말입니다.

Explanation

1. There is a widespread belief in Korea and Japan that blood type determines, or corresponds to, personality.

that은 belief와의 동격절을 이끄는 접속사입니다. correspond to/with는 '일치하다, 상응하다'라는 의미입니다.
Ex) The fact that he purchased a car has nothing to do with it.
(그가 차를 구입했다는 사실은 그것과 아무 관계가 없습니다.)

Ex) The diagram does not correspond to the answer.
(도표와 답이 일치 하지 않습니다.)

2. People in these countries tend to fit others into blood group stereotypes, and blood types are discussed as commonly as horoscopes and zodiac signs are in the West.

tend to는 '~을 하는 경향이 있다, ~하기 마련이다'라는 뜻입니다. as~ as는 '~만큼 ~한, ~와 같이'라는 의미입니다.

Ex) People tend to be less active in winter because of the low temperature.
(사람들은 겨울의 낮은 기온 때문에 덜 활동적이기 마련입니다.)

Ex) I do not go shopping as frequently as I used to.
(나는 예전만큼 자주 쇼핑을 하지 않습니다.)

3. They want to be leaders, and when they see something they want, they keep striving until they achieve the goal.

want 는 expect, demand, decide, appear, hope 등과 함께 to부정사를 목적어로 취하는 동사입니다. something they want 에서는 something 다음에 목적격 관계대명사 that이 생략되었는데, '그들이 원하는 어떤 것'이라고 해석하시면 됩니다. keep은 enjoy, admit, consider, finish 등과 함께 동명사를 목적어로 취하는 동사입니다.

Ex) I want to go home early today.
(나는 오늘 집에 일찍 가고 싶습니다.)

Ex) If you find something you like, tell me.
(당신이 좋아하는 것을 찾게 되면 나에게 말 해 주세요.)

Ex) The rain keeps falling. (비가 계속 내립니다.)

4. They are not good at following rules set by others, and they like to get their own way.

rules set by others에서는 rules 다음에 관계대명사와 be동사인 which are가 생략되었습니다. set by 는 '~에 의하여 정해진' 이라는 뜻을 가지고 있으며 여기에서 수동태에서 쓰이는 set은 과거분사형입니다. (set-set-set). like 는 want와 마찬가지로 to부정사와 ~ing형을 모두 목적어로 취할 수 있습니다.

Ex) The model house (which was) built by my dad was huge.
(아버지가 만든 모델 하우스는 매우 컸습니다.)

Ex) My family likes to eat at the Chinese restaurant on Saturday evenings.
(우리 가족은 토요일 저녁때 그 중국식당에서 식사하는 것을 좋아합니다.)

5. An individual's personality is affected by a complex mixture of genetic and environmental factors such as parents, education, and relationships with others.

be affected by 역시 수동태 표현으로 '~에 의해 영향을 받다' 라고 해석하시면 됩니다. such as 는 '~와 같은' 이란 의미로 뒤에 관련된 예가 나오게 됩니다.

Ex) My grades are definitely affected by how much time I spend studying.
(나의 성적은 분명내가 얼만큼의 시간을 공부하는 데 투자하느냐에 따라 영향을 받습니다.)

Ex) In the past I used to learn musical instruments such as the oboe and the flute.
(과거에 나는 오보에와 플룻 같은 악기를 배우곤 했습니다.)

6. While blood type is genetically determined, any influence on personality must be very small, if it exists at all.

while 은 접속사로써 '~을 하는 동안에, ~하는 반면에, ~할지라도' 라는 의미로 사용됩니다. at all이 if와 함께 조건/양보를 나타내는 문장에서 사용될 경우 '적어도, 조금이나마, 비록 ~하더라도' 라는 의미로 해석하면 됩니다.

Ex) While I admit the tasks are hard, we have to finish them on time.
(비록 나는 그 임무가 어렵다는 것을 인정하지만, 우리는 그것을 제시간에 끝마쳐야 합니다.)

Ex) If you believe in me at all, you will make the right decision.
(당신이 나를 조금이나마 믿는다면 당신은 옳은 선택을 할겁니다.)

Q.1 Choose the definition on the right that matches the word on the left.

1. strive	a) without complication, honest
2. correspond	b) exhibiting hesitation
3. reserved	c) to try extremely hard
4. indecisive	d) inclined to judge severely
5. critical	e) to be in agreement or harmony
6. genetic	f) keeping one's thoughts and emotions to oneself
7. straightforward	g) relating to genes

Q.2 Mark True (T) or False (F).

1. Type O people are confident, sensitive, and indecisive. ( )
2. Science supports the belief that personality is decided by blood type. ( )
3. Many Koreans and Japanese think that blood type determines, or corresponds to personality. ( )
4. Blood types influence people's career and partner choices around the world. ( )
5. Blood type is genetically and environmentally determined. ( )
6. In Western countries, people often talk about horoscopes and zodiac signs. ( )

Auxiliary Verbs 04 Unit

Introduction

Topic: Reunion (재회)

Lesson objectives:

Auxiliary verbs (조동사)

- can/could, may/might, will/would
- shall/should, must
- need, dare, used to, do

WARM-UP

After a chance encounter with his ex-girlfriend, Brett realizes it was a mistake to let her go. Despite his long-time friendship with Aaron, he decides to tell her this. In this lesson, we are going to listen in on a phone call between the two.

(phone ringing)

Camille : Hello? Is someone there? Hello?

(The phone rings again a minute or two later)

Brett : Hi, Camille?
Camille : Hello? Hello? Who is this?
Brett : It's Brett. Can you hear me? (can)
Camille : Did you just call a minute ago?
Brett : Who? Me? No. That must have been someone else. (must)
Camille : Um, okay. So, what's up?

Brett : May I have a few minutes of your time? (may)

Camille : Sure. What's on your mind?

Brett : I'm just calling to say "hello".

Camille : Well, hello.

(awkward silence)

Brett : Well, that's not exactly why I called.

Camille : Okay, so why did you call?

Brett : You know, we used to have a lot of fun together. (used to)

Camille : Yes. We did. But you needed to move to California for that big promotion. (need)

Brett : Well, now I think I might have made a mistake. (might)

Camille : I dare say I'm speechless. (dare)

Brett : I think you should give me another chance. (should)

Camille : Really, I would, but I'm seeing your friend, Aaron. (would)

Brett : I know, but I could talk to him. (could)

Camille : I don't think so.

Brett : Will you at least have dinner with me? (will)

Camille : I can't.

Brett : Shall we have coffee then? (shall)

Camille : I should go now. (should)

Brett : Do think about it. (do)

Camille : Goodbye, Brett.

Translation

예전 여자친구와 우연히 만나게 된 후, Brett은 그녀를 떠나 보낸 것이 실수라는 것을 깨달았습니다. Aaron과의 오랜 우정에도 불구하고, 그는 그녀에게 이것을 이야기하기로 결심합니다. 이번 과에서 우리는 둘 사이의 전화내용을 들을 것입니다.

(전화벨)

Camille : 여보세요? 누구세요? 여보세요?

(전화벨이 1, 2분 후 다시 울린다.)

Brett : 안녕, Camille?
Camille : 여보세요? 여보세요? 누구세요?
Brett : Brett이야. 들리니?
Camille : 좀전에 네가 전화했니?
Brett : 누구? 나? 아니야. 다른 사람이었을거야.
Camille : 음, 그래. 근데 무슨 일이야?
Brett : 잠깐 시간좀 내줄 수 있니?
Camille : 그럼, 무슨 일인데?
Brett : 그냥 안부인사하려고 전화했어.
Camille : 어, 안녕.

(어색한 침묵)

Brett : 그런데, 사실 이게 내가 정말 전화한 이유는 아니야.
Camille : 그래, 그럼 왜 전화했니?
Brett : 너도 알다시피, 우리 함께 좋은 시간을 많이 보냈었잖아.
Camille : 그래, 우린 그랬지. 하지만 네가 대규모 판촉행사 때문에 California로 떠나야 했었지.
Brett : 그래, 지금 와서 생각해보니 내가 그때 실수했던 것 같아.
Camille : 할말이 없는 것 같애.
Brett : 네가 나에게 기회를 한 번 더 주어야 한다고 생각해.
Camille : 정말 그러고 싶지만 나는 지금 네 친구 Aaron을 만나고 있어.
Brett : 알아, 하지만 내가 그에게 이야기할 수 있어.
Camille : 그렇지 않을거야.
Brett : 나랑 적어도 저녁식사는 해줄거지?
Camille : 안돼.
Brett : 그럼 커피 한 잔 할래?
Camille : 나 지금 나가봐야 해.
Brett : 꼭 생각해봐.
Camille : 안녕, Brett.

Comprehension Check

1. Brett's initial attitude is one of:
   (a) certainty
   (b) eagerness
   (c) confidence
   (d) hesitation

2. What is Brett's reason for calling Camille?
   (a) to admit a past mistake
   (b) to invite her to a holiday party at his office
   (c) to ask her to have dinner with him
   (d) both (a) and (c)

3. Camille likely __________ of Brett's decision to move to California.
   (a) talked
   (b) disapproved
   (c) regretted
   (d) approved

Useful Expressions

In this dialogue	Explanation
1. What's on your mind?	1. Curious what a friend is thinking? You can use this expression to find out. It's a great way to open up a conversation and can break an awkward silence. It's used most often between close friends; usually when one can sense the other would like to talk about something, but is unclear as to what it is. Though your boss might start a meeting like this if you've asked her for some time to discuss an important matter.
2. I'm just calling to say "hello."	2. Often, when you make a phone call, you state your purpose right away. Perhaps it's business related or maybe to invite a friend over to your house for dinner. But, sometimes, you call just because you feel like chatting. In that case, you can use this expression from today's dialogue.

In this dialogue	Explanation
3. Really, I would, but I'm seeing your friend, Aaron.	3. We all know what it means to see a movie or play, but, "see" takes on a special meaning when used with reference to a person. In today's dialogue, Camille says she's seeing Aaron, one of Brett's closest friends. She likely means that they're dating, but probably not too serious. At least not just yet.
4. I dare say I'm speechless.	4. You can probably tell that Brett's confession took Camille by surprise. If not, we need only look at her response to get a better sense of what she's thinking. While the expression "I dare say" sounds a bit old-fashioned, and isn't used all too often in everyday conversation, it indicates hesitation or uncertainty. And, given the circumstances, Camille didn't quite know what to say.

Grammar

조동사는 의문문, 부정문, 진행형, 완료형, 수동태 등을 만들 때 쓰이는 be, do, have 등의 조동사와 가능, 허가, 의무, 추측 등의 의미를 나타내는 데 쓰이는 법조동사 (Modal auxiliary verbs)로 나눌 수 있습니다. 법조동사에는 can/could, may/might, must, will/would, shall/should, ought to 등이 있습니다.

Focus 1 can/could, may/might, will/would

01 can / could

(1) can

'~을 할 수 있다' 라는 뜻으로, 능력, 허락, 요청, 가능성을 표현할 때 쓰이며, 가능성에 대한 강한 의문이나 부정을 나타내기도 합니다.

- We can do that for you. (능력)
  (당신을 위해 그렇게 해드릴 수 있습니다.)

- Can you hear me?
  (들리세요?)
- You can park here. (허가)
  (이 곳에 주차하셔도 괜찮습니다.)
- If you don't like it, you can exchange it for something else.
  (당신이 원하지 않는다면, 이것을 다른 것으로 교환하셔도 됩니다.)
- Can you pass the salt? (요청)
  (소금 좀 전달해주시겠어요?)
- Anybody can make a mistake. (가능성)
  (누구라도 실수는 하기 마련입니다.)
- What he says can't be true. (강한 부정)
  (그가 말한 것이 사실일 리 없습니다.)
- He can't have said so. (과거에 대한 강한 부정)
  (그가 그렇게 말했을 리 없습니다.)

(2) could

can의 과거형으로 과거시제나 좀더 정중한 표현에 쓰입니다. 또한 '~할 수도 있겠다' 라는 가능성을 표현하기도 합니다.

- I received some money, so I could go to university. (과거)
  (나는 돈을 좀 받았습니다. 그래서 대학에 갈 수 있었습니다.)
- Could you carry this luggage for me? (정중한 표현)
  (이 짐을 좀 들어주실 수 있습니까?)
- Could I have another minute to think about it?
  (저에게 생각할 시간을 좀주시겠습니까?)
- I know, but I could talk to him. (가능성: can 보다 좀 더 이론적 가능성)
  (알고 있습니다. 그러나 내가 그에게 이야기할 수도 있습니다.)
- You are very talented. You could be a famous singer.
  (당신은 재능이 뛰어납니다. 당신은 유명한 가수가 될 수도 있습니다.)

(3) can / be able to

현재의 능력을 나타낼 때는 can을 be able to로 바꾸어 쓸 수 있고, 과거의 능력을 나타낼 때도 could를 was/were able to로 바꾸어 쓸 수 있다. 그러나 과거에 실제로 일어났던 특정 행위에 대해 말할 때는 was/were able to만을 쓸 수 있습니다.

- The children could swim when they were quite young. (과거 능력)
  (그 아이들은 아주 어렸을 때 수영을 할 수 있었습니다.)
- The children were able to swim across the river. (과거 행위)
  (그 아이들은 그 강을 가로질러 수영할 수 있었습니다.)

02 may / might

(1) may

'~할 수도 있다' 라는 허락을 나타내거나 '~할 지도 모른다' 라는 뜻으로 추측의 의미를 가지기도 하며, 기원을 나타낼 때도 쓰입니다. so that~may 구문에서는 목적을 나타내기도 하고, 양보절에서 쓰이기도 합니다.

- May I have a few minutes of your time? (허락)
  (잠깐만 시간을 내줄 수 있나요?)
- She may only have the flu, but we're still waiting for her blood test results. (추측)
  (그녀는 단지 감기에 걸린 것일 수도 있지만, 우리는 아직 그녀의 혈액검사 결과를 기다리고 있습니다.)
- The man may have won the lotto.
  (그 남자는 로또에 당첨되었을 수도 있습니다.)
- May she rest in peace! (기원)
  (그녀가 평안하게 잠들기를!)
- May you live in interesting times.
  (당신이 즐거운 인생을 살기바랍니다.)
- Parents make sacrifices so that their children may have more opportunities in life. (목적)
  (부모님들은 그들의 아이들이 인생에서 좀 더 많은 기회를 얻도록 하기 위해 희생을 합니다.)
- They work on Sundays so that they may make more money.
  (그들은 더 많은 돈을 벌기 위해 일요일에도 일합니다.)
- Be that as it may, I'm not going to change my mind. (양보)
  (그렇더라도 저는 제 입장을 바꾸지 않을 것입니다.)
- Try as he may, he never succeeds.
  (그가 아무리 노력할지라도, 결코 성공하지는 못할 것입니다.)

(2) might

may의 과거형으로 쓰이거나, may의 대용어로서 보다 정중한 표현이나 좀 더 불확실한 것을 나타낼 때 쓰입니다. 가정법에서 쓰이기도 합니다.

- I hoped that she might accept my apology. (may 과거)
  (나는 그녀가 내 사과를 받아주기를 바랬습니다.)
- I shouted loudly so that she might hear me.
  (나는 그녀가 내 말을 들을 수 있게 크게 소리쳤습니다.)
- Well, now I think I might have made a mistake. (may 대용)
  (음, 이제와 생각하니 내가 실수를 한 것 같습니다.)

- We might be unable to get there in time for breakfast.

  (우리는 아침식사 시간에 맞춰 도착할 수 없을 것입니다.)

cf) I may go to Paris next month. (about a 50% chance)
(나는 다음달에 파리에 갈 것입니다.)
Peter might have dinner with us. (about a 30% chance)
(Peter는 우리와 저녁을 먹을지도 모릅니다.)
그러나 이 경우 많은 원주민들은 may와 might를 의미 차이 없이 쓰고 있습니다.

- If he had been there, you might have acted differently. (가정법)

  (그가 거기 있었더라면 당신은 다르게 행동했을지도 모릅니다.)

(3) may(might)의 관용표현

- You may/might well be proud of your daughter. (~하는 것도 당연하다.)

  (당신이 딸을 자랑스러워하는 것도 당연합니다.)
- We might as well accept the situation before us. (~하는 게 낫다.)

  (우리가 우리 앞에 놓여진 상황을 받아들이는 것이 낫습니다.)
- You might as well expect the sun to rise in the west as expect me to agree with you. (~하느니 차라리 ~하는 것이 낫다.)

  (내가 당신에게 동조하길 기대하느니 차라리 해가 서쪽에서 뜨길 기대하는 편이 낫습니다.)

03 will / would

(1) will

'~할 것이다' 라는 뜻으로, 미래시제를 표현할 때 쓰는 조동사 입니다. 또한 강한 의지, 요청, 습관, 필연적인 일을 나타낼 때 쓰입니다.

- If you are elected president, what will be your first initiative? (미래)

  (당신이 대통령으로 선출된다면, 가장 먼저 무엇을 할 것입니까?)
- Will the train be on time?

  (그 기차가 제 시간에 올까요?)
- I really will stop smoking. (의지)

  (나는 정말 담배를 끊을 작정입니다.)
- Will you at least have dinner with me? (요청)

  (나와 저녁 식사 정도는 해줄 수있지요?)
- Will you go to the dance with me?

  (저랑 춤추실래요?)
- She'll sit talking for hours. (습관)

  (그녀는 곧잘 여러 시간 동안 앉아 이야기하곤 합니다.)

- Everything will change as time goes by. (필연)
  (시간이 흐름에 따라 모든 것은 변하기 마련입니다.)
- Your time will eventually come.
  (기회는 결국 오게 됩니다.)

(2) would

will의 과거 형태로 쓰이거나, 화자의 의지나 바램 (would like to)의 의미로 주로 쓰입니다. 또한 과거의 습관, 공손한 요청, 추측, 현재에 대한 가정을 표현할 때도 사용됩니다.

- Jenny said she would be here by now. (will의 과거)
  (Jenny는 그녀가 지금쯤은 벌써 여기에 와 있을 거라고 말했습니다.)
- They tried for hours, but she wouldn't come out of her room. (의지)
  (그들이 몇시간째 노력했지만, 그녀는 방에서 나오려 하지 않았습니다.)
- I asked him many times, but he wouldn't tell me.
  (나는 그에게 여러 번 물었으나 그는 내게 말하지 않으려고 합니다.)
- Really, I would, but I'm seeing your friend, Aaron. (바램)
  (정말 나는 그러고 싶습니다. 그러나 나는 당신의 친구인 Aaron을 만나고 있습니다.)
- I would like to send the letter by express mail.
  (빠른 우편으로 편지를 보내고 싶습니다.)
- We'd like another minute to look over the menu, please.
  (우리는 메뉴를 좀더 보고 싶습니다.)
- When Rachael was younger, she would talk about becoming an actress. (과거습관)
  (Rachael이 더어렸을 때 그녀는 배우가 되겠다고 말하곤 했습니다.)
- He would go jogging every morning.
  (그는 매일 아침 조깅을 하곤 하였습니다.)
- Would you bring me some orange juice? (요청)
  (오렌지 주스 좀저에게 주시겠습니까?)
- Would you guide me around the museum?
  (박물관 안내를 좀 해주시겠습니까?)
- It would take over an hour to walk there. (추측)
  (거기까지 걸어가는데 한 시간 이상 걸릴 것입니다.)
- It would be a mile from here to the station.
  (여기서 그 역까지 1마일 정도 될 것입니다.)
- I wouldn't vote for him if you gave me a million dollars. (가정)
  (당신이 나에게 백만 달러를 준다면 그를 뽑지 않을 것입니다.)
- I would tell you if I knew.
  (내가 안다면 당신에게 알려줄 것입니다.)

Task 1

Choose the appropriate word(s) from the box to complete each sentence.

may	could	was able to	would	can

1. __________ you like some tea now?
   (지금 차를 좀 드시겠어요?)

2. You __________ as well make the best of the situation.
   (당신은 그 상황을 최대한 잘 이용하는 것이 낫습니다.)

3. Luckily, the driver __________ stop before he crashed into the bus.
   (다행히 그 운전사는 버스와 충돌하기 전에 차를 멈출 수 있었습니다.)

4. The story __________ not possibly be true.
   (그 이야기는 사실 일리가 없습니다.)

Focus 2 shall/should, must

01 shall

'~해주겠다, 하도록 하겠다' 라는 뜻으로 말하는 사람의 의지를 나타낼 때 사용됩니다. 또한 의문문으로 사용되었을 때에는 '~할까요? ~시킬까요?' 라는 뜻으로 사용됩니다.

- This invention shall revolutionize the way people think about transportation.
  (이 발명품은 사람들의 교통수단에 대한 사람들의 사고 방식에 혁명을 일으키게 될 것입니다.)
- We shall make a visit to Sue's.
  (Sue의 집을 방문하도록 하겠습니다.)
- He shall be punished for his crime.
  (그는 범죄의 대가를 치르게 될 것입니다.)

- Shall we have coffee then?
  (그렇다면 커피 한잔 할까요?)
- Shall we head over to the theater?
  (극장으로 갈까요?)

02 should

(1) should

의무, 추측, 목적 등으로 '~해야 한다, ~일 것이다, ~하지 않도록/ ~할까 봐 (lest~should)' 이라는 뜻을 가지고 있습니다. 또한 '~일 리가 있겠는가' 라는 뜻으로 뜻밖의 상황이나 의아스러움을 나타낼 때 사용하기도 합니다.

- I think you should give me another chance. (의무)
  (저는 당신이 저에게 또 다른 기회를 주어야 한다고 생각합니다.)
- I should go now.
  (나는 이제 가야만 합니다.)
- Judy should be here soon. She left home an hour ago. (추측)
  (Judy는 곧 여기에 오게 될 것입니다. 그녀는 한 시간 전에 집을 떠났습니다.)
- He's afraid lest the scandal should come to light. (lest~should)
  (그는 그 추문이 알려질까봐 두려워합니다.)
- I don't know how I should interpret his statement. (뜻밖의 상황)
  (그의 진술을 어떻게 해석해야 할지 모르겠습니다.)

(2) should have + p.p.

should have + p.p.: 과거에 일어나지 않은 일에 대한 유감
shouldn't have + p.p.: 과거에 일어난 일에 대한 유감

- The refund should have been credited to your account.
  (환불금액은 당신의 계좌에 입금되었어야 합니다.)
- You shouldn't have bought this car.
  (당신은 이 차를 사지 말았어야 합니다.)

(3) should가 쓰이는 that절

should는 중요성과 관련된 형용사(important, necessary, vital, essential, eager, anxious, concerned) 다음에 오는 that절에서 사용되고, 제안, 충고, 주장, 요구와 관련된 동사 (insist, order, urge, recommend, suggest, propose, request, demand) 다음에 오는 that절에서도 쓰입니다. 여기에서 should는 생략이 가능한 데, 생략이 되더라도 그 뒤에 오는 동사는 that절에서 원형으로 쓰입니다. 대개의 경우 should를 생략합니다.

- Is it necessary that his family (should) be informed?
  (그의 가족에게 알릴 필요가 있습니까?)
- He insisted that his wife (should) reduce her expenditures.
  (그는 아내가 지출을 줄여야 한다고 주장했습니다.)
- The doctor recommends you (should) rest for several weeks before returning to work.
  (의사는 당신에게 업무에 복귀하기 전에 여러 주 휴식을 취할 것을 권유합니다.)

03 must

(1) must / must have + p.p.

must는 '~해야 한다, 하지 않으면 안 된다' 라는 뜻으로 should보다 더 강한 의무를 나타낼 때 사용합니다. 또한 '~임에 틀림없다' 라는 뜻으로 추측을 나타낼 때 사용하기도 하는데 역시 should 보다 더 강한 추측을 나타냅니다. 과거에 대한 추측은 must have + p.p.로 표현합니다.

- Kelly must report to the principal's office immediately. (의무)
  (Kelly는 교장실에 즉시 보고해야 합니다.)
- All freshman students must attend a mandatory health and wellness seminar.
  (모든 신입생들은 의무적인 건강관리 세미나에 참석해야만 합니다.)
- Ann stayed up all night reading the book. She must be very tired. (강한 추측)
  (Ann은 그 책을 읽느라고 밤을 샜습니다. 그녀는 틀림없이 피곤할 겁니다.)
- That must have been someone else. (과거 일에 대한 강한 추측)
  (그것은 누군가 다른 사람이었음에 틀림없습니다.)
- The artist who produced this work must have been very talented.
  (이 작품을 만든 예술가는 틀림없이 재능이 있는 사람이었을 겁니다.)

(2) must/should/ought to

must는 강제적인 명령이나 강한 권유의 의미가 있고, should나 ought to는 그보다 약한 권유나 충고의 의미가 있습니다.

- You must stop smoking, or you'll die.
  (당신은 담배를 끊어야만 합니다, 그렇지 않으면 당신은 죽게 될 것입니다.)
- You should/ought to stop smoking. It's bad for you.
  (당신은 담배를 끊어야 합니다. 담배는 당신에게 해롭습니다.)
- You must get to bed, or you'll have trouble waking up for school tomorrow.
  (당신은 잠을 자야만 합니다. 그렇지 않으면 내일 학교 가기 위해 일어나는데 문제가 있을 것입니다.)
- We ought to consider some of the alternatives.
  (우리는 몇 가지 대안을 고려해야만 합니다.)

Task 2

Read each sentence carefully and decide whether it is correct (O) or incorrect (X).

	O	X
1. Joanna keeps crying. She should have a problem.	( )	( )
2. He suggested that she meet with her lawyer before signing the paper.	( )	( )
3. Passengers don't must smoke in the toilet.	( )	( )
4. Let's go to the movies, will we?	( )	( )
5. Your application arrived too late. You should have sent it in earlier.	( )	( )

Focus 3 need/dare, used to, do

01 need / dare

(1) 부정문과 의문문(조동사), 긍정문(일반동사)

need는 '~할 필요가 있다', dare는 '감히 ~하다' 라는 뜻을 가지고 있습니다. need/dare는 부정문과 의문문에서는 주로 조동사로 쓰여서 동사원형이 뒤에 오고, 긍정문에서는 일반 동사로 쓰여서 to부정사가 뒤에 옵니다. need not have + p.p.는 "~할 필요가 없었는데 했다" 라는 뜻입니다. I dare say는 '~인 것 같다,' dare + O + to do는 '감히 ~하도록 도전하다/내기하다' 의 뜻으로 쓰입니다.

- Investors need not be alarmed; our institution remains financially sound. (부정문)
  (투자자들은 놀랄 필요가 없습니다: 우리 시설은 재정적으로 건전합니다.)
- Need you listen to music at that volume? (의문문)
  (당신은 그렇게 크게 음악을 들을 필요가 있습니까?)

cf) Do you need to listen to music at that volume? - 더 자연스러운 표현

- You needed to move to California for that big promotion. (긍정문)
  (당신은 그 대규모 판촉 행사 때문에 California로 이주해야만 했습니다.)

- You needn't have cooked so much food. Nobody was hungry. (need have + p.p.)
  (당신이 그렇게 많은 음식을 할 필요는 없었습니다. 아무도 배고프지 않았습니다.)
- I dare not look at his face. (부정문)
  (나는 감히 그의 얼굴을 볼 수 없습니다.)
- Dare you question my authority? (의문문)
  (당신이 감히 나의 권한에 대해 의문을 제기한다는 것입니까?)
- She dares to shout at me?
  (그녀가 어떻게 감히 나에게 소리를 지른단 말입니까?)
- I dare say I'm speechless.
  (나는 할 말이 없는 것 같습니다.)
- Science continually dares us to challenge our fundamental assumptions about nature. (dare + O + to부정사)
  (과학은 끊임없이 우리에게 계속 자연에 대한 기본적인 가정에 감히도전하도록 합니다.)
- My friends once dared me to eat a live worm.
  (내 친구들은 언젠가 한번 내가 살아있는 벌레를 먹도록 내기를 하였습니다.)

(2) 부정문과 의문문(일반동사)

need와 dare는 부정문과 의문문에서도 일반 동사로 쓰여서 조동사 do를 동반하기도 합니다.

- You don't need to reserve seats on the train.
  (기차 좌석을 예약할 필요는 없습니다.)
- Do we need to eat the same thing for lunch every day?
  (우리는 매일 점심에 똑같은 것을 먹어야 합니까?)
- I would not dare to inquire about her ex-husband.
  (그녀의 전 남편에 대해 나는 묻을 엄두가 나지 않습니다.)
- Does he dare to do it?
  (그가 감히 그것을 할까요?)

02 used to

(1) used to / be used to / get used to

used to 는 과거의 어떤 기간에 걸쳐 행했던 동작이나 상태 혹은 습관을 나타냅니다. 특히 현재와 대비되는 과거의 상태 또는 사실을 나타냅니다. 주의해야 할 점은 be used to/get used to는 뒤에 동명사나 명사가 와서 '~에 익숙해져 있다' 라는 뜻으로 사용됩니다.

- You know, we used to have a lot of fun together. (과거 동작, 상태)
  (당신도 알다시피 우리는 많은 즐거운 시간을 함께 보냈습니다.)
- I used to go out to dinner all of the time, but these days I'm trying to save money.
  (나는 항상 저녁을 나가서 먹곤 했지만 요즘에는 돈을 아끼려고 하고 있습니다.)
- It used to be much easier to find a quality tailor. (대비)
  (예전에는 유능한 재단사를 찾는 일이 (지금보다) 훨씬 쉬웠습니다.)
- I'm used to driving in Seoul now, but it was hard at the beginning. (be used to)
  (나는 이제 서울에서 운전하는데 익숙해져 있습니다, 그러나 처음엔 힘들었습니다.)
- It normally takes a while to get used to the sounds of a foreign language. (get used to)
  (대개 외국어 소리에 익숙해지는데 시간이 좀 걸립니다.)

(2) 의문문과 부정문

격식체에서는 used to가 조동사로 쓰이기도 하나, 대개는 의문문과 부정문에서 조동사 do와 함께 쓰입니다.

- Did you used to smoke?
  (당신은 담배를 피우곤 했습니까?)
- I didn't used to like soap operas, but now I do.
  (나는 예전에 드라마를 좋아하지 않는 편이었으나 지금은 좋아합니다.)
- Didn't you used to have much longer hair?
  (당신은 예전에 훨씬 긴 머리를 갖고 있지 않았습니까?)

(3) used to / would

used to와 would 모두 과거의 반복적인 행동을 나타내지만, would는 언제든지 중단이 가능한 동사하고만 쓰이기 때문에 과거의 상태를 표현할 수는 없습니다. would는 생물체만 주어로 삼는 반면, used to는 무생물도 주어로 삼을 수 있습니다. used to는 길고 막연한 과거를 전제로 하기 때문에 명확한 과거 시점을 나타내는 부사구와는 쓰이지 않습니다.

- When we were children we used to go skating in winter. / When we were children we would go skating in winter.
  (우리가 아이였을 땐 겨울에 스케이트 타러 가곤 했습니다.)
- When I was a child I used to like candy. / *When I was a child I would like candy.
  (내가 아이였을 때 사탕을 좋아하곤 했습니다.)
- There used to be a pond over there. / *There would be a pond over there.
  (저쪽에 연못이 있었습니다. (지금은 없습니다.))
- I lived in Belgium for three years. / * I used to live in Belgium for three years.
  (나는 3년 동안 벨기에에 살았습니다.)

03 do

do는 의문문 혹은 부정문에 쓰이고, do +동사는 그 동사의 의미를 강조하게 됩니다. 또한 do는 앞에 나온 동사구를 대신하여 쓰이기도 하고, 도치구문에서도 쓰입니다.

- Do you enjoy going to the cinema? (의문문)
  (영화 보러 가는 것을 즐기세요?)
- The subway doesn't run after midnight. (부정문)
  (지하철은 자정 이후에는 운행되지 않습니다.)
- Do think about it. (강조)
  (그것에 대해서 꼭 생각해 보세요.)
- Do remember to check your answers after you've finished the exam.
  (시험을 다 본 후에 당신의 답을 검토하는 것을 꼭 기억하세요.)
- Washington University doesn't offer a major in chemical engineering, but Oregon State does. (= ...but Oregon State offers....)
  (Washington대학에는 화학 공학과가 없지만 Oregon대학에는 있습니다.)
- Rarely does he lose his temper. (도치)
  (그는 좀처럼 화를 내지 않습니다.)
- Only in the rarest of circumstances do sharks attack humans.
  (오직 가장 낯선 환경에서만 상어는 사람을 공격합니다.)

Task 3

Choose the correct word(s) in the blank.

1. A big house __________ (used to/would) stand there.
2. How dare he __________ (take/to take) my computer to his room?
3. They __________ (used to/be used to) go to church on Sundays.
4. You need __________ (handle/to handle) the package with care.
5. They dared me __________ (climb/to climb) to the top of the tree.

Reading　The Montessori School

In most classrooms, teachers lead and students follow. Tests are given to gauge progress, students are promoted according to grade and rank, and variations on this basic model have lasted for centuries and across many cultures. But around the end of the 19th century, Italian physician Maria Montessori proposed an educational paradigm in stark contrast with tradition.

The classroom she envisioned was a child-centered one; one in which the teacher's role is resigned to developing an environment conducive to learning. It is through interaction with this environment and repeated self-examination that learning takes place, she argued. The teacher places materials before the students, and the students review them at their own pace. Teachers demonstrate, but don't lecture. When a child becomes bored with a particular concept or task, they are considered ready to move on.

While the Montessori method is as controversial today as when it was first proposed, thousands of schools across the globe bear the founder's name. More than 8,000 exist in America alone, followed by Australia, with roughly 200; and the rest are dispersed throughout the world. Though these schools represent a broad range of educational philosophies they share a number of common goals: to awaken human curiosity, nurture creativity, and develop the imagination of students.

Translation　몬테소리 학교

대부분의 수업에서, 교사들이 주도를 하고 학생은 따라갑니다. 시험은 발달을 평가하기 위해 주어지며 학생들은 성적과 순위에 따라 진급하게 됩니다. 그리고 몇 세기 동안 많은 문화에 걸쳐 이러한 기본 형태가 변형되며 이어져 왔습니다. 하지만 19세기 말경에 이탈리아 의사인 Maria Montessori는 전통적인 방법과는 완전히 대조를 이루는 교육 체계를 주창했습니다.

그녀가 생각했던 교실은 아이들 중심이었습니다 그 안에서 선생님의 역할은 학습에 도움이 되는 환경을 만들어 주는 것입니다. 학습이 되는 것은 이러한 환경과의 상호작용과 반복되는 자기분석을 통해서라고 그녀는 주장합니다. 선생님이 학생 앞에 재료를 놓고 학생들은 그들의 속도에 맞게 그것을 잘 살펴봅니다.

선생님들이 시범을 보여주긴 하지만 강의를 하지는 않습니다. 아이들이 특정한 개념이나 임무에 지루함을 느낄 때 그들은 다음으로 옮겨 갈 준비가 된 것으로 간주됩니다.
Montessori방식은 이것이 처음 알려졌을 때만큼이나 오늘날에도 논란이 되고 있지만, 세계 수천 개의 학교들이 창시자의 이름을 붙이고 있습니다. 미국에서만 8,000개 이상이며 호주에서 대략 200개 정도 됩니다 그리고 나머지는 전세계에 퍼져 있습니다. 이러한 학교들은 다양한 범위의 교육 철학을 표현하지만, 많은 목표들을 공유합니다: 인간의 호기심을 깨우고, 창조성을 기르고, 학생들의 상상력을 발전시키는 것입니다.

Comprehension Check-up

True/False

1. The Montessori method is undisputed in the educational field. (T/F)
2. In the Montessori classroom, teachers serve as facilitators, not lecturers. (T/F)
3. The philosophy developed by Maria Montessori is one rooted in addressing individual student needs. (T/F)

Vocabulary Matching

1. physician	a. spread out, scattered
2. nurture	b. a medical doctor
3. conducive	c. to support and encourage
4. dispersed	d. favourable, helpful

Word Challenge

Quiz

Check Your Understanding: Choose the best word from the box to complete each sentence.

practice	study	learn

1. I don't know where I'm going to find time to __________ for next week's exam.
2. It's important for teachers to __________ their students' names.
3. I set aside an hour every day to __________ the piano.

Word Challenge

learn	Usage: While learning may involve studying, and studying may imply learning, there are certain instances where the verb "learn" is the better choice. This verb has several meanings, although they are closely related: to acquire knowledge or a skill; to memorize, as a child might do with the alphabet; and to gain knowledge or understanding through experience. examples: 1. After years of study, he finally learned to play the piano. (to acquire knowledge or a skill) (몇 년 간 공부한 후 그는 마침내 피아노 치는 법을 배웠습니다.) 2. He learned several famous speeches and could recite them at will. (to memorize) (그는 몇몇의 유명한 연설들을 외워서 그것들을 마음대로 인용할 수 있었습니다.) 3. Someday, I hope people will finally learn to live together peacefully? (to gain knowledge or understanding through experience) (언젠가, 나는 사람들이 함께 평화롭게 사는 방법을 마침내 터득하게 되기를 희망합니다.)
practice	Usage: In general, "practice" is used to refer to repetitive or habitual actions. Whereas "learn" or "study" often pertain to acquiring information or a new skill, "practice" implies a process. examples: 1. Perfecting your golf swing isn't easy; you'll have to practice repeatedly. (to perform habitually) (당신이 골프 스윙을 완벽하게 하는 것은 쉽지 않습니다. 당신은 반복적으로 연습해야 할 것입니다.) 2. All citizens have the right to practice whichever faith they choose. (to follow or observe) (모든 시민들은 그들이 선택한 어떠한 신앙이든 신봉할 수 있는 권리가 있습니다.) 3. In order to practice law, you'll need to pass the bar exam. (to partake in a profession) (변호사 개업을 하기 위해서는 변호사 자격시험을 통과해야 합니다.)
study	Usage: Though "learn" and "study" are close cousins, the latter implies effort and the application of one's mind to a task. And while you can learn to play basketball, you'll rarely hear that someone is studying basketball.

	examples: 1. Jeff studied for hours only to fail the exam. (application of the mind to the acquisition of knowledge) (Jeff는 몇 시간 동안 공부했지만, 시험에 실패하고 말았습니다.) 2. He studied the portrait intently. (to consider carefully or reflect deeply upon something) (그는 오로지 인물화만 공부했습니다.) 3. Great actors study their lines, but are able to improvise when needed. (to learn or memorize) (훌륭한 배우들은 그들의 대사를 외우지만, 필요할 때는 즉석에서 만들어 낼 수도 있습니다.)

Practice

Task 4

Fill in the blank with the most appropriate choice.

1. A: Can I help you with anything?
   B: I _______ like a glass of water.
   (a) should (b) would (c) may (d) could

2. A: I ________ be a ballerina, and I loved to dance.
   B: What about now?
   (a) would (b) shall (c) could (d) used to

3. A: I don't think you love her.
   B: I ________ love her. I swear.
   (a) would (b) do (c) may (d) must

4. A: Have you seen Matt?
   B: No, but he ________ be downstairs.
   (a) may (b) ought (c) do (d) can

5. A: Hurry up!
   B: We ________ not be in a hurry. We still have a lot of time.
   (a) should (b) dare (c) need (d) must

Task 5

Find the sentences that are incorrect and correct them. If the sentence is correct, leave it alone.

correct incorrect

1. It is required that students would go to the principle's office whenever they are late for school. ( ) ( )

   ____

2. We need buy a small gift to show our appreciation. ( ) ( )

   ____

3. Hannah couldn't find the Picasso art gallery. She should have visited the information center. ( ) ( )

   ____

4. He can't have finished the work in time. ( ) ( )

   ____

5. There's nothing more to do today, so you will go home. ( ) ( )

   ____

Culture Corner

Hair and Head

우리나라 말로 '당신의 머리가 좋다' 라고 하면 그것은 당신의 지능이 높다 라는 뜻으로 이해할 수 있습니다. 만약 이 것을 영어로 표현한다면 어떻게 될까요? Your head is good. 이렇게 말한다면 외국인의 입장에서는 매우 엉뚱하게 들릴 것입니다. 이는, 우리말로 머리는 실제 머리,

두뇌 그리고 머리칼을 다 의미하지만 영어에서는 이것을 구분하기 때문입니다. 그러므로 머리가 좋다는 You are intelligent. 또는 smart 등으로 표현 하는 것이 옳고, 머리가 아프다는 My head hurts. 라고 합니다. 또한 당신의 머리는 금발입니다 라고 말할 때, Your head is blonde. 라 하지 않고 Your hair is blonde. 라 하는 것입니다.

hair는 머리카락을 주로 의미하지만 신체에 나는 털을 가리키기도 합니다 그렇기 때문에 누군가가 "I am hairy." 라고 한다면 그것은 머리 숱이 많다는 뜻이 될 수도 있겠지만 몸 전체에 털이 많다는 뜻이 되는 것입니다.

우리가 흔히 말하는 흰머리는 gray hair라고 하며 우리말에 속상하거나 걱정거리가 있으면 흰머리가 늘어난다는 표현이 있는 것처럼 영어에서도 같은 의미로get gray hair, get gray 라는 숙어가 있습니다. Anxiety has turned my hair gray.는 '걱정 때문에 머리가 하얗게 세었다' 라는 뜻이 됩니다.

영어에서는 hair와 head와 관련된 관용적인 표현이 굉장히 많이 존재합니다. My brother is getting in my hair. 에서 get in my hair는 '나를 못살게, 성가시게 굴다' 라는 뜻입니다. 반대로 out of one's hair 는 '무엇으로부터 벗어나다' 라는 의미를 가지고 있습니다. let one's hair down 는 '머리를 늘어뜨리다, 긴장을 풀고 편하게 마음을 가진다' 란 뜻이고 split hairs는 '중요하지 않은 사소한 것을 마치 매우 중요한 듯 상세하게 파헤친다'는 뜻입니다. 그래서 He always splits hairs. 는 '그는 항상 쓸데없이 따지기만 좋아한다' 는 뜻이 됩니다. by a hair's breadth/ by a hair하면 '가까스로' 라는 뜻이 되어, He escaped by a hair's breadth. 는 '그는 간신히 탈출했다.' 라는 뜻입니다

머리(head)와 관련된 관용어 중 big head 는 문자 그대로 '머리가 크다' 란 말이 될 수도 있지만 주로 '잘난체하다, 우쭐해 하다' 라는 의미로 사용합니다. He has a big head after winning a trophy.는 '그는 트로피를 수상한 후 '잘난체한다' 라고 해석할 수 있습니다, 그렇다면 문자 그대로 '누구의 머리가 크다' 라고 표현하고 싶을 때엔 He has a big head. 보다는 His head is big. 이라고 하는 것이 뜻을 더 분명하게 전달할 수 있습니다.

hang one's head는 '부끄러워 고개를 숙이다' 이고 반대로 keep one's head는 '침착을 유지하다' 라는 뜻을 가지고 있습니다. keep one's head above water는 '빚지지 않고 겨우 살아가다' 의 의미가 됩니다. lose one's head 는 '흥분하다, 분별력을 잃다', off the top of one's head 는 '재빠르게, 즉각적으로 생각해내다' 의 의미를 가지고 있습니다. 또한 over one's head는 '~의 수준 이상이다. 이해하기 어렵다' 라는 뜻으로 쓰이고 있습니다. 한국말과 비슷한 표현으로는 eyes in the back of one's head, '머리 뒤에 눈이 달렸다', from head to toe '머리부터 발끝까지' 와 같은 것들이 있습니다.

- You are intelligent.
- My head hurts.
- Your hair is blonde.
- Anxiety has turned my hair gray.
- My brother is getting in my hair.
- He always splits hairs.

- He escaped by a hair's breadth.
- He has a big head after winning a trophy.
- His head is big.

Wrap-up

Key sentences

1. can/could
   - Can you hear me?
   - I could talk to him.

2. may/might
   - May I have a few minutes of your time?
   - I might have made a mistake.

3. will/would
   - Will you at least have dinner with me?
   - Really, I would, but I'm seeing your friend, Aaron.

4. shall
   - Shall we have coffee then?

5. should
   - I think you should give me another chance.

6. must
   - That must have been someone else.

7. need, dare
   - You needed to move to California for that big promotion.
   - I dare say I'm speechless.

8. used to

- You know, we used to have a lot of fun together.

9. do

- Do think about it.

REVIEW TEST

Choose the best choice to complete the sentence. (1-10)

1. A: I stayed up all night preparing for the exams.
   B: You ___________ be really tired.
   (1) can (2) will (3)must (4) need

2. A: Do you know where Mark left the car keys?
   B: He ___________ have left them on the table.
   (1) shall (2) will (3) had to (4) might

3. The movie was very impressive. You ___________ have seen it.
   (1) must (2) ought (3) should (4) can

4. Employees will ___________ accept the new conditions or be dismissed.
   (1) must (2) ought to (3) have to (4) can

5. A: Why is Barbara in her room?
   B: I don't know. She ___________ be doing her homework.
   (1) must (2) may (3) needs (4) should

6. I can't find my credit card. I have no idea where it is. I guess I ___________ call the credit card company.
   (1) used to (2) don't have to (3) had better (4) ought

7. It is important that she ___________ what her decision means.

(1) understands (2) understand (3) to understand (4) understanding

8. I __________ eat peanuts, but then I became allergic to them.

(1) may (2) have to (3) ought to (4) used to

9. All documents __________ to be submitted prior to May 1.

(1) need (2) can (3) dare (4) must

10. A: ____________ you like your new job?

B: Yes, I'm enjoying it.

(1) Would (2) Could (3) Do (4) Have

Supplementary Reading (보충 독해)

다음 글을 읽고 문제를 풀어 보세요.

Where Are the Babies?

Korea's National Statistical Office indicated that the country's birth rate has reached the lowest level ever recorded. The average woman has 1.17 children, significantly below the rate of 2.3 needed to keep the population at its current level.

Cultural trends might be playing a role in the declining birth rate. Forty years ago, South Korean women married young and had, on average six children. Now many women are marrying later or choosing to remain single, while those who do have children prefer to spend all their resources on one.

The population of South Korea is expected to diminish by two-thirds in the next century, dropping to 16 million from 48 million, and creating a national economic and labor-shortage disaster. In order to raise the fertility rate, the government has proposed offering cash incentives and childcare subsidies to parents. Parents of newborn children would be given a 200,000 won grant, and families with three or more children would be given priority when bidding for a new apartment. The government also plans to offer consulting services through civil organizations for married couples considering divorce because the rising divorce rate is partly blamed for the falling birth rate.

Translation 아기들은 어디에 있나요?

한국 국가통계청에서는 국가 출산율이 사상 최저 수치를 기록했다고 말했습니다. 평균 여성은 1.17명의 아이를 낳는 것으로 나타나서, 현재 인구수를 유지하기 위해 필요한 2.3의 비율보다 상당히 낮습니다. 출산율 하락에는 문화적 추세가 한 몫을 하고 있을 겁니다. 40년 전에는 대한민국 여성들이 어린 나이에 결혼을 하였고 평균적으로 여섯 명의 자녀를 낳았습니다. 많은 여성들은 이제 더 늦게 결혼을 하거나 미혼으로 남기를 선택하며 아이를 낳는 여성들은 한 아이에게 모든 자력을 투자합니다.
우리나라의 인구는 다음 세기에 4천800만에서 천600만으로 떨어져 3분의 2가 줄어들 것으로 예상되고 경제 파탄과 노동력 부족을 초래할 것입니다. 출산율을 증가시키기위하여 정부는 부모에게 장려금과 양육 보조비를 제공할 것을 제안하였습니다. 신생아의 부모에게는 20만원의 보조금이 지급되며 자녀가 셋 이상인 가족들에게 새 아파트 입찰시 우선권이 주어집니다. 정부는 또한 시민단체를 통하여 이혼을 고려중인 부부에게 제공하는 상담 서비스를 계획하고 있습니다. 하락하는 출산율의 이유로는 증가하는 이혼율이 일부를 차지하고 있기 때문입니다.

Explanation

1. Korea's National Statistical Office indicated that the country's birth rate has reached the lowest level ever recorded.

has reached 는 현재완료 시제로써 현재까지 행하여진 것의 결과를 나타내게 됩니다. 부사 ever는 이 문장에서 최상급 lowest level를 강조하는 역할을 합니다. ever recorded 앞에는 관계대명사와 be동사인 which has been이 생략된 형태로 보면 됩니다.

Ex) Korea has become one of the leading countries in IT.
(한국은 IT산업에 있어서 주요국가 중 하나가 되었습니다.)

Ex) That is the funniest story I've ever heard.
(그것은 내가 들어본 것 중에 가장 재미있는 이야기입니다.)

2. The average woman has 1.17 children, significantly below the rate of 2.3 needed to keep the population at its current level.

needed 앞에는 관계대명사와 be동사인 that is가 생략되어 있습니다. needed 뒤에 나오는 to부정사는 '~하기 위해서' 라는 목적을 나타냅니다.

Ex) Have you taken care of the preparations needed to complete the job successfully?
(이 일을 성공적으로 끝내기 위해서 필요한 준비사항들을 다 처리했습니까?)

3. Cultural trends might be playing a role in the declining birth rate.

조동사 may/might는 '~일수도 있다, ~의 가능성이 있다' 등의 뜻으로 추측을 나타냅니다. 현재나 미래에 대한 추측을 나타낼 때는 may/might + be + ~ing로 나타냅니다.

Ex) She might be working at home today.
(그녀는 아마 오늘 재택 근무를 할 수도 있습니다.)

4. Now many women are marrying later or choosing to remain single, while those who do have children prefer to spend all their resources on one.

prefer는 '~을 선호하다' 라는 의미를 가지고 있으며 to 부정사 혹은 ~ing 형과 함께 사용합니다. spend something on~은 '무엇을 ~에 쓰다' 라는 어구입니다.

Ex) We prefer to dine out on the weekends.
(우리는 주말에 외식하는 것을 즐깁니다.)

Ex) I spent all my time completing this project.
(나는 이 프로젝트를 끝내는 것에 시간을 다 보냈다.)
= I spent all my time on this project.

5. The population of the country is expected to diminish by two-thirds in the next century, dropping to 16 million from 48 million, and creating a national economic and labor-shortage disaster.

be expected to(= be likely to)는 '~할 것으로 예상되다' 라는 뜻이다. two-thirds는 2/3을 나타내며, 1/3은 one-third 입니다. dropping과 creating은 '~하면서, 그리고 ~하다' 라는 뜻으로 동시상황을 나타내는 분사구문입니다.

Ex) The shop is expected to open sometime next month.
(그 상점은 다음 달 중에 열릴 것으로 예상됩니다.)

Ex) I would like to buy just one fifth of that cake.
(나는 그 케이크의 1/5을 사기 원합니다.)

Ex) Running out of the room, she knocked over a vase.
(그녀는 방에서 뛰어나가면서 화병을 넘어뜨렸습니다.)

Ex) The boy wailed and wailed, creating havoc around him.
(그 소년은 울고 또 울어서 주위를 혼란스럽게 했습니다.)

6. In order to raise the fertility rate, the government has proposed offering cash incentives and childcare subsidies to parents.

propose는 '~을 제안하다' 라는 뜻으로 뒤에 to부정사와 ~ing형이 다 올 수 있습니다.

Ex) He proposed taking a rest there.
(그는 그 곳에서 휴식을 취할 것을 제안했습니다.)
I proposed to reduce the loan.
(나는 대부금을 줄일 것을 제안했습니다.)

7. The government also plans to offer consulting services through civil organizations for married couples considering divorce because the rising divorce rate is partly blamed for the falling birth rate.

plan 다음에는 to부정사가 목적어로 와서 '~을 할 것을 계획하다' 의 의미로 쓰입니다. considering 앞에는 관계대명사와 be동사인 who are 가 생략되었습니다. 수동태로 표현된 is blamed for는 '~에 대해서 비난을 받다' 라는 뜻입니다. 능동태 표현인 blame A for B는 'B에 대해서 A를 비난하다, 꾸짖다' 의 뜻입니다.

Ex) I plan to take my chances.
(나는 운에 맡기고 해볼 생각입니다.)

Ex) He is the one considering buying your antique lamp.
(그가 바로 당신의 골동품 램프를 구입할까 고려하는 사람입니다.)

Ex) Even though it wasn't her fault, they blamed her for the drop in sales.
(그녀의 탓이 아니었음에도 불구하고 그들은 매출하락을 그녀의 책임으로 돌렸습니다.)

Q.1 Choose the definition on the right that matches the word on the left.

1. corresponding	a) to ask for advice or information
2. resource	b) similar or equivalent
3. incentive	c) financial aid given by a person or government
4. fertility	d) means of support, especially money or property
5. subsidy	e) something that motivates effort or encourages action
6. bid	f) to seek to win or attain something
7. consult	g) the ability of a living organism to produce offspring

Q.2 Make True (T) or False (F).

1. The population of Korea is expected to diminish by one-third over the next century. ( )
2. Families with at least three children can be given priority when bidding for a new apartment under a proposed plan. ( )
3. The low birth rate of Korea supports economic development. ( )
4. The falling birth rate of Korea is a temporary phenomenon. ( )
5. The increasing divorce rate is also relevant to the decreasing birth rate. ( )

Participle 05 Unit

Introduction

Topic: Delays and disappointments (지연과 실망)

Lesson objectives:

Participle (분사)

- present participle and past participle (현재분사와 과거분사)
- participle construction (분사 구문)

WARM-UP

In this dialogue, Brett arrives a few minutes late to the office to find an important client waiting for him. It's a big day and there's a lot of pressure, but can Brett live up to expectations? We'll find out in just a moment.

Brett	: I'm sorry that I'm late. The subway…(interrupted by Mr. Daniels)
Mr. Daniels	: Let's get started. Brett, you know our client, Mr. Yuan. He has come all the way from Beijing to meet with us today. (past participle)
Brett	: Yes, sir. It's nice to see you again.
Mr. Daniels	: I hope you've got something good for us today, Brett.
Mr. Yuan	: Yes, Brett, I've heard you're a very talented young man. I want this ad campaign to be big, new, fresh, bold.
Brett	: Well, I thought we might feature a jogging panda bear; we'd dress him up with sunglasses and running shoes. (present participle / gerund)

Mr. Yuan	: What else do you have?
Brett	: If you take a look at the screen, I have a rough sample for you. This one is of a group of struggling scientists. (present participle) After a few sips of VERVE 3000 they discover life on a distant planet.
Mr. Yuan	: Frankly speaking, I'm not impressed. (impersonal absolute participle)
Brett	: There's more. Picture this: There's a guy who's late for work, his car stalls, he gets out, and then puts some of our energy drink into the gas tank. Next thing, he's speeding to the office.
Mr. Yuan	: Having come all the way from Beijing, I expected more from this meeting. (participle construction) Maybe I should be thinking about taking our business elsewhere. (present participle)
Brett	: Give me another shot. I can help you sell a billion of these drinks. (help + O + OC)
Mr. Yuan	: A billion?
Brett	: Yes. A billion.
Mr. Yuan	: Okay. But I want to see something amazing. (present participle)
Brett	: You won't be disappointed. (past participle)
Mr. Yuan	: Let's hope not.
Mr. Daniels	: Yes, Brett, let's hope Mr. Yuan is not disappointed.

Translation

이 대화에서 Brett은 사무실에 몇 분 늦게 도착하는데, 중요한 손님이 그를 기다리고 있는 것을 발견합니다. 중요한 날이며 큰 압박감이 있는데, Brett은 기대만큼 잘 할 수 있을까요? 잠시 후에 알게 될 것입니다.

Brett	: 늦어서 죄송합니다. 지하철이…(Daniels씨가 끼어든다.)
Mr. Daniels	: 시작합시다. Brett, 우리 고객 Yuan씨 알죠. 오늘 멀리 북경에서 우리를 만나러 여기까지 와주셨어요.
Brett	: 네, 다시 뵙게 되어 반갑습니다.
Mr. Daniels	: 당신이 오늘 우리에게 좋은 것을 결과를 가져다 주길 바랍니다. Brett씨.

Mr. Yuan	: 네, Brett씨, 당신이 유능한 젊은이라고 들었어요. 이번 광고 캠페인이 크고 새롭고, 신선하고 눈에 띄는 것이기를 바랍니다.
Brett	: 그러니까, 저는 우리가 조깅하는 팬더곰의 특징을 그릴 수 있다고 생각해봤습니다 선글라스와 러닝화로 치장을 하려고 합니다.
Mr. Yuan	: 또 다른 것은요?
Brett	: 화면을 보시면, 대략적인 샘플을 보실 수 있습니다. 이것은 열심히 노력하고 있는 과학자들 집단입니다. VERVE 3000을 몇 모금 마신 후 그들은 먼 행성에서 생명체를 발견합니다.
Mr. Yuan	: 솔직히 말해서, 별로 인상적이지 않군요.
Brett	: 더 있습니다. 이것을 그려보세요: 한 남자가 지각을 합니다. 차가 꼼짝 하지 않자 그는 내려서 우리 에너지 음료로 주유를 합니다. 그 다음, 그는 속력을 내서 사무실로 갑니다.
Mr. Yuan	: 멀리 북경에서 여기까지 왔기 때문에 오늘 미팅에 대해 더 많은 기대를 했어요. 아마도 우리 사업을 다른 곳에 맡기는 것에 대해 생각해 봐야겠습니다.
Brett	: 한번만 더 기회를 주세요. 제가 이 음료수 10억 개를 팔도록 도와 드리겠습니다.
Mr. Yuan	: 10억 개?
Brett	: 네, 10억 개요.
Mr. Yuan	: 알겠어요. 하지만 저는 뭔가 굉장한 것을 보고 싶어요.
Brett	: 실망하시지 않을 겁니다.
Mr. Yuan	: 그러지 않기를 바랍시다.
Mr. Daniels	: 그래요, Bret씨. Yuan씨가 실망하지 않기를 바랍니다.

Comprehension Check

1. What kind of ad campaign does Mr. Yuan want?
   (a) big, new, wild, bold
   (b) clever, fresh, bold, new
   (c) big, new, fresh, bold
   (d) bold, brilliant, cool, fresh

2. Which of the following adjectives best describes Mr. Yuan's general tone?
   (a) anxious
   (b) angry
   (c) disappointed
   (d) stern

3. How does Brett persuade Mr. Yuan to give him another chance?

(a) He promises big results.

(b) He promises to make him very rich and happy.

(c) He hints at his next idea.

(d) He begs and pleads.

Useful Expressions

In this dialogue	Explanation
1. It's nice to see you again.	1. Just about everyone knows that when you first make someone's acquaintance it's customary to say, "Nice to meet you." But you probably shouldn't use this greeting the second and third time you greet someone. In this instance, the expression "It's nice to see you again," will do nicely. Furthermore, it will let the person you're talking to know that you haven't forgotten the first time you met.
2. I hope you've got something good for us today, Brett.	2. When Brett arrives, Mr. Yuan is already waiting for him. He's made even more anxious by thefact that he doesn't know exactly what to expect since Brett has been given a great deal of creative freedom on the project at hand. Still, he wants to let Brett know that he's looking forward to an impressive presentation. He does so with this simple expression. Try it out the next time you have to rely on someone else's creativity or expertise.
3. Maybe I should be thinking about taking my business elsewhere.	3. Any good businessperson knows how important it is to keep customers happy. If they're not satisfied the first time around, there's a good chance they won't be back again. However, sometimes it's still hard to get exactly whatyou want. The next time this happens to you, use this expression to let the other person know they only have one more shot to make things right.

In this dialogue	Explanation
4. Give me another shot.	4. Sure, we all make mistakes. Most of the time we can learn from them and do a much better job the second time around. The problem is that others aren't always so forgiving. While we're not encouraging you to beg, it can never hurt to ask for another chance. Why not try out this expression the next time you find yourself in a similar predicament?

Grammar

Focus 1 Present and past participle (현재분사와 과거분사)

01 Present and past participle (현재분사와 과거분사)

(1) 분사는 형용사의 역할을 하는 것으로, 현재분사와 과거분사가 있습니다.

- an irritating experience (= an experience that irritates one)
  (화나게 하는 경험)
- a jogging panda bear (= a panda bear that is jogging)
  (조깅하는 팬더곰)
- a broken chair (= a chair which is broken)
  (부서진 의자)
- an excited spectator (= a spectator who is excited)
  (흥분된 관객)

(2) 현재분사 - 진행형, 과거분사 - 완료형과 수동형

- Maybe I should be thinking about taking our business elsewhere.
  (아마도 우리 사업을 다른 곳에 맡기는 것에 대해 생각해 봐야겠습니다.)
- He has come all the way from Beijing to meet with us today.
  (그는 오늘 멀리 북경에서 우리를 만나러 여기까지 와주셨습니다.)
- I'm not impressed.
  (별로 인상적이지는 않습니다.)

- You won't be disappointed
  (실망하시지는 않을 겁니다.)

02 Usages of participle (분사의 용법)

(1) 형용사적 용법

현재분사나 과거분사는 명사를 앞이나 뒤에서 직접 수식하는 형용사적 용법으로 사용되는데 이것을 한정적 용법이라 합니다. 현재분사는 능동의 의미를 나타내고, 과거분사는 수동의 의미를 지닙니다.

명사의 전치 수식: 분사가 단독으로 쓰일 경우

- I thought we might feature a jogging panda bear.
  (저는 우리가 조깅하는 팬더곰의 특징을 그릴 수 있다고 생각해봤습니다)
- Come and rake the fallen leaves.
  (이리 와서 낙엽을 긁어 모으세요.)

cf) I want to see something amazing.

명사의 후치 수식: 분사가 수식어구를 동반할 경우

- I helped the lady struggling with her luggage.
  (나는 짐 때문에 힘들어 하는 여인을 도왔습니다.)
- Mom served the chicken cooked in a mushroom sauce.
  (어머니께서는 버섯소스로 요리한 닭고기를 내놓으셨습니다.)

(2) 보어

주격보어, 목적격보어 등 보어로 쓰이는 것은 서술적 용법입니다. 주격보어는 be 동사와 불완전자동사 뒤에서 주로 사용됩니다.

- The mayor's speech was disappointing.
  (시장의 연설은 실망스러웠습니다.)
- We lay looking up at the night sky.
  (우리는 밤하늘을 바라보며 누웠습니다.)
- The entire arena was electrified with excitement.
  (경기장 전체가 흥분에 빠졌습니다.)
- He emerged from the ordeal unscathed.
  (그는 그 시련에서 무사히 빠져 나왔습니다.)

목적격보어로 쓰이는 것은 지각동사와 사역동사를 포함한 불완전타동사의 목적격 보어로 쓰인 경우인데, 능동의 경우 현재분사를 사용하고 수동의 경우 과거분사를 사용합니다.

- I'm sorry I've kept you waiting so long.
  (당신을 그렇게 오래 기다리게 해서 미안합니다.)
- You have to admit, that movie kept you guessing until the very end.
  (당신은 그 영화가 마지막까지 계속 추측을 하게 만들었다는 것을 인정해야 합니다.)
- He cannot make himself understood in English.
  (그는 영어로 의사소통을 할 수 없습니다.)
- It's important to have your voice heard.
  (당신의 목소리가 들리도록 하는 것은 중요합니다.)

지각동사 (see, hear, watch, smell, notice, etc.) 의 목적보어로는 보통 동사원형과 -ing형이 사용됩니다.

- I noticed you doing a lot of helpful work.
  (당신이 이로운 일을 많이 한다는 것을 알게 되었습니다.)
- I first noticed her walking her dog, and knew then I had to talk to her.
  (나는 처음에 그녀가 개를 산책시킨다는 것을 알아챘고, 그 다음엔 내가 그녀에게 말을 걸어야 한다는 것을 알았습니다.)
- I heard you sing the anthem.
  (나는 당신이 애국가를 부르는 것을 들었습니다.)
- Everyone saw you take the last cupcake.
  (모두들 당신이 마지막 컵 케익을 가져가는 것을 봤습니다.)

cf) She heard her name called.

사역동사 (make, have, let) 의 목적보어로는 동사원형과 과거분사가 사용되는데 능동관계일 경우엔 동사원형, 수동관계일 경우엔 과거분사를 사용합니다. -ing형은 사용하지 않습니다. 동사 help도 목적보어로 대개 동사원형을 취합니다.

- My friend Eva makes me laugh. (능동)
  (내 친구 Eva는 나를 웃게 만듭니다.)
- Our family has our milk delivered. (수동)
  (우리 가족은 우유를 배달시킵니다.)
- I can help you sell a billion of these drinks.
  (제가 이 음료수 10억 개를 팔도록 도와 드리겠습니다.)

cf) Let me introducing my husband. (x) (제 남편을 소개하겠습니다.)

(3) 부사적 용법

분사가 부사로 사용될 경우에는 매우(very)의 뜻을 지닙니다.

- The weather is freezing cold.
  (날씨가 정말 춥습니다.)
- He got soaking wet from exercising.
  (그는 운동으로 인해 흠뻑 젖었습니다.)

- The troops marched across the scorching hot desert for three days.
  (그 군대는 3일 동안 타는 듯이 뜨거운 사막을 가로질러 행진했습니다.)

03 Gerunds and present participle (동명사와 현재분사)

동사 원형+ing 형태 중에서는 동명사인 것이 있는데 이는 현재 분사와 혼동할 여지가 많습니다. 동명사는 문장에서 명사적인 용법으로 주어나 보어, 목적어와 같은 역할을 합니다.

- Evaluating your own work is never easy.
  (당신 자신의 일을 평가하는 것은 결코 쉽지 않습니다.)
- I thoroughly enjoy writing letters by hand.
  (저는 손으로 편지 쓰는 것을 정말 즐깁니다.)

동명사는 합성명사에서 쓰이고, 현재분사는 명사의 동작을 나타냅니다. 동명사 + 명사인 경우, 강세가 동명사에 오고, 현재분사 + 명사인 경우, 명사에 옵니다.

- rúnning shoes / running chéetah
  (운동화 / 달리는 치타)
- dáncing girl / dancing gírl
  (직업 댄서 / 춤추는 소녀)
- bóiling point / boiling wáter
  (비등점 / 끓는 물)
- sléeping car / sleeping báby
  (침대차 / 잠자는 아기)

Task 1

Choose the best word from the box to complete each sentence.

crash	crashed	shocking	shocked	displaying
displayed	using	used	relax	relaxing

1. We were __________ by the news about the tsunami.
2. Customers __________ their Discover Card will receive a ten percent discount on all purchases.
3. She felt her car __________ against the post.
4. Classical music helps me __________.
5. I'd like to purchase one of those pictures __________ on the wall.

Focus 2 Participle construction (분사구문) (1)

01 Participle construction (분사구문)

분사구문은 분사를 사용하여 절을 구로 만든 것입니다. 분사구문을 만들 때는 종속절의 접속사를 생략하고, 종속절의 주어가 주절의 주어와 같으면 종속절의 주어를 생략하고 다르면 써 줍니다. 종속절 동사의 경우 주절의 동사와 같은 시제일 경우 –ing 형을 사용하고 시제가 더 과거이면 having + p.p.를 사용하여 구문을 만듭니다. 주어와 동사의 관계가 수동이면 동사를 -ed로 써줍니다. 이 경우, 앞에 being은 생략될 때도 있습니다. 분사구문에는 시간, 이유, 조건, 양보, 부대상황을 표시하는 접속사의 뜻이 내포되어 있습니다.

(1) 시간

'~하는 때에, ~하면서, ~하는 동안에, ~한 후에' 라는 시간의 의미를 나타냅니다.

- Passing by the storefronts on Fifth Avenue, a pair of brown shoes caught my eye.
  (= While I passed by the storefronts on Fifth Avenue, a pair of brown shoes caught my eye.)
  (Fifth Avenue에 있는 상점 앞을 지나가다가 갈색 신발이 눈에 들어왔습니다.)
- Finishing my drink, I picked up the phone.
  (= As I finished my drink, I picked up the phone.)
  (음료수를 다 들이키면서 전화를 받았습니다.)
- Straightening my necktie, I walked toward the manager's office.
  (= As I straightened my necktie, I walked toward the manager's office.)
  (넥타이를 똑바로 하면서, 저는 부장의 사무실로 걸어갔습니다.)

(2) 이유

'~때문에, ~해서' 라는 이유를 나타냅니다.

- Having come all the way from Beijing, I expected more from this meeting.
  (= Since I had come all the way from Beijing, I expected more from this meeting.)
  (멀리 북경에서 여기까지 왔기 때문에 오늘 미팅에 대해 더 많은 기대를 했습니다.)
- Not knowing what to do, she asked for his advice.
  (= As she didn't know what to do, she asked for his advice.)
  (무엇을 해야 할 지를 몰라서 그녀는 그의 조언을 구했습니다.)
- Overwhelmed by the news, I could not do anything for a good while. (= Since I was overwhelmed by the news, I could not do anything for a good while.)
  (그 소식을 듣고 당황해서 나는 오랫동안 아무것도 할 수 없었습니다.)

- Worried about oversleeping, she set three different alarm clocks for the same time. (= Because she was worried about oversleeping, she set three different alarm clocks for the same time.)
  (늦잠자는 것이 걱정되어서 그녀는 세 개의 자명종시계를 같은 시각에 울리도록 해놓았습니다.)

(3) 양보

'~일지라도, 비록 ~이지만' 이라는 의미로 양보의 뜻을 나타냅니다.

- Apologizing for what I did, I still feel I'm not completely wrong. (= Although I apologizes for what I did, I still feel I'm not completely wrong.)
  (비록 내가 한 일에 대해서 사과는 하지만 나는 여전히 내가 완전히 잘못 한다고는 생각하지 않습니다.)
- Conceding that point, I still think I have the better argument. (= Though I concede that point, I still think I have the better argument.)
  (나는 그 점을 양보하기는 하지만, 나는 여전히 내 주장이 더 낫다고 생각합니다.)

(4) 조건

'~라면, ~한다면' 이라는 의미로 조건을 나타냅니다.

- Turning to the right, you'll see the new library. (= If you turn to the right, you'll see the new library.)
  (오른쪽으로 돌면 새로 지은 도서관을 볼 수 있을 것입니다.)
- A tweed sports coat, selected carefully, can add a fresh element of style to your wardrobe. (= A tweed sports coat, if it is selected carefully, can add a fresh element of style to your wardrobe.)
  (트위드 스포츠 코트는, 주의해서 잘 고르면, 당신의 의상에 다소 신선한 느낌을 더할 수 있습니다.)

(5) 부대상황 (동시동작/ 연속동작)

'~하면서, ~하고 나서' 라는 의미로 동시 동작이나 연속 동작을 나타냅니다.

- Gesturing toward the door, she asked him to leave. (= While she gestured toward the door, she asked him to leave.)
  (그녀는 문 쪽으로 손짓하며 그에게 떠날 것을 요구했습니다.)
- We started in the morning arriving in Busan at noon. (= We started in the morning and arrived in Busan at noon.)
  (우리는 오전에 출발해서 정오 에 부산에 도착했습니다.)

02 Perfect (완료형)

'having+과거분사 ~'의 형태를 취하는 완료분사구문은 주절의 시제보다 앞선 시제를 나타내게 됩니다.

- Having visited Paris three times already, the couple decided to go to Rome for their anniversary this year.
  (= Since they had already visited Paris three times, the couple decided to go to Rome for their anniversary this year.)
  (이미 파리에 세 번이나 가 보았기 때문에, 그 커플은 이번 기념일에는 로마로 가기로 결정했습니다.)
- Having been adopted, I don't love my parents any less.
  (= Though I was adopted, I don't love my parents any less.)
  (비록 나는 입양되었지만, 그렇다고 나의 부모님을 그 만큼 덜 사랑하는 것은 아닙니다.)

Task 2

Change the following sentences into a participle construction.

1. Though I sat in the sun, I felt cold.
   ____________________, I felt cold.

2. If you use these numbers to create an estimate, you'll find that the result is positive.
   ______________________________ to create an estimate, you'll find that the result is positive.

3. Some books, if they are read carelessly, will do more harm than good.
   Some books, ____________________, will do more harm than good.

4. As Tim walked up the stairs, he reflected back upon the meeting.
   __________________________, Tim reflected back upon the meeting.

5. As I had learned to knit, I was able to make a sweater for my daughter.
   ______________, I was able to make a sweater for my daughter.

Focus 3 Participle construction (분사구문) (2)

01 with ~ing / with ~ed

with + ~ing/with ~ed 의 형식을 취해서 주절에 대한 이유나 동시상황을 나타냅니다. 이 경우, with와 ~ing/~ed 사이에 주어가 오게 됩니다.

- With one eye bandaged, I couldn't see properly.
  (Because one eye was bandaged, I couldn't see properly.)
  (한쪽 눈을 붕대로 감아서 나는 정확하게 볼 수가 없었습니다.)
- With Kathy living in France, we don't see her often.
  (= Since Kathy lives in France, we don't see her often.)
  (Kathy는 프랑스에 살고 있기 때문에, 우리는 그녀를 자주 볼 수가 없습니다.)
- She sat on the chair with her legs crossed.
  (그녀는 다리를 꼰 채로 의자에 앉아 있었습니다.)

02 Absolute participle construction (독립분사구문)

분사구문의 의미상 주어와 주절의 주어가 일치하지 않은 경우에는 분사 앞에 주어를 밝혀 주어야 합니다. 즉, 분사구문이 분사자체의 주어를 갖는 것을 독립분사구문이라 합니다.

- The aquarium being closed, he had to find another place to visit.
  (= As the aquarium was closed, he had to find another place to visit.)
  (수족관이 닫혀있어서 그는 방문할 다른 곳을 찾아야 했습니다.)
- All things being equal, you should always choose the simplest solution.
  (= If all things are equal, you should always choose the simplest solution.)
  (모든 것이 같다면, 당신은 항상 가장 간단한 해결책을 선택해야 합니다.)

03 Impersonal absolute participle construction (비인칭 독립분사구문)

독립분사구문의 의미상 주어가 필요하지만, 그것이 we, you, they, people 등 일반인을 나타낼 때는 주어를 생략하고 쓰는 것이 보통입니다. 이를 비인칭 독립분사구문이라 합니다.

- Generally/Strictly/ Frankly/ Roughly/ Broadly speaking
  (일반적으로/ 엄격히/ 솔직히/ 대략/ 넓게 말하자면)
- Granting that~
  (~을 인정한다면 , ~이라고 할지라도)
- Talking/Speaking of~
  (~에 관해 말하자면)
- Compared with~
  (~을 비교하면)
- Putting it mildly,
  (완곡한 표현을 쓰자면)
- Supposing that~
  (만약 ~라면, 만약 ~하더라도)
- Given~
  (만약 ~라면)
- Provided (that)~ = Providing (that)~
  (만약 ~라면)
- Considering ~
  (~을 고려하면, ~치고는)
- Judging from~
  (~으로 판단하건대)
- Taking all things into consideration,
  (만사를 고려하면)
- Frankly speaking, I'm not impressed.
  (솔직히 말씀드리면 별로 인상적이지 않습니다.)
- Speaking of ethics, have you heard about the most recent scandal at Samsung?
  (윤리에 대해 말하자면, 당신은 가장 최근에 삼성의 스캔들을 들어봤습니까?)
- Provided (that) all your work is done, you may go home.
  (당신의 일이 모두 끝나면 당신은 집에 갈 수 있습니다.)
- Compared with last year, prices of dairy products have risen by 25 percent.
  (작년과 비교한다면, 유제품의 가격이 25퍼센트나 상승하였습니다.)
- Supposing you and I were lovers, what would happen?
  (당신과 내가 연인이라면 어떤 일이 일어날까요?)
- Considering her behavior, I'd say you are well within your right to be angry.
  (그녀의 행동을 고려하면, 당신이 화를 내는 것도 당연합니다.)

Task 3

Choose the correct words(s) to complete the sentences.

1. (Supposing, Supposed) that you could go overseas tomorrow, where would you go?
2. (Comparing, Compared) with his brother, he is not a good player.
3. With night (coming, came) on, the wind began to blow.
4. (Being, It being) warm inside the cinema, I fell asleep.
5. (Giving, Given) the current economic climate, you might want to consider going back to school.

Reading Where Do You Get Your News?

This past year has been packed with big news stories: elections, scandals, and economic turmoil. At the same time, news bureaus around the world have been downsizing at a record pace as more and more people are shunning the newspaper and choosing the Internet as their primary news source.

The problem boils down to the fact that a newspaper's web site simply can't generate the same level of advertising revenue as its print version. What's more, newspapers used to publish their biggest stories in the morning edition, but the Internet has helped to create a 24 hour news cycle that constantly demands new and interesting content. This costs newspapers more at a time when they're already strapped for advertising cash.

With news organizations trimming down or shutting down in droves, many people are left wondering what's in store for printed news. Some newspapers, like The Wall Street Journal, have started charging for the content offered on their web site, whereas other papers have decided to eschew the Internet all together. It's hard to say exactly what the future holds for the newspaper, but surely we'll be able to read about it online.

Translation 당신은 어디에서 소식을 얻습니까?

지난해는 큰 뉴스거리들로 가득 찼었습니다: 선거, 스캔들 그리고 경제대란. 동시에 점점 더 많은 사람들이 신문을 멀리 하고, 그들의 인터넷을 주요한 뉴스 출처로 선택하면서 전 세계 편집국들은 기록적인 속도로 축소되고 있습니다.

그 문제는 결국 신문 웹사이트가 단지 인쇄판이 광고 수익을 내는 것만큼의 효과를 내지 못한다는 사실로 요약됩니다. 게다가 신문은 가장 큰 뉴스거리를 아침에 인쇄했지만, 인터넷은 새롭고 재미있는 내용을 지속적으로 요구하는 24시간 뉴스 흐름을 만드는데 도움을 주고 있습니다. 신문은 이미 광고 수입도 다 떨어졌는데, 이것 때문에 한꺼번에 더 많이 지출을 해야 합니다.

언론사들이 삭감을 하거나 함께 휴업을 하면서 많은 사람들은 인쇄되는 뉴스에 대해서 어떤 일이 닥칠지 의문을 품게 됩니다. Wall Street Journal과 같은 일부 신문들은 그들의 웹 사이트에서 제공되는 내용들에 대해 요금을 부과하기 시작했습니다. 반면에, 다른 신문들은 모두 인터넷을 피하기로 결정했습니다. 앞으로 신문이 어찌될지 확실히 말하기는 어렵지만, 분명히 우리는 온라인 상에서 그것에 관해서 읽을 수 있을 겁니다.

Comprehension Check-up

True/False

1. A newspaper's web site is often more profitable than its print version. (T/F)
2. The constant demand for new content on a newspaper's web site adds to costs for many organizations. (T/F)
3. Some newspapers have decided not to publish their content on the Internet. (T/F)

Vocabulary Matching

1. strapped	a. cast off, avoid
2. pace	b. in financial need
3. droves	c. rate
4. eschew	d. large crowds or groups

Word Challenge

Quiz

Check Your Understanding: Choose the best word from the box to complete each of the following sentences. Use each word only once.

recognize	remember	recall

1. __________ to bring your textbook along with a pen or pencil to every class.
2. After discovering the defect, the company tried to __________ the product before it reached stores.
3. I had been away so long that I could hardly __________ my own father when I saw him.

Word Challenge

remember	Usage: The verb "remember" can be used in a variety of ways. While you might find its usage in examples one and two negligibly different, pay close attention to the third example. examples: 1. It's difficult to remember words in a foreign language. (to recall) (외국어 단어를 기억하는 것은 어렵습니다.) 2. Please remember to bring your textbooks to every class. (to keep in mind) (수업할 때마다 교과서를 가져오는 것을 기억해주세요.) 3. My husband always remembers our anniversary. (to bear in mind as deserving of a gift or special attention) (나의 남편은 항상 우리 기념일을 기억합니다.)
recognize	Usage: In the following examples a few of the diverse uses of the verb "recognize" are demonstrated. You're probably familiar with the usage found in the first example, but perhaps examples two and three are a little bit confusing. Let's take a look. examples: 1. It's been so long; I hardly recognized you. (to identify from previous knowledge) (오래된 일입니다. 전 당신의 거의 알아볼 수 없었습니다.)

	2. Each year the city recognizes leaders in business and government for their outstanding contributions. (to show appreciation) (매년 시에서 사업과 정부에 우수한 기여를 한 지도자들을 공식적으로 인정합니다.) 3. Some schools refuse to recognize the theory of evolution. (to perceive as true) (일부 학교들은 진화론을 사실로 받아들이기를 거부합니다.)
recall	Usage: The verb "recall" has several meanings. In some cases, it can be used almost interchangeably with "remember," but in others the meaning is quite different. examples: 1. If you recall our last meeting, you said I'd be given a raise within three months. (to consider a previous matter) (당신이 우리의 지난 회의를 기억하신다면, 제 임금이 3개월 안에 인상될 거라고 당신이 말씀하셨습니다.) 2. Can you recall the telephone number for the pizza shop down the street? (to bring back from memory) (길 아래에 있는 피자 집 전화번호를 기억합니까?) 3. Last year, Sony recalled thousands of notebook computers owing to a problem with their batteries. (to call back; summon to return) (작년, Sony는 배터리상의 문제로 수천 개의 노트북을 회수했습니다.)

Practice

Task 4

Choose the best expression to complete each of the following sentences.

1. ___________ twice already, Angie was reluctant to try again.

(a) Having rejected (b) Having been rejected

(c) Had rejected (d) Had been rejected

2. ___________ from the work, he went to bed earlier than usual.

(a) As he was tired (b) Though he was tired

(c) Even if he was tired (d) While he was tired

3. The result of the election left many people ___________.

(a) dissatisfying (b) to dissatisfy

(c) to be dissatisfied (d) dissatisfied

4. ___________ , we went out for a walk.

(a) Being warm outside (b) Warm outside

(c) It being warm outside (d) It having been warm outside

5. ___________ what to say, I remained silent.

(a) Didn't knowing (b) Have not knowing

(c) Knowing not (d) Not knowing

Task 5

Find the parts where the verb forms are used incorrectly, and correct them.

1. I was irritating by the endless noise coming from the second floor.

___________ → ___________

2. The target animal stood still surrounding by hunters.

___________ → ___________

3. We saw him played the electric violin at the concert tonight.

___________ → ___________

4. I wish you all a very interested and enjoyable stay.

___________ → ___________

5. My parents could not utter a word when I told them my surprised secret.

___________ → ___________

Culture Corner

Idioms with Face (얼굴과 관련된 숙어)

영어에서의 face는 얼굴뿐만 아니라 안색이나 표정 등 여러 의미로 사용됩니다. 영어에서는 기분이 언짢거나 불쾌해하는 사람을 보고 'Why the long face?' 라는 말을 잘 하는데 이를 '왜 얼굴이 길어?' 라고 해석하시면 안됩니다. 이 표현은 불쾌할 때 입 꼬리가 내려와 얼굴 모양이 길어 보인다는 데서 생겨난 표현으로 '왜 우울한 표정을 하고 있지? 안 좋은 일이라도 있어?' 라고 해석하는 것이 맞습니다. 즉 'Why so down?' 'Why do you look so blue?' 와 같은 의미로 보면 됩니다.

얼굴 표정과 관련된 표현으로는 make a face, pull a face 등이 있는데 '얼굴을 찡그리거나 인상을 쓰다'라는 뜻입니다. make a face 는 'The clown at the circus made faces at the audience' 에서와 같이 복수로 사용할 수 도 있는데, '남을 웃게 하려고 우스꽝스러운 표정을 짓다' 라는 의미로 사용됩니다. 이와는 반대로 웃지 않고 진지한 표정을 하거나 감정을 억제할 때엔 keep a straight face라는 표현을 사용합니다. 또한 a poker face는 포커(도박의 일종)을 하는 사람처럼 무엇을 숨기는, 낌새를 알아챌 수 없는 무표정함을 나타낼 때 자주 사용합니다.

Face에는 또한 '표면, ~에 직면하다' 라는 뜻도 있는 데, face to face는 '대면하여' 라는 뜻이고, in the face of 는 '~의 면전에서' 라고 해석할 수 있습니다. 화폐나 수표 주식 채권 등의 액면가를 이야기 할 때에도 face를 이용하여 face value 라고 합니다. face reality, face the music 이 두 표현은 모두 '현실에 직면하다' 란 의미를 지니고 있습니다. 예를 들어, 'He faced the music like a man.' 은 '그는 남자답게 어려움에 대처했다' 는 뜻이 됩니다.

Face 는 체면을 이야기할 때 사용하기도 하는데 save face 와 lose face는 각 '체면을 살리다, 수치나 모욕을 면하다' 와 '체면을 구기다, 면목을 잃다' 라 해석할 수 있습니다. 'In many Asian cultures, it is important to save face in front of peers.' 특히 우리나라를 비롯한 아시아권 문화에서는 동료들 앞에서 체면을 살리는 것을 중요하게 여기죠.

- The clown at the circus made faces at the audience.
- He faced the music like a man.
- In many Asian cultures, it is important to save face in front of peers.

Wrap-up

Key sentences

1. He has come all the way from Beijing to meet with us today.
2. I thought we might feature a jogging panda bear; we'd dress him up with sunglasses and running shoes.
3. Frankly speaking, I'm not impressed.
4. Having come all the way from Beijing, I expected more from this meeting.
5. Maybe I should be thinking about taking our business elsewhere.
6. I can help you sell a billion of these drinks.
7. But I want to see something amazing.
8. You won't be disappointed.

REVIEW TEST

Find the correct answers in the blanks. (1-5)

1. __________ closer, you'll see that the artist has painted himself in the background.
   (1) Look (2) Looking (3) Looked (4) Being looked

2. ___________ the book, I returned it to him.
   (1) Read (2) Had read (3) Having read (4) Having been read

3. His new book is a ____________ mystery story which has a very ____________ ending.
   (1) fascinating - surprising (2) fascinating - surprised
   (3) fascinated - surprising (4) fascinated - surprised

4. Aspirin can be dangerous when ____________ in excessive amounts.
   (1) take (2) taking (3) taken (4) having taken

5. I made it ___________ to all my friends.

(1) know (2) knowing (3) knew (4) known

Complete the sentences with the *-ing* or *-ed* forms of the verbs in parentheses. (6-10)

6. A: Is Alice going to the movies with us tonight?

   B: No, I don't think she's ______________ in going. (interest)

7. These directions are ______________. I don't understand them. (confuse)

8. I was quite ___________ by her singing. She's quite a good singer. (impress)

9. Korean citizens ___________ abroad should carry the phone number and address of the local embassy. (travel)

10. ___________ the eldest son, I am responsible for taking care of my parents. (be)

Supplementary Reading (보충 독해)

다음 글을 읽고 문제를 풀어 보세요.

Kangaroo Tribe

A deep economic recession has produced a new tribe in South Korea, the kangaroo tribe. The term "kangaroo tribe" describes a new trend among young people in their 20s or 30s who are dependent on their parents although they have reached the age to find a job after graduating from college. Like a baby kangaroo living in the pouch of its mother, these young people are still in the protection of their parents.

Recently, increasing numbers of unemployed young people have fallen into the kangaroo tribe category. They rely on their parents financially and psychologically. A survey found that only 68 percent of young adults living with their parents found jobs, while 87 percent of those who lived independently got jobs. It is said that 40 out of 100 jobless young people voluntarily stay unemployed because they are seeking better wages and working conditions.

Having grown up in affluent homes, many young people are reluctant to work in jobs they consider dirty, dangerous, or difficult. They do not even want to work at small companies. So many smallor medium-sized enterprises suffer from a lack of workers. Meanwhile, the elderly express concern for young people who shun achieving something through hard work.

Translation 캥거루족

심각한 경기 침체로 인해 한국에는 캥거루 족이라는 또 하나의 신조어가 생겼습니다. "캥거루족" 이란 대학 졸업 후 취업할 나이가 되었음에도 불구하고 부모님에게 의지하는 2,30 대의 젊은이들 사이에서 새로운 풍조를 일컫는 용어입니다. 엄마의 주머니 속에서 사는 아기 캥거루처럼 이 젊은이들은 아직 부모의 보호 아래 있습니다.
최근 증가하는 상당수의 청년 실업자들이 이 부류에 해당됩니다. 그들은 경제적으로, 정신적으로 그들의 부모에게 의지합니다. 한 설문지에 의하면 부모와 함께 사는 젊은이들 중에서는 68%만이 취직을 한 반면 독립해서 사는 젊은이들 중에서는 87%가 취직을 한 것으로 나타났습니다. 직업이 없는 100명 중 40명은 보다 좋은 연봉과 근무환경을 찾으려 하기 때문에 자의적인 실업상태로 있다고 합니다.
풍족한 집안 환경에서 성장했기 때문에 많은 청년들이 더럽고 위험하거나 어렵다고 생각되는 (3D) 직업은 꺼려합니다. 소규모 회사에서 일하기 조차 싫어해서 여러 중소기업들은 인력 부족으로 고생합니다. 한편 중장년층은 힘든 일을 통하여 무엇을 성취하려는 것을 피하는 젊은이들에 대하여 염려를 표합니다.

Explanation

1. The term "kangaroo tribe" describes a new trend among young people in their 20s or 30s who are dependent on their parents although they have reached the age to find a job after graduating from college.

be dependent on 은 '~에 의지(의존)하다' 라는 뜻입니다. reach는 ~에 닿다, 도달(도착)하다 란 뜻의 타동사로 뒤에 전치사를 쓰지 않는 것에 유의해야 합니다.

Ex) We mustn't be completely dependent on an allowance from our parents.
(우리는 우리 부모님으로부터 받는 용돈에 완전히 의존해서는 안됩니다.)

Ex) The financial crisis in Asia has reached its peak.
(아시아의 금융 공황은 극에 달했습니다.)

2. Recently, an increasing number of unemployed young people have fallen into the kangaroo tribe category.

numbers of + 복수가산명사는 '많은, 상당수의' 라는 뜻으로, a (great/large) number of + 복수가산명사도 같은 뜻으로 쓸 수 있습니다. fall into 는 '~에 빠지다, ~하기 시작하다' 란 의미이며, 여기서는 현재완료형으로 쓰였습니다.

Ex) We lost numbers of pictures.

(우리는 많은 수의 사진을 잃어버렸습니다.)

Ex) She has fallen into a big trap.

(그녀는 큰 함정에 빠졌습니다.)

3. A survey found that only 68 percent of young adults living with their parents found jobs, while 87 percent of those who lived independently got jobs.

living앞에는 관계대명사와 be동사인 who were가 생략되어 있습니다. while은 접속사로써 '~하는 반면' 이라는 뜻으로 보면 됩니다.

Ex) The girl living with my cousin is Susie.

(나의 사촌과 같이 살고 있는 그 여자애는 Susie입니다.)

4. Having grown up in affluent homes, many young people are reluctant to work in jobs they consider dirty, dangerous, or difficult.

having grown up은 분사구문의 완료형으로 주절 동사보다 앞선 시제를 나타내고, 이유를 나타내는 접속사가 생략되었다고 보면 됩니다. 즉, As they have grown up~을 분사구문 형태로 나타낸 것입니다. jobs 다음에는 which나 that 따위의 목적격 관계대명사가 생략되었습니다. consider는 목적어, 목적보어와 함께 쓰여 '~을 ~이라고 생각하다, 여기다' 라는 뜻이며, 여기에서 dirty, dangerous and difficult는 흔히 3D 업종을 지칭하는 말입니다.

Ex) Having been there before, I can show you around.

(그곳에 가본적이 있으니 당신을 구경시켜 줄께요.)

Ex) This is a responsibility that I consider important.

(이것이 바로 내가 중요하게 여기는 책임감입니다.)

5. Many small- or medium-sized enterprises suffer from a lack of workers.

suffer from은 '~을 앓다, ~으로부터 고통을 받다' 라는 뜻의 어구입니다.

Ex) Children in Africa suffer from fatal diseases such as AIDS and malaria.

(아프리카의 아이들은 에이즈나 말라리아와 같은 치명적인 질병으로 고통을 받습니다.)

Q.1 Find the word that can be replaced with the underlined word.

1. A deep economic <u>recession</u> produced the kangaroo tribe.

a) departure b) slump c) lack d) progress

2. Some jobless young people <u>voluntarily</u> stay unemployed.

a) temporarily b) hastily c) willingly d) unfortunately

3. They have grown up in affluent homes.

a) wealthy b) influential c) subsequent d) enough

4. Some people are reluctant to work at small companies.

a) relevant b) disappointed c) disinclined d) rejected

5. Young people shun achieving something through hard work.

a) attempt b) support c) aspire d) avoid

6. They tried to achieve their goal.

a) fail b) attain c) climb d) proceed

Q.2 Mark True (T) or False (F).

1. The kangaroo tribe is a term to describe young people who graduate from college.
2. Young people who belong to the kangaroo tribe receive assistance from their parents.
3. The number of young people who are categorized as the kangaroo tribe is decreasing.
4. Young people who are independent show a higher percentage of employment than those who aren't.
5. Young people don't like to have dirty or difficult jobsdue to their comfortable lifestyles while growing up.
6. The elderly are worried that young people lack ambition.

Adjectives and Adverbs 06 Unit

Introduction

Topic: A Desperate Attempt (무모한 시도)

Lesson objectives:

Adjectives and adverbs (형용사와 부사)

- usage of adjectives (형용사 용법)
- comparison (비교)
- usage of adverbs (부사 용법)

WARM-UP

In today's lesson, Brett shows up unannounced at Camille's house. What he doesn't know is that Aaron is also on his way over. Will he be upset when he finds out what Brett has been up to? Read on to find out.

(knock on the door)

Camille : Who is it?

Brett : It's me, Brett. Can I come in?

Camille : Only for a second. Aaron is coming over; we're going to the movies.

Brett : I'll speak quickly then. (adverbs)

(knock on the door)

Camille : Who is it?

Aaron : It's me, Aaron. Can I come in?

Camille : Sure. Brett just stopped over to say hello.

Aaron : Oh, that's nice.

Brett : That's not exactly why I stopped by. (adverbs)

Camille : Well, why did you stop by?

Aaron : Yeah, why did you stop by, Brett?

Brett : I came by to tell Camille that I'd like a second chance. (adjectives)

Camille : And I already told you that's not possible. (adjectives)

Aaron : Right, Brett, that's not possible. (adjectives)

Brett : Well, Camille, I'd like you to know that I think you're as beautiful as the sunsets in Sweden, and I'd like another shot. (adjectives)

Aaron : Well, Camille, I'd like you to know that I think you're more beautiful than the sunsets in Sweden, and I don't think you should give Brett another shot. (adjectives)

Camille : Gentlemen! This is the most ridiculous thing I've ever heard. (adjectives)

Aaron : Are you ready to go?

Camille : Yes. Let's go.

Brett : I think I'll go along as well. (adverbs) I'm sure there's an available seat. (adjectives)

Aaron : I don't think so. It's a sold out show and there won't be a seat available. (adjectives)

Brett : Aaron, you're being a total jerk. (adjectives)

Aaron : Well, you're being an utter fool. (adjectives)

Camille : Frankly, I think you're both silly. (adverbs, adjectives)

Aaron : Are we going to see this movie or not?

Camille : I'm not in the mood to go anymore.

Brett : Me, neither.

Translation

오늘 강의에서는 Brett이 예고없이 Camille의 집에 나타납니다. Brett은 Aaron 역시 오고 있다는 사실을 몰랐습니다. Brett이 방문한 것을 알면 Aaron은 화를 낼까요?

(문을 두드림)

Camille : 누구세요?
Brett : 나야, Brett. 들어가도 되니?
Camille : 잠시만이야. Aaron이 오고 있어 우리는 영화 보러 갈 거야.
Brett : 그럼 빨리 이야기할께.

(문을 두드림)

Camille : 누구세요?
Aaron : 나야, Aaron. 들어가도 되니?
Camille : 물론. Brett이 이제 방금 인사하려고 들렸어.
Aaron : 오, 잘 됐다.
Brett : 사실 그게 내가 온 이유는 아니야.
Camille : 그럼, 왜 왔어?
Aaron : 그래, 무슨 일로 온거니, Brett?
Brett : Camille에게 또 한 번의 기회를 달라고 말하러 왔어.
Camille : 이미 그건 불가능하다고 말했잖아.
Aaron : 그래, Brett. 그건 안돼.
Brett : 그래도, Camille, 나는 네가 스웨덴의 노을 진 하늘만큼이나 아름답다고 생각하고 있다는 것을 알아주길 바래. 그리고 나는 다시 시작하고 싶어.
Aaron : 어, Camille, 나는 네가 스웨덴의 노을 진 하늘보다 더 아름답다고 생각하고 있다는 것을 알아주길 바래. 그리고 나는 네가 Brett에게 또 다른 기회를 주어서는 안 된다고 생각해.
Camille : 신사양반들! 이건 지금까지 내가 들어본 것 중에 가장 바보 같은 얘기야.
Aaron : 나갈 준비 됐니?
Camille : 그래. 나가자.
Brett : 나도 같이 가는 것이 좋겠어. 분명히 남는 자리가 있을거야.
Aaron : 아니야. 전 좌석 매진됐어. 남는 자리는 없을거야.
Brett : Aaron, 넌 정말 바보야.
Aaron : 아니, 너야말로 완전 바보야.
Camille : 솔직히, 너희 둘 다 어리석은 것 같아.
Aaron : 우리 영화 보러 갈 거야, 말 거야?
Camille : 더 이상 갈 기분이 아니야.
Brett : 나도 그래.

Comprehension Check

1. When Aaron tells Brett there won't be an available seat at the movies, he's making a(n):
   (a) excuse
   (b) story
   (c) reservation
   (d) offer

2. During the course of the dialogue, Camille's attitude toward Brett changes from __________ to __________.
   (a) disappointed - angry
   (b) cordial - angry
   (c) angry - forgiving
   (d) pleasant – disappointed

3. Which statement of the following is true?
   (a) Brett came by Camille's house just to say hello.
   (b) Brett had an appointment with Camille.
   (c) Aaron invited Brett to come along.
   (d) Camille decided not to go to the movies.

Useful Expressions

In this dialogue	Explanation
1. This is the most ridiculous thing I've ever heard.	1. What's the funniest thing you've ever heard? You probably don't remember. Most people don't. Still, when someone tells a good joke, so good that you're doubled over laughing, you might say, "That's the funniest thing I've ever heard." This is just another way of saying that something is incredibly funny. It doesn't necessarily mean that you've carefully considered all the jokes you've ever heard, and deemed this one the best.

In this dialogue	Explanation
2. I think I'll go along as well.	2. The phrase "go along" can be used to mean "accompany," as seen in today's dialogue, or it can be used to express agreement with an idea. Since we're already familiar with the first usage, let's take a look at the second. If someone says, "I can't go along with that plan," it doesn't mean they're not willing to travel. In this case, this expression indicates that someone isn't willing to support an idea that they don't agree or concur.
3. It's a sold out show and there won't be a seat available.	3. Have you ever rushed to the theater only to find out that the movie you wanted to see was sold out? This particular verb phrase indicates that all tickets usually for a performance or event, have been sold. Some adjectives can be used before or after the noun they modify without changing the meaning. "Available" is one. Some others include above, possible, and capable.
4. Aaron, you're being a total jerk.	4. There's an old saying, "To find a friend one must close one eye; to keep him, two." In other words, to find a friend, you'll have to overlook someone's faults. Still, there are times when even the best of friends will get on your nerves. In this case, you might like to let them know what you're thinking. But be careful how you do it. There's a big difference between, "You're being stupid," and "You are stupid." The first one implies that the stupidity is confined to an isolated incident, whereas the latter indicates it might be more permanent.
5. I'm not in the mood to go anymore.	5. You might hear people using this expression when talking about food they'd like to eat or places they'd like to go. If you feel like going to a movie, you might say, "I'm in the mood to see a movie." When you get there, you might be in the mood for popcorn. (Go light on the butter; it's bad for your health.) In today's example, "not" is included. So, we're talking about someplace someone would not like to go.

Grammar

Focus 1 Adjectives (형용사)

01 Attributive use and predicative use (한정적 용법과 서술적 용법)

형용사에는 명사를 직접 수식하는 한정적 용법과 주격보어나 목적격보어로 쓰이며 명사를 간접 수식하는 서술적 용법이 있습니다. 대부분의 형용사는 두 가지 용법으로 다 쓸 수 있습니다.

(1) 한정적 용법

- I'd like a second chance.
  (나는 또한번의 기회를 갖고 싶습니다.)
- She's going out with a rich businessman.
  (그녀는 돈 많은 사업가와 사귀고 있습니다.)
- The film has an unhappy ending.
  (그 영화는 불행한 결말을 포함하고 있습니다.)
- The president usually wears a blue tie.
  (그 대통령은 보통 파란색 넥타이를 맵니다.)
- My computer has a wireless mouse.
  (나의 컴퓨터는 무선 마우스를 이용합니다.)

(2) 서술적 용법

be, seem, become, come, get, grow, appear, remain, prove, look, feel, sound 등의 뒤에 나옵니다.

- I already told you that's not possible.
  (나는 그것이 가능하지 않다고 이미 당신에게 말했습니다.)
- The sales forecast for the fourth quarter remains bleak.
  (4분기 판매 예상은 여전히 어둡습니다.)
- The baby looks healthy.
  (그 아기는 건강해 보입니다.)
- When it's hot outside, the dogs become lazy.
  (밖이 더울 때는 개들이 게을러집니다.)
- The worst case scenario appears likely.
  (최악의 상황이 될 것 같습니다.)

(3) 한정적 용법에만 쓰이는 형용사

강의어 (intensifier)

mere(단지), extreme(극도의), lone(혼자의), principal(주요한), entire(전체의), sheer(순수한), total(절대적인), utter(완전한)

- Aaron, you're being a total jerk.
  (Aaron, 당신은 정말 바보입니다.)
- Well, you're being an utter fool.
  (아니, 당신이야말로 완전한 바보입니다.)
- He sometimes talks sheer nonsense.
  (그는 가끔씩 정말 어처구니 없는 말을 합니다.)
- Our company's products can withstand even the most extreme conditions.
  (우리 회사의 제품은 가장 극한 상황도 견디어 낼 수 있습니다.)
- The scandal is likely to affect the entire business community.
  (그 추문은 전체 업계에 영향을 미칠 것 같습니다.)

비교급에서 파생한 형용사

my elder sister(나의 언니), a former principal(전 교장), lower/upper class(하류/상류 계층), an inner court(안뜰), an outer wall(외벽)

'지정'의 의미

a certain man(어떤 사람), the following day(다음 날), the late Mr. Park(고 미스터 박), the next day(다음 날), the same pianist(같은 피아니스트), the right book(바로 그 책), the only day(유일한 날)

명사에서 파생된 형용사

the dramatic situation(극적인 상황), criminal law(형사법), civil law(민사법), a medical school(의과대학), a sub-urban house (교외에 있는 집)

기타

a daily newspaper(일간 신문), a monthly magazine(월간지), a wooden box(나무 상자), woolen socks(모직 양말), Western Europe(서유럽), a live concert(라이브 콘서트), a spare tire (예비용 타이어)

(4) 서술적 용법에만 쓰이는 형용사

접두사 a-로 시작하는 형용사

ablaze(불타는), afloat(떠있는), afraid(두려운), alike(비슷한), alive(살아있는), alone(홀로), ashamed(부끄러운), asleep(잠든), awake(깨어난), aware(의식이 있는)

- It is said that no two snowflakes are alike.
  (어떤 두 개의 눈송이도 같지 않다고 합니다.)

- In less than two hours, the entire structure was ablaze.

(두 시간도 안 되어서 전체 구조물이 불길에 휩싸였습니다.)

- The baby is asleep.

(아기는 잠들어 있습니다.)

cf) a sleeping baby (잠든 아기)

- The ship is still afloat.

(배는 아직 떠있습니다.)

cf) a floating ship (떠있는 배)

- He was afraid.

(그는 두려웠습니다.)

cf) a frightened man (겁을 먹은 사람)

전치사구, that절, to부정사구를 수반하는 형용사

able to(~할 수 있는), afraid of/about/to/that(~이 두려운), aware of/that(~을 의식하는), fond of(~을 좋아하는), conscious of/that(~을 자각하고 있는), glad about/to/that(~을 기쁘게 여기는), subject to(~되기 쉬운)

- Someday scientists will be able to find a cure for cancer.

(언젠가는 과학자들은 암을 치료하는 약을 찾을 수 있을 것입니다.)

cf) She is an able politician.

(그녀는 유능한 정치인입니다.)

건강상태와 관계 있는 형용사

ill(아픈), well(건강한), unwell(건강하지 않은), pale(창백한), faint(어지러운)

- He is seriously ill.

(그는 위독합니다.)

cf) *an ill man

02 Premodification and postmodification (전위수식과 후위수식)

명사를 수식하는 형용사는 명사의 앞에 오는 것이 보통이지만, 다음과 같이 명사의 뒤에 오기도 합니다.

(1) 후위 수식

–one, –thing, –body, those, all

- The army called on everyone capable.

(군대는 가능한 모든 사람을 소집했습니다.)

- All present were happy.

(참석했던 모든 이들은 행복했습니다.)

- I want to drink something hot.

(나는 무언가 뜨거운 것을 마시고 싶습니다.)

cf) I'd like to drink hot tea.

(나는 뜨거운 차을 마시고 싶습니다.)

– able/–ible로 끝나는 형용사

- It's a sold out show and there won't be a seat available.

(전 좌석이 매진되어서 남는 자리가 없을 거야.)

cf) I'm sure there's an available seat.

(분명히 남는 자리가 있을 거야.)

- As a young police officer, I made just about every mistake possible.

(젊은 경찰이기 때문에, 나는 많은 갖가지 실수를 했습니다.)

- We ate everything edible.

(우리는 먹을 수 있는 모든 것을 먹었습니다.)

기타

- The book has stories both amusing and instructive.

(그 책에는 재미도 있고 유익한 이야기들이 있습니다.)

- We needed a rope fifty-five meters long.

(우리는 55 미터 길이의 밧줄이 필요했습니다.)

- They met the president elect.

(그들은 대통령 당선자를 만났습니다.)

- Have you ever talked to the woman upstairs?

(당신은 윗층 여자와 이야기 해본 적이 있습니까?)

(2) 전위 수식과 후위 수식에 따른 의미 차이

- the members present (출석한 회원)

  the present members (현 회원)

- the authorities concerned (관계당국)

  concerned look (근심 어린 표정)

- stars visible (눈에 보이는 별)

  visible stars (가시거리에 있는 별)

Task 1

Choose the correct word or expression to complete each sentence.

former	live	total	afraid	fond of	well	frightened	like

1. The ________ child was crying in the corner of the room.
2. The ________ coach of our team is back.
3. It's good to see you are ________.
4. The children seem ________ the nanny.
5. Last year's Christmas party turned out to be a ________ disaster.

Focus 2 Comparison (비교)

01 Comparison of equality (동등 비교)

(1) as~as

as ~ as: ~ 만큼 ~한

as ~ as any+(명사): 누구(어느 것) 못지않게 ~한

as ~ as possible / as ~ as one can: 가능한 ~하게

as ~ as ever: 변함없이 ~한

- I'd like you to know that I think you're as beautiful as the sunsets in Sweden.
  (나는 당신이 스웨덴의 노을 진 하늘만큼이나 아름답다고 내가 생각하고 있다는 것을 알아주었으면 합니다.)
- Was the movie as good as you expected?
  (당신이 생각한 것만큼 영화가 괜찮았습니까?)
- Please get here as soon as possible.
  (여기로 가능한 한 빨리 오세요.)
- You are as beautiful as ever.
  (당신은 변함없이 아름답군요.)

(2) 부정문

not as ~ as: ~만큼 ~ 하지 않은
no +명사 is as ~ as: 어느 무엇도 ~만큼 ~하지 않은

- That film wasn't as frightening as I expected.
  (그 영화는 내가 기대했던 것만큼 무섭진 않았습니다.)
- Learning a foreign language isn't as difficult as some people think.
  (외국어를 배우는 것은 몇몇 사람들이 생각하는 것만큼 어려운 것은 아닙니다.)
- No one in our class is as tall as he. (= He is the tallest one in our class.)
  (우리 반에 그만큼 키가 큰 아이는 없습니다.)

(3) 배수비교

- You're not half as clever as you think you are.
  (당신은 자신이 생각하는 것의 반 정도도 똑똑하지 않습니다.)
- When you buy a ticket at the airport, you'll pay twice as much as you would online.
  (당신이 공항에서 표를 사면 온라인에서 사는 것보다 두 배를 지불할 것입니다.)
- The university received at least ten times as many applications as it did last year.
  (그 대학은 지난 해보다 적어도 열 배나 많은 지원자를 받았습니다.)

(4) 관용적 표현

- Her hands are as cold as ice.
  (그녀의 손은 얼음같이 차갑습니다.)
- He's as hard as nails.
  (그는 못처럼 딱딱한 사람입니다.)
- He is as innocent as a lamb.
  (그는 양처럼 순한 사람입니다.)

02 Comparison of superiority (우등 비교)

(1) 비교급 + than

형용사 원급에 –er를 붙여 비교급을 만들고, 형용사가 y로 끝나는 경우엔 y를 빼고 ier을 쓰며, 2음절 이상의 경우엔 more를 붙입니다.

cheap – cheaper, easy – easier, comfortable – more comfortable

- Blood is thicker than water.
  (피는 물보다 진하다.)
- Sending a package via postal mail is slower than using a courier service.
  (우편으로 소포를 보내는 것은 택배를 이용하는 것보다 느립니다.)
- I'd like you to know that I think you're more beautiful than the sunsets in Sweden.
  (나는 당신이 스웨덴의 노을 진 하늘보다 더 아름답다고 내가 생각하고 있다는 것을 알아주었으면 합니다.)
- Diesel fuel is more expensive than gasoline.
  (디젤은 가솔린보다 더 비쌉니다.)
- I'm late for work more often than not.
  (나는 지각할 때가 더 많습니다.)

(2) more 비교급

2음절의 형용사나 부사의 경우에도, 다음의 경우에는 비교급에 more를 씁니다.

- She is more wise than kind. (동일인물이나 사물의 성질 비교)
  (그녀는 친절하기 보다는 지혜로운 편입니다.)
- He is more fond of her than her sister. (afraid of, alike, alive, alone, fond of등)
  (그는 그녀의 언니보다 그녀를 더 좋아합니다.)
- I feel more alive now than ever.
  (나는 전보다 생동감을 느낍니다.)
- Joe runs more slowly than Sam. (-ly가 붙은 부사)
  (Joe는 Sam보다 느리게 뜁니다.)

cf) She felt tired last night, so she went to bed earlier than usual.
(그녀는 어젯밤에 피곤해서 평소보다 더 일찍 잠자리에 들었습니다.)

(3) 부정

not은 대부분 비교급 자체를 부정합니다. 열등 비교에는 less + than을 씁니다.

- I'm not slimmer than my mother.
  (나는 나의 엄마보다 더 날씬하지는 않습니다.)
- Oxygen is not lighter than hydrogen.
  (산소는 수소보다 더 가볍지는 않습니다.)
- They are less happy than me.
  (그들은 나보다 행복하지 못합니다.)
- Older cars are often less reliable than new ones.
  (오래된 차는 새 차보다 종종 안정감이 떨어집니다.)

(4) 비교의 차이

- She is two inches taller than you.
  (그녀는 당신보다 2인치 더 큽니다.)
- He weighs three pounds more than an average boy of his age.
  (그는 그 나이 또래의 보통 아이들보다 3파운드 더 무겁습니다.)

(5) 비교급 강조

비교급을 강조할 때는 much, far, even, a lot 등을 비교급 앞에 쓰게 되는데 '훨씬, 더욱' 의 의미를 갖습니다.

- Flying is actually much safer than driving.
  (비행하는 것이 사실 운전하는 것보다 훨씬 더 안전합니다.)
- This problem is far more complicated than the previous one.
  (이 문제는 전의 것보다 훨씬 더 복잡합니다.)
- Alex is a lot more mature than most teenagers.
  (Alex는 대부분의 십대들보다 훨씬 더 성숙합니다.)

(6) the + 비교급

'두 개중 더 ~한'의 의미로 쓰일 때는 비교급에 the를 붙입니다.

- The coach will choose the faster one of the two boys.
  (그 코치는 두 소년 중 더 빠른 아이를 선택할 것입니다.)
- Algebra is the more confusing of the two.
  (대수학이 둘 중에서 더 복잡합니다.)
- The Amazon is the longer of the two rivers.
  (Amazon은 두 강 중에서 더 깁니다.)

(7) the + 비교급, the + 비교급

'~하면 할수록 더 ~하다'라는 의미로 쓰입니다.

- The more, the better.
  (많을수록 좋습니다.)
- The older you get, the wiser you become.
  (당신은 나이가 더 들수록 더 지혜로워집니다.)
- The better you prepare for it, the safer your trip will be.
  (당신이 준비를 더 잘 할수록 당신의 여행은 더 안전할 것입니다.)
- The more difficult the government makes it for children to purchase cigarettes, the less they'll smoke.
  (정부가 아이들이 담배 구매하는 것을 더 어렵게 할수록 그들은 담배를 덜 피울 것입니다.)

(8) 라틴어 비교

비교대상 앞에 than 대신에 to를 씁니다: superior to(~보다 뛰어나), inferior to(~보다 못한), junior to(~보다 손아래의), senior to(~보다 손위의), prior to(~보다 앞선)

- Our new line of products is far superior to existing lines.
  (우리의 신제품은 기존 제품보다 훨씬 더 우수합니다.)
- He is senior to me by three years.
  (그는 저보다 세 살이 많습니다.)
- Some people believe that economically priced wines are inferior to expensive ones.
  (어떤 사람들은 값이 저렴한 와인이 비싼 와인보다 못하다고 믿습니다.)

(9) 관용적 표현

no more than, not more than (=at most): 많아야

no less than,not less than (=at least): 적어도

no longer: 더 이상 ~아니다

- He has not more than 5,000 won. / He doesn't have more than 5,000 won.
  (그는 많아야 5000원을 가지고 있습니다.)
- He has not less than 5,000 won. / He doesn't have less than 5,000 won.
  (그는 적어도 5000원을 가지고 있습니다.)
- They are no longer living here.
  (그들은 더 이상 이곳에 살지 않습니다.)

(10) 두 가지 의미

종속절에 나온 명사를 주격으로 보는 지, 목적격으로 보는 지에 따라 의미가 달라집니다.

- He loves his cat more than his children.
  (그는 그의 아이들보다 더 고양이를 좋아합니다.)
  (아이들이 고양이를 좋아하는 것보다 더 고양이를 좋아합니다. / 아이들을 좋아하기보다 고양이를 더 좋아합니다.)

03 Superlative (최상급)

(1) the + 최상급

형용사 원급에 est를 붙여 최상급을 나타내고, 형용사가 y로 끝나는 경우엔 y를 빼고 iest 를 쓰며, 2음절 이상의 형용사의 경우엔 most를 붙입니다.

fast - fastest, happy - happiest, intelligent - most intelligent

- She is the fastest girl on her team.
  (그녀는 팀 중에서 가장 빠릅니다.)
- At one time, the Sears Tower was the tallest building in the world.
  (한때는, Sears Tower가 세계에게 가장 높은 건물이었습니다.)
- This is the most ridiculous thing I've ever heard.
  (이건 지금까지 내가 들어본 것 중에 가장 바보 같은 얘기입니다.)
- That's certainly not the most intelligent thing you've ever said.
  (그것은 확실히 지금까지 당신이 한 말 중에서 가장 현명한 것은 아닙니다.)

(2) 최상급 + of all 복수 명사

- This is the most delicious of all chocolates.
  (이것은 모든 초코렛 중에 가장 맛있습니다.)
- Of all the elements, silver is the best conductor of electricity.
  (모든 원소 중에서 은은 전류에 대한 가장 뛰어난 전도체입니다.)

(3) 최상급의 뜻을 지닌 표현

원급이나 비교급으로도 최상급의 의미를 나타낼 수 있습니다. 또한 부정어와 함께 원급이나 비교급을 쓰면 최상급을 의미합니다.

- Betty had better marks than any other student in her class. (= Betty has the best marks in her class.)
  (Betty는 그녀 학급에서 어떤 아이들보다도 점수가 높았습니다.)
- No one is as accomplished in the world of chess as Gary Kasparov.
  (Gary Kasparov만큼 세상에서 체스를 잘 두는 사람은 없습니다.)
- I couldn't be happier.
  (나는 이 이상 행복할 수 없을 겁니다.)
- There's nothing better than a cold drink on a hot day.
  (더운 날씨에는 차가운 음료수보다 더 좋은 것은 없습니다.)

(4) the를 붙이지 않는 최상급

- The lake is deepest at this point. (동일물의 속성을 비교)
  (이 호수에서는 여기가 가장 깊습니다.)
- The sun is hottest near the equator.
  (태양은 적도 부근에서 가장 뜨겁습니다.)
- I like this song best. (부사의 최상급)
  (나는 이 노래를 가장 좋아합니다.)

Task 2

Read each sentence carefully and decide whether it is correct (O) or incorrect (X).

		O	X
1.	At work, Friday is the busier day of the week.	(　)	(　)
2.	The most nervous he gets, the faster he drives.	(　)	(　)
3.	Your baby brother couldn't get any cuter.	(　)	(　)
4.	It took three times as long as we had expected.	(　)	(　)
5.	Of the two candidates, I think Mr. Wilson is the best one.	(　)	(　)

Focus 3 Adverbs (부사)

01 부사의 기능

부사는 동사, 형용사, 다른 부사, 명사, 또는 문장 전체를 수식합니다.

- During the past decade, China's economy has expanded rapidly. (동사 수식)
  (지난 10년 동안, 중국의 경제는 급속히 팽창했습니다.)
- She quite likes him, but not enough to marry him. (동사 수식)
  (그녀는 그를 꽤 좋아하지만 결혼할 만큼 좋아하지 않습니다.)
- It's extremely important that you mail your application well in advance of the deadline. (형용사 수식)
  (기한 전에 당신의 지원서를 보내는 것이 매우 중요합니다.)
- He ran unusually fast. (부사 수식)
  (그는 보통 때와 달리 빨리 뛰었습니다.)
- Even Mary didn't see him this morning. (명사 수식)
  (Mary 조차도 오늘 아침 그를 보지 못했습니다.)
- Frankly, I think you're both silly. (문장 수식)
  (솔직히 나는 당신 둘 모두 어리석다고 생각합니다.)

02 부사의 위치

(1) 부사는 동사와 목적어 사이에 올 수 없습니다.

- He found yesterday the book. (X)
  He found the book yesterday. (O)
  (그는 어제 책을 찾았습니다.)

(2) 문장 앞/중간/끝에 올 수 있습니다.

- Please remember to read chapter six before coming to class tomorrow.
  (내일 수업 오기 전에 6장을 읽어오는 것을 기억해 주세요.)
- My brother completely forgot about the appointment.
  (나의 남동생은 약속에 대해서 완전히 잊어버렸습니다.)
- The Kremlin released a statement early yesterday.
  (러시아 정부는 어제 일찍 성명서를 발표했습니다.)

(3) 빈도 부사 (always, usually, often, frequently, sometimes, seldom, never, hardly)

be동사나 조동사 다음, 일반동사 앞에 옵니다.

- You can always come and stay with us if you want to.
  (원한다면 언제든지 와서 우리와 지내도 됩니다.)
- Albert Einstein is frequently cited as the founder of modern physics.
  (Albert Einstein은 자주 현대 물리학의 창시자로 언급됩니다.)
- He sometimes visits his grandparents.
  (그는 가끔 그의 조부모님들은 방문합니다.)
- My students seldom do their homework.
  (나의 학생들은 거의 숙제를 하지 않습니다.)

(4) 부정의 뜻인 hardly, rarely, scarcely, seldom, never 등이 문장 서두에 오면 주어와 조동사가 도치됩니다.

- Never have we eaten such a delicious meal.
  (이렇게 맛있는 식사를 한 번도 해본 적이 없습니다.)
- Hardly ever did we hear him raise his voice in anger.
  (우리는 그가 화가 나서 목소리를 높이는 것을 거의 들은 적이 없었습니다.)

- Rarely does she lose her self-control.

(그녀는 좀처럼 자제심을 잃지 않습니다.)

(5) 초점부사

수식하는 어구 앞에 놓아서, 그 부분에 주목하게 합니다. especially, mainly, even, particularly 등은 좀 더 구체적으로 기술하기 위해 쓰이고, just, only, simply, alone 등은 하나의 사물이나 사람에 국한시키기 위해 쓰입니다.

- He always wears a jacket, even in summer.

(그는 늘 그 자켓을 입는 데, 여름에도 입습니다.)

- The population is mainly concentrated in large urban areas.

(인구는 큰 도시 주변 지역에 주로 집중하게 됩니다.)

- It's not just a job; it's a lifestyle.

(그것은 단지 직업이 아니라, 생활방식입니다.)

- Only you could do such a good job.

(그렇게 일을 잘할 수 있는 사람은 당신뿐입니다.)

03 다양한 의미를 갖는 부사

(1) generally

- Answer the next question generally, not in detail.

(다음 질문에 대해 자세하지 않게 대강 답하십시오.)

- He generally talks too fast.

(그는 보통 말을 너무 빨리 합니다.)

- Generally, I think your work is great.

(전반적으로 당신의 작품은 훌륭하다고 생각됩니다.)

(2) badly

- The barber cut your hair badly.

(그 이발사는 당신의 머리를 형편없이 잘랐습니다.)

- Your hair needs cutting badly.

(당신은 머리를 꼭 자르셔야 할 것 같습니다.)

(3) bitterly

- She bitterly criticized his attitude.

(그녀는 그의 태도에 대해 신랄하게 비판을 하였습니다.)

- It is bitterly cold today.
  (오늘은 무척 춥습니다.)
- Bitterly, he admitted his mistake.
  (씁쓸하게, 그는 그의 잘못을 인정했습니다.)

(4) naturally

- We naturally assumed the worst.
  (우리는 자연스럽게 최악의 경우를 가정했습니다.)
- Naturally, we went with the least expensive option.
  (당연히 우리는 최소한의 비용이 드는 쪽을 선택했습니다.)
- The air we breathe is filtered naturally by trees and others plants.
  (우리가 숨쉬는 공기는 나무와 다른 식물들을 통해 자연의 힘으로 여과됩니다.)

04 두 가지 형태의 부사

hard /hardly(열심히 / 거의 ~하지 않다), high / highly(높이 / 매우), just / justly(틀림없이 / 공정하게), most / mostly(가장 / 대개), near / nearly(가까이 / 대략), late / lately (늦게 / 최근에)

(1) hard /hardly

- He works hard these days.
  (그는 요즘 열심히 일합니다.)
- I can hardly believe it.
  (나는 도저히 그것을 믿을 수가 없습니다.)

(2) high / highly

- Throw it as high as you can.
  (가능한 한 높이 던져 올리세요.)
- I can highly recommend it.
  (나는 그것을 적극 추천할 수 있습니다.)

Task 3

Choose the correct word(s) to complete the sentence.

1. The proposal I made was very (good, well) received.
2. We were (absolute, absolutely) shocked by the accident.
3. You should try as (hard, hardly) as you can to overcome that problem.
4. It's (terrible, terribly) cold today.
5. He (always talks, talks always) about the writer Kafka.

Reading Playing with Words

Trends come and go, but the crossword puzzle, which debuted in 1913 in the *New York World*, looks like it's here to stay. The first crossword, or "word-cross" as it was called back then, looked much different from the black and white grids we know today. Arthur Wynne, an English expatriate working at the *World*, modeled his puzzle after an ancient brainteaser, but his version was diamond shaped and didn't make use of blank squares.

Today, the crossword can be found in daily newspapers all around the world. However, don't assume that they all look the same. In North America, most puzzles are symmetrical, meaning that when you turn them upside down, the grid looks the same. The Australians prefer more black squares, whereas the Japanese have adopted the North American style, although they've added a few rules of their own: no two black cells may touch and the corner blocks must be white.

Perhaps the most revered crossword in contemporary times is found in the Sunday edition of *The New York Times*. Former American President Bill Clinton has professed to be a loyal fan of the puzzle, and has even written one for publication himself.

Translation 낱말놀이

유행은 왔다가 가지만, 1913년 *New York World*에 처음 등장한 글자 맞추기 놀이는 그대로 여기에 머물러 있는 듯 합니다. 처음 크로스워드 또는 그 당시에 말인 "워드-크로스"는 오늘날 우리가 알고 있는 검정색 흰색 격자모양과는 꽤 다른 모습이었습니다. 영국에서 이주하여 *World*에서 일하던 Arthur Wynne은 고대에서부터 있었던 퍼즐(머리로 생각하는 놀이)을 본떠서 그의 퍼즐을 만들었습니다. 그가 만든 것은 다이아몬드 모양이었으며 빈 네모 칸을 이용하지도 않았습니다.

오늘날 크로스워드는 매일 전세계 신문에서 볼 수 있습니다. 하지만, 모두 똑같다고 생각해서는 안됩니다. 북미에서는 대부분의 퍼즐이 대칭적이어서 그것을 뒤집어도 그 격자는 똑같이 보입니다. 호주인들은 검정색 네모 칸이 더 많은 것을 선호하고, 반면에 일본인들은 북미스타일을 채택하기는 했지만, 그들만의 약간의 규칙을 추가했습니다: 두 개의 검정색 칸이 닿아 있을 수 없으며 모퉁이 부분은 흰색이어야 합니다.

아마도 현대에 있어서 가장 인기 있는 크로스워드는 *The New York Times*의 일요일 판에 나오는 것 일 겁니다. 전 미국 대통령 Bill Clinton은 이 퍼즐의 열렬한 팬이 되겠다고 선언했으며, 심지어 직접 간행물을 쓰기도 했습니다.

Comprehension Check-up

True/False

1. The crossword puzzle has been around since ancient times. (T/F)
2. In Australia, the crossword puzzle is perfectly symmetrical. (T/F)
3. Bill Clinton writes as well as solves crossword puzzles. (T/F)

Vocabulary Matching

1. debut	a. a person living in a foreign country
2. expatriate	b. the same on both sides
3. symmetrical	c. to appear for the first time
4. loyal	d. faithful

Word Challenge

Quiz

Check Your Understanding: Use the words in the box to complete each of the following sentences.

some	little	any

1. You can ask __________ German and they'll tell you the same thing.
2. I'd like __________ more coffee, please.
3. She won by a huge margin, and encountered __________ difficulty along the way.

Word Challenge

some	Usage: The first adjective we're going to look at today, "some," can be used to modify both countable and uncountable nouns. It can refer to an undetermined degree, a specific amount, or an amount that is quite significant. examples: 1. I agree with that statement to some extent. (an uncertain degree) (어느 정도는 그 말에 동의합니다.) 2. Some toys require batteries. (specific) (어떤 장난감들은 건전지가 필요합니다.) 3. We shopped for some time before deciding on a Hyundai. (considerable but unspecified) (우리는 현대로 결정하기 전에 얼마 동안 물색을 했습니다.)
little	Usage: Unlike "some," we can only use "little" to modify uncountable nouns. This list of nouns includes things like water, juice, money, and cake. "Little" can indicate degree, importance, or time, as seen in the examples below. examples: 1. Little inventory remained after the convention. (small in amount or degree) (그 집회 이후 재고품이 거의 남지 않았습니다.) 2. Little comfort was to be had knowing the storm would strike soon. (small in consideration) (폭풍우가 엄습하리라는 것을 아는 그에게 어떤 것도 위로가 되지 않았습니다.) 3. There was little time to come up with a plan. (short in duration) (계획을 세울 시간이 거의 없었습니다.)

any	Usage: Like "some," the third adjective we'll look at today, "any," can be used to modify both countable and uncountable nouns. Its usage is versatile and can take on the meaning of "all," "one," or "whichever." examples: 1. Any good citizen knows the pledge of allegiance. (all; every) (모든 훌륭한 시민은 누구나 충성 맹세를 알고 있습니다.) 2. It's the same price in any store. (whichever or whatever) (어느 상점에서나 똑같은 가격입니다.) 3. Do you have any money left? (one, any, a, some) (남은 돈이 좀 있습니까?)

Practice

Task 4

Choose the correct expression to complete each sentence.

1. Please give me __________ to drink.
   (a) hot something (b) something hot

2. Jack Russells are the smartest __________.
   (a) alive dogs (b) dogs alive

3. The newly-constructed highway is said to be __________.
   (a) twenty miles long (b) twenty miles of length

4. A dog's intelligence is much greater __________.
   (a) than a cat (b) than that of a cat

5. I'll try to learn __________.
   (a) as much as I can (b) as possible as I can

Task 5

Find the sentences that are incorrect and correct them. If the sentence is correct leave it alone.

		correct	incorrect
1.	Your Chinese ability is superior than mine. ____________________	( )	( )
2.	Of the two, he is the nicer one. ____________________	( )	( )
3.	This movie is worst one I've ever seen. ____________________	( )	( )
4.	She is very faster than her friends. ____________________	( )	( )
5.	He is not less intelligent than his sisters. ____________________	( )	( )

Culture Corner

미국의 결혼풍습

미국은 다양한 문화의 사람들이 모여 사는 곳인 만큼 결혼식도 다양하게 치러집니다. 남녀 둘이 시청에 가서 서류에 서명만 하고 나서 부부로써 사는 사람들도 있고 법적 결혼 후 교회에서 종교적인 의식을 갖춰서 성대하게 치르기도 합니다.

우리나라에서는 예식장에서 결혼식이 많이 거행되는 반면 미국에서는 교회, 호텔, country club(컨트리 클럽), 야외 또는 신부의 집에서 결혼식이 열리기도 합니다. 예식장이라는 별도의 장소가 없는 것 입니다. 대개의 경우 집 근처의 교회에서 식이 올려지는 데, groom(신랑)이 먼저 입장 한 후 bride(신부)가 아버지에 의해 priest(목사)나 bishop(주교) 등의 성직자에게 인도되는 것은 한국과 비슷합니다. 신부가 입장할 때엔 bridesmaid(들러리)를 대동하고 입장하는데, bridesmaid는 bride의 친한 친척이나 친구들로서 서너 명 정도 됩니다. 이들도 드레스를 입고 머리에 꽃 화환을 두르고 입장한 후에는 신부의 옆쪽에 서있습니다. 또한 bridesman 혹은 best man 이라 불리는 들러리들이 신랑 쪽에 서게 되는데 신랑 쪽 들러리의 역할은 반지를 건네주는 것입니다.

성직자는 입장한 신부의 손을 신랑의 손 위에 겹치게 하고 남편과 아내의 의무에 관한 성경구절을 낭독하고 결혼의 의의에 관한 메시지를 전합니다. 그리고 나서 신랑신부의 결혼서약이 이뤄지는데 이때 성직자는 Do you (신랑/신부 이름) take this man 혹은 woman (신랑/신부 이름) to be your lawful wedded wife 혹은 husband? 라고 합니다. 예를 들어 Do you, Mike Peters, take this woman, Julie Estevan, to be your lawful, wedded wife?라 하고, 질문을 받은 신랑은 I do.라고 대답합니다. 가끔 신랑이나 신부가 너무 긴장한 나머지 I will. 이라고 대답하는 경우도 있습니다. 서약 다음 반지교환이 있은 후 성직자는 이들이 부부가 되었음을 선포함으로써 식을 마치게 됩니다. 식이 끝나면 하객들이 교회 문밖에 있다가 Wedding Reception(결혼 피로연)으로 가기 위해 교회 문을 나서는데 이때 쌀알을 신랑신부에게 던집니다. 쌀알을 던지는 관습은 신부의 다산과 가계의 번영을 상징한다고 합니다. Reception은 신부의 집 정원, 교회의 집회홀, 컨트리클럽, 호텔에서 이뤄집니다. 교회에서는 대부분 가벼운 스낵 정도의 피로연을 열고 호텔에서는 뷔페식 피로연을 하는데 우선 a toast for the bride and groom(신랑신부를 위한 건배) 가 있고 그 후엔 춤을 추게 됩니다. 춤은 첫 번째로 신랑 신부, 두 번째는 신부와 부친, 신랑과 모친, 세 번째는 신부와 시아버지, 신랑과 장모, 네 번째는 신랑아버지와 신부 어머니, 신랑 어머니와 신부 아버지, 마지막으로, 하객들 순으로 춥니다. Reception이 끝날 때쯤 신랑신부는 연회장을 빠져 나와 빈 깡통이나 헌 구두를 달고 "just got married"(이제 막 결혼 했음)이라고 낙서한 자동차를 타고 honeymoon(신혼여행) 길에 오릅니다.

- Do you, Mike Peters, take this woman, Julie Estevan, to be your lawful, wedded wife?
- Do you, Julie Estevan, take this man, Mike Peters, to be your lawful, wedded husband?

Wrap-up

Key sentences

1. 형용사의 한정적 용법과 서술적 용법
   - She's going out with a rich businessman.
   - The baby looks healthy.

2. 형용사의 전위 수식과 후위 수식
   - I'm sure there's an available seat.
   - It's a sold out show and there won't be a seat available.
   - I want to drink hot tea.
   - I want to drink something hot.

3. 비교
   - I'd like you to know that I think you're as beautiful as the sunsets in Sweden.
   - I'd like you to know that I think you're more beautiful than the sunsets in Sweden.
   - This is the most ridiculous thing I've ever heard.

4. 부사
   - I'll speak quickly then.
   - Frankly, I think you're both silly.

REVIEW TEST

Choose the best word(s) to complete each sentence. (1-5)

1. Tom spoke very ______________ of the mechanic who repaired his car.
   (1) high (2) highly (3) higher (4) highest

2. Susan often laughed ____________ when talking with people.
She seemed ____________ today.
(1) cheerful - cheerful (2) cheerful - cheerfully
(3) cheerfully - cheerful (4) cheerfully - cheerfully

3. The telephone line was so bad that I could __________ hear what he was saying.
(1) near (2) nearly (3) hardly (4) hard

4. Melissa appears much ___________ now that she has started her new job. She didn't like her old job as much.
(1) happy (2) happier (3) more happily (4) happiest

5. Jane has three daughters. Of the three girls, Marge is the _________ and she looks _________ like her mother.
(1) older - more (2) older - most
(3) oldest - more (4) oldest - most

Complete each sentence with the appropriate form of the word in parentheses. (6-10)

6. I thought the restaurant would be expensive, but it was ______________ than expected. (cheap)

7. She _________ admitted that she wasn't doing a good job. (frank)

8. Nothing is _________ than traveling with friends. (pleasant)

9. This movie is really well made. It's one of the ____________ movies I've ever seen recently. (good)

10. It's not difficult to get this magazine in any bookstore. It's ____________ available. (wide)

Supplementary Reading (보충 독해)

다음 글을 읽고 문제를 풀어 보세요.

Morning Person

Are you a morning person or a late riser? In Korea, as books that have a message about morning people become bestsellers, more and more people are getting up early to prepare for the day. They take a walk, go to fitness centers, read books, or study foreign languages. They are so pleased with all the things they can accomplish in the early morning. They can even use this time to relax while other people are busy getting ready for work.

Saisyo Hiroshi, a Japanese doctor, is the author of the book, "Morning-Type Person." He says that utilizing morning time makes (1) it possible for us to manage the whole day effectively, and the successful management of each day paves the way for long-term success. He provides numerous examples of successful people who wake up early in the morning.

Some scientists believe they may know why some of us are early risers while others prefer to stay up late at night. They found a link between a gene and people's preference for mornings or evenings. The gene is one of those involved in regulating the body's internal clock. However, the scientists also say that the day or night preference is obviously a complex behavioral trait. Our lifestyle choices also play a significant role, and the genetic factor can be overridden. We can actually become morning people if we really want to.

Translation 아침형 인간

당신은 아침형 인간입니까? 아니면 늦게 일어나는 형입니까? 한국에는 아침형 인간에 관한 메시지가 수록된 책들이 베스트셀러가 됨에 따라 하루를 준비하기 위해 아침 일찍 일어나는 사람들이 갈수록 늘어나고 있습니다. 그들은 산책을 하고, 헬스장에 가며 책을 읽거나 외국어를 공부합니다. 그들은 아침 일찍 그들이 해낼 수 있는 모든 것에 대해 매우 뿌듯해 합니다. 그들은 다른 사람들이 보통 직장 갈 준비로 바쁠 때, 쉴 수 있는 여유까지 가질 수 있습니다.

사이쇼 히로시라는 일본 의사는 "아침형 인간" 이라는 책의 저자입니다. 그는 아침 시간을 활용하는 것은 하루 전체를 효과적으로 관리하는 것을 가능케 한다고 합니다. 그리고 하루하루를 성공적으로 관리하는 것은 장기적인 성공의 지름길이라고 합니다. 그는 성공한 사람들, 일찍 일어나는 사람들의 여러 사례를 제공합니다.
어떤 과학자들은 왜 어떤 이들은 일찍 일어나는 반면 어떤 이들은 밤에 늦게까지 앉아있는 것을 좋아하는지에 대한 이유를 알 것 같다고 주장합니다. 그들은 유전자와 아침과 저녁에 대한 사람들의 선호도 사이의 연결관계를 발견하였습니다. 그 유전자는 몸의 생체시계를 조절하는 것과 연관된 것 중 하나입니다. 그러나 과학자들은 낮과 밤에 대한 선호도는 물론 복잡한 행동적 성향이라고도 합니다. 우리의 생활 방식의 선택도 중요한 역할을 하기 때문에 유전적인 요소는 무시할 수도 있습니다. 우리는 사실 정말 원한다면 아침형 인간이 될 수 있는 것입니다.

Explanation

1. As books that have a message about morning people become bestsellers, more and more people are getting up early to prepare for the day.

as 는 접속사로써 이유나 때를 표시하기도 하고, 이 문장에서처럼 '~함에 따라서, ~할수록' 이라는 뜻을 나타내기도 합니다. prepare for 는 '~을 준비하다, ~에 대비하다' 라는 표현입니다.

Ex) As we went up, it was getting colder.
(우리가 높이 올라감에 따라 점점 더 추워졌습니다.)

Ex) I will help you prepare for our picnic today.
(오늘 소풍을 위해 준비하는 것을 도와 줄게요.)

2. They are so pleased with all the things they can accomplish in the early morning.

be pleased with 는 '~에 대해 매우 흡족해하다, 기뻐하다' 라는 뜻의 표현입니다. 전치사 by 외에 다른 전치사를 쓰는 수동태 표현으로는 be bored with (~에 지루해하다), be obsessed with (~에 사로잡히다), be satisfied with (~에 만족하다) 등이 있습니다.

Ex) We are so pleased with your exam results.
(우리는 당신의 시험 결과에 매우 기분이 좋습니다.)

3. They can even use this time to relax while other people are busy getting ready for work.

while 은 접속사로써 '~하는 동안에, ~하는 반면' 라는 의미를 지닙니다. be busy ~ing 는 '~을 하느라 바쁘다' 라는 뜻입니다.

Ex) While you play the guitar, I will play the drums.
(당신이 기타를 칠 동안 나는 드럼을 칠 겁니다.)

Ex) They were busy cleaning up the house.
(그들은 집을 치우느라 바빴습니다.)

4. Utilizing morning time makes it possible for us to manage the whole day effectively, and the successful management of each day paves the way for long-term success.

이 문장에서 it은 가목적어, for us는 의미상의 주어, to manage 이하는 진목적어로 쓰이고 있습니다. 주어나 목적어가 긴 경우, 흔히 가주어나 가목적어를 사용합니다. pave the way to/for 는 '~을 향한 길을 열다, 준비하다' 라는 의미입니다.

Ex) The noise made it difficult for me to solve the problem.
(그 소리 때문에 나는 문제를 풀기가 어려웠습니다.)

Ex) An internship can often pave the way to a full-time job.
(인턴쉽은 종종 전임 직장을 얻는 길이 될 것입니다.)

5. Some scientists believe they may know why some of us are early risers while others prefer to stay up late at night.

why는 의문부사로 쓰일 수도 있고, 관계부사로 쓰일 경우, 그 앞에 선행사 the reason은 흔히 생략됩니다. prefer는 '오히려 ~하는 것을 선호하다' 라는 뜻으로 뒤에 to부정사가 따라옵니다. stay up이란 '자지 않고 깨어있다' 라는 뜻입니다.

Ex) Tell me why you rejected the plan.
(왜 그 계획을 거절 했는지 나에게 말해주세요.)

Ex) I prefer to go to the cinema alone.
(나는 영화관에 혼자 가는 것을 선호합니다.)

6. Our lifestyle choices also play a significant role, and the genetic factor can be overridden.

override(overrode– overridden)는 '~보다 우위에 서다, 무시하다' 라는 뜻으로 여기서는 수동태로 쓰여 '무시될 수도 있다' 라는 뜻이 됩니다.

Ex) President Andrew Johnson's veto was overridden.
(Andrew Johnson 대통령의 거부권이 무효로 되었습니다.)

Q.1 Match each word with its definition.

1. accomplish	a) characteristic, feature
2. utilize	b) form a surface with stone or brick
3. pave	c) overrule, dominate
4. regulate	d) make use of
5. trait	e) control, adjust
6. override	f) achieve

Q.2 Answer the following questions.

1. Which of the following is not true according to the passage?
   a) Managing each day effectively will lead to success.
   b) People who get up early can take a walk, go to fitness centers and also relax.
   c) Scientists found a link between a gene and people's preferences for morning or evening.
   d) There is an internal clock within people, which regulates the gene.

2. Choose the sentence in which "it" is used in the way seen in (1).
   a) It is one of their best sellers.
   b) I felt it my duty to help his children.
   c) How far is it from the campus to the city?
   d) He told me it was not true.

3. It is not suggested in the passage that early risers have extra time to:
   a) take a walk
   b) relax
   c) do laundry
   d) study a foreign language

4. The passage states that genetics
   a) are related to people's internal clock
   b) are the most important factor in determining our lifestyle
   c) determine one's success or failure in life
   d) cannot be controlled

Pronouns & Review

07 Unit

Introduction

Topic: Booking a date (데이트 예약)

Lesson objectives:

Pronouns (대명사)

- personal pronoun/possessive pronoun/reflexive pronoun (인칭 대명사/소유대명사/재귀대명사)
- usage of 'it'/demonstrative pronoun (it의 용법, 지시대명사)
- indefinite pronoun/interrogative pronoun (부정대명사/의문대명사)

WARM-UP

In this scene, Brett is at the bookstore paging through a novel by one of his favorite authors when he is approached by another shopper. Will he leave the store with a story of his own? Let's find out.

Carrie : Excuse me. Is that Phillip Roth's new novel that you're holding? (demonstrative pronoun)

Brett : Yes, just taking a look. Have you read it? (it)

Carrie : I have read all of his books. (possessive pronoun)

Brett : Really? Which is your favorite? (interrogative pronoun)

Carrie : I like all of them. But, if I had to choose one, it would be Goodbye, Columbus. (it / indefinite pronoun)

Brett : That's his first novel, right? (demonstrative pronoun)

Carrie : Yes. But he really established himself as a writer with that novel. (reflexive pronoun)

Brett : I agree. That's a beautiful story. (demonstrative pronoun)

Carrie : It's so nice to meet someone interested in good literature. (it)

Brett	: I know. It seems that we have that in common. (it)
Carrie	: I'm sorry; I didn't even catch your name. (personal pronoun)
Brett	: It's Brett. (it) Nice to meet you. (personal pronoun)
Carrie	: I'm Carrie.
Brett	: I don't usually do this, but would you like to get a coffee with me? (demonstrative pronoun)
Carrie	: Sure. I'd like that. (demonstrative pronoun)
Brett	: Good. I know a great little café just around the corner.

Translation

이번 장면에서, 책을 사러 온 또 다른 사람이 그에게 다가왔을 때, Brett은 서점에서 그가 좋아하는 작가중 한 사람의 소설을 넘겨 보고 있습니다. 그는 그 자신의 이야기를 가지고 서점을 떠나게 될까요? 살펴봅시다.

Carrie	: 실례합니다. 당신이 들고 있는 것이 Phillip Roth의 새로운 소설인가요?
Brett	: 네, 그냥 보고 있어요. 당신은 읽어보셨어요?
Carrie	: 그 사람 책은 다 읽어봤어요.
Brett	: 당신이 가장 좋아하는 것이 어떤 것인가요?
Carrie	: 저는 그의 모든 책을 다 좋아해요. 하지만 굳이 하나를 골라야 한다면, *Goodbye, Columbus*라고 할 수 있죠.
Brett	: 그게 그의 첫 번째 작품이죠?
Carrie	: 네. 그러나 그는 그 소설로 작가로써 입지를 굳혔죠.
Brett	: 맞아요. 아름다운 이야기죠.
Carrie	: 좋은 문학 작품에 관심 있는 분을 만나서 반갑네요.
Brett	: 그러네요, 우리는 그것을 공통의 관심사로 갖고 있는 것 같군요.
Carrie	: 죄송해요, 이름도 여쭤보지를 않았네요.
Brett	: Brett입니다. 만나서 반가워요.
Carrie	: 저는 Carrie입니다.
Brett	: 제가 보통 이러지 않는데, 저와 커피 한잔 하시겠어요?
Carrie	: 물론이죠. 좋아요.
Brett	: 좋아요. 모퉁이 근방에 작고 멋진 카페를 하나 알고 있습니다.

Comprehension Check

1. What excuse does Carrie use to begin the conversation?
   (a) an interest in a book
   (b) a mutual friend named Phillip
   (c) a lost wallet
   (d) a song playing in the background

2. At the beginning of the conversation, Brett is:
   (a) shopping for a gift
   (b) talking with a friend
   (c) studying for an exam
   (d) looking through a novel

3. Brett and Carrie:
   (a) fall in love
   (b) have something in common
   (c) are old classmates
   (d) disagree on an important topic

Useful Expressions

In today's dialogue	Explanation
1. He really established himself as a writer with that novel.	1. Did you know that Leonardo DiCaprio used to do bubble gum commercials before he made it big? Most people don't know much about his career before the hugely successful Titanic. This, you could say, is the film in which he established himself as an actor. In other words, the film that got everyone's attention.

In today's dialogue	Explanation
2. I'm sorry I didn't even catch your name.	2. Have you ever struck up a conversation at a bus stop or maybe with a fellow museum-goer admiring the same piece you were looking at? You end up talking for an hour and learning about their family, friends, and how they like to spend their free time. At this point, asking their name may seem like an embarrassing task. Use this expression to make it a little easier.
3. I don't usually do this, but would you like to have a coffee with me?	3. Even in a culture as casual as America's, asking someone you just met out on a date can still seem a little too forward at times. For this reason, Brett prefaces his invitation by saying that this type of thing isn't something he does often. In a way, it's sort like an apology for what's to come.

Grammar

대명사는 명사의 반복을 피하기 위하여 사용하는 것으로, 인칭대명사, 지시대명사, 부정대명사, 의문대명사, 관계대명사 등으로 나누어 볼 수 있습니다.

Focus 1 Personal pronoun (인칭대명사)

01 Personal Pronoun (인칭대명사)

(1) 형태

		주격	소유격	목적격	소유대명사	재귀대명사
1인칭	단수	I	my	me	mine	myself
	복수	we	our	us	ours	ourselves
2인칭	단/복수	you	your	you	yours	yourself/yourselves
3인칭	단수	he/she/it	his/her/its	him/her/it	his/hers	himself/herself/itself
	복수	they	their	them	theirs	themselves

(2) 주격

주격 대명사는 주어, 주격보어 자리에 사용합니다.

- Excuse me. Is that Phillip Roth's new novel that you're holding?
  (실례합니다. 당신이 들고 있는 것이 Phillip Roth의 새로운 소설인가요?)
- She was the first female to be elected Prime Minister of Britain.
  (그녀는 영국수상으로 선출된 첫 여성입니다.)
- He is the most charming fellow I've ever met in my life.
  (그는 내 인생에서 만나본 사람 중 가장 매력적인 사람입니다.)
- It was they who had seen the accident.
  (사고를 목격한 것은 그들입니다.)

소유격 대명사는 명사 앞에서 사용합니다.

- I have read all of his books.
  (나는 그의 모든 책을 읽었습니다.)
- I'm sorry; I didn't even catch your name.
  (죄송해요, 이름도 여쭤보지를 않았네요.)
- They were told to leave their tools in the room.
  (그들은 방에 그들의 도구들을 놓아두라고 들었습니다.)

목적격 대명사는 (타동사/전치사의) 목적어 자리에 사용합니다. be동사 다음에 주격보어 자리에도 목적격이 자주 쓰입니다.

- It's me.
  (저예요.)
- I like all of them.
  (나는 그들 모두를 좋아합니다.)
- Between you and me, I think he will be fired.
  (우리끼리 말인데, 내 생각에 그는 해고당할 것 같습니다.)
- My mother still treats me like a child.
  (나의 어머니는 여전히 나를 아이처럼 다룹니다.)

(3) 일반인을 나타내는 we, you, they

- You never know what may happen.
  (무슨 일이 일어날지는 결코 알 수가 없습니다.)

- We had a lot of rain last summer.
  (지난 여름에 비가 많이 왔습니다.)
- Do they speak Spanish in Mexico?
  (멕시코에서 스페인어를 말합니까?)

02 Possessive pronoun (소유대명사)

(1) 소유격 + 명사 = 소유대명사

- This is her bag. = This is hers.
  (이것은 그녀의 가방입니다. = 이것은 그녀의 것입니다.)

(2) 이중소유격: 한정사 (a, an, the, this, some) + 명사 + of + 소유대명사

- I met an old friend of mine.
  (나는 나의 오래된 친구를 만났습니다.)
- My boss is a good friend of my father's.
  (나의 사장은 내 아버지의 좋은 친구입니다.)
- I don't want to hear any more about this crush of yours.
  (나는 당신이 누군가에게 반했다는 것에 대해서 더 이상 듣고 싶지 않습니다.)
- This is a beautiful picture of hers.
  (이것은 그녀가 소유한 아름다운 그림입니다.)

cf) This is a beautiful picture of her.
(이것은 그녀를 그린 아름다운 그림입니다)

(3) 소유격 + own: 소유 강조

- She had wanted her own apartment.
  (그녀는 자신의 아파트를 갖고 싶어했습니다.)
- This is my own (room).
  (여기는 내 방입니다.)
- His dream was to build his family a house of their own.
  (그의 꿈은 그의 가족에게 그들만의 집을 지어주는 것이었습니다.)

03 Reflexive pronoun (재귀대명사)

(1) 재귀용법: 주어와 목적어가 동일한 경우 목적어로 쓰인다.

- He really established himself as a writer with that novel.
  (그는 그 소설로 작가로써 입지를 굳혔습니다.)

- I managed to convince myself that moving to Australia would be good for my career.
  (나는 호주로 이주하는 것이 나의 경력에 도움이 될 것이라고 스스로를 간신히 납득시켰습니다.)
- She is old enough to take care of herself.
  (그녀는 그녀 자신을 돌볼 만한 나이가 되었습니다.)
- He thinks very highly of himself.
  (그는 자기 자신을 매우 높게 평가합니다.)

(2) 강조용법: 주어, 목적어, 보어 강조

- I offered to carry the bags myself. (= I myself offered to carry the bags.)
  (제 스스로가 가방을 운반하겠다고 제안했습니다.)
- The design is simplicity itself. (= The design is very simple.)
  (그 디자인은 매우 단순하였습니다.)

(3) 관용적 표현: 동사 + 재귀대명사

- He excused himself from the meeting.
  (그는 양해를 구하고 회의를 빠져 나왔습니다.)
- Did you enjoy yourself at the party?
  (파티에서 좋은 시간 보냈습니까?)
- Do you often catch yourself daydreaming at work?
  (당신은 종종 근무 중에 공상을 하다가 갑자기 멈춥니까?)

cf) amuse oneself/ content oneself/ avail oneself/ overwork oneself
(즐기다/ 만족하다/ 이용하다/ 과로하다)

(4) 관용적 표현: 전치사 + 재귀대명사

- The children aren't old enough to be left by themselves.
  (그 아이들은 그들만 남아 있을 수 있을 만큼 나이가 들지 않았습니다.)
- You look beside yourself this morning. Is everything all right?
  (당신은 오늘 아침에 제정신이 아닌 것 같아 보입니다. 괜찮습니까?)
- I think it's about time you started to do these things for yourself.
  (저는 당신 스스로의 힘으로 이 일을 시작할 때가 되었다고 생각합니다.)

cf) of itself/ in itself (= in its own nature)/ between ourselves
(저절로/ 본질적으로/ 우리끼리 이야기지만)

Task 1

Choose the best word from the box to complete each sentence. Some words can be used more than once.

she	her	hers	herself

1. Your bag looks nicer than __________.
2. She called __________ a master of negotiations, which was true.
3. It is one of __________ best sellers this year.
4. Joe, Robert, and __________are planning a weekend trip to the mountains.
5. Joan was beside __________ with joy when she heard the news.

Focus 2 It, Demonstrative pronoun (It, 지시대명사)

01 Usage of 'it' (it의 용법)

(1) 어떤 사물, 행위, 상황 또는 신원이 밝혀지지 않은 사람

- Carrie: Is that Phillip Roth's new novel that you're holding?
  (당신이 손에 들고 있는 것은 Phillip Roth의 새로운 소설인가요?)
  Brett: Yes, just taking a look. Have you read it?
  (네, 그냥 한번 보고 있어요. 읽어본 적이 있나요?)
- A: Did someone ring?
  (누가 전화했나요?)
  B: It was Vicky. She just called to say she's arrived safely.
  (Vicky였습니다. 그녀는 안전하게 도착했다고 막 전화했습니다.)
- Skiing is an expensive hobby, isn't it?
  (스키는 비용이 많이 드는 취미입니다. 그렇지 않나요?)
- It isn't entirely your fault.
  (그것은 전적으로 당신의 잘못은 아닙니다.)

(2) 비인칭 it

- It's half past five already. (시간)
  (벌서 다섯 시 반입니다.)
- It was much warmer yesterday. (날씨)
  (어제는 훨씬 더 따뜻했습니다.)
- How far is it to the station? (거리)
  (역까지 얼마나 먼가요?)
- It won't be long now.
  (이제 얼마 안 남았습니다.)

(3) 가주어, 가목적어

- It's so nice to meet someone interested in good literature.
  (좋은 문학 작품에 관심 있는 분을 만나서 반갑습니다.)
- It seems that we have that in common.
  (우리는 그것을 공통의 관심사로 갖고 있는 것 같습니다.)
- It's a pity (that) you can't come with us.
  (당신이 우리와 갈 수 없다니 유감입니다.)
- I found it difficult to tell him the news.
  (내가 그에게 그 소식을 말하기는 어려울 것 같습니다.)
- Didn't you find it rude that she didn't even say "hello" when we walked into the room?
  (우리가 그 방으로 들어갔을 때 그녀가 "안녕하세요" 라고 인사조차 하지 않은 것은 무례한 짓이라고 생각하지 않으셨나요?)

(4) It~that 강조

- It was John who got drunk at the party last night.
  (어젯밤 파티에서 취한 사람은 John이었습니다.)
- It is because of you that I came back.
  (내가 돌아온 것은 당신 때문입니다.)
- I'm sure it was the sushi that made me sick.
  (나는 내가 먹은 회 때문에 아팠다고 확신합니다.)
- It was a cold day in the middle of November when she told me she was leaving.
  (그녀가 떠날 거라고 나에게 말했던 때는 11월 중순의 어느 추운 날이었습니다.)

02 Demonstrative Pronoun (지시대명사)

(1) this/these, that/those

this는 앞이나 뒤의 구, 절을 받습니다.

- I don't usually do this, but would you like to get a coffee with me?
  (제가 보통 이러지 않는데, 저와 커피 한잔 하시겠어요?)
- Listen to this! The meeting was cancelled.
  (주목하세요! 회의는 취소되었습니다.)

that은 앞에 나온 명사의 반복을 피하기 위해 쓰입니다.

- The climate of Florida is like that of Hawaii.
  (플로리다의 기후는 하와이의 기후와 같습니다.)
- The ears of a rabbit are longer than those of a wolf.
  (토끼의 귀는 늑대의 귀보다 깁니다.)

those + who: he/one who~는 단수로 쓰이고 those who는 복수로 쓰입니다.

- One who is not diligent will never prosper.
  (부지런하지 않은 사람은 결코 성공하지 못할 것입니다.)
- Heaven helps those who help themselves.
  (하늘은 스스로 돕는 자를 돕습니다.)
- One who constantly speaks does not have time to listen.
  (계속 말을 하는 사람은 들을 시간이 없습니다.)
- A counselor will be provided for those who need someone to talk to about today's traumatic events.
  (오늘 정신적으로 큰 충격을 받은 사건에 대해 이야기를 나눌 사람이 필요한 분들을 위하여 상담자가 제공될 것입니다.)

(2) such

앞에 나온 구, 절을 받습니다.

- I offended her, but such was not what I meant. (= this)
  (나는 그녀를 화나게 하였지만 이것은 내가 의도한 것은 아니었습니다.)
- Such is not the case.
  (이것은 그런 일이 아닙니다.)

such as, as such

- I like summer fruits such as watermelons, peaches, and grapes. (= for example)
  (나는 수박, 복숭아, 포도와 같은 여름 과일을 좋아합니다.)
- Copyrighted materials represent the hard work and creative efforts of artists. As such, we must take further initiative to uphold the laws that protect these products. (= considering this; this said)
  (저작권이 있는 작품은 예술가들의 힘든 노동과 창조적인 노력을 나타냅니다. 이것을 고려하여 우리는 이러한 작품들을 보호하는 법을 지지하기 위해 더 솔선수범해야 합니다.)

(3) so, not

- A: Do you think it will be cold?
  B: I think so. (= I think that it will be cold.)
  (당신 생각에 추울 것 같습니까? 그럴 것 같습니다.)
- A: Is he punctual?
  B: I think not. (= I don't think he is punctual.)
  (그는 시간을 잘 지킵니까? 제 생각엔 아닌 것 같습니다.)

(4) same

- A: Have a nice day!
  B: (The) same to you.
  (좋은 하루 보내세요! 당신두요.)
- The holidays aren't the same without you.
  (당신이 없으면 휴일도 똑같지가 않습니다.)
- Things just aren't the same anymore.
  (모든 것이 더 이상 예전과 같지 않습니다.)
- That's not change, that's more of the same.
  (그건 변한 게 아니라 매 한가지입니다.)

Task 2

Read each sentence carefully and decide whether it is correct or incorrect. If the sentence is incorrect, correct it.

	correct	incorrect
1. It was my uncle whom took my brother to the hospital yesterday.	( )	( )
2. It's strange that John didn't come to the class.	( )	( )
3. Is there cold outside?	( )	( )
4. A: Is the museum open on Saturdays? B: Yes, I think so.	( )	( )
5. Scientists so as Einstein are rare.	( )	( )

Focus 3 Indefinite pronoun, interrogative pronoun

(부정대명사, 의문대명사)

01 Indefinite Pronoun (부정대명사)

all, both, either, neither, each, some, any, none, one, other, another, anyone, someone, nobody, anybody, everybody, somebody, anything, everything

(1) All

- All is fair in love and war.
  (사랑과 전쟁은 수단을 가리지 않습니다.)

- All's well that ends well.
  (끝이 좋으면 다 좋습니다.)
- Is that all you have for me today?
  (그것이 오늘 당신이 나를 위해 준비한 전부입니까?)

(2) both, either, neither

- Both of us shouted out the answer at the same time. (둘 모두)
  (우리 둘 다 동시에 답을 외쳤습니다.)
- It could be either of them; there's no way to tell. (둘 가운데 하나)
  (둘 중 하나일 수 있습니다. 알 수가 없습니다.)
- Neither of them replied to my email. (둘 가운데 어느 하나도 ~아닌)
  (그들 모두 내 이메일에 답변하지 않았습니다.)

(3) each

each는 단수동사와 함께 쓰입니다.

- Each of us sees the world differently.
  (우리 각자는 세계를 다르게 봅니다.)
- Each brings a unique skill to the team.
  (각자가 팀에게 특별한 기술을 제공합니다.)

(4) some, any

원칙적으로는 some은 긍정문에, any는 부정문과 의문문에 쓰입니다.

- Some say that the tax system unfairly burdens the poor.
  (어떤 이들은 세금체계가 가난한 사람들에게 불공평하게 부담을 준다고 말합니다.)
- The new energy plan benefits some more than others.
  (새로운 에너지 계획은 누군가에게는 다른 사람들에게보다 더 많은 이익을 줍니다.)
- There is hardly any left.
  (남아있는 것이 거의 없습니다.)
- Are there any upstairs?
  (위층에 누군가 있습니까?)

cf) 형용사로 쓰이는 경우

- I need to buy some new pants. (나는 새 바지를 사야 할 필요가 있습니다.)
- Is there any milk left? (우유가 남아 있습니까?)
- I found the building without any difficulty. (나는 어려움 없이 그 건물을 찾았습니다.)
- Please call me any time. (양보) (언제든지 나에게 전화하세요.)
- Would you like some more coffee? (권유) (커피를 좀 더 하시겠어요?)

(5) none

none = no + 명사

- None of my brothers remembered my birthday.
  (내 형제 아무도 내 생일을 기억하지 못했습니다.)
- None of the passengers were injured.
  (승객중에 부상을 입은 사람은 없었습니다.)
- When I moved to the city twenty years ago there were hundreds of record shops; now there are none.
  (20년 전에 내가 도시로 이주했을 때 수백 개의 레코드 가게가 있었습니다. 이제는 하나도 없습니다.)

(6) one

one은 일반인을 가리키기도 하고, 앞에 나온 가산명사 대신 사용하기도 합니다.

- I like all of them. But, if I had to choose one, it would be *Goodbye, Columbus*.
  (저는 그것들 모두 다 좋아합니다. 하지만 굳이 하나를 골라야 한다면, Goodbye, Columbus라고 할 수 있죠.
- That's the one that I want.
  (그것이 내가 원하는 것입니다.)
- I hear that Samsung is coming out with a new one this year.
  (올해 삼성이 새 제품을 출시할 것이라고 합니다.)
- John Donne was one of the Metaphysical Poets.
  (John Donne은 형이상학파 시인중 한 사람이었습니다.)
- One should never underestimate his opponent.
  (사람들은 자신의 상대방을 결코 과소평가해서는 안됩니다.)

(7) another

기본의미는 '하나 더, 다른 것'입니다. 관용표현으로 'A와 B는 별개이다'라고 말할 때 사용되기도 합니다.

- I don't like this one; show me another.
  (전 이건 별로 입니다. 다른 것을 보여주세요.)
- To know is one thing; to teach is another.
  (아는 것과 가르치는 것은 별개입니다.)
- My sister jumps from one job to another with no thought of her future.
  (제 여동생은 그녀의 미래를 생각지도 않고 계속 이직을 합니다.)

(8) other

기본 의미는 '그 밖의 것, 다른 것'입니다.

- We both know what the other wants.
  (우리 둘 다 상대방이 원하는 것을 압니다.)
- Perhaps you should interview others who were there that day.
  (아마 당신은 그 날 거기에 있었던 다른 사람들을 인터뷰해야 할 것입니다.)
- That's one reason, among others, that I've decided to quit my job.
  (그것이 내가 일을 그만 두기로 한 이유들 중 하나입니다.)

one~, the other (둘 중에서 하나는~, 또 하나는)

- I have two pens; one is green, and the other is blue.
  (나는 펜이 두 개 있습니다. 하나는 녹색이고 다른 하나는 파란색입니다.)
- You'll have to choose one or the other.
  (당신은 이 것이나 저 것 중 하나를 선택해야 할 것입니다.)
- The difference between the two is that one finds solutions, and the other makes problems.
  (그 둘 사이의 차이점은 한 명은 해결책은 찾는다는 것이고 다른 한 명은 문제를 만든다는 것입니다.)

one~, another (다수 중에서 두 개를 지칭하여 하나는~, 또 하나는)

- There are many eggs; one is big, and another is small.
  (계란이 많이 있습니다. 하나는 크고 또 하나는 작습니다.)
- The dominoes fell one after another.
  (도미노가 잇따라서 무너졌습니다.)

one~, the others (다수의 정해진 수 중에서 하나는~, 나머지는)

- There are four cars. One is mine, and the others belong to my company.
  (차가 네 대 있습니다. 하나는 내 것이고 나머지는 회사가 소유한 것입니다.)

some~, others (다수 중에서 몇 개를 지칭하여 어떤 것은~, 다른 것은)

- There are ten students; some study English, and others study Japanese.
  (학생이 열 명 있습니다. 몇 명은 영어를, 다른 사람들은 일본어를 공부합니다.)
- Some are in stock while others need to be ordered.
  (어떤 것들은 재고로 쌓여져 있고, 반면에 다른 것들은 주문이 되어야 합니다.)

some~, the others (다수의 정해진 수 중에서 몇 명은~, 나머지는)

- There are five books. Some of them are written in Chinese, and the others are in Japanese.
  (책이 다섯 권 있습니다. 그 중 몇 개는 중국어로 쓰여있고, 나머지 다른 것들은 일본어로 쓰여 있습니다.)

02 Interrogative Pronoun (의문대명사)

의문대명사의 용법에는 who, what 과 which가 있습니다.

(1) who

이름, 신원, 신분을 물을 때 사용합니다.

- Who exactly do you think you are?
  (당신은 엄밀하게 당신이 누구라고 생각합니까?)
- Who would you feel more comfortable working with?
  (당신은 누구와 일하는 것이 더 편합니까?)

(2) what

직업, 신분을 물을 때 사용하거나, '무엇, 어떤 것'이라는 의미로 쓰입니다.

- What is she?
  (그녀는 무슨 일을 합니까?)
- What else do you like to read?
  (그 외에 무엇을 읽는 것을 좋아하십니까?)
- What is the difference between these two monitors?
  (이 두 모니터의 차이는 무엇입니까?)
- What are you waiting for?
  (당신은 무엇을 기다리고 있습니까?)

(3) which

일정 수의 물건, 사람 중에서의 선택에 사용합니다.

- Which is your favorite?
  (당신이 가장 좋아하는 것은 어떤 것인가요?)
- Which of them do you want?
  (저것들 중 어떤 것을 당신은 원합니까?)

- I don't know which is worse.
  (어느 쪽이 더 나쁜지 모르겠습니다.)
- It's hard to say which is more enticing.
  (어느 쪽이 더 매력적인지 말하기가 힘듭니다.)

(4) who와 whom

목적격 whom 대신에 who가 많이 사용되지만, 전치사 다음에는 whom만 사용합니다.

- Who are you looking for?
  (당신이 찾고 있는 사람은 누구입니까?)
- With whom are you coming?
  (당신은 누구와 함께 옵니까?)
- To whom is that letter addressed?
  (저 편지는 누구 앞으로 왔습니까?)
- There are plenty of people for whom medical care is still too costly.
  (진료비가 아직도 너무 비싼 사람들이 많습니다.)

(5) 간접의문문

의문문이 다른 문장의 일부가 되어 주어, 목적어, 보어로 쓰이는 경우입니다. 일반의문문과 간접의문문은 어순이 다르므로 주의해야 합니다.

- Do you know who he is?
  (당신은 그가 누구인지 압니까?)
- You'll never believe who I ran into today.
  (내가 오늘 누구를 마주쳤는지 당신은 절대 믿지 못할 겁니다.)

간접의문문이 나오는 문장에서 think, believe, guess, consider, suppose, imagine의 동사가 사용될 경우는 의문사가 문두로 나갑니다.

- Who do you think will get there first?
  (당신은 누가 제일 먼저 그 곳에 갈 거라고 생각합니까?)

Task 3

Choose the best word to complete each sentence.

1. He lost (everything, anything) in the fire.
2. I tried every key in the lock, but (no, none) of them fit.
3. I don't like (either, neither) of my English teachers.
4. They were (every, both) waiting for her.
5. I don't have a pen. Can you lend me (one, another)?

Practice

Task 4

Fill in the blanks with the most appropriate choice.

1. __________ is strange that Sarah didn't come to the party.
   (a) This (b) What (c) It (d) She

2. If you want some orange juice, she'll get you __________ at the shop.
   (a) those (b) none (c) any (d) some

3. Is that your key, or is it __________?
   (a) hers (b) her (c) her's (d) herself

4. No one is allowed except __________ who have an invitation card.
   (a) those (b) them (c) that (d) the one

5. People know very little about __________ Shakespeare was or how he lived.
   (a) whom (b) who (c) whose (d) which

Task 5

Find the sentences that are incorrect and correct them. If the sentence is correct, leave it alone.

	correct	incorrect
1. I have two brothers; one is in Canada, and the other is in France. ______	( )	( )
2. Whom do you think will participate in the contest? ______	( )	( )
3. The population of Cheonan is smaller than that of Busan. ______	( )	( )
4. Her opinion is different from him. ______	( )	( )
5. Would you like any coffee? ______	( )	( )

Wrap-up

Key sentences

1. 인칭대명사
   - Excuse me. Is that Phillip Roth's new novel that you're holding?
   - I'm sorry; I didn't even catch your name.
   - He really established himself as a writer with that novel.

2. It, 지시대명사
   - Have you read it?
   - It's nice to meet someone interested in good literature.
   - I don't usually do this, but would you like to have a coffee with me?

- The climate of Floridais like that of Hawaii.

3. 부정대명사, 의문대명사
   - I like them all. But, if I had to choose one, it would be *Goodbye, Columbus*.
   - Some say that the tax system unfairly burdens the poor.
   - What else do you like to read?
   - Which is your favorite?

Review 1-7

Unit 1

Choose the appropriate verb tense to complete each of the following sentences.

1. The commission already __________ next year's budget.
   (a) approved (b) approve
   (c) approves (d) approving

2. Her speeches __________ millions of people over the years.
   (a) inspire (b) have inspired
   (c) inspiring (d) be inspiring

3. Next Thursday, we __________ a new president.
   (a) chose (b) have chosen
   (c) choosing (d) will choose

4. The latest poll results __________ that most people favor the conservative candidate.
   (a) suggests (b) had suggested
   (c) suggest (d) suggesting

5. At next week's debate, candidates __________ some tough questions.
   (a) face (b) faced
   (c) will face (d) have faced

6. Oliver Percovich __________ in Kabul in 2007.
   (a) arrives (b) will arrive
   (c) is arriving (d) arrived

7. It ___________ all day. I wonder when it will stop.

(a) rains (b) is raining

(c) was raining (d) has been raining

8. Janice and Alice ____________ about something when I walked into the room. I had some trouble trying to stop them.

(a) are arguing (b) were arguing

(c) have argued (d) had argued

9. A: Is Marge working this Saturday?

B: I'm not sure, but she _________ usually off on Saturdays.

(a) is (b) was

(c) had been (d) has been

10. If you _________ now, you'll be able to catch the last train.

(a) left (b) will leave

(c) leave (d) have left

Unit 2

Choose the correct verb to complete each of the following sentences.

1. I think you need to have the brakes in your car _________.

(a) check (b) checked

(c) checking (d) to check

2. They _________ the matter for a long time, but their efforts __________ failure.

(a) discussed about – resulted (b) discussed – resulted

(c) discussed about – resulted in (d) discussed – resulted in

3. Their parents encouraged them _________ good, honest citizens.

(a) becoming (b) became

(c) become (d) to become

4. He didn't ________ the meeting because he was sick.

(a) attend (b) attended

(c) attend to (d) attended to

5. Would you get a beer ________?

(a) to me (b) me

(c) for me (d) of me

6. After I briefly looked over the papers, I ___________ them on the table.

(a) laid (b) lay

(c) lied (d) laying

7. I ________ him my proposal to get some advice.

(a) said (b) explained

(c) suggested (d) showed

8. Why didn't you let him _____________ what you were thinking?

(a) know (b) knows

(c) knew (d) knowing

9. I was able to watch them ________ a new parking lot from my office window.

(a) built (b) to build

(c) building (d) to be built

10. I think this jacket looks _______ on you. The green color suits you ________.

(a) good – good (b) good – well

(c) well – good (d) well – well

Unit 3

Choose the appropriate word(s) to complete each sentence.

1. My father refused __________ me to go to the concert.
   (a) to allow (b) allowing
   (c) allow (d) allowed

2. The Bill and Melinda Gates Foundation aims __________ disease in developing nations.
   (a) eradicate (b) to eradicate
   (c) eradicates (d) eradicating

3. The goal of education is __________ independent thinking.
   (a) encouragement (b) encourage
   (c) of encouragement (d) to encourage

4. It's easy __________ sight of what's important.
   (a) losing (b) loses
   (c) to lose (d) lose

5. I'm not in the habit of __________ a diary.
   (a) keep (b) to keep
   (c) keeping (d) kept

6. I wanted __________, but I had to work late.
   (a) coming (b) to come
   (c) comes (d) came

7. You don't always need __________ a lot of money to travel abroad.
   (a) to spend (b) spent
   (c) spend (d) spending

8. Would you mind __________ out this garbage?

(a) take (b) took

(c) to take (d) taking

9. I kept ________________ you this morning. But your line was busy.

(a) trying to call (b) trying calling

(c) to try to call (d) to try calling

10. I don't think that I'll ever finish ___________ this book. It's boring and confusing.

(a) read (b) to read

(c) reading (d) with reading

Unit 4

Choose the appropriate word(s) to complete each sentence.

1. A: Do you speak French?

B: I _________ speak a little.

(a) can (b) shall

(c) could (d) should

2. A: What can we do about this?

B: I think we _________ hold a meeting to get everyone's input.

(a) do (b) should

(c) dare (d) did

3. A: Are you going to class tomorrow?

B: I think I _________ skip.

(a) dare (b) could

(c) might (d) do

4. A: I was able to do long division at the age of four.
   B: Well, I __________ do algebra by the time I was five.
   (a) can (b) could
   (c) may (d) might

5. A: Nothing seems to be working.
   B: We __________ to try something new.
   (a) do (b) need
   (c) may (d) can

6. A: Can you help me out here?
   B: I would if I __________, but I can't.
   (a) could (b) can
   (c) should (d) may

7. A: I've had this cold for more than a week.
   B: You really __________ get that checked out.
   (a) did (b) shall
   (c) dare (d) ought to

8. Before starting any diet plan, you ____________ talk to your doctor.
   (a) should (b) dare
   (c) shall (d) need

9. We ___________ swim and fish in the river before it became polluted. It's unfortunate that we cannot swim or fish there any more.
   (a) had (b) must
   (c) should (d) used to

10. If you had been there, he _____________ have acted differently.
   (a) can (b) will
   (c) have to (d) might

Unit 5

Choose the appropriate word(s) to complete each sentence.

1. The woman __________ with my cousin is Susan.
   (a) living (b) to live
   (c) live (d) lived

2. Did you see the woman __________ caricatures in the park?
   (a) drawing (b) to draw
   (c) drawn (d) drew

3. Today's lunch special is flaky salmon __________ over brown rice.
   (a) serve (b) served
   (c) to serve (d) serving

4. __________ China, did you hear about the country's plan to build the world's fastest commuter train?
   (a) Given that (b) Provided that
   (c) Speaking of (d) Granting that

5. The mood on Wall Street was __________.
   (a) depressed (b) depress
   (c) to depress (d) depressing

6. __________ there before, I can show you around.
   (a) Having been (b) Having
   (c) Been (d) To be

7. __________, managers tend to focus too much on experience and not enough on problem solving abilities.
   (a) Compared with (b) Generally speaking
   (c) Provided that (d) Talking of

8. ______________ for the surgery, I got very nervous and agitated.
(a) Waited (b) Waiting
(c) Had waited (d) Having been waited

9. His new book is fairly _____________, if not his best.
(a) interest (b) interests
(c) interested (d) interesting

10. ______________ with other places nearby, this hotel is rather expensive but quiet and comfortable.
(a) Compare (b) Comparing
(c) Compared (d) Comparison

Unit 6

Choose the appropriate word(s) to complete each sentence.

1. Nothing is ______________ as your safety.
(a) as important (b) the most important
(c) more important (d) important

2. Temperatures are ______________ around this time of year.
(a) the coldest (b) coldest
(c) colder than (d) more cold

3. Real estate is ______________ in Seoul than in Tokyo.
(a) the most expensive (b) expensive
(c) much expensive (d) more expensive

4. Many of the residents are ____________ against building a plant in the neighborhood.
(a) strongly (b) strong
(c) stronger (d) strength

5. Have you seen any movies __________?

(a) later (b) latest
(c) lately (d) last

6. It seems that Edna is getting used to her work. These days, she makes __________ mistakes.

(a) not much (b) fewer
(c) a little (d) least

7. The rain started when we arrived at the theater. It was __________ raining when the movie had finished.

(a) yet (b) still
(c) already (d) ever

8. I tasted the soup __________ because it was too hot. The soup tasted a little __________ for me.

(a) careful - salty (b) careful - salt
(c) carefully - salty (d) carefully - salt

9. Jake is really humorous. He's one of __________ people I've ever known.

(a) more funny (b) funnier
(c) the most funny (d) the funniest

10. The more he talked, __________.

(a) the more bored I became (b) the most I was bored
(c) the more bored I becomes (d) the most bored I was

Unit 7

Choose the appropriate word(s) to complete each sentence.

1. There were __________ left by the time we arrived.

(a) none (b) no
(c) any (d) every

2. I don't enjoy __________ of them.

(a) neither (b) every
(c) either (d) no

3. The victim's own blood was different from __________ found on the kitchen floor.

(a) that (b) one
(c) ones (d) those

4. I suggest that we finish reviewing __________ of the contract amendments by next Tuesday.

(a) every (b) all
(c) it (d) they

5. The police are still investigating __________ did it.

(a) which (b) that
(c) whom (d) who

6. It's unclear __________ is the proper course of action.

(a) whom (b) which
(c) that (d) who

7. The Chinese branch has already finished its sales totals, but you have not finished calculating __________ yet.

(a) you (b) your
(c) yours (d) yourself

8. __________ does a flight to Mexico cost these days?

(a) It (b) That
(c) Which (d) What

9. This is the __________ cell phone that my brother lost.

(a) same (b) such
(c) so (d) each

10. The children amused __________ by playing games.

(a) himself (b) herself

(c) themselves (d) ourselves

Culture Corner

Numbers

나라마다 사람들이 좋아하는 숫자도 있고 꺼려하는 숫자가 있습니다. 삼천리 금수강산, 삼원색, 만세삼창, 삼세번, 삼신할매, 삼칠일 금기 등의 표현에서 알 수 있듯이, 우리나라 사람들은 숫자 3을 안정과 조화를 나타내는 수로 여겨 좋아합니다. 그러나 4는 한자에서 죽을 사(死)와 발음이 같다고 하여 싫어하고, 건물 등에서도 4층을 F로 표시하는 것을 흔히 볼 수 있습니다.

미국에서는 7을 lucky seven이라 하여 행운의 숫자로 여기는 반면, 13은 제일 불길한 숫자로 생각합니다. 잘 알려진 동화 Snow White (백설공주) 이야기에서도 seven dwarfs (7명의 난장이)가 등장하고, 007 시리즈 주인공은 정말 운 좋게도 온갖 함정을 잘 헤쳐 나갑니다.

숫자 9가 쓰인 표현도 많이 있습니다. '더할 나위 없이 좋다' 는 I'm on cloud nine'이라고 합니다. 9가 들어간 다른 말로는, nine out of ten 이 있는데, 우리말의 '십중팔구' 라는 말과 똑같습니다. 우리가 알고 있는 속담에도 9가 들어간 것이 몇 가지 있습니다. A stitch in time saves nine. (제 때의 한 바늘이 아홉 바늘을 던다/ 적시에 하는 것이 많은 수고를 던다.)., A cat has nine lives (고양이는 아홉 목숨을 가졌다/ 쉽게 죽지 않는다) 등입니다.

자주 등장하는 숫자 중에 12를 나타내는 dozen이 있는데, 많은 수를 가리킬 때 dozens of라고 하기도 하고, 여섯이라는 숫자를 가리킬 때는 a half dozen이라고 합니다. Six of one and half a dozen of the other라는 표현을 보면, six of one은 어떤 물건 여섯 개를 의미하고 half a dozen of the other는 다른 물건 반 타스, 즉 여섯 개를 뜻하니까, 결국 '이거 여섯 개나 저거 반 타스나 그게 그거다' 대동소이 하다는 말이 됩니다. A dime a dozen은 한 타스에 10센트에 불과하니까, '흔해 빠진' 이라는 의미로 쓰이고, a baker's dozen 혹은 devil's dozen은 13개를 나타냅니다. 즉, A baker's dozen is thirteen 입니다.

- I'm on cloud nine.
- A stitch in time saves nine.
- A cat has nine lives.
- A baker's dozen is thirteen.

Supplementary Reading (보충 독해)

다음 글을 읽고 문제를 풀어 보세요.

Cosmetic Surgery in Asia

It wasn't many generations ago that Asian people had no control over their looks. According to Confucian tenets, damaging any part of the body was viewed as a violation of filial duty. For example, Koreans considered their hair a gift from their parents, and they did not have it cut. Cosmetic surgery, however, is now booming throughout Asia. In Taiwan, a million procedures are performed every year. In Korea, surgeons estimate that at least one in ten adults have received some form of surgical upgrade. The government of Thailand has taken to marketing plastic surgery tours which attract many foreigners with low costs. In Japan, top plastic surgeons are raking in $100 million a year. Recently, China even hosted the country's first beauty contest in which every contestant had undergone plastic surgery.

As the job market becomes more competitive, people think that enhancing their looks will give them a cutting edge over their rivals. Doctors say they are seeing more and more men trying to take years off their looks. More men than ever before are convinced cosmetic surgery can improve their career prospects. And, as operations have become cheaper, increasing numbers of men undergo surgery.

Part of the problem with cosmetic surgery is that it is much harder to exact legal retribution in Asia than in the West, where medical malpractice suits often yield enormous settlements. Most Asian lawyers avoid malpractice cases, since so few result in victory and financial payout.

Translation 아시아의 성형수술

몇 세대 전만 해도 아시아인들은 자신의 외모에 대해 통제권이 없었습니다. 공자의 교의에 의하면, 신체의 어느 부분이라도 상하게 하는 것은 자식으로서의 도리를 다하지 못하는 것이었습니다. 예를 들어서, 한국인들은 머리카락을 부모로부터의 선물로 생각하여 자르지 않았습니다. 그러나 이제 아시아 내에서 성형수술은 붐을 이루고 있습니다. 대만에서는 매년 백만 번의 수술이 시술되고 있습니다. 한국에서는 성형외과 전문의들이 성인 10명 중 적어도 1명은 어떤 형태로든지 수술로 효과를 보았다고 추측합니다. 태국 정부는 성형수술 투어 마케팅에 전념하여 낮은 비용으로 많은 외국인들을 끌어 드립니다. 일본에서는 톱 성형외과 전문의는 한 해에 1억 달러를 벌어들입니다. 최근에 중국은 심지어 성형 수술을 받은 후보들만이 참가하는 미인 대회를 열었습니다.
취업 시장이 더욱 경쟁적이 되면서 사람들은 외모를 돋보이게 하는 것이 경쟁자들을 물리치는 길이라고 생각합니다. 의사들은 점점 더 많은 남성들이 젊어 보이려는 노력을 하고 있다고 말합니다. 유례없이 많은 남성들이 성형수술이 직업의 장래성을 향상시킬 것이라 믿습니다. 또한 시술비용이 저하되면서 수술을 받는 남성의 수가 증가하고 있습니다.
성형수술의 한 문제점은 서양에서보다 아시아에서 법적인 보상을 요구하는 것이 더 어렵다는 것입니다. 서양에서는 의료과실에 대한 소송이 대개 타결점을 찾게 됩니다. 대부분의 아시아인 변호사들은 의료과실 사건들을 회피합니다. 왜냐하면 굉장히 적은 수의 소송만이 승리를 거두고 재정적 보상을 받기 때문입니다.

Explanation

1. It wasn't many generations ago that Asian people had no control over their looks.

It은 가주어, that절이 진주어로 쓰인 경우입니다. have control over/of~는 '~을 관리하다/ 제어하다' 의 의미입니다.
Ex) Don't worry about things you have no control over. (어쩔 수 없는 일입니다.)

2. According to Confucian tenets, damaging any part of the body was viewed as a violation of filial duty.

according to는 '~에 따르면, ~에 의하면' 이라는 뜻입니다. 'view + 목적어 + as'는 '~을 ~이라고 간주하다' 입니다. 위 문장에서는 수동태로 쓰였습니다.
Ex) We should not view a minor setback as a disaster.
(우리는 사소한 실패를 재난으로 보아서는 안됩니다.)

3. For example, Koreans considered their hair as a gift from their parents, and they did not have it cut.

'consider + 목적어 + as~'는 '~을 ~으로 간주하다' 는 뜻입니다. 'consider + 목적어 + to be~' 으로 표현할 수도 있습니다.
ex) They considered him as a retarded child. = They considered him to be a retarded child.
(= They thought of him as a retarded child.)
(그들은 그를 지진아로 간주했습니다.)

have + 목적어 + p.p.는 '목적어를 ~하게 시키다, 당하다' 는 뜻입니다.
ex) They had him investigated by the police.
(그들은 그가 경찰의 조사를 받게 하였습니다.)

4. China even hosted the country's first beauty contest in which every contestant had undergone plastic surgery.

관계대명사가 전치사의 목적어인 경우, 전치사는 주로 관계대명사 앞에 옵니다. 관계대명사 that 앞에는 전치사가 올 수 없습니다.

in which는 관계부사 where로 바꿔 쓸 수 있습니다.
ex) This is the city in which I grew up. = This is the city where I grew up.

5. As the job market becomes more competitive, people think that enhancing their looks can give them a cutting edge over their rivals.

as는 '~함에 따라' 의 뜻입니다. a cutting edge는 '최첨단, 날카로움' 이라는 뜻인데, give somebody a cutting edge over는 '우위를 점하게 하다'는 말입니다.
ex) Italian designers are on the cutting edge of fashion.
(이태리 디자이너들은 패션의 최첨단에 있습니다.)

Q.1 Choose the definition on the right that matches the word on the left.

1. violation	a) to guess
2. estimate	b) to make greater
3. undergo	c) the breaking of a law or a promise
4. enhance	d) relating to a son or a daughter
5. prospect	e) something given or demanded in repayment
6. exact	f) to experience
7. retribution	g) a possibility, chance
8. filial	h) to force or demand

Q.2 Mark True (T) or False (F).

1. Koreans thought damaging their body was to disobey their parents. ( )
2. Influenced by Confucianism, most Asians are still against cosmetic surgery. ( )
3. Only women are interested in cosmetic surgery in Korea and Japan. ( )
4. Even though operation costs have risen, more men are undergoing plastic surgery. ( )
5. It is harder in Asia than in the West to receive legal retribution in a malpractice case. ( )

Relatives

Unit 08

Introduction

Topic: Great Expectations (엄청난 기대)

Lesson objectives:

Relatives (관계사)

1. Relative pronouns (관계대명사)
   - who, whose, whom, which
   - that, what
   - whoever, whomever, whichever, whatever
2. Restrictive and Nonrestrictive usage / Ellipsis of relative pronouns / Quasi- relative pronouns (제한적 용법과 비제한적 용법 / 관계대명사의 생략 / 유사 관계대명사)
3. Relative adverbs (관계부사)
   - when, where, why, how
   - whenever, wherever, however

WARM-UP

In their second meeting, Brett presents Mr. Yuan with a proposal for the new ad campaign. To Brett's surprise, it is accepted, and his work life seems likely to improve.

Mr. Daniels : Let's hope this goes better than did last time. (quasi-relative pronoun)

Brett : I've been up all night, and I can't decide which idea to open with.

Mr. Daniels : Open with whichever idea is going to get us this contract. (relative pronoun) Mr. Yuan will be here any second. I hope you're not going to let us down, Brett.

Brett : I hope so too.

(Mr. Yuan enters the room.)

Mr. Daniels : Please, have a seat.

Mr. Yuan : Thanks. I hope what you have for me today is spectacular. (relative pronoun)

Brett : I think you'll like it, sir.

Mr. Yuan : Okay. Please begin whenever you're ready. (relative adverb)

Brett : Well, um, I have some illustrations here for you to take a look at. This is a character that we have developed just for this campaign. (relative pronoun) He's been awake for more than a year.

Mr. Yuan : Please, continue.

Brett : He's powered by the VERVE 3000 energy drink. And he's no longer the same ordinary guy he used to be. (ellipsis: relative pronoun)

Mr. Yuan : All right. Tell me more about him.

Brett : Okay. He's the guy who has the corner office at the hottest firm in town, the guy whom everyone looks up to, the guy whose life everyone aspires to lead. (relative pronoun) He's got everything you could want: great apartment, sports car, and a beautiful girlfriend. (ellipsis: relative pronoun)

Mr. Yuan : I like it so far.

Brett : What's his advantage? I'll tell you. When the rest of the world is sleeping, he's awake, sipping your product, and this is why he's able to stay ahead of the competition. (relative adverb)

Mr. Yuan : Is that all?

Brett : Um, well, yes, sir, it is.

Mr. Yuan : I love it.

Translation

그들의 두 번째 만남에서 Brett는 Mr. Yuan에게 새로운 광고 캠페인에 대한 계획을 제시하였습니다. 놀랍게도 그의 제안이 받아들여졌고 그의 직장 생활은 개선될 것 같습니다.

Mr. Daniels : 이번에는 지난번보다 나아지길 기대합니다.
Brett : 밤을 꼬박 새웠습니다. 어떤 아이디어부터 꺼내야 할 지 모르겠어요.
Mr. Daniels : 어떤 아이디어든 이번 계약을 성사시킬 수 있는 것으로 시작하세요. Mr. Yuan이 여기 곧 도착할 겁니다. 당신이 우리를 실망시키지 말았으면 좋겠군요, Brett.
Brett : 저도 그랬으면 좋겠습니다.

(Mr. Yuan 이 방으로 들어옵니다.)

Mr. Daniels : 자리에 앉으시지요.
Mr. Yuan : 감사합니다. 오늘 절 위해 준비한 것이 굉장한 것이었으면 좋겠군요.
Brett : 마음에 드실 겁니다.
Mr. Yuan : 좋습니다. 준비되시면 시작하시죠.
Brett : 음, 여기 제가 한 번 보시라고 삽화를 준비해 놓았습니다. 저희가 이번 캠페인만을 위해 만든 캐릭터입니다. 그는 일년 이상 깨어 있습니다.
Mr. Yuan : 계속 하시죠.
Brett : 이 사람은 에너지 음료인 VERVE 3000을 마시면 힘이 납니다. 그는 더 이상 예전과 같은 평범한 사람이 아닌 거죠.
Mr. Yuan : 그렇군요. 그에 대해서 좀 더 설명해 주십시오.
Brett : 네. 그는 도시에서 가장 인기 있는 회사의 코너에 사무실을 가지고 있고, 사람들의 존경을 받으며, 모든 사람들이 동경하는 삶을 살고 있습니다. 여러분이 원할 수 있는 모든 것을 가지고 있습니다. 멋진 아파트와 스포츠카 그리고 아름다운 여자 친구가 있죠.
Mr. Yuan : 지금까지는 마음에 드는군요.
Brett : 그의 장점은 무엇일까요? 제가 말씀 드리겠습니다. 다들 잠들어 있을 때 그는 귀사의 상품을 마시며 깨어 있습니다. 이게 바로 그가 경쟁에서 앞설 수 있는 이유입니다.
Mr. Yuan : 끝난 겁니까?
Brett : 음, 네. 그렇습니다.
Mr. Yuan : 마음에 드는군요.

Comprehension Check

1. Brett suggests a character that customers will likely __________.
   (a) dislike
   (b) envy
   (c) find mysterious
   (d) ignore

2. The advertising campaign Brett proposes hints that __________.
   (a) VERVE 3000 will help you find true love
   (b) VERVE 3000 will make you more attractive
   (c) VERVE 3000 will help you find success
   (d) none of the above

Useful Expressions

In this dialogue	Explanation
1. I hope you're not going to let us down, Brett.	1. In today's dialogue, both Mr. Yuan and Mr. Daniels have high expectations. The expression "to let down" means to disappoint, which both men hope he does not. Here, we should probably also mention that "letdown" can be used as a noun, meaning "a disappointment" or "a discouragement." "The film turned out to be a big letdown," for example.
2. He's the guy who has the corner office at the hottest firm in town, the guy whom everyone looks up to, the guy whose life every-one aspires to lead.	2. We all need a role model, someone to look up to, or revere. In today's warm up dialogue, Brett appeals to his audience with a character everyone will surely admire. In other words, he's saying, "Buy this product, and you can be like him!" "Hot" was probably one of the first English words you learned as an elementary school student. But who knew it could mean so many things? In this case, it

In this dialogue	Explanation
	means "favorable" or "desirable." Some additional examples of this usage might include: a. LeBron James is the hottest thing in professional sports right now. b. Capri pants are a hot trend this year.
3. He's got everything (that) you could want: great apartment, sports car, and a beautiful girlfriend.	3. In this sentence, "that" is omitted after "everything," which most often occurs when the relative pronoun is used as an object. The omission almost always occurs when the dependent clause begins with a personal pronoun or a proper name. "The work he produced early in his career is some of the most widely known," for example.
4. When the rest of the world is sleeping, he's awake, sipping your product, and this is why he's able to stay ahead of the competition.	4. Business can be tough, especially in these hard economic times. That's why everyone is looking for a competitive advantage in order to stay ahead of the competition. If a product promised to help you do just that, wouldn't you buy it?

Grammar

Focus 1 Relative pronouns (관계대명사)

01 who, whose, whom, which

관계대명사는 두 문장을 연결하는 접속사의 역할을 겸한 대명사로, 다음의 (a)는 의미상 (b)와 (c)가 합쳐진 문장입니다.

(a) I have a friend who is an actor.
(b) I have a friend + (c) The friend is an actor.

(a)는 (c)에서 중복되는 the friend를 생략하고 그 자리에 대신 주격 관계 대명사 who를 써서 (b)와 (c)를 하나로 합친 문장입니다. 관계 대명사 앞에 오는 명사를 선행사(antecedent)라고 합니다.

선행사	주 격	소유격	목적격
사람	who/that	whose	who(m)
사물, 동물	which/that	whose/of which	which
사람, 사물, 동물	that		that

- He's the guy who has the corner office at the hottest firm in town, the guy whom everyone looks up to, the guy whose life everyone aspires to lead.
  (그는 도시에서 가장 인기 있는 회사의 코너에 사무실을 가지고 있고, 사람들의 존경을 받으며, 모든 사람들이 동경하는 삶을 살고 있습니다.)
- The woman who lives next door is a widow.
  (옆집에 사는 여자는 과부입니다.)
- I met a man whose sister knows you.
  (나는 당신을 알고 있는 사람의 오빠를 만났습니다.)
- The professor whom I wanted to see was away on holiday.
  (내가 만나고 싶던 교수님께서는 휴가를 떠나셨습니다.)
- It's a cartoon which interests children of all ages.
  (그것은 모든 연령의 아이들에게 인기 있는 만화영화입니다.)

02 that

that은 사람, 동물, 사물 등을 모두 선행사로 삼을 수 있습니다. 특히 선행사가 형용사의 최상급, only, all, any, every, no, little, few, much, the first, the last, the same, 형용사로 쓰이는 very 등의 수식을 받을 때나, who로 시작하는 의문문일 경우에는 관계대명사 who나 which보다 that이 선호됩니다.

- This is a character that we have developed just for this campaign.
  (저희가 이번 캠페인만을 위해 만든 캐릭터입니다.)
- Everything that we worked so hard for was destroyed in the flood.
  (우리가 그렇게 열심히 작업했던 모든 것들이 홍수로 인해 파괴되었습니다.)
- Not everything that glitters is gold.
  (반짝이는 모든 것이 금은 아닙니다.)
- I gave her all the money that I had.
  (나는 그녀에게 내가 가지고 있던 돈을 다 주었습니다.)
- Who that has worked with you as long as I have does not understand your situation?
  (나만큼 오랫동안 당신과 일한 사람이라면 누가 당신의 상황을 이해하지 못하겠습니까?)
- There are few people that still practice the art of calligraphy.
  (아직도 서예를 연습하는 사람은 거의 없습니다.)

03 what

what은 선행사를 포함한 관계대명사로, the thing which, all that의 뜻을 갖습니다. 관계대명사 what은 명사절을 이끌어서 주어, 목적어, 보어 자리에 위치할 수 있습니다.

- I hope what you have for me today is spectacular.
  (오늘 절 위해 준비한 것이 굉장한 것이기를 바랍니다.)
- What happened yesterday has nothing to do with Cindy.
  (어제 일어난 일은 Cindy와 아무런 상관이 없습니다.)
- I hope you will like what I bought.
  (내가 산 물건이 당신 마음에 들었으면 좋겠습니다.)
- That's not what I'm talking about.
  (제 얘기는 그게 아닙니다.)

04 복합관계대명사: whoever, whomever, whichever, whatever

복합 관계대명사는 명사적 용법, 형용사적 용법, 부사적 용법으로 쓰입니다.

(1) 명사적 용법

'누구든지, 무엇이든지, 도대체 누가' 라는 뜻으로 명사절을 이끕니다.

- Whoever did this will be punished to the fullest extent of the law.
  (이런 짓을 한 사람은 누구든 법의 테두리 내에서 최대한 처벌을 받을 것입니다.)
- You may invite whomever you like.
  (당신이 좋아하는 사람은 누구든지 초대해도 괜찮습니다.)
- Whoever thought this day would come?
  (이 날이 오리라고 도대체 누가 생각했겠습니까?)
- Whatever you decide will be fine with me.
  (당신이 어떤 결정을 내리든 저는 괜찮습니다.)
- Order whichever you want.
  (당신이 원하는 어떤 것이든 주문하십시오.)

(2) 형용사적 용법

명사 앞에서 쓰여서 명사를 수식하는 데, 'whichever + 명사'는 정해진 것 중에서의 선택을 의미하고, 'whatever + 명사'는 막연한 선택을 의미합니다.

- Open with whichever idea is going to get us this contract.
  (어떤 아이디어든 이번 계약을 성사시킬 수 있는 것으로 시작하십시오.)
- I will help you in whatever way I can.
  (내가 할 수 있는 어떠한 방법으로든 당신을 도울 것입니다.)
- I'll accept whichever proposal reaches my desk first.
  (내 책상에 제일 먼저 도착하는 제안서가 무엇이든 그것으로 받아들이겠습니다.)
- You may read whatever book you like.
  (당신이 좋아하는 어떤 책이든 읽을 수 있습니다.)

(3) 부사적 용법

'~이든지 간에, 비록 ~일지라도' 라는 양보의 의미를 가진 부사절을 이끕니다.

- Whatever happens, I'll always be with you.
  (무슨 일이 생기든 전 항상 당신과 함께 할 겁니다.)
- Whoever said so, they were lying.
  (누가 그렇게 말했던지 간에 그들은 거짓말을 하고 있었습니다.)
- Whichever side wins, you won't be satisfied.
  (어떤 쪽이 이기든 당신은 만족하지 못할 것입니다.)

Task 1

Choose the correct relative pronoun from the box to complete the sentences.

what	who	which	whom	whose

1. He has written a book _________ name I forgot.
2. The girl _________ was injured in the accident is now in the hospital.
3. She is married to an actor of _________ you may have heard.
4. The building _________ was destroyed in the fire has now been rebuilt.
5. _________ she did is inexcusable.

Focus 2 Restrictive and Nonrestrictive usage / Ellipsis of relative pronouns / Quasi-relative pronouns

(제한적 용법과 비제한적 용법 / 관계대명사의 생략 / 유사관계대명사)

01 Restrictive and Nonrestrictive usage (제한적 용법과 비제한적 용법)

(1) 제한적(한정적) 용법과 비제한적(계속적) 용법

a. John's brother who lives in Chicago is a lawyer. (제한적)

(시카고에 사는 John의 형은 변호사입니다.)

b. John's brother, who lives in Chicago, is a lawyer. (비제한적)

(John에게는 형이 있는데, 그는 시카고에 살며 변호사입니다.)

(a)에서는 관계사절인 who lives in Chicago가 선행사인 John's brother를 한정하고 있으며, John에게는 Chicago가 아닌 다른 곳에서 살고 있는 형이 또 있을 수 있습니다. (b)에서는 관계사절이 삽입되어 선행사를 설명하고 있으며, John에게는 다른 형이 없습니다. 비제한적인 용법의 경우, 관계대명사 앞에 콤마(,)가 필요합니다.

- *The Portrait of the Artist as a Young Man* by James Joyce, which was first published in 1916, is a semi-autobiographical novel.

  (James Joyce의 *The Portrait of the Artist as a Young Man*은 1916년에 최초로 발간되었는데 이것은 반자서전적인 소설입니다.)

(2) that

관계대명사 who, which는 제한적 용법, 비제한적 용법에 모두 쓰이지만, that은 비제한적 용법에 쓰이지 않습니다.

- Is that your car that's parked outside?

  (밖에 주차되어 있는 것이 당신의 차입니까?)

- Is that your phone that's ringing?

  (지금 울리고 있는 것이 당신 핸드폰입니까?)

cf) Mr. Rogers, who founded the hospital, grew up in a poor family. (o)
(Mr. Rogers는 그 병원을 세웠는데, 가난한 가정에서 자라났습니다.)
Mr. Rogers, **that** founded the hospital, grew up in a poor family. (x)

(3) which

계속적 용법의 which는 앞에 나온 문장 전체나 보어를 선행사로 삼을 수 있습니다.

- He was late again, which upset the chairman.

  (그는 또 지각을 하였는데, 이것이 의장을 화나게 하였습니다.)

- She's a vegetarian, which is why you'll never see her order meat.
  (그녀는 채식주의자인데 이것이 그녀가 고기를 주문하는 모습을 절대 볼 수 없는 이유입니다.)
- I enjoy traveling, which is why I don't want to have children.
  (나는 여행을 좋아하는데 이것이 내가 아이를 갖지 않는 이유입니다.)

(4) 고유명사

고유명사 다음에는 비제한적 용법의 관계대명사가 나옵니다

- Tom Cruise, who parted with Nicole Kidman, is now married to another woman.
  (Tom Cruise는 Nicole Kidman과 헤어지고 지금은 다른 여자와 결혼하였습니다.)

(5) 접속사 + 대명사

계속적 용법의 관계대명사는 '접속사+대명사'로 바꾸어 쓸 수 있습니다.

- I had a long talk with my father, who really helped me make the right decision.
  I had a long talk with my father, and he really helped me make the right decision.
  (나는 아버지와 긴 대화를 나누었는데 아버지는 내가 옳은 결정을 할 수 있도록 큰 도움을 주셨습니다.
- Kyle said that he had missed my party because he was working, which was hardly a good excuse.
  Kyle said that he had missed my party because he was working, but it was hardly a good excuse.
  (Kyle은 일 때문에 내 파티에 불참하였다고 말했지만 그것은 좋은 변명이 되지 않았습니다.)

02 Ellipsis of relative pronouns (관계대명사의 생략)

(1) 타동사의 목적어

- He's got everything (that) you could want: great apartment, sports car, and a beautiful girlfriend.
  (그는 여러분이 원할수 있는 모든 것을 가지고 있습니다: 멋진 아파트와 스포츠카 그리고 아름다운 여자 친구가 있죠.)
- This morning I met somebody (whom) I hadn't seen for ages.
  (오늘 아침에 나는 오랫동안 만나지 못했던 사람을 만났습니다.)
- I took the advice (that) you gave me.
  (난 당신이 해 준 충고를 받아들였습니다.)

- All inquiries (that) customers send to this address will be answered in the order they are received.
  (고객들이 이 주소로 보낸 모든 문의에 대해서 도착한 순서대로 답변할 것입니다.)
- Surely, everyone has things in their past (which) they'd like to forget.
  (확실히 사람들은 모두 잊고 싶은 과거가 있기 마련입니다.)

cf) 그러나, 관계대명사가 비제한적 용법으로 쓰일 때는 생략할 수 없습니다.

- We stayed at the Lotte Hotel, which Rosemary recommended to us.
  (우리는 롯데호텔에 묵었는데 그곳은 Rosemary가 추천해준 곳이었습니다.)
  We stayed at the Lotte Hotel, Rosemary recommended to us. (x)

(2) 전치사의 목적어

- Every country has its own flag (which) it is proud of.
  (모든 나라에는 자랑스럽게 여기는 국기가 있습니다.)

관계대명사가 전치사 바로 뒤에 오는 경우는 생략할 수 없습니다.

- The woman with whom he fell in love left him after a few weeks. (o)
  (그가 사랑에 빠진 그 여자는 몇 주 후에 그를 떠났습니다.)
  The woman with he fell in love left him after a few weeks. (x)
  The woman (whom) he fell in love with left him after a few weeks. (o)
- These are people with whom the president hopes to form alliances.
  (이 분들은 대통령께서 동맹을 맺고 싶어하시는 분들입니다.)
  These are people (whom) the president hopes to form alliances with.

(3) be 동사의 보어

- He's no longer the same ordinary guy (that) he used to be.
  (그는 더 이상 예전과 같은 평범한 사람이 아닙니다.)
- He is not the cheerful boy (that) he used to be.
  (그는 예전처럼 명랑한 소년이 아닙니다.)
- This isn't the same city (that) it once was.
  (이 곳은 예전과 같은 도시가 아닙니다.)

(4) 주격 관계대명사 + be동사

- The fossil (that was) discovered is suggested to be of the Jurassic Age.
  (그 발견된 화석은 쥐라기 시대 때의 것으로 추정됩니다.)

- The girl (who is) standing next to him is the nicest person I've ever met.
  (그의 옆에 서 있는 여자는 내가 지금까지 만나본 가장 멋진 사람입니다.)
- The test results (which were) posted on the web site contain errors.
  (웹사이트에 올라와 있는 시험결과에는 오류가 있습니다.)

03 Quasi-relative pronouns (유사 관계대명사)

(1) as

선행사 앞에 same이나 such가 붙는 경우, as는 관계대명사와 유사한 구실을 하고, as 앞에 나오는 절이 선행사가 되기도 합니다.

- You're sitting in the same chair as Thomas Jefferson once did.
  (당신은 Thomas Jefferson이 한 때 앉았던 것과 같은 의자에 앉아있습니다.)
- I'm not such a perfect fool as you thought.
  (나는 당신이 생각했던 그런 바보는 아닙니다.)
- Ann's going to join us, as was agreed last week.
  (Ann은 우리와 동참할 것인데, 그것은 지난 주에 합의한 바입니다.)
- She spends more time talking on the phone than doing her homework, as is often the case with teenage girls.
  (그녀는 숙제보다 전화통화하는데 더 많은 시간을 보내는데 이는 10대 소녀들이 종종 보이는 모습입니다.)

(2) than

선행사에 비교급이 있을 때 than이 관계 대명사처럼 쓰입니다.

- Let's hope this goes better than (it) did last time.
  (이번에는 지난번보다 나아지길 기대합니다.)
- Five hours of sleep is less than is recommended by most health experts.
  (다섯 시간을 자는 것은 대부분의 건강 전문가가 추천하는 것보다 적은 시간입니다.)
- The amount you have here is more than is permitted under the current law.
  (당신이 여기에 가지고 있는 총액은 현행법에서 인정하는 것보다 많습니다.)

Task 2

Read each sentence carefully and decide whether it is correct or incorrect.

	correct	incorrect
1. This is the town which I was born.	( )	( )
________________________________		
2. My brother, you once met, is visiting us tomorrow.	( )	( )
________________________________		
3. Half of the people invited to the party didn't turn up.	( )	( )
________________________________		
4. The man I talked to was very friendly.	( )	( )
________________________________		
5. The contract was cancelled, which was what he wanted.	( )	( )
________________________________		

Focus 3 Relative adverbs (관계부사)

01 관계부사

선행사가 시간, 장소, 이유, 방법에 대한 명사일 때, 관계부사 when, where, why, how 등을 쓸 수 있습니다. 관계부사는 전치사 + which로 바꿀 수 있습니다.

(1) when, where

- This is the house. + Tom lives in the house.
  This is the house in which Tom lives.
  This is the house where Tom lives.
  (이곳은 Tom이 사는 집입니다.)

- I can't forget the day when I first arrived in Russia.
  (나는 처음으로 러시아에 도착했던 날을 잊지 못합니다.)
- This is the place where he was last seen alive.
  (여기는 그가 살아서 모습을 보인 마지막 장소입니다.)

(2) how, why

방법을 나타내는 관계부사 how의 경우, 선행사 the way와 how 둘 중 하나를 생략하고 쓰며 the way that이라고 쓸 수도 있습니다. 이유를 나타내는 why의 경우, 선행사 the reason 뒤에 나오는 why를 생략하기도 하고, 선행사 없이 why가 '~하는 이유' 라는 뜻으로 명사절을 이끌기도 합니다.

- When the rest of the world is sleeping, he's awake, sipping your product, and this is why he's able to stay ahead of the competition.
  (다들 잠들어 있을 때 그는 귀사의 상품을 마시며 깨어 있습니다. 이게 바로 그가 경쟁에서 앞설 수 있는 이유입니다.)
- I don't like the way (that) she speaks to me.
  (= I don't like how she speaks to me.)
  (나는 그녀가 나에게 말하는 방식이 싫습니다.)
- I don't know the reason (why/that) he left early.
  (나는 그가 빨리 떠난 이유를 모르겠습니다.)
- This is why he was so nervous.
  (이것이 그가 매우 초조해 하는 이유입니다.)

02 복합관계부사

(1) 관계부사+ever

관계부사에 ever가 결합된 형태로, whenever (= at any time when), wherever (= at any place where), however (= no matter how)가 있습니다.

- Please begin whenever you're ready.
  (준비되면 언제든 시작하세요.)
- It was hot wherever we went.
  (우리가 가는곳마다 더웠습니다.)
- Feel free to contact me whenever you need help.
  (도움이 필요하면 언제든지 연락하세요.)

(2) 양보의 의미

복합관계부사는 양보의 의미를 지닌부사절을 이끌기도 합니다. (~하든지 간에).

- I will follow you wherever you go.
  (당신이 어디를 가든지 따라가겠습니다.)
- Whenever you come, I'm ready for it.
  (당신이 언제 오든, 나는 항상 준비가 되어 있습니다.)
- However much it costs, I'm willing to pay the price.
  (그것의 가격이 얼마가 되든 나는 기꺼이 돈을 지불하겠습니다.)
- It's important to be professional, however unreasonable your boss may be.
  (당신의 상사가 아무리 비이성적이라도 프로의 모습을 갖추는 건 중요합니다.)

Task 3

Choose the correct word from the box to complete each of the following sentences.

when	where	why	whenever	however

1. The hotel __________ we stayed wasn't very clean.
2. This is _________ I refuse to go.
3. Do you know the day __________ exams begin?
4. They should have called him, __________ busy they were.
5. He helps me __________ I'm in trouble.

Reading　The Power of Words

We all know that what we say is important. But, according to psychologist James W. Pennebaker, how we say it also matters. For example, the use of first-person pronouns such as "I" might indicate dominance in an interaction. Similarly, frequent use of words like "except," "but" or "without" might indicate that someone is lying.

Early on, Dr. Pennebaker observed health improvements in patients who used causal words to talk about traumatic experiences. For increased precision, he developed computer software to count words, including pronouns and articles, which he calls style words, and sort them into more than 70 categories. He started out with song lyrics, examining a few of the Beatles' greatest hits, and has since counted and categorized words in political campaigns, newspapers, classic novels, and even terrorist video recordings. He measures things like anxiety, self-discrepancies, inhibitions, causation, and anger, among others.

So, you're probably wondering what all of this means in practical terms. Well, Dr. Pennebaker and his team of researchers say that this technology can aid in the diagnosis of depression, tell us whether someone may be prone to suicide, or even reveal how likely a couple is to stay together over time.

Translation 단어의 힘

우리가 무슨 말을 하는지가 중요하다는 것은 모두 알고 있습니다. 그러나 심리학자인 James W. Pennebaker에 따르면 어떻게 말하는지 역시 중요하다고 합니다. 예를 들어, 1인칭 대명사인 "I"를 사용하면 상호작용에 있어서 우월함을 나타낼 수 있습니다. 비슷하게 "except, but" 또는 "without" 같은 단어를 자주 사용하면 거짓말을 하고 있다는 증거가 될 수 있습니다.

일찍부터 Pennebaker 박사는 정신적인 충격이 컸던 사건에 대해 이야기할 때 인과관계를 나타내는 단어를 사용하는 환자의 건강이 좋아진다는 사실을 알아냈습니다. 좀 더 정확히 알아보기 위해 그는 단어의 수를 세어보려고 컴퓨터 소프트웨어를 개발했는데 여기에는 그가 스타일 단어라고 명명한 대명사와 관사가 포함되어 있으며, 이 단어들을 70개 이상의 범주로 분류하였습니다. 그는 노래 가사부터 시작하였는데 Beatles의 히트곡 몇 개를 조사하였고, 그 후에는 정치운동, 신문, 고전소설, 심지어 테러범들의 비디오에서 나오는 단어의 수까지 세어보고 이를 분류하였습니다. 그는 여기서 불안, 자가당착, 금지, 인과관계, 분노와 같은 것들을 측정합니다.

그래서, 이것들이 실질적인 면에서 무엇을 의미하는지 궁금하실 겁니다. Pennebaker 박사와 그의 연구팀은 이 기술이 우울증 진단에 도움이 되고, 누가 자살하기 쉬운지를 우리에게 알려주고, 어떤 한 부부가 오랜 시간 동안 함께 잘 지낼 수 있는지도 밝혀낼 수 있다고 합니다.

Comprehension Check-up

True/False

1. Liars use different language than people who are telling the truth. (T/F)
2. Dr. Pennebaker believes that what we say is more important than how we say it. (T/F)
3. This technology may be applied to the diagnosis of mental disorders. (T/F)

Vocabulary Matching

1. psychologist	a. psychologically painful
2. prone	b. someone trained to analyze the mind and mental processes
3. practical	c. having a natural tendency toward something
4. traumatic	d. useful

Word Challenge

Quiz

Check Your Understanding: Use the words in the box to complete each of the following sentences.

affect	effect

1. Pollution can __________ a population's health.
2. The new corporate tax policy is intended to __________ changes in the way we do business.
3. Don't let your emotions __________ your decision.

Word Challenge

affect	Usage: "Affect" and "effect" are frequently confused, even by native English speakers. In general, "affect" means "to influence," "change," "impress," or "act upon." Examples: 1. Political events frequently affect stock prices. (to produce an effect or change) (정치적인 사건은 자주 주가에 영향을 미칩니다.) 2. She was affected by that film in a way that she had never been before. (to impress or move) (그녀는 예전에 경험하지 못했던 방식으로 그 영화를 보고 감명을 받았습니다. 3. Alcohol can affect one's judgment. (to attack or grasp) (술은 사람의 판단력을 침범할 수 있습니다.)
effect	Usage: Like "affect," "effect" is always used as a transitive verb, meaning that it requires an object. It means "to bring about," "to produce an effect," or, "to put into operation." Examples: 1. Scientists will attempt to effect new particles using the Large Hadron Collider. (to cause to come into existence) (과학자들은 Large Hadron Collider을 사용하여 새로운 입자를 만들기 위해 노력할 것입니다.) 2. Nanotechnology will likely effect new and interesting research in the field of medicine. (to bring about) (나노기술은 의약분야에서 새롭고 흥미로운 연구를 가져올 것입니다.) 3. It is nearly impossible to effect change without the support of the people. (to put into operation) (그 사람들의 지원 없이 변화를 일으키는 것은 거의 불가능합니다.)

Practice

Task 4

Choose the best expression to complete each of the following sentences.

1. This food should be stored in a dry place ______ temperature extremes are minimal.
   (a) which (b) how
   (c) what (d) where

2. ______ book you may read, you will find it helpful.
   (a) Whomever (b) However
   (c) Whichever (d) Whoever

3. All ______ is a sufficient supply of fuel oil.
   (a) that is needed (b) is needed
   (c) what is needed (d) for their needed

4. Sandy is the woman ______ husband is in prison.
   (a) who's (b) whoever
   (c) whose the (d) whose

5. The secretary _______ very kind.
   (a) we talked was (b) to whom we talked him was
   (c) whom we talked to were (d) we talked to was

Task 5

Find and replace the incorrectly used relative pronouns with correct ones.

1. A pacifist is a person whom believes that all wars are wrong.

   ________ → ________

2. He offered me the job, that I declined.

   ________ → ________

3. Do you know a restaurant which we can have a really good meal?

   ________ → ________

4. Whatever angry you may be, you should not shout at them.

   ________ → ________

5. I will never forget the time where we got stuck in an elevator.

   ________ → ________

Culture Corner

Return과 Rebate

미국에서는 물건을 구입한 후, 일정 기간 내에는 영수증만 제시하면 환불을 해주거나(refund), 같은 종류의 새 물건으로 바꾸어 주는(exchange) 제도가 보편화되어 있습니다. 물건을 교환하는 경우에도 먼저 환불 용지 (refund check)에 주소, 전화번호를 기입하고 서명을 한 다음, 현금 출납원 (cashier)에게 가서 돈을 돌려받고, 다시 마음에 드는 것을 골라서 사는 경우가 많습니다. 보통 누구에게 어떤 물건을 선물 할 때는 gift receipt를 따로 만들어 선물과 함께 넣어주는데 여기에는 값은 써 있지 않지만 아이템 번호 등이 명시되어 있어서 이 영수증만 있으면 다른 것으로 교환을 할 수가 있습니다. 비슷한 제도로 rebate라는 게 있습니다. 제 값을 다 치르고 난 상품의 가격 일부를 판매자가 구입자에게 다시 돌려주는 것으로 일종의 가격 할인 제도입니다. 적게는

1달러에서부터 가격이 비싼 것을 구입할 경우는 몇 백 달러까지도 돌려 받습니다. 광고문에서 "$10 mail-in rebate" 라는 문구를 흔히 볼 수가 있는데, 물건을 일단 구입하고 난 후, 우편 환불 신청서(mail-in rebate form), 영수증, 물건 상자에 붙어있는 UPC (Universal Product Code) 스티커 등을 우편으로 보내면 두 달쯤 후에 $10 check을 받게 됩니다. 환불 신청서는 물건 속에 들어 있기도 하고, 영수증과 함께 현금 출납원이 건네 주기도 합니다. 또 미국은 우리나라와 마찬가지로 세금을 일단 걷어 갔다가도 그 사람의 일년간 수입과 가족 수 등을 다시 계산하여 세금을 돌려주는 tax return제도가 있습니다. 저임금에 부양 가족이 많을 경우에는 자기가 낸 세금의 전액이나 그 이상을 돌려 받기도 합니다. 대학생들이 낸 등록금, 아이를 day care center에 맡기는 데 드는 돈, 병원비 등에서 세금 환불 혜택을 받을 수 있습니다. 세금 환불 혜택을 받기 위해서는 소득세 신고서(income tax return)를 작성해서 우편으로 보내기도 하고, 직접 컴퓨터 웹 사이트에 들어가서 소정의 양식을 작성해서 제출하기도 합니다. 세금 환불 신청을 대행해 주는 곳도 많이 있습니다.

Wrap-up

Key sentences

1. 관계대명사
   - He's the guy who has the corner office at the hottest firm in town, the guy whom everyone looks up to, the guy whose life everyone aspires to lead.
   - This is a character that we have developed just for this campaign.
   - I hope what you have for me today is spectacular.
   - Open with whichever idea is going to get us this contract.

2. 제한적 용법과 비제한적 용법 / 관계대명사의 생략 / 유사관계대명사
   - *The Portrait of the Artist as a Young Man* by James Joyce, which was first published in 1916, is a semi-autobiographical novel.
   - He's got everything (that) you could want: great apartment, sports car, and a beautiful girlfriend.
   - He's no longer the same ordinary guy (that) he used to be.
   - I'm not such a perfect fool as you thought.

3. 관계부사

- When the rest of the world is sleeping, he's awake, sipping your product, and this is why he's able to stay ahead of the competition.
- Please begin whenever you're ready.

REVIEW TEST

Choose the best word to complete each sentence. (1-10)

1. They bought her ________ she really wants.
   (1) who (2) which (3) that (4) what

2. I said nothing, __________ made him angry.
   (1) who (2) which (3) that (4) what

3. This is the best picture __________ he's ever painted.
   (1) who (2) whom (3) that (4) what

4. Jane has never left the town __________ she was born.
   (1) when (2) where (3) why (4) how

5. My son wants to go to a PC room __________ he gets the chance.
   (1) whenever (2) wherever (3) whoever (4) whatever

6. Is there any student __________ name hasn't been called?
   (1) whom (2) who (3) whose (4) what

7. Your shoes are the same size __________ mine.
   (1) as (2) which (3) that (4) what

8. I didn't get a pay raise, but this wasn't the reason ________ I left the job.

(1) that (2) which (3) how (4) where

9. ________ suggested we fly on Delta Airlines obviously doesn't travel much.

(1) Who (2) Whoever (3) Whatever (4) What

10. Who __________ has common sense can commit such a folly?

(1) who (2) which (3) what (4) that

Supplementary Reading (보충 독해)

다음 글을 읽고 문제를 풀어 보세요.

Internet Dating

The Internet is becoming more and more popular with people who are interested in finding new friends or romantic partners around the world. Advertising for love is not new. The first official personal ad was published in England in 1727, in which the never-married Helen Morrison advertised her desire for companionship in the local weekly. At that time, her actions were considered so strange that she was sent to a mental hospital for a month. Nowadays, millions of people visit online dating websites, and Internet dating is big business.

People believe that online dating is more open and liberating because they can reach a variety of people that they could never hope to reach via friends, work, or even the newspaper. Shy men and women may find it easier to communicate through a keyboard than face-to-face interaction because they can express themselves freely, and the fear of rejection is reduced. Internet dating is also helpful for handicapped people who are seeking to marry. However, people are not immune from scams and those pretending to be somebody else in cyberspace. Some Internet users may adopt false identities with accompanying photos or leave out important details about their lives.

The following are a few Internet dating safety tips. Do not reveal personal details until you are confident that it is safe. Never meet a first date for anything more than a casual drink or cup of coffee. The first time you meet someone in person, take a friend along, or meet in a public place. Experts say that personals ads on the Internet can either be a great way to meet new people or the beginning of a nightmare.

Translation 인터넷 만남

인터넷은 국경을 넘어 새로운 친구나 애인을 찾고 싶어하는 사람들에게 점점 더 인기를 얻고 있습니다. 이제 애인을 구하는 광고는 전혀 새로울 것이 없습니다. 공식적인 최초의 개인 광고는 1727년 영국에서 나왔는데, 그것은 한 번도 결혼을 하지 않은 Helen Morrison이 그 지방 주간지에 마음 맞는 친구를 구하는 희망 사항을 광고한 것이었습니다. 당시에는 그녀의 행동이 너무 이상하게 여겨져서 그녀는 한달 동안 정신병원에 보내지기도 하였습니다. 오늘날에는 수백만 명이 온라인 만남 웹사이트에 접속을 하고 인터넷 만남 주선 사이트도 번창하고 있습니다.

사람들은 온라인 만남이 더 개방적이고 자유롭다고 여깁니다. 왜냐하면 친구들이나 직장, 심지어 신문을 통해서는 만남을 기대할 수 조차 없었던 다양한 사람들과 만날 수 있기 때문입니다. 내성적인 남녀들은 직접 만나는 것 보다 키보드를 통한 채팅으로 말하는 것이 더 쉽다는 것을 알게 될 겁니다. 왜냐하면 마음을 터 놓고 대화를 나눌 수 있고, 거절 당할지도 모른다는 두려움은 한결 줄어들기 때문입니다. 인터넷 만남은 또한 결혼을 하려고 하는 장애인들에게 도움을 줍니다. 그러나 사람들은 사기꾼과 가상 공간에서 다른 사람으로 위장하는 사람들을 만날 수도 있습니다. 어떤 사람들은 가짜 ID(신분증)과 사진을 이용하기도 하고, 또 그들의 인생에서 중요한 세부사항을 빼 버리기도 합니다.

다음은 인터넷 만남에 있어 유용한 몇 가지 안전 수칙들입니다. 안전하다는 확신이 들기 전까지는 당신의 개인 정보를 공개하지 마십시오. 첫 번째 만남에서는 간단히 술을 마시거나 커피를 마시는 것 이상의 것을 하지 마십시오. 누군가를 개인적으로 처음 만나는 자리에는 친구를 데리고 가거나 공개적인 장소에서 만나는 것이 좋습니다. 전문가들은 인터넷 상의 개인 광고가 새로운 사람을 만나는 멋진 방법일 수 있지만 악몽의 시작이 될 수도 있다고 말합니다.

Explanation

1. The Internet is becoming more and more popular with people who are interested in finding new friends or romantic partners around the world.

be interested in은 '~에 관심이 있다. 흥미가 있다' 는 뜻입니다.
원래는 '누군가의 흥미, 관심을 끌다.' 라는 타동사 interest에서 출발하여, 흥미나 관심을 끄는 사물이 주어가 되면, It is interesting. 흥미나 관심을 갖게 되는 사람이 주어가 되면, I'm interested in it.이 됩니다.

Ex) Salesperson: Does it interest you? (그것 마음에 드세요?)
Customer: Well, I'm interested in Samsung products.
(글쎄요, 전 삼성제품이 끌리던데요.)

Ex) Anyone interested in joining the school band should come to the student union building and sign up by the end of this month.
(학교밴드에 들어오는데 관심이 있는 사람은 이번 달 말까지 학생회관으로 와서 신청해야 합니다.)

2. The first official personal ad was published in England in 1727, in which the never-married Helen Morrison advertised her desire for companionship in the local weekly.

관계대명사로 연결된 문장으로, 원래의 다음 두 문장이 한 문장으로 연결된 것입니다.
The first official personal ad was published in England in 1727.
The never-married Helen Morrison advertised her desire for companionship in **the first official personal ad** in the local weekly.
뒷문장에서는 중복되는 명사를 관계대명사 which로 바꾸고 전치사 in과 함께 문장 앞으로 이동한 것입니다. 여기서는 관계대명사가 비제한적 용법으로 쓰이고 있습니다. 또한 in which는 장소를 나타내는 관계부사 where로도 바꿀 수 있습니다.
Ex) I love the movie *Out of Africa*, in which Robert Redford and Meryl Streep starred.
(나는 영화 Out of Africa를 정말 좋아하는 데, 그 영화에는 Robert Redford와 Meryl Streep이 주연으로 나왔습니다.)

3. People believe that online dating can be more open and liberating because they can reach a variety of people that they could never hope to reach via friends, work or even the newspaper.

위의 문장에서 앞의 that은 believe의 목적절을 이끄는 접속사이고, 뒤의 that은 선행사 people을 한정해 주는 관계사절을 이끄는 관계대명사 that입니다.
Ex) I think that there was little that interested the boy at the exhibition.
(그 전시회에서 그 소년의 흥미를 끈 것은 거의 없었다고 생각합니다.)

4. Shy men and women find it easier to communicate through a keyboard than face-to-face interaction.

to communicate through a keyboard가 find의 진목적어인데, 너무 길기 때문에 가목적어, 혹은 형식목적어인 it을 앞에 쓰고, 진목적어는 후치 됩니다. 이것은 영어의 큰 원칙 중에 하나인 end-weight 원칙인 데, 정보가 무거우면 문장의 뒷부분으로 빠진다는 것입니다.
Ex) I found it very foolish to climb the mountain without a guide.
(가이드 없이 등산하는 것은 매우 어리석은 짓이라는 것을 알았습니다.)

5. People are not immune from scams and those pretending to be somebody else in cyberspace.

be immune from은 '~로부터 면제된, ~당할 염려가 없는'의 의미입니다.
pretend '~인체 하다'는 뜻으로 to부정사나 that절이 목적어로 옵니다. those pretending은 원래 those (who are) pretending인데, 관계대명사와 be동사가 생략된 것입니다.
Ex) He was fortunately immune from the disease.
(그는 운 좋게 그 질병으로부터 면역되었습니다.)
The girl (who is) skating over there is my niece.
(저쪽에서 스케이트를 타고 있는 소녀가 내 조카입니다.)

Q.1 Match the word in column A with its definition in column B.

A	B
1. companionship	a) being certain in one's abilities
2. liberating	b) suffering from a mental or physical disability
3. handicapped	c) a dishonest plan for making money
4. scam	d) fellowship
5. confident	e) an experience that is very frightening or unpleasant
6. nightmare	f) exempt or protected
7. immune	g) freeing from the restrictions

Q.2 Mark True (T) or False (F).

1. The Internet is mainly used by people interested in finding new jobs. ( )
2. The first official personal ad was published in the United States in 1727. ( )
3. The number of people who visit online dating websites is decreasing. ( )
4. Handicapped people use Internet dating websites to meet someone they want to marry. ( )
5. For shy people, it is very difficult to speak through a keyboard. ( )
6. People should reveal their personal information when they first communicate with someone in cyberspace. ( )

The Passive Voice 09 Unit

Introduction

Topic: Go Away (떠나다)

Lesson objectives:

The passive voice (수동태)

- active versus passive (능동태와 수동태)
- usages of the passive (수동태 용법)
- passive without 'by' (by를 쓰지 않는 수동태)

WARM-UP

This week, Camille invites Aaron to have coffee with her on short notice. It turns out that she has some surprising news to deliver. What could it be? Let's take a look.

Aaron : Hello.
Camille : Aaron?
Aaron : Oh, hi. I was just thinking about you.
Camille : Oh, really? Well, I need to see you right away.
Aaron : Okay. Is everything all right?
Camille : Um. Well, can you meet me at Cafe Emporio in 20 minutes?
Aaron : Sure. I guess.

(twenty minutes later)

Aaron : Hi.
Camille : Hi.

Aaron : So, can you tell me what this is about?

Camille : Sure. I'll get right to the point. I was presented with an outstanding opportunity by my agent. (passives)

Aaron : Congratulations. What is it?

Camille : It's a dream come true. I will be photographed by the great Sergio Valentine. (passives)

Aaron : That's great.

Camille : It's in Europe.

Aaron : I guess it's expected that you'll be there for a while. (passives)

Camille : At least a year.

Aaron : When do you leave?

Camille : I was asked to leave immediately by my agent. (passives)

Aaron : So, I take it the dinner reservation we made for next week has been cancelled? (passives)

Camille : Oh, I forgot all about that.

Aaron : You forgot? The reservation was made for your birthday! (passives)

Camille : Oh, I am absorbed in my work these days. (passives)

Translation

이번 주에 Camille은 같이 커피를 마시자며 급히 Aaron을 초대합니다. 그녀는 놀라운 소식을 갖고 있는 것으로 밝혀지는데요. 과연 무슨 일일까요? 한 번 살펴 봅시다.

Aaron : 여보세요?

Camille : Aaron?

Aaron : 안녕? 나 방금 너 생각하고 있었어.

Camille : 정말? 지금 당장 좀 봤으면 하는데.

Aaron : 좋아. 무슨 일 있는 건 아니지?

Camille : 음, 20분 후에 Emporio 카페에서 만날래?

Aaron : 그러자.

(20분 후)

Aaron : 안녕?

Camille : 안녕?
Aaron : 무슨 일인지 말해줄 수 있어?
Camille : 응, 본론부터 말할게. 내 대리인 덕에 나는 굉장히 좋은 기회를 갖게 되었어.
Aaron : 축하해. 무슨 기회인데?
Camille : 내 꿈이 실현됐어. 위대한 Sergio Valentine이 내 사진을 찍을거야.
Aaron : 멋지다.
Camille : 유럽에서 할 거야.
Aaron : 한 동안 거기 있겠구나.
Camille : 적어도 1년은 있을것 같아.
Aaron : 언제 떠나?
Camille : 바로 떠나달라고 대리인이 요청을 했어.
Aaron : 그럼 우리가 예약한 다음주 저녁은 취소되는 거네?
Camille : 아, 완전히 잊고 있었어.
Aaron : 잊고 있었다고? 그 예약은 네 생일을 축하하기 위한 것이었잖아!
Camille : 나 요즘 일 때문에 정신 없어서 그래.

Comprehension Check

1. Why does Camille need to see Aaron so urgently?
   (a) She has some news for him.
   (b) She has a family emergency.
   (c) She's leaving town.
   (d) Both (a) and (c)

2. Camille tells Aaron that this opportunity is something she:
   (a) has always dreamed about
   (b) is nervous about
   (c) has some reservations about
   (d) has not thought much about

3. Aaron is surprised that Camille forgot about their plans because:
   (a) they fall on a special occasion
   (b) he's reminded her three times
   (c) she made the plans
   (d) none of the above

Useful Expressions

In this dialogue	Explanation
1. I'll get right to the point.	1. Sometimes it's best to skip the small talk and get right down to business. In today's dialogue, Camille doesn't want to waste any more time, so she decides to give Aaron the news straight away. Use this expression when you want to cut out all the formalities and get to the matter at hand.
2. It's a dream come true.	2. This expression describes a wish, hope, or goal that has materialized. You can use it to describe nouns, usually people or things. In our example, "it" refers to Camille's big modeling opportunity. And if the sentence structure seems somewhat odd at first, try reading it again as, "It's a dream (that has) come true."
3. I take it the dinner reservation we made for next week has been cancelled?	3. The verb "take," as it is used here, means "understand" or "infer." Let's take a look at a few additional examples: a. I take it you're not happy with the results. (= I can tell you're not happy with the results.) b. Please don't take this the wrong way. (=Please don't misunderstand what I'm about to say.)
4. I am absorbed in my work these days.	4. Like a sponge, one thing can suck up all of your time. In today's dialogue, Camille tells us that work requires all of her attention with this simple metaphor. Let's take a look at a few additional examples: a. During the day, she worked on the farm, but at night, she was absorbed in tales about faraway lands. b. I was so absorbed in my work that I simply forgot to eat lunch.

Grammar

Focus 1 The Active vs. Passive Voice (능동태와 수동태)

01 능동태와 수동태의 선택

(1) 능동태와 수동태

능동태란 '주어+동사+목적어'의 형식으로, 주어(행위자)가 동작을 행하여 '~하다' 라는 능동의 의미를 갖는 문장을 말합니다.

- I need to see you right away.
  (당신을 당장 만나야겠습니다.)
- I invited him to my house.
  (나는 그를 우리 집으로 초대하였습니다.)
- The thief stole the expensive car.
  (그 도둑이 값비싼 차를 훔쳤습니다.)

수동태란 능동태의 목적어를 주어로 삼아서 'be +과거분사 + by 행위자'의 형식을 취하며, '(주어가) ~ 당하다, ~하여지다' 라는 의미를 갖는 문장을 말합니다.

능동태: My father built the house.

수동태: The house was built by my father.
(내 아버지가 그 집을 지었습니다.)

- My agent presented me with an outstanding opportunity.
  I was presented with an outstanding opportunity by my agent.
  (내 대리인이 나에게 좋은 기회를 주었습니다.)

자동사는 목적어가 없어서 수동태를 만들 수 없습니다: arrive, rise, disappear, die, lie, exist, seem, become, remain 등

- We arrived at the station. (O)
  (우리는 역에 도착했습니다.)
  We were arrived at the station. (X)

타동사 중에서도 상태를 나타내는 동사 (stative verbs)는 수동태를 만들 수 없습니다: fit, have, lack, resemble, suit 등

- They have a nice house. (O)
  (그들은 멋진 집을 가지고 있습니다.)
  A nice house is had by them. (X)

(2) 수동태를 주로 쓰는 경우

능동태의 주어가 분명하지 않을 때.

- Her husband was killed in World War II.
  (그녀의 남편은 2차 세계대전에서 죽었습니다.)
- A man was murdered in his apartment.
  (한 남자가 그의 아파트에서 살해 당했습니다.)

능동태의 주어가 막연한 일반인을 나타낼 때.

- French is spoken in France, Belgium and Switzerland.
  (불어는 프랑스, 벨기에 그리고 스위스에서 쓰입니다.)
- We are not allowed to smoke here.
  (여기에서 담배를 피워서는 안 됩니다.)
- The Koran is written in Arabic.
  (코란은 아랍어로 쓰여 있습니다.)
- Patrons are requested to refrain from taking photographs.
  (고객들은 사진 찍는 것을 삼가도록 요청 받았습니다.)
- Orion can be seen on a clear night.
  (날씨가 좋은 날 밤에는 오리온자리를 볼 수 있습니다.)

능동태의 주어보다 수동태 주어에 관심이 클 때.

- The thief was caught by a police officer.
  (그 도둑은 경찰에게 붙잡혔습니다.)
- Our cat was run over by a car.
  (우리 고양이가 차에 치였습니다.)
- The traffic was made worse by the rain.
  (비 때문에 교통상황이 더욱 나빠졌습니다.)
- The impact of the crisis was compounded by the failure of several large banks.
  (그 재정위기의 충격은 몇몇 대형 은행의 도산으로 더욱 악화되었습니다.)

- Today's presentation was brought to you by The Coca-Cola Company.

  (오늘의 발표는 코카콜라 회사에서 준비했습니다.)

수동의 의미가 거의 없이 자동사로 느껴지는 경우, 즉, 종사, 위치, 사망, 출생, 피해 등을 나타낼 때: be engaged(종사하다, 약혼하다), be absorbed(마음을 빼앗기다, 심취하다), be situated(위치해 있다), be born(태어나다), be drowned(익사하다), be damaged(피해를 입다) 등

- I am absorbed in my work these days.

  (난 요즘 내 일에 몰두해 있습니다.)
- He is engaged in writing a novel.

  (그는 소설 쓰는 일을 하고 있습니다.)
- She was born on June 2nd.

  (그녀는 6월 2일에 태어났습니다.)
- Pamplona is situated in the northern part of Spain.

  (Pamplona는 스페인의 북부에 위치해 있습니다.)

앞에 나온 주어와 연결될 경우

- She spoke and was applauded by the audience.

  (그녀는 강연을 했고 청중들에게 박수갈채를 받았습니다.)
- He went there but was not welcomed.

  (그는 거기에 갔지만 환영을 받지 못했습니다.
- In 1998, Bill Clinton committed perjury and was impeached by Congress.

  (1998년에 Bill Clinton은 위증죄를 범하여 국회에서 탄핵 소추를 당하였습니다.)
- She loved and was loved by all.

  (그녀는 모두를 사랑했고 또한 그들에게 사랑 받았습니다.)

02 by 행위자의 생략

수동태는 행위의 대상을 강조하는 구문이므로 행위자는 중요시되지 않는 것이 일반적입니다. 따라서 수동태 문장에서 「by+목적어」의 행위자 표시는 생략되는 경우가 많습니다. 행위자를 생략하는 경우는 행위자를 확실히 알 수 없을 때, 굳이 말 할 필요가 없을 때 그리고 능동태 문장의 주어가 일반적인 사람들을 나타낼 때 입니다.

- Kimchi is eaten here in Korea. (일반적인 사람일 때)

  (이 곳 한국에서는 김치를 먹습니다.)
- Our house was robbed last Thursday. (행위자를 모를 때)

  (지난 목요일에 우리 집이 털렸습니다.)

- The criminal was arrested this morning. (누구나 알 수 있을 때)
  (그 범죄자가 오늘 아침에 체포되었습니다.)
- The reservation was made for your birthday!
  (그 예약은 당신의 생일을 축하하기 위해 한 것이었습니다.)
- The case was dismissed before it reached the high court.
  (그 사건은 고등법원에 가기 전에 기각되었습니다.)
- The national flag was flown at half-mast all last month.
  (지난달 내내 국기가 반기로 게양되었습니다.)

Task 1

Choose the correct expression from the box to complete each passive sentence.

been discussed	be solved	was announced	were told	is not sold

1. A new theory ___________ by Einstein.
2. We ____________ by the tour guide to have a look around.
3. The problem has already ____________ by the board of directors.
4. Alcohol ____________ in this shop.
5. This problem can _________ by Jan.

Focus 2 Usages of the passive voice (수동태 용법)

01 S + V + IO + DO (4형식 문장)

목적어가 두 가지일 때, 즉 간접목적어와 직접목적어를 동시에 취하는 4형식의 문장에서는 두 가지 형태의 수동태 문장을 얻을 수 있습니다.

- Luke gave us information about the assignment.
  We were given information about the assignment by Luke.
  Information about the assignment was given to us by Luke.
  (Luke는 우리에게 그 과제에 관한 정보를 주었습니다.)
- He gave me a present.
  I was given a present by him.
  A present was given to me by him.
  (그는 나에게 선물을 주었습니다.)

make, read, get, sell, write, buy, cook, bring 등의 동사가 쓰인 4형식 문장에서는 직접목적어를 주어로 한 수동태만이 가능합니다.

- I wrote her a letter.
  A letter was written to her by me.
  She was written a letter by me. (x)
  (나는 그녀에게 편지를 썼습니다.)
- He bought his mother the muffler.
  The muffler was bought for his mother by him.
  His mother was bought the muffler by him. (x)
  (그는 어머니께 그 머플러를 사드렸습니다.)

4형식 문장의 수동태에서 직접목적어가 주어로 쓰이면 간접목적어 앞에는 동사에 따라 보통 to나 for같은 전치사가 쓰입니다.

- They sent me a postcard.
  A postcard was sent to me.
  (그들이 나에게 엽서를 보냈습니다.)
- Loud music gives me headaches.
  Headaches are given to me by loud music.
  (시끄러운 음악때문에 머리가 아픕니다.)
- Tom bought her a new jacket.
  A new jacket was bought for her by Tom.
  (Tom이 그녀에게 새 자켓을 사주었습니다.)

02 S + V + O + OC (5형식 문장)

「주어+동사+목적어+목적보어」 의 5형식 문장에서 목적어가 수동태의 주어가 되면 목적격 보어는 그 자리에 그대로 둡니다.

- My agent asked me to leave immediately.
  I was asked to leave immediately by my agent.
  (나의 대리인이 나에게 즉시 떠나달라고 부탁했습니다.)
- They found him guilty.
  He was found guilty.
  (그들은 그가 유죄임을 알아냈습니다.)
- His presence made the situation worse.
  The situation was made worse by his presence.
  (그의 출현이 상황을 더욱 악화시켰습니다.)
- We elected him captain of our team.
  He was elected captain of our team (by us).
  (우리는 그를 우리 팀의 주장으로 선출하였습니다.)

그러나 목적 보어를 주어로 하는 수동태는 가능하지 않습니다.

- We called him the matchmaker.
  (우리는 그를 중매쟁이라고 불렀습니다.)
  He was called the matchmaker. (o)
  The matchmaker was called him. (x)

let, make, have 등의 사역동사는 「주어+동사+목적어+원형부정사」 구문으로 쓰이는 데, 수동태가 되면, 부정사 앞에 to를 쓰게 된다.

- Her boss made her stay until the work was finished.
  She was made to stay (by her boss) until the work was finished.
  (그녀의 상사는 그 일이 끝날 때까지 그녀를 남아있게 하였습니다.)
- They let me enter the building.
  I was allowed to enter the building.
  (그들은 내가 그 건물로 들어갈 수 있게 해 주었습니다.)

03 타동사구

「자동사+전치사」, 「타동사+명사+전치사」의 동사구는 타동사 역할을 하므로 수동태로 바꿀 수 있습니다. 이때는 동사구는 한 단어처럼 취급하므로 전치사 등의 요소가 누락되지 않도록 주의해야 합니다.

- They looked at the baby boy. (자동사+전치사)
  The baby boy was looked at (by them).
  (그들은 그 남자 아기를 쳐다보았습니다.)
- We paid careful attention to what he was saying. (타동사+명사+전치사: 두 가지 수동태 가능)
  Careful attention was paid to what he was saying.
  What he was saying was paid careful attention to.
  (우리는 그가 말하는 것에 세심한 주의를 기울였습니다.)

04 that절

목적어가 that절인 문장의 수동태의 경우, 1) 가주어 it를 쓰거나, 2) that 절 속의 주어를 수동태 주어로 합니다. 이때 that 절은 주어가 없으므로 구(to 부정사)로 고칩니다. that절을 목적어로 취하는 동사에는 say, know, believe, expect, think, hope, feel, fear, consider, find, intend, suppose 등이 있습니다.

- We expect that you'll be there for a while.
  It's expected that you'll be there for a while.
  You are expected to be there for a while.
  (우리는 당신이 얼마 동안 거기 있을 거라고 예상합니다.)
- People believe that she is innocent.
  It is believed that she is innocent.
  She is believed to be innocent.
  (사람들은 그녀가 결백하다고 믿습니다.)
- They thought that he was the right person for the position.
  It was thought that he was the right person for the position.
  He was thought to be the right person for the position.
  (그들은 그가 그 자리에 적임자라고 생각했습니다.)

- We know that the universe is expanding.
  It is known that the universe is expanding.
  The universe is known to be expanding.
  (우리는 우주가 계속 팽창하고 있다는 사실을 알고 있습니다.)

05 진행형, 완료형, 조동사

진행형 수동태는 「be being + p.p.」 형태로 만들어집니다.

- A stranger is following us.
  We are being followed by a stranger.
  (낯선 사람이 우리를 따라오고 있습니다.)
- He is making a dog's house.
  A dog's house is being made by him.
  (그는 개 집을 만들고 있습니다.)
- Four independent companies are seeking a lucrative contract.
  A lucrative contract is being sought by four independent companies.
  (각기 다른 4개의 회사가 유리한 계약을 찾고 있습니다.)
- The boys are arguing over the bigger bedroom.
  The bigger bedroom is being argued over by the boys.
  (남자 아이들이 더 큰 침실을 두고 다투고 있습니다.)

완료형 수동태는 「have/had been + p.p.」 형태로 만들어집니다.

- We have cancelled the dinner reservation we made for next week.
  The dinner reservation we made for next week has been cancelled.
  (우리가 다음주에 하기로 한 저녁 예약은 취소되었습니다.)
- They had shown the police officer Ian's photo.
  Ian's photo had been shown to the police officer.
  (그들은 Ian의 사진을 그 경찰관에게 보여주었습니다.)

조동사가 있는 문장의 수동태 만들 때엔 조동사는 그대로 두고 동사원형만 「be+p.p.」 로 바꿉니다.

- The great Sergio Valentine will photograph me.
  I will be photographed by the great Sergio Valentine.
  (위대한 Sergio Valentine이 내 사진을 찍을 것입니다.)

- You must finish it by today.
  It must be finished by today.
  (당신은 오늘까지 그것을 끝내야 합니다.)
- You should keep your word.
  Your word should be kept.
  (당신은 약속을 지켜야 합니다.)

Task 2

Read each pair of sentences carefully and decide whether the passive sentence is correct or incorrect.

	O	X
1. We will deal with this matter soon. This matter will be dealt with soon.	( )	( )
2. They expect that you will get high grades. It is expected you to get high grades.	( )	( )
3. Mom is carrying the groceries. The groceries are being carried by Mom.	( )	( )
4. I gave the money to John. The money was given to John by me.	( )	( )
5. You must return the video on time. The video must returned on time.	( )	( )

Focus 3 Passives without 'by' (by를 쓰지 않는 수동태)

01 by 이외의 전치사를 쓰는 경우

by 이외에도 with, in, at, to, of 등 다른 전치사가 수동태에 사용되어 하나의 숙어처럼 쓰입니다.

(1) with를 사용하는 경우

be filled with (~으로 가득차다)
be covered with (~으로 덮이다)
be delighted with (~에 기뻐하다)
be pleased with (~에 기뻐하다)
be concerned with (~와 관계가 있다)
cf) be concerned about (~을 걱정하다)
be fed up with (~에 싫증나다)
be bored with (~에 싫증나다)
be satisfied with (~에 만족하다)

- The room is filled with guests.
  (방이 손님들로 꽉 찼습니다.)
- He was bored with the card game.
  (그는 카드게임 하는 것이 지겨워졌습니다.)
- My parents were pleased with the news that I passed the exam.
  (부모님은 내가 시험에 통과했다는 소식을 듣고 기뻐하셨습니다.)
- I am bored with school these days.
  (난 요즘 학교에 싫증이 납니다.)
- The strawberries are covered with chocolate after they are chilled.
  (그 딸기는 얼린 다음 초콜릿으로 덮여 있습니다.)
- Physics is concerned with the workings of the natural world.
  (물리는 자연 세계의 움직임과 관계가 있습니다.)

(2) in을 사용하는 경우

be interested in (~에 관심이 있다)
be absorbed in (~에 몰두하다)
be engaged in (~에 종사하고 있다)
cf) be engaged to (~와 약혼 중이다)

- I was so absorbed in the story that I didn't hear the phone ringing.
  (나는 그 이야기에 너무 몰두하고 있어서 전화가 울리는 것도 듣지 못했습니다.)

- He is engaged in the project.
  (그는 그 프로젝트에 참여하고 있습니다.)
- Most teenage boys are interested in girls.
  (대부분의 10대 남자아이들은 여자아이에게 관심이 있습니다.)

(3) at을 사용하는 경우

be surprised at/ by/ with (~에 놀라다)
be startled at/ by (~에 깜짝 놀라다)
be amazed at/ by (~에 놀라다)
be disappointed with/by/at (~에 실망하다)
be embarrassed at/by/with (~에 당황하다)

- Everyone was surprised at her admission on the witness stand.
  (그녀가 증인석에 입장하자 모두 깜짝 놀랐습니다.)
- Public opinion polls showed that a majority of citizens were disappointed by the government's failure to act.
  (여론조사에 따르면 대다수의 시민들이 정부가 제대로 일 처리를 못한 것에 대해 실망한 것으로 나타났습니다.)
- He was embarrassed by her question.
  (그는 그녀의 질문에 당황했습니다.)

(4) to를 사용하는 경우

be devoted to (~에 전념하다)
be exposed to (~에 노출되다)
be married to (~와 결혼해 있다)

- Amnesty International is devoted to ending abuses of human rights worldwide.
  (국제 사면 위원회는 전세계적으로 인권남용을 없애기 위해 헌신합니다.)
- Public figures are frequently exposed to harsh criticism.
  (공인은 강도 높은 비판에 자주 노출됩니다.)

(5) of를 사용하는 경우

be tired of (~에 싫증나다)
be convinced of (~을 확신하다)
be composed of (~로 구성되다)
be ashamed of (~을 부끄러워하다)

- Most people are tired of the bitter divisiveness which characterizes politics today.
  (대부분의 사람들이 요즘 정치의 특성인 지독한 불화에 싫증이 났습니다.)
- The jury is already convinced of his guilt.
  (그 배심원은 이미 그의 유죄를 확신하고 있습니다.)

- The United Arab Emirates is composed of seven states.

(아랍에미리트연방은 7개의 주로 구성되어 있습니다.)

cf) Canada consists of various ethnic groups.

(캐나다는 다양한 민족으로 구성되어 있습니다.)

- She was ashamed of eating too much in front of him.

(그녀는 그의 앞에서 너무 많이 먹어서 부끄러웠습니다.)

(6) 기타

be caught in the rain (비를 만나다)
be known as/ by/ for/ to (~으로 알려지다/ ~에 의해 알 수 있다/ ~으로 유명하다/ ~에게 알려지다)

- Perhaps Samuel Clemens is better known as Mark Twain.

(아마도 Samuel Clemens은 Mark Twain으로 더 잘 알려져 있을 겁니다.)

- A man is known by the company he keeps.

(사람은 그가 사귀는 친구를 보면 알 수 있습니다.)

- Elba is known for being the site of Napoleon's first term in exile, not to mention its breathtaking views of the Mediterranean.

(Elba는 지중해의 아름다운 장관은 말할 것도 없고, 나폴레옹의 첫 번째 유배지로도 유명합니다.)

- The actor is well known to the Japanese.

(그 배우는 일본인들에게 잘 알려져 있습니다.)

02 동작 수동태와 상태 수동태

수동태는 「be+과거분사」 의 형태를 취하는 것이 원칙이지만 be동사 대신에 get, grow, become이 쓰여 「get/grow/become+과거분사」 의 형태가 되는 경우도 있습니다. 이때에는 상태의 변화나 동작의 의미를 강조하는 문장이 되는데 이를 동작 수동태라고 합니다.

be, lie, stand, remain, + p.p.: 상태강조 (~되어져 있다)
get, grow, become + p.p.: 동작강조 (~ 되어지다)

- My house is painted blue.

(내 집은 파란색으로 칠해져 있습니다.)

My house gets painted every year.

(내 집은 매년 페인트 칠이 됩니다.)

- He has been married for 16 years.

(그는 결혼한지 16년 되었습니다.)

He got married last year.

(그는 작년에 결혼했습니다.)

- The man was drunk last night.
  (그 남자는 지난 밤에 취해 있었습니다.)
  The man got drunk last night.
  (그 남자는 지난 밤에 취했습니다.)
- Finding reliable information on the Internet can be difficult.
  (인터넷에서 신뢰할만한 정보를 찾는 것은 어렵습니다.)
  Finding reliable information on the Internet has become difficult.
  (인터넷에서 신뢰할만한 정보를 찾는 것은 어렵게 되었습니다.)

Task 3

Choose the correct preposition to complete each sentence.

1. The room is filled (with / by / to / for) fresh air.
2. James was surprised (in / on / to / at) the test result.
3. I was sick and tired (with / to / of / at) my job.
4. He has been exposed (with / to / for / by) danger.
5. She got married (to / with / by / at) a computer programmer last fall.

Reading　Solar Energy

Humans have depended on the sun's energy for thousands of years. They have relied on it for warmth, to grow crops, and for the light by which they worked. Following a century and a half of industrial development powered by coal, oil, and other fossil fuels, people are once again turning to the sun as a chief source of energy.

In the wake of mounting concerns over a global energy crisis, converting the sun's energy into usable power is high on the agenda of government leaders around the world. In Europe, and in Germany and Spain in particular, solar energy has started to gain traction. However, in the United States, the world's largest consumer of fossil fuels, solar power accounts for only one percent of the total energy supply due to its relatively high cost.

While in the eyes of some,the expense of solar power still makes it an impractical replacement for fossil fuels, the sky is the limit when it comes to its applications. Because the sun's reach extends just about everywhere, the Solar Turbine Group hopes solar energy will help reduce developing economies' dependence on the energy grid for growth. And if you don't consider helping impoverished nations fashionable enough, you could always throw down $350 for one of Joe Hynek's solar power generating purses. As a graduate student in Iowa State University's mechanical engineering department, Hynek developed a handbagthat can generate enough energy in three hours to power an iPod, camera, or cell phone.

Translation 태양에너지

수 천년 동안 인간은 태양에너지에 의존해 왔습니다. 사람들은 온기를 얻기 위해, 작물을 재배하기 위해, 일하는데 필요한 빛을 얻기 위해 태양에너지에 의지해 왔습니다. 석탄, 기름 그리고 다른 화석 연료를 이용해 산업을 발전시킨 지 1세기 반 만에 사람들은 에너지의 주요원천으로 다시 한 번 더 태양 쪽으로 돌아서고 있습니다.

세계적으로 에너지 위기에 대한 걱정이 증가함에 따라 태양에너지를 쓸 수 있는 에너지로 변환시키는 것이 전 세계 지도자들의 주요 안건이 되었습니다. 유럽에서, 특히 독일과 스페인에서는 태양에너지가 인기를 끌기 시작했습니다. 그러나 세계에서 화석연료를 가장 많이 소비하는 미국에서는 상대적으로 높은 가격 때문에 태양에너지가 전체 에너지 공급량의 1퍼센트밖에 차지하지 않습니다.

일부에서는 비용 때문에 태양에너지가 화석연료를 대체하는 것이 아직도 비현실적이라고 생각하지만, 그 용도에 있어서는 제한이 없습니다. 태양은 거의 모든 곳에 영향을 미치기 때문에 Solar Turbine Group은 개발도상국이 성장을 위해 에너지 시설망에 의존하는 것을 줄이는데 도움을 줄 것이라고 희망합니다. 가난한 국가를 돕는 것이 충분히 매력적이라고 생각하지 않는다면, 당신은 언제든지 Joe Hynek의 태양열 발전 지갑 하나를 사는데 350 달러를 쓸 수도 있습니다. 아이오와 주립대학의 기계공학과 대학원생인 Hynek는 아이팟, 카메라 또는 핸드폰이 3시간 동안 작동할 수 있도록 충전해주는 에너지를 발생시키는 핸드백을 개발했습니다.

Comprehension Check-up

True/False

1. Solar power is on everyone's mind because of a worldwide energy shortage. (T/F)
2. The Solar Turbine Group thinks solar energy is a good temporary solution for developing economies. (T/F)
3. The potential uses of solar energy are varied and wide. (T/F)

Vocabulary Matching

1. fossil fuels	a. use
2. impractical	b. petroleum, coal, and natural gas
3. impoverished	c. unwise or inefficient
4. application	d. poor

Word Challenge

Quiz

Check Your Understanding: Use the words in the box to complete each of the following sentences.

deny	refuse	reject

1. The defendant continues to __________ his guilt.
2. Each year, universities are forced to __________ hundreds of qualified applicants due to budget constraints.
3. I __________ to be treated like this.

Word Challenge

deny	Usage: Use "deny" when you want to negate the truth of a claim, withhold something, or refuse an agreement. Remember, it's always used with an object. Examples: 1. He denied any knowledge of the accounting fraud that took place while he was chief executive. (to state that something is not true) (그는 그가 최고 경영진에 있는 동안 발생했던 분식회계에 대해 아는 바가 없다고 말했습니다.) 2. In many countries, women are still denied the rights normally afforded their male counterparts. (to withhold possession, use, or enjoyment of) (많은 국가에서 여성들은 남성에게 정상적으로 제공되는 권리를 여전히 받지 못합니다.) 3. The defendant's request for parole has been denied. (to refuse to agree to or accede) (가석방을 요청한 피고인의 요구는 거절되었습니다.)
refuse	Usage: You can use "refuse" with regard to a declined invitation or item, or to indicate the intention not to do something. It can be used both with and without an object. Examples: 1. The president refused our invitation to speak at this year's commencement ceremonies. (to decline to accept something offered) (그 총장은 올해 졸업식사를 발표해 달라는 우리의 초대를 거절했습니다.) 2. We reserve the right to refuse admission to anyone who appears to be under the influence of alcohol or drugs. (to decline to give, to deny) (우리는 술이나 마약에 취한 것처럼 보이는 사람의 입장을 거부할 권리를 가지고 있습니다.) 3. I refuse to answer that question. (to express determination not to do something) (그 질문에 대답하기를 거부하겠습니다.)
reject	Usage: The meaning of "reject" isn't all that different from "refuse." But there are certain instances in which it's more appropriate. Those include times when you're talking about an idea or submission. Examples: 1. I strongly reject the idea that life exists on other planets. (to refuse to have, take, or recognize) (나는 다른 행성에도 생명체가 존재한다는 의견에 강하게 반대합니다.) 2. The estimate for the Dubai project was rejected. (to refuse to accept) (두바이 프로젝트에 대한 견적서는 받아들여지지 않았습니다.)

Practice

Task 4

Choose the appropriate expression to complete each passive sentence.

1. An article __________ by her for the magazine.
   a) was writing　　b) was being written
   c) being written　　d) was being writing

2. The work ___________ on time.
   a) has to finished　　b) has been to finish
   c) has to be finished　　d) has to finish

3. A skyscraper __________ by our company.
   a) will be constructed　　b) will have constructed
   c) will been constructed　　d) will constructed

4. Angela __________ come to dinner this evening.
   a) is expecting　　b) expects
   c) is to expect　　d) is expected to

5. The baby __________ by him.
   a) has be looked after　　b) has looked after
   c) has been look after　　d) has been looked after

Task 5

Read each sentence carefully. If it is incorrect, correct it. If the sentence is correct, leave it alone.

	correct	incorrect
1. Children are resembled by their parents.	( )	( )
2. You can't come in now. The office is being cleaned.	( )	( )
3. I must have my watch repairing.	( )	( )
4. I am not satisfied by my life nowadays.	( )	( )
5. All the workers involved in the demonstration were dismissed.	( )	( )

Culture Corner

Houses

우리가 흔히 '집'이라고 부르는 주거의 형태에도 여러 가지가 있습니다. 또한 주거 형태를 가리키는 말로 우리나라에서 쓰는 용어와 영어의 용법과는 차이가 있습니다. 먼저 우리가 흔히 아파트라고 부르는 것은 apartment에서 ment 부분이 잘려 나가고 뜻이 변형된 것입니다. apartment란 국가나 기업이 공동 주택을 지어 놓고 임대하여 주는 것이고, 개인 사업자가 분양하는 아파트는 condominium이라고 합니다. apartment의 경우 아래층에는 office(관리인의 살림집), 세탁실(laundry room), 창고(storage) 등이 있고, 2층부터는 세 들어 사는 사람(tenant)들이 삽니다. 미국은 아파트를 입주할 때 임대의 형식이 대부분으로, 건물주는 입주자의 직업, 소득, 가족관계 등을 조사하여 다달이 월세를 받는데 문제가 없는지를 확인한 다음 임대여부를 결정합니다.

콘도(condo, condominium)는 원래 영어로 집을 의미하기보다는 '공동 통치'라는 뜻으로 유럽에서 시작된 새로운 경영 기법입니다. 이것이 점차 개인이 소유할 수 있는 공동 주택이라는 뜻으로 변했습니다. 우리 나라에서는 일반인들이 회원권을 가지고 이용할 수 있는 휴양시설을 콘도미니엄이라고 부르지만 사실 대부분의 아파트는 개인이 소유하게 되므로 condominium이라고 볼 수 있습니다.

타운 하우스(town house)는 우리 나라의 연립주택과 비슷하지만 주거단지 내부의 주택 배치 형태와 주택 모형이 연립주택에 비해 다양하고 독특한 모양으로 설계됩니다. 일반주택과 거의 같은데 줄줄이 붙어 있다는점만 다르며 그래서 값이 싼 편입니다.

맨션(mansion)이란 'a large house, usually belonging to a wealthy person'으로 한마디로 부자들의 대저택을 가리키는 말입니다. 우리나라에서는 보통의 아파트인 경우도 '~맨션'이라는 이름을 붙이기도 하지만, 미국사람들은 mansion이라고 하면 커다란 저택을 상상하게 됩니다.

빌라(villa)란 주로 시골에 있는 정원이 딸려있는 쾌적한 주택, 별장 등으로 대개 휴가 중에 사용합니다. 이탈리아 르네상스 시기에 성행한 빌라는 이탈리어로는 빌라 수부르바나(villa sub-urbana)나, 프랑스어로는 빌레쥐아튀라(villegiatura)로 불립니다. 우리나라에서 '빌라'란 이름은 여기에서 따온 것이지요. 하지만 우리가 말하는 '빌라'는 미국의 duplex(두 세대용 연립주택)에 가까운 말입니다.

별장(cottage)이란 'a small old house,especially in the country'로 주로 피서지의 조그만 별장, 오두막집 등을 가리킵니다. 정해진 형태는 없으나 건축과 자연이 어울려 그 특색이 나타납니다. 한국에서도 경치가 좋은 터를 잡아 별장을 지었는데 조선시대에는 별저, 별서라고 불렀습니다. 조선시대 별장은 살림집에서 그리 멀지 않은 곳에 지었으나 오늘날은 좀더 먼 곳에 지어 주말용, 창작활동용, 레저용 등으로 용도가 다양해졌습니다.

펜션(pension)은 호텔의 편의성과 민박의 가정적 분위기를 갖춘 새로운 숙박 시설입니다. 펜션은 원래 '연금'의 뜻으로 유럽에서 노인들이 여생을 연금과 민박 경영으로 보내는 데서 그 이름이 붙었다고 합니다. 유럽에 오래 전부터 있었던 민박풍의 작은 호텔로, 가족 경영에 의한 전 가족의 서비스가 특징입니다. 엄밀히 말하자면 타인을 위한 숙박시설이지만 가족들이 직접 펜션에서 살며 경영해 나가는 경우도 많습니다.

펜트하우스(penthouse)는 옥상가옥이라는 뜻입니다. 우리말로 흔히 '옥탑집, 옥탑방'으로 불리지요. 이 말은 라틴어의 'appendere'에서 온 말로 그 뜻은 'to cause to be suspended (as if from the sky)'입니다. 즉, '하늘로부터 매달려 있게 한다'는 의미입니다.

Wrap-up

Key sentences

1. 능동태와 수동태
   - I was presented with an outstanding opportunity by my agent.
     (My agent presented me with an outstanding opportunity.)
   - The reservation was made for your birthday!
   - I'm absorbed in my work these days.

2. 수동태 용법
   - I was asked to leave immediately by my agent.
   - So, I take it the dinner reservation we made for next week has been cancelled?
   - I will be photographed by the great Sergio Valentine.
   - I guess it's expected that you'll be there for a while.

3. by를 쓰지 않는 수동태
   - I am bored with school these days.
   - Most teenage boys are interested in girls.

REVIEW TEST

Find the correct answers in the blanks. (1-5)

1. I was asked ___________ back early by him.
   (1) come (2) be come (3) coming (4) to come

2. He got married __________ a woman of the same age.
   (1) by (2) on (3) to (4) with

3. The name and address of each applicant should ___________ on the form.

(1) be writing (2) be written (3) have written (4) write

4. Do you know what ___________ to her yesterday?

(1) happened (2) was happened (3) happens (4) is happened

5. I ____________ good care of when I was at my grandmother's house.

(1) took (2) was taken (3) have taken (4) am being taken

Change the verb in the parenthesis to the correct formto complete each passive sentence. (6-10)

6. All of the details have __________ by them. (arrange)

7. My bicycle __________ a few days ago. (steal)

8. No one likes to __________ in front of their friends. (embarrass)

9. She __________ with her exam result now. (satisfy)

10. A new mall will __________ downtown soon. (build)

Supplementary Reading (보충 독해)

다음 글을 읽고 문제를 풀어 보세요.

Do Animals Have a Sixth Sense?

The tsunamis triggered by a massive earthquake in the Indian Ocean in 2004 killed thousands of people. Animals, however, seemed to have escaped the disaster. Wildlife officials in Sri Lanka were stunned because giant waves swept into Yala National Park,

Sri Lanka's biggest wildlife reserve, uprooting trees and flipping cars onto their roofs, but they couldn't find any dead animals. According to eyewitness accounts, elephants screamed and ran for higher ground; dogs refused to go outdoors; flamingoes abandoned their low-lying breeding areas; and other zoo animals rushed into their shelters. These facts indicate that animals may have sensed the massive wave coming.

It has been believed for centuries that animals can predict natural catastrophes. There have been reports that animals exhibit peculiar behavior before earthquakes, hurricanes, and volcanic eruptions. For example, dogs howl in the night mysteriously; caged birds become restless; chickens stop laying eggs and nervous cats hide. Some people claim they possess a sixth sense for impending danger in addition to the five senses of sight, hearing, touch, taste and smell. However, precisely what animals sense, if they feel anything at all, is still a mystery. They may be able to sense subtle changes in the earth's magnetic field or changes in the air pressure. Further research could reveal secrets about animal behavior that would allow humans to develop a more accurate early warning system.

Translation 동물들은 육감이 있을까요?

2004년 인도양의 거대한 지진으로 인하여 일어난 쓰나미는 수천 명의 목숨을 앗아갔습니다. 하지만 동물들은 이 재앙을 피해간 것 같습니다. 스리랑카의 야생동물 관계자는 매우 놀랐습니다. 왜냐하면 가장 큰 야생동물 보호 구역인 얄라 국립 공원에 대형 파도가 밀려오면서 나무의 뿌리가 뽑히고 차가 뒤집어졌으나 사망한 동물들은 한 마리도 발견할 수 없었던 것입니다. 목격자들의 증언에 의하면, 코끼리는 큰 울음소리를 내며 높은 지대로 달려갔고, 개들은 밖으로 나가려 하지 않았고, 플라밍고는 낮은 지대에 있는 그들의 번식지를 떠났으며, 동물원의 다른 동물들은 그들의 은신처로 서둘러 대피하였다고 합니다. 이 사실은 동물들이 큰 파도가 접근해오고 있음을 감지했을 거라는 것을 나타냅니다.

수세기 동안 사람들은 동물들이 자연 재앙을 예견할 수 있다고 믿고 있습니다. 동물들이 지진, 허리케인, 그리고 화산 폭발 이전에 특이한 행동을 보인다는 보고가 있었습니다. 예를 들어, 개들은 밤에 이상하게 울고, 새장 안의 새들은 안절부절 못하고, 닭은 알을 낳지 않으며, 신경이 곤두선 고양이들은 숨는다고 합니다. 어떤 사람들은 동물들이 시각, 청각, 촉각, 미각 그리고 후각이라는 오감 외에 다가올 위험을 감지하는 육감을 지니고 있다고 주장합니다. 그러나 동물들이 조금이나마 무언가를 느낀다면 그들이 정확히 무엇을 감지하느냐 하는 것은 아직 풀리지 않고 있습니다. 그들은 지구 자기장의 미묘한 진동이나 공기 압력의 변화를 감지할 수도 있습니다. 더욱 깊이 연구한다면 동물 행동에 관한 비밀을 밝혀내어 더욱 정확한 조기 주의 시스템을 발전시킬 수 있을 것입니다.

Explanation

1. The tsunamis triggered by a massive earthquake in the Indian Oceanin 2004 killed thousands of people.

trigger 는 '~일으키다, 유발하다' 라는 뜻의 동사이며 triggered by는 수동태로서 '~으로 인해 유발되었다' 란 뜻입니다. triggered 앞에는 관계대명사와 be동사인 which were가 생략되어 있습니다.

Ex) The protest triggered by the mayor's action was quelled within minutes.

(사장의 조치로 인해 야기된 시위는 몇 분 내로 진압되었습니다.)

2. Wildlife officials in Sri Lanka were stunned because giant waves swept into Yala National Park, Sri Lanka's biggest wildlife reserve, uprooting trees and flipping cars onto their roofs, but they couldn't find any dead animals.

stun은 surprise 와 비슷한 뜻으로 '깜짝 놀라게 하다, 실신시키다, 기절시키다'란 의미를 가집니다. surprise와 비교해서 더욱 강한 놀라움을 나타낸다 할 수 있습니다. 여기서는 'be 동사 + 과거분사'의 수동태 형태로 사용되어 '깜짝 놀랐다' 의 의미가 됩니다.

Ex) People in the building were stunned by the loud noise.

(건물에 있는 사람들은 큰 소음으로 인해 매우 놀랐습니다.)

uprooting 과 flipping은 부대상황을 나타내는 분사구문으로 동시에 일어나고 있는 일들을 설명하고 있습니다. uproot는 '뿌리채 뽑다'라는 뜻이고, flip은 '튀겨 올리다, 뒤집다' 라는 뜻으로 앞뒤를 정하기 위해 동전을 튀기는 것을 flip a coin 이라고 합니다.

Ex) I walked along the street looking at my feet.

(나는 내 발을 보며 도로를 따라 걸었습니다.)

3. These facts indicate that animals may have sensed the massive wave coming.

may have sensed는 추측을 나타내는 may의 과거형으로'~을 감지 했었을 수 있다' 란 의미가 됩니다.

Ex) She may have sensed the uneasy atmosphere in the office this morning.

(그녀는 오늘 아침 사무실의 불안스러운 분위기를 느꼈을 수도 있습니다.)

4. It has been believed for centuries that animals can predict natural catastrophes.

It has been believed that 은 '~라 믿어져 왔다' 란 뜻으로 수동태 문장입니다. 주어가 that절로 길기 때문에, 가주어 it을 사용한 문장입니다.

Ex) It has been confirmed that your business trip will be next month.

(당신의 출장은 다음달에 있을 거라고 확정되었습니다.)

5. However, precisely what animals sense, if they feel anything at all, is still a mystery.

what animals sense는 '동물들이 무엇을 감지하는 지'라는 뜻의 간접의문문입니다. '의문사 + 주어 + 동사'의 순으로 전체 문장에서 주어의 역할을 하고 있습니다. 또한 조건 절에서 at all은 '적어도, 조금이나마'의 뜻을 가지고 있습니다.

Ex) Tell me what the teacher said.

(선생님이 무엇이라고 말씀 하셨는지 나에게 알려주세요.)

Q. 1 Choose the expression that can replace the underlined word.

1. The tsunamis were triggered by a massive earthquake in the Indian Ocean.
   a) caused b) resulted c) stunned d) bought

2. The animals may have sensed the massive wave coming.
   a) noisy b) huge c) surprising d) quiet

3. He was stunned by the film's tragic ending.
   a) shocked b) pleased c) excited d) shortened

4. Animals can predict a natural catastrophe.
   a) event b) environment c) happiness d) disaster

5. Animals exhibit peculiar behavior before earthquakes or hurricanes.
   a) normal b) unusual c) boring d) exciting

6. Caged birds become restless.
   a) satisfied b) sad c) agitated d) surprised

Q.2 Choose the right answer for each question.

1. What was the cause of the tsunamis?
   a) giant waves in Yala park
   b) a big earthquake
   c) uprooted trees and flipped cars
   d) animals

2. Why were the wildlife officials so surprised?
   a) because waves swept into the park
   b) because the animals acted strangely
   c) because the zoo animals ran to their shelters
   d) because no animals died

3. In the article, which was not cited as evidence for the sixth sense in animals?
   a) Dogs howl mysteriously at night.
   b) Caged birds become restless.
   c) Hens lay eggs.
   d) Cats hide.

4. According to the article, which of the following is true?
   a) The sixth sense that animals may have is for impending danger.
   b) Reports say that animals show normal behavior before disasters.
   c) Many animals died because of the tsunamis.
   d) Scientists found out what animals sense before disasters.

5. According to the article, which of the following has long been held true?
   a) Animals can predict natural catastrophes.
   b) Animals can trigger disasters.
   c) Animals can be used to prevent natural catastrophes.
   d) Animals can sense subtle changes in the earth's magnetic field.

Subjunctive Mood 10 Unit

Introduction

Topic: Climbing the Corporate Ladder (회사의 승진 사다리 오르기)

Lesson objectives:

Subjunctive Mood (가정법)

- Subjunctive Past and Subjunctive Past Perfect (가정법 과거와 가정법 과거완료)
- Subjunctive Future and Ellipsis of 'if' (가정법 미래와 if의 생략)
- Other Structures for Subjunctive Mood (가정법의 다른 구문)

WARM-UP

Things seem to be going well for Brett lately. However, it's not usually a good sign when the boss requests a one-on-one meeting first thing in the morning. Will his streak of good luck come to an end? Listen in on Brett's conversation with Mr. Daniels to find out.

Mr. Daniels : Brett, I think we should talk.

Brett : Is everything all right?

Mr. Daniels : Absolutely. I have to say, your presentation the other day was remarkable. I felt as though I were watching myself at your age. (subjunctive mood – as though)

Brett : Thank you, sir.

Mr. Daniels : I should be thanking you. If it weren't for your brilliant work, we would have lost this contract. (subjunctive past)

Brett : I was just doing my job.

Mr. Daniels : Don't be so modest. I think it's about time you got a promotion. (subjunctive mood – it's time)

Brett	: Really? A promotion?
Mr. Daniels	: Certainly. I recommend that you serve as Vice President of Marketing for our Asia Division. (subjunctive mood)
Brett	: Vice President of Marketing? Isn't that Tom's position?
Mr. Daniels	: Only until the end of the day. If he had secured this contract, he'd be receiving the promotion. (subjunctive past perfect/past)
Brett	: I wish it were not this way. (subjunctive mood – I wish)
Mr. Daniels	: Be here at 6:30 a.m. tomorrow for a conference call with your counterparts at our overseas offices. If you should have any questions, let my secretary know. (subjunctive future)
Brett	: I'll be here; ready to go.
Mr. Daniels	: Good. And one more thing: If you should run into Tom, tell him to come to my office. (subjunctive future)
Brett	: Yes, sir.

Translation

요즘 Brett의 일이 잘 풀리는 것 같습니다. 하지만 상사가 아침에 제일 먼저 단독 회의를 하자고 하는 것은 보통 좋은 신호가 아닙니다. 그의 행운의 느낌도 끝이 나는 걸까요? Brett과 Mr. Daniels의 대화를 듣고 무슨 일인지 알아봅시다.

Mr. Daniels	: Brett, 우리 이야기 좀 합시다.
Brett	: 모든 것이 잘 되어가나요?
Mr. Daniels	: 물론입니다. 지난 번 당신이 한 프레젠테이션은 아주 뛰어났어요. 마치 당신 나이일 때의 내 자신을 보는 듯 했습니다.
Brett	: 감사합니다.
Mr. Daniels	: 감사의 표시를 해야 할 것 같군요. 당신의 뛰어난 성과가 없었다면 우리는 이 계약을 성사시키지 못했을 겁니다.
Brett	: 전 제가 해야 할 일을 했을 뿐입니다.
Mr. Daniels	: 겸손해 할 필요 없어요. 당신이 승진할 때가 된 것 같군요.
Brett	: 정말요? 승진이요?
Mr. Daniels	: 물론입니다. 나는 당신을 우리 아시아담당 부서의 마케팅팀 부사장으로 추천합니다.
Brett	: 마케팅팀 부사장이요? 그건 Tom의 직책 아닙니까?
Mr. Daniels	: 오늘까지는 그렇죠. 만약 그가 이 계약을 성사시켰더라면 그가 승진을 했을 겁니다.
Brett	: 이런 식을 바란 것은 아닙니다.

Mr. Daniels	: 해외부서에 있는 같은 직책의 담당자와 전화 회의가 있으니 내일 아침 6시 30분까지 여기로 오세요. 궁금한 사항 있으면 내 비서에게 말하면 됩니다.
Brett	: 알겠습니다. 가보겠습니다.
Mr. Daniels	: 좋아요. 그리고 하나 더. 만약 Tom과 만나게 되면 내 사무실로 오라고 전해 줘요.
Brett	: 네, 알겠습니다.

Comprehension Check

1. Mr. Daniels called this meeting to __________ Brett.

   (a) encourage
   (b) scold
   (c) praise
   (d) humiliate

2. Brett is going to __________ Tom.

   (a) fire
   (b) replace
   (c) promote
   (d) suggest

3. In this dialogue, Mr. Daniels' attitude toward Brett is best described as one of:

   (a) reverence
   (b) respect
   (c) appreciation
   (d) all of the above

Useful Expressions

In this dialogue	Explanation
1. I have to say, your presentation the other day was remarkable.	1. We've all heard the old adage, "Honesty is the best policy." At times when the conventions of honesty compel you to speak your mind, you can preface your comments with, "I have to say…" Or, "I must say…," works just as well.
2. I was just doing my job.	2. In today's dialogue, Mr. Daniels showers Brett with compliments. Trying to show that he has a sense of humility, Brett says that he was only doing what was required of him. Try out this expression the next time you find yourself a little uncomfortable with the excessive praise conferred upon you.
3. Don't be so modest.	3. At times, talking too much about your own achievements can make you seem boastful or arrogant. However, that doesn't mean that we need to downplay allof our accomplishments. Use this expression to let someone know that it's okay to accept credit when it's due.
4. I think it's about time you got a promotion.	4. The expression, "it's about time," is one that means either approximately the right time or long past the right time, depending on the context. You'll have to pay attention to subtle cues to figure out which definition is most suitable for a particular situation.

Grammar

Focus 1 Subjunctive past and subjunctive past perfect

(가정법 과거와 가정법 과거완료)

01 가정법과 직설법

직설법과 가정법은 문장의 형태와 의미에 있어 큰 차이를 보입니다.

(1) 직설법의 조건문: if절에서 현재형 동사가 쓰이고, 실현가능성이 있는 조건을 나타냅니다.

- If I find it, I'll tell you.
  (내가 만일 그걸 찾으면, 당신에게 알려주겠습니다.)
- If he is honest, we will employ him.
  (그가 정직하면, 우리는 그를 고용할 것입니다.)

(2) 가정법: if절에서 과거형 동사가 쓰이고, 실현가능성이 적은 순수 가정을 나타냅니다.

- If I won the lottery, I would quit my job tomorrow.
  (만약 내가 복권에 당첨되면 내일 직장을 그만둘 겁니다.)
- If it weren't raining, I would be more inclined to go outside and do something.
  (비가 오지 않는다면 나는 밖에 나가서 뭔가를 하려고 할 겁니다.)
- If I were a bird, I would fly to her.
  (내가 새라면 그녀에게 날아갈 겁니다.)

02 Subjunctive Past (가정법 과거)

(1) Form and Meaning

가정법 과거는 현재 사실의 반대를 가리키거나, 혹은 현실과 다른 상황을 가정하는 것을 말합니다. 주의할 점은 가정법 과거의 형태는 과거시제이지만 실제 시제는 현재라는 것입니다.

If + 주어 + 동사의 과거형, 주어 + would/should/could/might + 동사의 원형

- If I were in your position, I would make the same choice.
  (내가 만약 당신의 위치에 있다면 나도 같은 선택을 했을 겁니다.)

- If I were a parent, I would encourage my children to study a foreign language from a young age.
  (내가 만약 부모라면 내 아이들이 어렸을 때부터 외국어를 공부하도록 장려했을 겁니다.)
- If I knew his address, I could write to him.
  (내가 그의 주소를 안다면, 그에게 편지를 쓸 수 있을 텐데요.)

(2) If it were not for … (…가 없다면, …가 아니면)

현재 상황을 '~가 없다면' 하고 가정하는 것입니다. 과거에 있었던 것을 가정할 때는 if it had not been for 라고 써야 하지만, 이 경우에도 if it were not for를 쓰기도 합니다. 비슷한 표현으로 But for…, Without…, 등이 있습니다.

- If it were not for the upcoming conference, I'd have a lot more free time.
  (다가오는 회의가 없다면 나에겐 더 많은 자유시간이 있을 겁니다.)
- If it were not for their children, they would get divorced.
  (아이들이 없다면 그들은 이혼할 겁니다.)

cf) If it weren't for your brilliant work, we would have lost this contract.
(당신의 놀라운 성과가 없었다면 우리는 이 계약을 성사시키지 못했을 겁니다.)
- But for your help, we could not finish in time.
  (당신의 도움이 없다면 우리는 제시간에 끝내지 못할 겁니다.)
- Without the umbrella, I would get wet.
  (그 우산이 없다면, 나는 젖게 될 겁니다.)

03 Subjunctive Past Perfect (가정법 과거완료)

(1) Form and Meaning(형태와 의미)

가정법 과거완료는 과거의 사실과 반대되는 상황을 가정하거나, 과거에 있었던 일을 부정하거나, 또는 없었던 일에 대한 유감 혹은 소망을 나타냅니다. 주의할 점은 형태는 과거완료이지만 실제 시제는 과거라는 것입니다.

If + 주어+ had +동사의 과거분사형(p.p.), 주어+ would/should/could/might + have + p.p.

- If the police had caught him sooner, this incident might have been prevented.
  (경찰이 그를 좀 더 빨리 잡았다면 이번 사고는 예방할 수 있었을 겁니다.)
- If I had been aware of the details, I would have reacted differently.
  (내가 세부사항을 알고 있었다면 난 다르게 행동했을 겁니다.)
- If Joe Carter hadn't hit the famous game-winning homerun in the 1993 World Series, the Phillies might have won the pennant.
  (Joe Carter가 1993년 월드시리즈의 그 유명했던 게임에서 승리를 확정짓는 홈런을 치지 않았다면 the Phillies가 우승기를 차지했을 겁니다.)

- My boss would not have fired me if I had attended the monthly meeting.
  (내가 월례 회의에 참석만 했더라도, 사장이 나를 해고하지는 않았을 겁니다.)

(2) If it had not been for…(…가 없었다면, …가 아니었다면)

과거 현실에 존재했던 것을 '만약 ~가 없었다면' 하고 가정하는 것입니다.

- If it had not been for the traffic on Route 11, we might have been on time.
  (11번 도로에서 교통사고가 없었다면 우린 정각에 도착했을 겁니다.)
- If it were not for your past indiscretions, things might have been different.
  (당신의 지난 경솔한 행동만 없었다면 상황은 달라졌을 겁니다.)
- If it had not been for your advice, I would have failed.
  (당신의 조언이 없었다면, 나는 실패하고 말았을 것입니다.)
- Without your help, I could not have succeeded.
  (당신의 도움이 없었다면 난 성공하지 못했을 겁니다.)
- But for the storm, I would have been home earlier.
  (폭풍우가 없었더라면, 좀 더 일찍 집에 도착할 수 있었을 겁니다.)

04 혼합구문

가정법 문장에서 주절과 종속절의 시제가 서로 다를 때 이를 '혼합 가정'이라 합니다.

(1) 가정법 과거완료와 가정법 과거의 혼합구문

과거에 일어난 사건이 현재까지 영향을 미칠 때 가정법 과거완료-가정법 과거의 혼합가정구문을 사용하는데 그 형식은 다음과 같습니다.

If + 주어 + had + p.p., 주어 + would/should/could/might + 동사원형

- If you had not helped me then, I would not be here now.
  → 가정법 과거완료(실제 과거시점), 가정법 과거(실제 현재시점)
  (그때 당신이 나를 도와주지 않았다면, 전 여기 이 자리에 없었을 겁니다.)
- If he had secured this contract, he'd be receiving the promotion.
  (만약 그가 이 계약을 성사시켰더라면 그가 승진을 했을 겁니다.)
- If only we had written the address down, we would be there by now.
  (우리가 그 주소를 적어만 놨어도 우린 지금쯤 도착해 있을 겁니다.)
- If he had taken the doctor's advice, he might still be alive.
  (그가 그 의사의 충고를 들었다면 지금까지도 살아있을 겁니다.)

(2) 직설법과 가정법의 혼합구문

이루지 못한 소망에 대한 유감을 표할 때 직설법-가정법의 혼합구문을 사용합니다. 보통 가정법 구문에서 if절의 가정하는 부분이 이미 분명히 결정되었으므로, 생략하고 그 대신에 현실 상황을 덧붙여 주는 것입니다.

- (If I had enough time,) I would go, but I have no time.
  (시간이 있으면 가겠지만, 전 시간이 없습니다.)
- (If it had not been so noisy last night,) She would have slept well, but it was too noisy last night.
  (지난 밤에 그렇게 소란하지 않았더라면 그녀가 푹 잤겠지만, 어젯밤엔 너무 시끄러웠습니다.)
- (If there had been seats available on the four o'clock flight from Detroit,) We would have arrived sooner, but there were no seats available on the four o'clock flight from Detroit.
  (디트로이트에서 출발하는 4시 비행기에 자리가 있었다면 좀 더 일찍 도착했겠지만 남아있는 좌석이 없었습니다.)
- (If I had known you were coming over,) I would have made dinner, but I didn't know you were coming over.
  (당신이 오는 걸 알았더라면 저녁을 만들어 놓았겠지만 당신이 올 줄 몰랐습니다.)

Task 1

Choose the best expression to complete each sentence.

1. If I had known you were coming, I (would have baked, would bake) a cake.
2. If I had enough money to buy a house, I (would have married, would marry) her.
3. If Dorothy (had had, had) time, she would have written a much more interesting essay.
4. If he (had been, were) promoted, his family would have moved to an affluent neighborhood.
5. The flower (could have grown, could grow) well, but I did not water it.

Focus 2 Subjunctive Future and Ellipsis of 'if'

(가정법 미래와 'if'의 생략)

01 Subjunctive Future (가정법 미래)

(1) Form and Meaning

가정법 미래는 앞으로 일어날 가능성이 희박한 일을 나타낼 때 쓰입니다. '가정법 과거'와 '가정법 과거완료' 라는 명칭이 조건절에서 쓰이는 동사의 형식을 근거로 한다면, '가정법 미래' 라는 것은 의미에 초점을 두고 있습니다. if절에서 should나 happen to를 쓰는 것은 미래에 대한 강한 의심을 나타내고, were to를 쓰는 것은 미래에 실현이 불가능한 일을 상상할 때 쓰입니다. should가 들어간 if절과 함께 쓰이는 주절에는 직설법 문장이 오기도 합니다.

If + 주어 + should/were to /happen to + 동사원형, 주어+ will/ would/should/could/might/may/must + 동사원형

- If you should have any questions, let my secretary know.
  (만약 의문점이 생기면 제 비서에게 알려주세요.)
- If you should run into Tom, tell him to come to my office.
  (만약 Tom을 마주치면, 그에게 내 사무실에 오도록 말해주세요.)
- If it should rain tomorrow, the party will be cancelled.
  (내일 만약 비가 오면, 그 파티는 취소될 것입니다.)
- If you (should) happen to pass the supermarket, could you get some milk?
  (만약 슈퍼마켓을 지나가게 되면 우유를 좀 사오실 수 있나요?)
- If the Australian team were to lose, England would advance to the finals.
  (호주팀이 진다면 영국이 결승전에 진출할 겁니다.)
- If Lehman Brothers were to fail, the consequences would be devastating.
  (Lehman Brothers가 실패한다면 그 결과는 엄청날 겁니다.)

02 Ellipsis of 'if' (if의 생략)

가정법 구문에서 조건절의 if가 생략되면 동사+주어의 도치 구문이 만들어 집니다. 이러한 생략과 도치는 if절에 should, were, had가 나오는 경우에 주로 나타납니다.

- Were I rich, I could buy you a diamond ring.
  (=If I were rich, I could buy you a diamond ring.)
  (내가 부자라면, 당신에게 저 다이아몬드 반지를 사줄 수 있을 겁니다.)

- Should you change your mind, let me know.
  (= If you should change your mind, let me know.)
  (만약에 마음이 바뀌면, 알려주세요.)
- Had I had enough money, I could have lent him some.
  (= If I had had enough money, I could have lent him some.)
  (충분한 돈이 있었다면, 그에게 좀 빌려줄 수 있었을 겁니다.)
- Had I seen him at school today, I would have told him how I really felt.
  (= If I had seen him at school today, I would have told him how I really felt.)
  (오늘 학교에서 그를 봤다면 그에게 내가 정말 어떻게 느꼈는지 말했을 겁니다.)
- Were I to pass up this opportunity, it could be years before another comes along.
  (= If I were to pass up this opportunity, it could be years before another comes along.)
  (이 기회를 놓치면 다음 기회가 오기까지 수 년이 걸릴 수도 있습니다.)

03 if절의 대용

가정법 구문에서 조건절이 없이도 아래와 같은 형태에서 조건을 나타내는 표현이 됩니다.

(1) 명사구

- A woman of wisdom would not do such a foolish thing.
  (지혜로운 여인이라면, 그런 어리석은 짓은 하지 않을 겁니다.)
- A closer examination of it might have revealed a new fact.
  (면밀한 조사를 했으면 새로운 사실을 밝혀 냈을 것입니다.)

(2) 부사(구)

- Ten years ago not a single doctor could have cured the disease.
  (십 년 전이었더라면, 어떤 의사도 그 병을 치료 할 순 없었을 겁니다.)
- Without air, nothing could survive on the Earth.
  (공기가 없다면, 지구상에 어떠한 것도 살아 남지 못할 겁니다.)
- He is very busy this week; otherwise he would come to the meeting.
  (이번 주에 그가 매우 바쁘지 않았으면, 그 모임에 갈 겁니다.)

(3) 부정사

- To hear her speak English, you would take her for a British person.
  (당신이 만일 그녀가 영어로 말하는 것을 들으면, 그녀를 영국사람으로 생각 할 겁니다.)

- It would have been better for him to have kept silent.
  (그가 그냥 조용히 있었다면 훨씬 나았을 겁니다.)

(4) 분사구문

- Born in better times, I could have lived in ease and comfort.
  (더 좋은 시절에 태어났다면, 안락하고 편안하게 살 수 있었을 겁니다.)
- The same thing, happening in wartime, would amount to disaster.
  (만약에 똑같은 일이 전쟁 중에 일어난다면, 큰 참사가 될 겁니다.)

(5) 접속어구

- Supposing you couldn't write, what would you do?
  (만약 쓸 수가 없다면, 어떡하시겠습니까?)
- You can borrow my bike provided you bring it back.
  (만약 돌려만 준다면, 내 자전거를 빌려도 됩니다.)

Task 2

Read each sentence carefully and decide whether it is correct or incorrect. If it is incorrect, correct it. If it is correct, leave it alone.

	O	X
1. If you should see Sarah, please give her my regards. ______________________________	( )	( )
2. If his father has died, what will become of him? ______________________________	( )	( )
3. If should you be interested in this project, send me an email. ______________________________	( )	( )
4. If it rain tomorrow, we'll stay at home. ______________________________	( )	( )
5. It would be wrong if you were to steal. ______________________________	( )	( )

Focus 3 Other Structures for Subjunctive Mood

(가정법의 다른 구문)

01 I wish (expressing wishes)

(1) I wish + 가정법 과거

바라는 시점에서, 현실과 반대의 상황을 가정하여 이루어질 가능성 없는 소망을 표현합니다.

- I wish it were not this way.
  (이런 식이 아니길 바랍니다.)
- I wish I were a genius.
  (내가 천재이면 얼마나 좋겠습니까?)
- I wish I were able to talk to girls.
  (나도 여자아이들과 이야기 할 수 있으면 좋겠습니다.)
- I always wished I had a sister.
  (난 항상 여동생이 한 명 있기를 원했습니다.)

(2) I wish + 가정법 과거완료

바라는 시점보다 과거에 이루어지지 못했던 것에 대한 아쉬움을 표현합니다.

- I wish I had spoken English fluently in the last interview.
  (내가 바로 얼마 전 그 인터뷰에서 영어를 유창하게 말했으면 (지금) 얼마나 좋겠습니까? (아마 취업을 했겠죠))
- I wish I had never met you!
  (당신을 만나지 않았더라면 하고 바랍니다.)
- I wished I had not been born in a poor family.
  (나는 가난한 가정에서 태어나지 않았으면 좋았을 것이라고 바랬습니다.)
- I immediately wished I had not said that.
  (나는 곧바로 내가 그 말을 하지 않았으면 하고 바랬습니다.)

02 as if/ as though

as if/ as though 가정법 구문은 사실에 반대되는 모양이나 상태를 나타내는 표현입니다. 주절 동사가 나타나는 때와 동일한 때를 가정하는 경우는 가정법 과거를 쓰고, 주절 동사보다 앞선 때의 일을 나타내는 경우에는 가정법 과거완료를 씁니다.

(1) S+ V+ as if (as though) + 가정법 과거 (마치 ~인 것처럼)

- I felt as though I were watching myself at your age.
  (마치 당신만한 나이였을 때의 내 자신을 보고 있는 듯했습니다.)
- Paul acts as if he were not sad.
  (Paul은 슬프지 않은 것처럼 행동합니다.)
- She acts as if it were no big deal.
  (그녀는 그것이 별 거 아닌 것처럼 행동합니다.)
- He talks as if he were the authority on every subject ever known to man.
  (그는 마치 그가 사람들에게 알려진 모든 분야의 대가인 것처럼 말합니다.)
- It seemed as though she was avoiding the question.
  (그녀가 그 질문을 피하고 있는 것처럼 보였습니다.)

(2) S+ V+ as if (as though) + 가정법 과거완료 (마치 ~였던 것처럼)

- Jinni talks as if she had passed the bar exam.
  (Jinni는 마치 자신이 사법 고시를 합격한 것처럼 말합니다.)
- Suzie turned pale as though she had seen a ghost.
  (Suzie는 마치 유령이라도 본 것처럼 얼굴이 하얗게 질렸습니다.)
- I felt as if someone had punched me in the stomach.
  (나는 마치 누군가가 내 배를 때린 것 같은 느낌을 받았습니다.)

03 It's time

It's time + 가정법 과거 구문은 '~할 시간이다' 란 의미로, '(마땅히 ~할 때가 되었는데, 안하고 있을 때) 이제 ~하여야 지' 란 의미입니다.

- I think it's about time you got a promotion.
  (당신이 승진할 때가 된 것 같습니다.)
- It's time you went to bed.
  (이제 잘 시간입니다.)
- It's about time you had your hair cut!
  (머리를 자를 때가 되었습니다.)
- It's about time you stepped into the 21st century and bought a cell phone.
  (이제 당신은 21세기에 발을 들여놓고 핸드폰을 살 때가 되었습니다.)

04 as it were

'말하자면' 의 뜻으로 one might say 또는 so to speak로 바꾸어 쓸 수 있습니다.

- He is, as it were, a grown-up baby.
  (그는 말하자면 다 큰 애기입니다.)
- The Bible is, as it were, the lamp of life.
  (성경은 말하자면 인생의 등불입니다)
- Life is not, as it were, perfect as it is in the movies.
  (삶은 말하자면 영화에서 보이는 것처럼 완벽하지 않습니다.)
- As a young child, he often found himself, as it were, lost in a world of his own.
  (어렸을 때 그는 종종 말하자면 자신만의 세상에서 길을 잃은 자신의 모습을 발견하였습니다.)

05 suggestion or demand (제안, 요구) (should) + 동사원형

(1) 요구, 간청, 주장, 권고 등을 나타내는 술어동사

(order, command, request, require, ask, demand, stipulate, insist, urge, propose, suggest, move, recom-mend, agree, consent, desire) 다음에 오는 종속절에서는 (should) 동사원형이 오게 됩니다.

주어 + 동사 + that + 주어 + (should) 동사원형

- I recommend that you (should) serve as Vice-president of Marketing for the Asia Division.
  (나는 당신을 우리 아시아담당 부서의 마케팅팀 부사장으로 추천합니다.)
- I suggest that she (should) not apply for the job.
  (나는 그녀가 그 일에 지원해서는 안 된다고 건의했습니다.)
- The officer ordered that the robber (should) put the weapon down.
  (경찰관은 강도에게 무기를 내려 놓으라고 명령했습니다.)
- We ask that everyone (should) contribute a minimum of 15 hours per week.
  (우리는 모든 사람들이 일주일에 최소 15시간 기여하도록 요구합니다.)
- I insist that you (should) stay here; it's not a problem at all.
  (당신은 여기 있어야 합니다. 그건 전혀 문제가 아닙니다.)

(2) 당연, 필요, 적절, 중요 등의 주관적 판단을 나타내는 형용사

(natural, necessary, essential, imperative, good, better, desirable, advisable, proper, right, just, fair, rea-sonable, important, vital) 다음에 오는 종속절에서도 (should) 동사원형이 오게 됩니다.

It + be동사 + 형용사 + that + 주어 + (should)동사원형

- It is natural that a baby (should) cry when he or she doesn't feel well.
  (아기가 아플 때 우는 것은 당연합니다.)
- It was urgent that she (should) leave the place immediately.
  (그녀가 바로 그 곳을 떠나는 것이 다급한 것이었습니다.)

Task 3

Choose the correct expression.

1. I've eaten too much. I wish I (had not eaten, did not eat) so much.
2. It's about time the city (start, started) recycling.
3. I don't like my brother. He sometimes behaves as if he (be, were) my father.
4. (Had they prepared, Did they prepared) better, the team would have won the game.
5. The experts insist that the loan (would be, be) reduced.

Reading The World's Most Famous Spy

Ask most people who the world's most famous spy is, and they'll likely tell you the sometimes sensitive and endearing, sometimes ruthless and clever, British secret agent, James Bond.

Bond first appeared on the big screen in 1962's Dr. No, played by actor Sean Connery. Since then secret agent 007 has been featured in 21 official titles, and is considered the inspiration for countless other projects. Through the years, several big name actors have signed on to the Bond franchise, with Daniel Craig being the most recent. Notably, Craig's depiction of Bond in Casino Royale was the first installment of the series to be released in China, indicative of 007's undying appeal.

While people around the world have flocked to theaters for more than three decades to partake in Bond's latest adventure, it all began with a series of novels and short stories by British fiction writer, Ian Fleming. Fleming began writing the first Bond novel 10 years before his most famous character was seen on screen while vacationing in the Caribbean. Many have inquired as to the real-life inspiration for Bond, but Fleming has always denied that he existed anywhere but his imagination. Still, many devotees allege that Bond is likely a romanticized version of Fleming, who was well-known for his affection for exotic locales and beautiful women.

Translation 세상에서 가장 유명한 스파이

세상에서 가장 유명한 스파이가 누구인지 대부분의 사람들에게 물어보세요. 그러면 아마 가끔은 섬세하고 사랑스러우며 또 어떨 때는 냉혹하고 영리한 영국의 비밀요원 제임스 본드라고 대답할 겁니다.
제임스 본드는 1962년 Dr. No에서 최초로 대형 스크린에 모습을 비췄는데 그 때는 배우 숀 코너리가 주연을 맡았습니다. 그 후 비밀요원 007은 21개의 공식적인 제목을 단 영화에서 주연으로 등장했고, 다른 무수한 프로젝트의 영감이 되기도 했습니다. 수 년 동안 몇 몇 톱스타들이 Bond의 브랜드 네임에 계약을 했는데, 가장 최근에는 Daniel Craig가 이 역을 맡았습니다. 특히 그가 묘사한 Casino Royale편의 제임스 본드는 중국에 진출한 최초의 편으로, 사라지지 않는 007 시리즈의 인기를 보여줍니다.
30년이 넘도록 전 세계 사람들이 제임스 본드의 최신 모험을 함께하기 위해 극장으로 모였지만 모든 것은 영국 소설가인 Ian Fleming의 시리즈 소설과 단편소설에서 출발하였습니다. Ian Fleming은 그의 가장 인기있는 캐릭터가 스크린에 나타나기 10년 전에 캐리비안으로 휴가 가 있는 동안 최초의 본드 소설을 썼습니다. 많은 사람들이 실제 본드의 모델이 누군지 물어보았으나 Ian Fleming은 자신의 상상 속이 아닌 다른 곳에 본드가 존재한다는 사실을 항상 부인해 왔습니다. 아직도 많은 애호가들은 제임스 본드가 아마 Ian Fleming 자신의 낭만적인 버전이라고 주장하는데 그는 이국적인 장소와 아름다운 여성을 좋아하는 것으로도 유명합니다.

Comprehension Check-up

True/False

1. The popularity of the Bond character seems to be diminishing. (T / F)
2. The Bond character is based on a real life spy. (T / F)
3. Bond and his creator, Ian Fleming, share similar personality traits. (T / F)

Vocabulary Matching

1. franchise
2. partake
3. inspiration
4. ruthless

a. cruel, merciless
b. a brand name
c. motivation, influence
d. participate

Word Challenge

Quiz

Check Your Understanding: Use the words in the box to complete each of the following sentences.

imply	infer

1. I hope that you're not trying to _________ that this was my fault!
2. Please feel free to __________ your own conclusions.
3. I don't mean to __________ that we are anything more than friends.

Word Challenge

imply	Usage: While "infer" is often confused with "imply," the meanings are quite different. If a sentence or speaker implies something, information or meaning is conveyed without being stated directly. Examples: 1. The chairman's choice of words implied confidence in the initiative. (indicate or suggest) (회장의 단어 선택은 발의 안에 자신감을 나타냈습니다.) 2. A creation implies a creator. (to involve by logical necessity) (창조는 창작자를 포함합니다.)

infer	Usage: When a reader or listener infers, they draw conclusions that are not stated directly in what is said. Examples: 1. We can infer that Swift disapproved of the way Ireland's poorwere treated. (to conclude from evidence) (우리는 Swift가 아일랜드의 가난한 사람들이 대접받는 방식에 반대하는 것을 결론적으로 알 수 있습니다.) 2. Rewards often infer responsibilities. (lead to) (보상은 종종 책임감으로 이끕니다.) 3. One should not infer too much based on appearances alone. (guess, speculate) (너무 외모 하나만 바탕으로 추측하면 안 됩니다.)

Practice

Task 4

Choose the word or phrase that best completes each sentence.

1. Robbie would play tennis if he __________ a racket.
   a. has b. didn't have
   c. had d. would have

2. We were really late. I wish we __________ earlier.
   a. start b. starting
   c. will start d. had started

3. If I had had more money, I __________ a Mercedes Benz.
   a. can have bought b. will have bought
   c. would have bought d. would buy

4. You'll be in trouble if you __________ your passport.
   a. lost b. lose
   c. will lose d. had lost

5. Would you have written this essay for me if I __________ you to?
   a. ask b. has asked
   c. have asked d. had asked

Task 5

Read each sentence carefully. If it is incorrect, correct it. If the sentence is correct, leave it alone.

	correct	incorrect
1. If that coat were not so expensive, I bought it. ______________________	( )	( )
2. If you should run into Bill, tell him to come by my office. ______________________	( )	( )
3. The teacher requested that her students read lots of books. ______________________	( )	( )
4. If I were not sick, I would have met you yesterday. ______________________	( )	( )
5. It's boring to live in the countryside. I wish I live in a big city. ______________________	( )	( )

Culture Corner

식품관련 복지 정책

미국의 사회복지 정책 중 좋은 평가를 받고 있고 우리나라에도 도입필요성이 제기되고 있는 복지사업 가운데, The Special Supplemental Nutrition Program for Women, Infants, and Children (여성, 유아 그리고 아동을 위한 특별 영양 프로그램) 줄여서 WIC 라는 프로그램이 있습니다. WIC는 low-income families (저소득층)의 임신한 여성이나 5세 이하 아동을 위해 우유, 분유, 치즈, 주스, 계란 등을 무료로 지급하는 제도입니다. 이 시기의 영양상태가 평생 건강을 좌우한다는 이론을 배경으로, 이 시기에 무료로 우유 등을 제공해 줌으로써 나중에 저소득층에게 들어갈 의료비용을 줄일 수 있다는 명분 하에 실시되고 있습니다.

미국에는 또 정부가 low-income families를 위하여 시행하는 영양 관련 제도가 있는데요, 유명한 Food stamp라는 제도가 그것입니다. 식량 교환권이라고 번역할 수 있는데, 요즘에는 종이 쿠폰 대신 Electronic Benefits Transfer (EBT) 라고 하는 카드를 많이 사용하는 추세입니다. 이 식량 교환권을 내면 원하는 곳에서 식료품을 구입할 수 있습니다. 물론 nonfood item (비식품) 즉, 애완동물 사료, 비누, 문구류나 술 같은 제품은 살 수 없도록 제한하고 있습니다. 이 밖에도 미국에는 food banking (식품 기부) 라는 제도가 있습니다. 사람들이 통조림과 면류 등 유통기한이 장기간인 제품을 food banking organization에 기부하면 이것이 저소득층 가족들에게 제공되는 형태인데 학교에서 기부 받는 날을 정하여 식품을 모으거나 혹은 교회 같은 곳에서 식품을 모으기도 합니다. 이것은 1960년대에 시작되어 현재는 America's second harvest 라는 이름의 전국적인 organization으로 발전하였는데 연방 정부의 지원 없이 지역 봉사 단체의 도움으로 전국적으로 끼니를 해결 못하는 가난한 사람들에게 무료로 식품을 공급해 줍니다.

- Around the holidays, many schools sponsor food drives.
- Food banks distribute food and other essentials to needy families.

Wrap-up

Key sentences

1. 가정법 과거와 가정법 과거완료
   - If I were in your position, I would make the same choice.
   - If the police had caught him sooner, this incident might have been prevented.
   - If he had secured this contract, he'd be receiving the promotion.
   - If it weren't for your brilliant work, we would have lost this contract.

2. 가정법 미래와 if의 생략
   - If you should have any questions, let my secretary know.
   - If you should run into Tom, tell him to come to my office.
   - Had I had enough money, I could have lent him some.
   - I recommend that you serve as Vice President of Marketing for our Asia Division.

3. 가정법의 다른 구문

- I wish it were not this way.
- I felt as though I were watching myself at your age.
- I think it's about time you got a promotion.

REVIEW TEST

Choose the best answer to complete each of the following sentences. (1-5)

1. ____________ your help, I would fail in my business.
   (1) In (2) To (3) With (4) Without

2. If I ___________ the lotto, I would donate to the CUFS fund.
   (1) win (2) won (3) should win (4) might win

3. If you _____________ more careful, you wouldn't have lost the bag.
   (1) are (2) have be (3) would be (4) had been

4. I proposed that the vote a secret ballot.
   (1) is (2) be (3) will be (4) would be

5. I wish I ___________ to play a musical instrument when I was young.
   (1) should be (2) learn (3) had learned (4) learned

Change the verbs in the parentheses into the correct form. You can have one or two word(s) in the blank. (6-10)

6. It's time that you __________ off the TV. (turn)

7. __________ it not for water, life would not exist. (be)

8. I wish I __________ spend more time with my family now. (can)

9. Ifthe user agreement __________, all subscribers will be notified via email. (change)

10. The party was great! If you __________ with us, you would have had a wonderful time. (come)

Supplementary Reading (보충 독해)

다음 글을 읽고 문제를 풀어 보세요.

Yoga in Korea

In Korea, yoga has become popular among those who desire to be healthier both physically and mentally. Rather than heavy training like weight lifting, people now prefer yoga as a gentler alternative. In addition, more and more yoga centers are opening across the country. The yoga practice consists of physical exercise (asana), breathing, (branayama) and meditation. A yoga devotee strives to live in an ongoing and progressively more joyous state of harmony. Body, mind, and emotions are brought in attunement with one another and with one's soul, or spiritual self.

Koreans' familiarity with yoga does not have a long history. In the 1960s, Buddhist monks began to incorporate yoga practices into their studies to some extent. But it wasn't until a few years ago that a wider segment of the population began to show an interest in yoga. While the media is promoting yoga as part of the health craze, and some supermodels and actresses have gotten into the "yoga business" selling books and videotapes, yoga centers are also becoming more popular. Some yoga teachers, however, express concern over the current fad of yoga in Korea, citing unqualified yoga trainers who teach yoga in fitness centers despite having studied it for just three to six months. According to an Indian saying, yoga takes at least 12 years to learn, even if a person devotes all of his or her time to it. Yoga teachers should be familiar with yoga's philosophical principles in order to guide their students in the right direction. Losing weight and correcting posture is not yoga in a strict sense. Yoga is about finding peace of mind by overcoming mental and physical obstacles.

Translation 한국의 요가

한국에서 요가는 신체적으로 그리고, 정신적으로 보다 건강해 지고 싶어하는 사람들에게 인기가 있습니다. 사람들은 이제 역도 같은 격한 운동 보다는 좀더 부드러운 운동으로서 요가를 선호합니다 나아가 요가 센터들도 전국적으로 점점 더 많이 생겨나고 있습니다. 요가 수련은 신체 운동(아사나), 호흡(브라나야마), 그리고 명상으로 이루어 집니다. 요가 수련자들은 계속해서 그리고 점점 더 행복한 조화의 상태에서 살아가려고 애씁니다. 이를 통해서 몸, 정신, 감정이 서로서로와 또한 자신의 영혼, 즉 영적 자아와도 조화를 이루게 됩니다.

한국인들에게 요가가 알려진 것은 그리 오래 전 일이 아닙니다. 1960년대에 불교 스님들이 그들의 수행에 요가 수련을 어느 정도 넣기 시작했습니다. 그러나 몇 년 전까지는 많은 사람들이 요가에 관심을 보이지 않았습니다. 대중 매체들이 건강 유행에 대한 일부로 요가를 부추기고, 몇몇 슈퍼 모델들과 여배우들이 요가관련 책과 비디오를 팔아 '요가 산업'에 뛰어드는 동안 요가 센터들은 더욱 인기를 얻게 되었습니다. 그러나 몇몇 요가 숙련자들은, 겨우 3개월에서 6개월 정도를 배워서 헬스 클럽 등에서 요가를 가르치는 무자격 요가 강사들을 예로 들면서, 최근 한국에서의 요가 유행에 대해 우려를 표합니다. 한 인도의 격언에 따르면, 요가는 어떤 사람이 자신의 온 시간을 수련에 투자한다 하더라도 12년은 족히 걸린다고 합니다. 요가 강사들이 수강생들을 제대로 이끌어 주기 위해서는 요가의 철학적인 면에 대해 잘 알아야 합니다. 단순히 살을 빼거나 자세를 교정하는 것은 엄격히 말해 요가가 아닙니다. 요가는 정신적, 육체적인 장애를 극복함으로써 마음의 평화를 찾는 것입니다.

Explanation

1. Rather than heavy training like weight lifting, people now prefer yoga as a gentler alternative.

이 문장의 주어는 people, 동사는 prefer인데 rather than heavy training like weight lifting이 문두로 와서 topicalize된 것입니다. 즉, 구를 강조하기 위해 문장의 맨 앞으로 전치를 시킨 겁니다. 'prefer A rather than B' 라고 하면, 'B보다 오히려(차라리) A를 선호하다.'란 의미입니다.

Ex) I prefer this red T-shirt rather than that pink one.
(저 핑크색 티셔츠 보다는 차라리 이 빨간색 셔츠가 낫겠어요.)

2. Yoga practice consists of physical exercise (asana), breathing (branayama) and meditation.

consists of는 'of 이하의 것들로 이루어져 있다.'는 의미입니다.
be composed of~ 도 같은 뜻이므로 함께 알아두시면 좋겠습니다.

Ex) Most chapters consist of several practice tests.
(대부분의 단원들은 몇 개의 연습 문제들로 이루어져 있습니다.)

3. A yoga devotee strives to live in an ongoing and progressively more joyous state of harmony. Body, mind, and emotions are brought into attunement with one another and with one's soul, or spiritual self.

strive to는 try to(~하려고 애쓰다)보다 훨씬 강한 의미로, '어려운 일을 달성하기 위해 진지하게 온갖 노력을 다하다' 라는 뜻입니다.
두 번째 문장은 'by + 행위자' 가 생략된 수동태 문장입니다. 능동태 문장에서 주어인 행위자가 별로 중요하지 않거나, 불분명하거나, 의도적으로 가리고 싶을 때는 수동태 문장을 씁니다. attunement는 '조화, 조율' 의 의미이므로, be brought into attunement with는 '~와 조화를 이루게 되다' 라는 뜻입니다.

Ex) We should strive to build a more peaceful world.
(우리는 더 평화로운 세계를 만들기 위해 노력해야 합니다.)

Ex) No smoking is allowed in this area.
(이 곳은 금연 구역입니다.)

4. Some yoga teachers, however, express concern over the current fad of yoga in Korea, citing unqualified yoga trainers who teach yoga in fitness centers despite having studied it for just three to six months.

express concern over ~는 '~에 대해 걱정, 우려를 표하다' 입니다.
citing 이하는 분사구문입니다. 주절의 주어인 some yoga teachers와 종속절의 주어가 같기 때문에 생략하고 분사구문으로 바꾼 것입니다.

Ex) Environmentalists express concern over the future of earth.
(환경학자들은 지구의 미래에 대해 우려 합니다.)

Ex) He explained it at length, citing specific cases.
(그는 구체적인 경우를 예로 들면서, 그것을 상세하게 설명했습니다.)

5. According to an Indian saying, yoga takes at least 12 years to learn, even if a person devotes all of his or her time to it.

'according to~'는 '~에 따르면'이라는 뜻입니다. 여기에서 if절은 even if~와 마찬가지로 '~하더라도'라는 의미의 양보절로 쓰였습니다.

Ex) According to the weather report, it will rain tomorrow. (일기예보에 따르면 내일 비가 올 것입니다.)

Q.1 Choose the answer that best describes the meaning of each underlined word.

1. I have no alternative.
   (a) something considered to be very significant
   (b) something you treat as more important than anything else
   (c) a choice among other options
   (d) something considered to have little importance, value, or significance

2. I like to <u>meditate</u> before an important exam.
   (a) to think deeply, usually in silence
   (b) to try to settle an argument between more than two people or groups
   (c) to prescribe medicine that is used to cure or treat illness
   (d) to make people behave in a violent or illegal way

3. Buddhist <u>monks</u> lead simple lives.
   (a) a member of a female political group
   (b) a person who predicts something will happen in the future
   (c) a member of a male religious community
   (d) a person who is chosen to make decisions on behalf of other people

4. Mini skirts are the <u>fad</u> now.
   (a) a custom or belief that has existed for a long time
   (b) something that is very popular for a short time
   (c) a set of principles or beliefs, especially religious ones
   (d) something that is used to clean or protect things

5. Ann was a <u>devotee</u> of Buddhism.
   (a) a person who is most successful
   (b) a person who has suffered as a result of someone else's actions
   (c) a person who has a legal right to vote in an election
   (d) a person who is very enthusiastic about something

6. We have managed to <u>overcome</u> the first obstacle.
   (a) to keep leaving things you should do until later
   (b) to succeed in dealing with a problem
   (c) to stay somewhere, such as a friend's home, for one night
   (d) to create a particular aim or effect

Q.2 Mark True(T) or False(F).

1. Yoga is more effective for losing weight than heavy training like weight lifting.
2. In recent years, the number of yoga centers has increased in Korea.
3. Koreans' familiarity with yoga has a long history.
4. In the 1960s, some Buddhist monks began to teach yoga to believers.
5. In Korea, some unqualified trainers teach yoga in fitness centers.
6. It takes less than 10 months to master yoga.
7. In principle, yoga helps people lose weight and it corrects their posture.

Prepositions 11 Unit

Introduction

Topic: Reunited At Last (마침내 화해하다)

Lesson objectives:

Prepositions (전치사)

- Prepositions: time, place, direction (시간, 장소, 방향 전치사)
- Prepositions: theme, cause, job, etc. (다른 전치사: 주제, 원인, 직업 등)
- Usage of prepositions (전치사 용법)

WARM-UP

Things are going pretty well for Brett these days. He seems to have gotten over Camille and has decided that it might be time to patch things up with Aaron. Can he salvage their friendship? Let's find out.

Brett : I'm glad you came.
Aaron : I'd rather be at home. (preposition: at)
Brett : I want to talk about the argument we had. (preposition: about)
Aaron : Okay. What about it?
Brett : Well, first, I'm sorry.
Aaron : That's a good start.
Brett : You know, we've been friends since we were kids. (conjunction: since)
Aaron : Yes, I know.
Brett : And I don't think good friends should ever fight over a girl. (preposition: over)
Aaron : Perhaps you're right.
Brett : And we've never had a fight before; never.

Aaron : That's true.

Brett : And I won't interfere with your relationship with Camille anymore. I promise. (preposition: with)

Aaron : It doesn't matter now.

Brett : What do you mean?

Aaron : She left for Europe yesterday. (preposition: for)

Brett : Is she coming back?

Aaron : I have no idea.

Brett : This seems so sudden.

Aaron : It surprised me, too.

Brett : What is she doing there?

Aaron : She's the centerpiece of a huge modeling campaign. (preposition: of)

Brett : So, that's it?

Aaron : I think so. The next time I see her will probably be on a billboard or in a magazine. (preposition: on, in)

Brett : Are you still mad, then?

Aaron : No. I forgive you. But feel free to show how sorry you are by buying dinner. (preposition: by)

Brett : You got it. Despite your troubles, I'm glad we got to talk things over. (preposition: despite)

Aaron : Me, too. Let's go get something to eat.

Translation

최근 Brett의 일이 꽤 잘 풀리고 있습니다. 그는 Camille과의 문제는 해결한 듯 보이고 Aaron과의 일을 수습할 때가 되었다고 결심하게 됩니다. Brett은 그들의 우정을 회복할 수 있을까요? 알아봅시다.

Brett : 와 줘서 고마워.

Aaron : 차라리 집에 있을 것 그랬다.

Brett : 전에 우리가 했던 논쟁에 대해 이야기를 했으면 해.

Aaron : 좋아. 뭔데?

Brett : 음, 먼저 미안하다.

Aaron : 시작은 괜찮네.

Brett : 너도 알다시피 우린 어릴 때부터 친구였잖아.
Aaron : 그래, 알지.
Brett : 내 생각에 여자 때문에 싸우는 건 진정한 친구가 아닌 것 같아.
Aaron : 아마 그럴지도 모르지.
Brett : 그리고 우리 예전에는 한 번도 안 싸웠잖아. 절대로.
Aaron : 맞아.
Brett : 너와 Camille 사이에 다시는 끼어들지 않을게. 약속해
Aaron : 이제 상관없어.
Brett : 무슨 말이야?
Aaron : Camille은 어제 유럽으로 떠났어.
Brett : 다시 돌아온대?
Aaron : 모르겠어.
Brett : 너무 갑작스럽네.
Aaron : 나도 놀랐어.
Brett : 거기서 그녀가 무엇을 하는데?
Aaron : 큰 규모의 모델 캠페인에서 가장 중요한 역할인가 봐.
Brett : 그래서 그게 다야?
Aaron : 그런 것 같아. 아마도 다음에 내가 그녀를 보는 건 광고 게시판이나 잡지에서 일거야.
Brett : 아직도 화났어?
Aaron : 아냐. 용서할게. 하지만 저녁을 사는 것으로 네가 얼마나 미안한 마음을 갖고 있는지 보여줘도 돼.
Brett : 알았어. 너한테 좀 안 좋은 일이 있긴 하지만 그래도 이렇게 얘기해서 기쁘다.
Aaron : 나도 그래. 뭐 먹으러 가자.

Comprehension Check

1. Which of the following best describes Aaron's tone throughout most of the dialogue?
   (a) reluctant
   (b) cordial
   (c) furious
   (d) warm

2. What does Brett promise to do?
   (a) to stop calling Camille
   (b) to buy Aaron a celebration dinner
   (c) to give Aaron and Camille privacy
   (d) to end the friendship on good terms

3. Which is NOT a reason Brett gives for ending the feud?

(a) that the guys have never quarreled before

(b) that Camille is out of the picture

(c) that friendship is more important than a crush

(d) that their friendship is a longstanding one

Useful Expressions

In this dialogue	Explanation
1. I don't think good friends should ever fight over a girl.	1. In today's dialogue, Brett tells us that good friends shouldn't quarrel over a girl at any time, under any circumstances. Of course, he could have also said, "Good friends should never fight over a girl." Use this construction to express ideas you believe to be universally true. (1) I don't think it's ever right to steal. (2) It's not ever a good idea to lie to someone you love.
2. I won't interfere with your relationship with Camille anymore. I promise.	2. In this week's dialogue, Brett tells Aaron that he'll stop trying to come between him and Camille. The verb phrase "interfere with" might be new to some of you, so let's take a look at a few additional examples. (1) Cell phones can interfere with the proper functioning of airline equipment. (2) I would prefer that my mother didn't interfere with my personal life.
3. She's the centerpiece of a huge modeling campaign.	3. Centerpieces aren't just for dinner tables. Let's a take a look at some other instances where this word is used to mean "the most central or important feature." (1) An Italian sculpture will serve as the centerpiece of the design. (2) Health care reform was the centerpiece of his last campaign.

In this dialogue	Explanation
4. The next time I see her will probably be on a billboard or in a magazine.	4. If you recall, we took a detailed look at the varied usage of "see" earlier this semester. One of the uses we learned was "to meet and converse with." Aaron tells us a bit spitefully that he probably won't meet Camille in person anytime soon, but he might come across one of her photos. In this case, "see" takes on a double meaning. Here, it means both "to read or view" and to "meet or visit."

Grammar

Focus 1 Prepositions– time, place, direction

(시간, 장소, 방향 전치사)

01 시간 표시 전치사

(1) 시간: at, on, in

① at은 때의 한 순간이나 시각을 나타냅니다.

- We went out for a walk at night.
  (우리는 밤에 산책을 하러 나갔습니다.)
- I'll leave at ten tomorrow morning.
  (나는 내일 아침 10시에 떠날 것입니다.)
- Let's meet at lunch time.
  (점심시간에 만납시다.)

② on은 날짜, 요일 등 특정한 날을 나타냅니다.

- His birthday is on May 22nd.
  (그의 생일은 5월 22일입니다.)
- We'll see her (on) the following evening.
  (우리는 그녀를 내일 저녁에 볼 것입니다.)

- I'd like to go to the park on Saturday, but it's supposed to rain all weekend.
  (토요일에 공원가고 싶지만 주말 내내 비가 올 거랍니다.)
- On an average day, more than 10,000 people visit the Colosseum.
  (하루평균 10,000명 이상의 사람이 콜로세움에 방문합니다.)

cf) 월 만을 이야기 할 때엔 in을 사용하지만 월, 일을 다 말할 경우 on을 사용합니다.
Ex) in August, on August 20th, on the 20th of August

③ in은 년, 월, 계절 등 비교적 긴 시간이나 하루 중의 한 부분을 나타냅니다.

- In summer I like to go surfing.
  (나는 여름에 서핑 하러 가는 것을 좋아합니다.)
- In 1521, Magellan was killed in a fight that broke out on the Spice Islands.
  (1521년에 Magellan은 Spice Islands에서 발생한 싸움에 목숨을 잃었습니다.)
- I should be there in an hour or two. (= an hour or two from now)
  (나는 한 두 시간 후에 거기에 있을 겁니다.)

cf) 밤은 at과 사용하는 반면 오전, 오후, 저녁은 in과 함께 사용합니다.
Ex) at night, in the morning, in the afternoon, in the evening
cf) on time은 '정각에' 라는 뜻이고, in time은 '시간에 늦지 않게, 알맞은 때' 라는 뜻입니다.
ex) The 9:15 train left on time. (9시 15분 기차가 정시에 출발했습니다.)
ex) I hope the parcel will arrive in time. (그 소포가 늦지 않게 도착했으면 좋겠습니다.)

(2) 기간: for, during

① for는 '~동안' 이라는 시간의 길이를 나타내고, 숫자가 포함된 기간에 자주 사용됩니다.

- My family will be in France for a year.
  (우리 가족은 프랑스에서 1년간 있을 것입니다.)
- We've been waiting for approval for more than 90 days.
  (우리는 승인이 나기를 90일이 넘도록 기다려 왔습니다.)
- Bake at 350 degrees for 25 minutes.
  (350도에서 25분간 구우시오.)
- Cell phone use is not permitted for the duration of the flight.
  (비행하는 동안에는 핸드폰 사용이 금지됩니다.)

② during은 특정한 기간을 나타냅니다.

- We hope you will have a good time during your stay.
  (우리는 당신이 머무르는 동안 즐거운 시간을 보내기를 바랍니다.)

- Women who smoke during pregnancy run a greater risk of complications.
  (임신했을 때 흡연을 하는 여성은 합병증이 생길 위험이 큽니다.)
- Support among union workers diminished significantly during the course of the campaign.
  (그 캠페인이 진행되는 동안 조합원들 사이에서의 지지가 급격히 감소했습니다.)

(3) 기한: till/until/up to, by

till과 until은 '~까지' 라는 어느 시간까지의 동작이나 상태의 계속을 나타냅니다. by는 '~까지, ~보다 늦지 않게'라는 뜻으로 동작 또는 상태가 완료되는 시점을 나타냅니다. '~부터 ~까지'라는 뜻으로 from~ to/until/till~ 라는 표현을 쓰기도 합니다.

- The new timetable will remain in operation till/until June 30th.
  (새 시간표는 6월 30일까지 시행될 것입니다.)
- Can you get here by noon?
  (12시 까지 여기에 올 수 있습니까?)

cf) Can you get here until noon? (x)

- They usually work from nine to/until/till five.
  (그들은 보통 9시 에서 5시 까지 일합니다.)
- This policy will remain in effect until further notice.
  (이 정책은 다른 공지가 있을 때까지 유효할 겁니다.)
- It may take up to three weeks to process your application.
  (당신의 지원서를 처리하는데 최대 3주가 걸릴 수 있습니다.

(4) since

'~이래로' 라는 뜻으로 주절에 완료형이 자주 쓰입니다. 물론 주절에 현재형이나 과거형이 올 수도 있습니다.

- Since last Sunday, I haven't been able to stop thinking about you.
  (저번 일요일 이래로 줄곧 당신 생각을 하고 있습니다.)
- We've been best friends since freshman year of high school.
  (우리는 고등학교 1학년일 때부터 매우 친한 친구입니다.)

cf) You know, we've been friends since we were kids. (since - 접속사)
(당신도 알다시피, 우리는 어린 아이였을 때부터 친구로 지냈습니다.)

02 장소 표시 전치사

(1) at, on, in

① at: '~에' 라는 뜻으로 비교적 좁은 장소나 지점을 나타냅니다.

② on: '~(위)에' 라는 뜻으로 표면에 접촉된 상태에서의 위를 나타냅니다.

③ in: '~에' 라는 뜻으로 나라, 도시 같은 비교적 넓은 장소나 지역을 나타냅니다.

- I'd rather be at home.
  (집에 있는 편이 나을 것 그랬습니다.)
- The fair was held at the park.
  (축제는 공원에서 열렸습니다.)
- Turn right at the next corner.
  (다음 길모퉁이에서 우회전을 하세요.)
- The next time I see her will probably be on a billboard or in a magazine.
  (아마도 다음 번엔 그녀를 광고게시판이나 잡지에서 보게 될 것 같습니다.)
- There's a big spider on the ceiling.
  (천장에 큰 거미가 있습니다.)
- I'm pretty sure that I lost my wallet somewhere on campus.
  (내가 캠퍼스 어딘가에서 지갑을 잃어버렸다고 확신합니다.)
- The 2008 Olympic Games were held in Beijing.
  (2008년 올림픽 경기는 베이징에서 열렸습니다.)
- This is the best deal you'll find at any retailer in the city.
  (당신이 이 도시에서 찾을 수 있는 어떤 소매상인과도 이렇게 좋은 거래는 할 수 없을 겁니다.)

(2) before, after, in front of, behind, at the back of

'앞에, 뒤에' 라는 의미입니다.

- My mother has never cried in front of me.
  (우리 어머니는 제 앞에서 우신 적이 한 번도 없습니다.)
- David is running behind Jane.
  (David은 Jane 뒤에서 달리고 있습니다.)
- There's an interesting story behind her nickname. (There's an interesting story about how she got her nickname.)
  (그녀의 별명에 얽힌 재미있는 사연이 있습니다.)
- The food court is at the back of the store.
  (푸드코트는 그 가게 뒤에 있습니다.)

(3) above, over, below, under

above는 '(전체적으로, 먼 거리) ~보다 위쪽에, (수량 등이) ~을 넘는' 이라는 뜻이고, over는 '(수직으로) ~바로 위에' 라는 뜻입니다. below와 under도 비슷한 관계에 있습니다. 즉, below가 '(먼 거리) ~보다 아래에' 라는 뜻이고, under는 '(수직으로) ~바로 아래에' 라는 뜻입니다.

- We saw the moon above the hill.
  (우리는 언덕 위의 달을 보았습니다.)

- The current temperature is just above zero.

(현재 기온은 0도를 살짝 넘습니다.)

- There is a bridge over the river.

(강 위로 다리가 있습니다.)

- Parts of Holland are below sea level.

(네덜란드의 일부분은 해수면보다 낮습니다.)

- Nearly 20 percent of the population lives below the poverty line.

(인구의 거의 20퍼센트는 빈곤선 이하의 삶을 삽니다.)

- She is hiding under the tree.

(그녀는 나무 밑에 숨어 있습니다.)

(4) by, beside, near, close to

'곁에, 옆에, 근처에, 가까운 곳에' 라는 의미를 지니고 있습니다.

- My parents have a house by the lake.

(우리 부모님께서는 호수 옆에 집을 한 채 갖고 계십니다.)

- There's a small café beside the highway where a lot of travelers stop before crossing the border.

(많은 여행객들이 국경선을 넘어가기 전에 멈추게 되는 큰 길 옆에 조그만 카페가 하나 있습니다.)

- Why is it warmer near the equator?

(왜 적도 부근은 더 따뜻할까요?)

cf) besides는 '~외에도' 하는 뜻으로 이미 알려진 것에 덧붙여 다른 것을 말할 때 쓰입니다.

– Besides having a very influential father, what has he accomplished in life?
(매우 영향력 있는 아버지를 둔 것 외에 그는 삶에서 무엇을 성취했습니까?)

(5) between, among

between는 '둘 사이'라는 뜻입니다. 따라서 둘을 뜻하는 복수형, 또는 둘을 연결하는 and가 있는 목적어가 뒤따릅니다. among은 '셋 이상의 사이에' 라는 뜻입니다. 그러나 구어체에서는 셋 이상의 경우에도 확연히 구분할 수 있는 것에는 between을 쓰고, 집단이나 무리를 가리킬 때는 among을 씁니다.

- Sweden is located between Norway and Finland.

(스웨덴은 노르웨이와 핀란드 사이에 놓여 있습니다.)

- The house was hidden among the trees.

(그 집은 나무 사이에 가려졌었습니다.)

- Latvia is located among the Northern European Baltic states.

(Latvia는 북유럽 발트 제국들 사이에 위치해 있습니다.)

(6) across, along, through

across는 '~의 건너편에' 라는 뜻이고, along은 '~을 따라서' 라는 뜻입니다.

through는 '~을 통과하여, 지나서' 라는 의미입니다.

- It is prohibited to carry certain agricultural products across international borders.
  (특정 농산품을 지니고 국경선을 넘는 것은 금지되어 있습니다.)

- The stores along Fifth Avenue are known all over the world.
  (5번가를 따라 있는 가게들은 전 세계적으로 알려져 있습니다.)
- Lake Powell spans almost 200 miles through northern Arizona and Utah.
  (Powell호는 북부 아리조나와 유타를 통과하여 거의 200 마일에 이릅니다.)

03 방향 표시 전치사

(1) to, for, toward

① to: '~쪽으로' 라는 방향을 나타냅니다.

② for:'~을 향하여' 라는 목적지를 나타냅니다.

③ toward:'~ 쪽으로, ~을 향하여' 라는 운동의 방향을 나타냅니다. '~ 쪽으로' 향하는 것이지 그 지점에 도달 여부와는 관계가 없는 표현입니다.

- I'd like to go to Jamaica this winter if I can get some time off from work.
  (이번 겨울에 직장에서 휴가를 얻을 수 있다면 자메이카에 가고 싶습니다.)
- She left for Europe yesterday.
  (그녀는 어제 유럽으로 떠났습니다.)
- My older brother is leaving for the army this week.
  (우리 형은 이번 주에 입대할 겁니다.)
- It's time to start moving toward sustainable energy solutions.
  (고갈되지 않는 에너지 해결책을 향해 움직이기 시작할 때입니다.)
- It's getting late; we should probably start heading toward home.
  (날이 어두워지고 있습니다. 집에 가야 할 것 같습니다.)

(2) onto, into

'~에 , ~로' 라는 이동의 방향을 나타내는 말로, 구어체에서 on과 in으로 대치됩니다.

- We turned onto a dark side street on the outskirts of the city.
  (우리는 도시 변두리의 어두운 거리로 들어섰습니다.)

- The economy officially went into recession in the fourth quarter of last year.
  (공식 발표상으로 작년 제4사분기의 경제는 불황기에 접어들었습니다.)
- Passersby often toss spare change into the fountain.
  (행인들은 종종 여분의 잔돈을 분수대 안으로 던집니다.)

(3) up, down

up은 '~의 위로', down은 '~아래로' 라는 뜻으로 운동의 방향을 나타냅니다.

- I started to feel nervous as I walked up the stairs and onto the stage.
  (계단을 올라 무대위로 가면서 나는 긴장하기 시작했습니다.)
- I think the restaurant you're looking for is further down the road.
  (당신이 찾고 있는 식당은 더 내려가야 할 것 같습니다.)

(4) around

around는 '~의 주위에, ~을 둘러싸고 ~의 주위를 돌아' 라는 뜻이고, 시간을 나타내는 말과 함께 쓰일 때는 '~무렵, ~경' 이라는 뜻이 됩니다.

- A crowd of onlookers began to gather around the scene of the accident.
  (한 무리의 구경꾼들이 그 사고 현장 주위로 모이기 시작했습니다.)
- The number of tourists usually drops off around this time of year.
  (해마다 이맘때면 관광객의 수는 보통 줄어듭니다.)

Task 1

Choose the correct preposition to complete each of the following sentences.

through	across	since	on	at

1. I plan to eat lunch __________ noon.
2. It has been a long time __________ the last meeting.
3. __________ a hot day like today, I like to sleep under a big tree.
4. It costs two dollars to drive __________ the tunnel.
5. I swam ______ the river to get to the other side.

Focus 2 Prepositions– theme, cause, job, etc.

(주제, 원인, 직업, 수단, 양보, 예외, 재료, 대가를 나타내는 전치사)

01 주제: about, on, of

'~에 관하여' 라는 뜻을 가지고 있습니다.

- I want to talk about the argument we had.
  (나는 우리가 했던 논쟁에 대해서 말하고 싶습니다.)
- I wrote an article on/ about the environment.
  (나는 환경에 관한 글을 썼습니다.)
- What do you think of/ about his offer?
  (그의 제의에 대해 어떻게 생각하십니까?)
- My grandfather talks fondly of his childhood in Germany.
  (우리 할아버지께서는 독일에서의 어린시절에 대해 다정하게 말씀하십니다.)

02 원인: from, of, at, over, for, with

from: 직접적 원인

of: 사망이나 병의 원인

at: 감정의 원인 '~을 보고서 (듣고서) 기쁘다(슬프다)'

over: 감정이나 행위의 원인 '~로 인해서'

for: 행위의 이유 '~때문에'

with: 행위의 원인 '~때문에 (추위, 두려움, 무서움, 흥분)'

- He suffered from a bad headache.
  (그는 심한 두통으로 고통을 받았습니다.)
- He died of lung cancer.
  (그는 폐암으로 죽었습니다.)
- I feel like I'm going to faint at the first sight of blood.
  (피를 처음 보면 난 기절할 것 같습니다.)
- I don't think good friends should ever fight over a girl.
  (진정한 친구는 여자 때문에 싸워서는 안 된다고 생각합니다.)
- It would be a shame to end a lifelong friendship over such a petty disagreement.
  (그런 사소한 의견차이로 평생의 우정을 끝내는 것은 부끄러운 일일 것입니다.)

- I'm sorry for being late.

(늦어서 미안합니다.)

- She was shuddering with cold.

(그녀는 추위로 인해 떨고 있었습니다.)

cf) 원인이나 이유를 나타내는 전치사구에는 because of, on account of, owing to, due to 등이 있습니다.

- It is sad to see a child held back because of an illness.
  (병 때문에 제지를 당하는 아이를 보는 것은 슬픈 일입니다.)
- We'll have to postpone this year's carnival on account of the rain.
  (우리는 비 때문에 올해의 축제를 연기해야 할 것입니다.)
- The chairman was forced to resign, owing to pressure from shareholders.
  (그 회장은 주주들의 압력 때문에 퇴임하도록 요구되었습니다.)
- The price of imported goods is likely to increase due to fluctuations in the exchange rate.
  (수입품 가격은 환율변동으로 인해 오를 것 같습니다.)

03 직업, 소속: at, of, to, in, with

- I'm no longer at that company.

(나는 더 이상 그 회사에서 일하지 않습니다.)

- She is the centerpiece of a huge modeling campaign.

(그녀는 규모가 큰 모델 캠페인의 가장 중요한 인물입니다.)

- Vladimir Putin is prime minister of Russia.

(Vladimir Putin은 러시아의 총리입니다.)

- She is the secretary to our Dean.

(그녀는 우리 학장의 비서입니다.)

- I used to work in publishing.

(나는 출판업계에서 일하곤 했습니다.)

- Alex Rodriquez is no longer with the Seattle Mariners.

(Alex Rodriquez는 더 이상 Seattle Mariners에서 뛰지 않습니다.)

04 수단: by, with, through

① by: (수단, 방법) '~으로, 에 의하여'

② with: (도구) '~을 가지고, ~으로'

③ through: (매개, 수단) '을 통하여'

- My friends and I went there by bus and returned by taxi.

(내 친구들과 나는 버스를 타고 그곳에 갔다가 택시를 타고 돌아왔습니다.)

- The Hyundai Genesis is powered by a 3.8 liter V6 engine.
  (현대 제네시스는 3.8 리터 V6엔진으로 가동됩니다.)
- In most major cities, it's often faster to go through a real estate agent than look for an apartment on your own.
  (대부분의 주요도시에서는 혼자 아파트를 구하는 것보다 부동산을 통하는 것이 종종 더 빠릅니다.)
- The man was killed with/ by a gun.
  (그 남자는 총을 맞아 죽었습니다.)

05 양보: in spite of, despite, for, with all, for all

- The train was one hour late. In spite of this, we managed to get to the meeting in time.
  (기차는 한 시간이 늦었습니다. 이것에도 불구하고 우리는 제 때에 회의에 도착할 수 있었습니다.)
- Despite your troubles, I'm glad we got to talk things over.
  (비록 당신에게 어려운 일이 있지만, 우리가 이야기를 하게 되어서 기쁩니다.)
- He was found innocent, despite the overwhelming evidence against him.
  (압도적인 증거에도 불구하고 그는 무죄인 것으로 밝혀졌습니다.)
- With all (of) his faults, I still like him.
  (그의 단점에도 불구하고, 난 여전히 그를 좋아합니다.)
- For all his faults, he's basically a good person.
  (그의 모든 잘못에도 불구하고 기본적으로 그는 좋은 사람입니다.)

06 예외: except, except for, but

- I saw all (of) the pieces of art in the gallery except for Picasso's Dream.
  (나는 미술관에서 피카소의 "꿈"을 제외하고 모든 작품을 관람하였습니다.)
- That doesn't happen anywhere except in the movies.
  (그것은 영화가 아닌 다른 곳에서는 일어나지 않습니다.)
- Everybody's here but George.
  (George를 제외한 모두가 여기에 있습니다.)

07 재료: of, from/out of, with

원료를 나타낼 때는 from, 재료를 나타낼 때는 of를 씁니다. 일상체에서는 out of를 쓰기도 합니다.

- Numerous household items are made of plastic.
  (수많은 가정용품들은 플라스틱으로 만들어집니다.)
- Wine is made from grapes.
  (와인은 포도로 만듭니다.)
- Architects Jinhee Park and John Hong built their Cambridge, Massachusetts home out of more than 600,000 pounds of recycled materials.
  (건축가인 박진희와 John Hong은 60만 파운드 이상의 재활용 물질로 Massachusetts주의 Cambridge 집을 만들었습니다.)
- Some scientists have claimed that the pyramids of Egypt were actually built with concrete and not stones.
  (일부 과학자들은 이집트의 피라미드가 사실 돌이 아니라 콘크리트로 지어졌다고 주장합니다.)

08 대가: at, for

- He bought the house at a good price.
  (그는 좋은 가격에 그 집을 샀습니다.)
- I paid $200 for the camcorder.
  (나는 그 캠코더를 사는데 200불을 지불했습니다.)
- In 2007, Microsoft offered more than $44 billion for Yahoo.
  (2007년에 마이크로소프트는 야후를 사들이기 위해서 440억 달러 이상을 제안하였습니다.)

Task 2

Read each sentence carefully and decide whether the preposition is used correctly or incorrectly.

	correct	incorrect
1. He gave a lecture on environmental issues. ____	( )	( )
2. There is a bridge on the lake. ____	( )	( )
3. In spite my good intentions, everything went wrong. ____	( )	( )
4. If you have any trouble, you can reach me at this number. ____	( )	( )
5. I'm afraid from being left by myself. ____	( )	( )

Focus 3 Usage of prepositions (전치사의 용법)

01 전치사의 목적어

전치사 뒤에 오는 목적어는 목적격이어야 하며, 전치사의 목적어에는 명사, 대명사, 명사 상당어구(동명사, 부정사)가 옵니다.

- I am happy for your success.
  (나는 당신의 성공을 기쁘게 생각합니다.)
- Feel free to show how sorry you are by buying dinner.
  (저녁을 사는 것으로 당신이 얼마나 미안한 마음을 갖고 있는지 보여주셔도 됩니다.)

- He left without saying good-bye.

  (그는 작별 인사도 없이 떠났습니다.)

- That's good except that it is too long.

  (너무 길다는 것을 제외하고 그것은 좋습니다.)

- There was nothing we could do but offer a few kind words.

  (몇 마디 다정한 말을 건네는 것 외에 우리가 할 수 있는 일은 아무것도 없었습니다.)

- He had no choice but to accept the offer.

  (그는 그 제안을 받아들일 수 밖에 없었습니다.)

02 전치사의 후치

전치사는 목적어가 되는 어구 앞에 놓이지만, wh-의문문, 관계사절, 감탄문, 수동문에서는 문장 끝에 오기도 합니다.

- Which house is he staying at?

  (그가 머무는 집이 어느 집입니까?)

- You're just the person (whom) I was looking for.

  (당신은 내가 찾던 바로 그 사람입니다.)

- Music is what I live for.

  (음악은 내가 살아가는 이유입니다.)

- Where are you coming from?

  (어디서 오는중입니까?)

- She's fun to be with.

  (그녀는 같이 있으면 즐겁습니다.)

03 전치사의 생략

(1) 전치사는 다음과 같은말 앞에서는 생략됩니다.

next / last / this / some / every

today / tomorrow / yesterday

home / overseas / upstairs / downstairs

- The meeting will be held this afternoon.

  (회의는 오늘 오후에 개최될 것입니다.)

- I'm going upstairs now.

  (나는 지금 위층으로 올라갑니다.)

- Most of our clients are located overseas.
  (우리 고객의 대부분은 해외에 있습니다.)
- Sometimes I think about my friends back home.
  (때때로 나는 고향에 있는 친구들을 생각합니다.)

(2) 다음 구문에서 in은 보통 생략됩니다.

- She had trouble (in) catching a taxi.
  (그녀는 택시를 잡는데 어려움이 있었습니다.)
- He has difficulty (in) remembering names and phone numbers.
  (그는 이름과 전화번호를 기억하는 것이 어렵습니다.)
- Many small businesses are experiencing difficulty (in) securing credit.
  (많은 소규모 사업들은 대출금을 확보하는데 어려움을 겪고 있습니다.)
- Most people are too busy (in) worrying about the future to enjoy the present.
  (대부분의 사람들은 미래를 걱정하느라 너무 바빠서 현재를 즐기지 못합니다.)

03 중요 전치사구

(1) according to (~에 따라)

- According to Sabrina, you were in Paris last week.
  (Sabrina의 말에 따르면 당신은 지난 주에 파리에 있었더군요.)
- According to the new tax code, individuals with two or more children will receive a special deduction.
  (새로운 세금법에 따르면 두 명 이상의 자녀가 있는 사람들은 특별 공제를 받을 겁니다.)

(2) anxious about/for

- Many soon-to-be college graduates are anxious about their job prospects.
  (곧 졸업할 많은 대학생들이 직업 전망에 대해 걱정합니다.)
- We're all anxious for an end to this misunderstanding.
  (우리 모두는 이번 오해가 끝나기를 간절히 바랍니다.)

(3) apart from (~와 별도로)

- Apart from the obvious health risks associated with smoking, it can damage your teeth, skin, and even your fingernails.
  (흡연과 연관된 명백한 건강 위험을 별도로 하고도 흡연은 치아와 피부 그리고 심지어 손톱까지 손상시킬 수 있습니다.)

- Apart from a brief interlude in the early sixties, she's never been out of work.
  (60세 초반의 짧은 기간을 제외하고 그녀는 항상 일을 했습니다.)

(4) at the risk of (~의 위험을 무릅쓰고)

- He jumped into the river to save the boy at the risk of his own life.
  (그는 죽을 위험을 무릎 쓰고, 그 소년을 구하기 위해 강으로 뛰어들었습니다.)
- At the risk of sounding naive, can someone please give me some advice about asking a girl out?
  (비록 내가 하는 말이 고지식하게 들리겠지만 누군가 여자에게 데이트 신청하는 방법에 대해서 제게 충고해 주실 수 있습니까?)

(5) far from (~에서 멀리 / 조금도 ...않다.)

- I'm far from perfect, but you're in no position to talk. (= I'm far from perfect, but you are in no position to criticize me.)
  (내가 결코 완벽하지는 않지만 당신이 날 비판할 입장은 아닙니다.)
- He is far from being a fool.
  (그는 결코 바보가 아닙니다.)

(6) in accordance with (~에 따라서)

- We intend to finish the project in accordance with our original agreement.
  (우리는 기존 협의에 따라 프로젝트를 마칠 계획입니다.)
- The government acted in accordance with public opinion.
  (정부는 여론에 맞게 행동했습니다.)

(7) in case of (~의 경우에는, ~에 대비하여)

- It's always a good idea to carry a credit card in case of an unforeseen emergency.
  (뜻하지 않은 긴급상황에 대비하여 신용카드를 가지고 다니는 것이 좋습니다.)
- Take an umbrella with you in case of rain.
  (비가 올 경우에 대비해서 우산을 가져가세요.)

cf) I'll prepare some more food in case she comes.
(그녀가 올 경우에 대비해서 (오든 안 오든) 음식을 좀 더 준비할 것입니다.)
I'll prepare some more food if she comes.
(만약 그녀가 온다면 음식을 좀 더 준비할 것입니다.)

(8) in comparison with(to) ~와 비교해 볼 때(compared with/to)

- These petty bribes are nothing in comparison to the widespread corruption that exists throughout the region.

  (이 사소한 뇌물은 그 지역 도처에 만연하는 부패에 비하면 아무것도 아닙니다.)

- Even Tom looks small in comparison with/to John.

  (Tom도 John에 비하면 작아 보입니다.)

(9) in conclusion (결론적으로)

- In conclusion, I'd like to ask everyone to do their part in making sure that poverty in Africa becomes a thing of the past.

  (결론적으로, 나는 아프리카에서 가난이 확실히 과거의 일이 되도록 모든 사람이 자신의 본분을 다하기를 부탁드리고 싶습니다.)

- In conclusion, none of us will go.

  (결론적으로 말하면 우리 중 아무도 가지 않을 겁니다.)

(10) on behalf of (~대신해)

- A class action lawsuit has been filed on behalf of those patients who took the drug prior to its recall.

  (그 약을 회수하기 전에 이미 복용한 환자들을 대신해 집단 소송이 제기되었습니다.)

- I am appealing on behalf of the poor.

  (나는 가난한 사람들을 대신해 호소하고 있습니다.)

(11) regardless of (~에 상관없이)

- Kant argued that it is important to tell the truth, regardless of the consequences.

  (칸트는 결과에 상관없이 진실을 말하는 것이 중요하다고 주장했습니다.)

- She does as she wants regardless of others.

  (그녀는 다른 사람을 개의치 않고 자기가 하고 싶은 대로 합니다.)

(12) with regard to (~에 관해서는)

- Israel has issued a new statement with regard to the recent Hamas victory.

  (이스라엘은 최근 하마스의 승리에 대해 새로운 성명을 발표했습니다.)

- I know nothing with regard to the matter.

  (나는 그 일에 대해서는 아무 것도 모릅니다.)

Task 3

Choose the appropriate preposition.

1. (According, In accordance) to Doctor Park, I have to take this medicine (for, in) a week.
2. I cried myself (in, to) sleep because (to, of) a fight with my boyfriend.
3. (From, Due to) the storm, the plane could not land (on, for) time.
4. This letter was written (in, of) ink (by, from) my grandfather.
5. (For, In) case of an emergency, use the stairs instead (on, of) the elevator.

Reading Old Country Cuisine, New Country Concepts

The landscape of the American city is dotted with Japanese restaurants. For years, Americans have appreciated their careful simplicity and sophistication. And while some individual Korean restaurateurs have garnered praise in the past, the trend has been slow to catch on and mostly confined to neighborhoods comprising ethnic Koreans. Until now, that is.

In recent years, both second-generation Korean Americans and newer transplants have done a lot to bring Korea's culinary traditions into the mainstream. Korean and Korean American chefs are offering up new variations on traditional cuisine or drawing on other great traditions for inspiration. Whereas older generations tended to cater to fellow Koreans, the younger one is putting its familiarity with American culture to good use and reaching out to an entirely new clientele.

The Orchid restaurant in New York offers a uniquely Korean karaoke experience with a database of more than 18,000 songs, but is probably best known for its fusion of the California and Korean food heritage. On the other side of the country, in Los Angeles, people wait in line for more than an hour for tacos at the Kogi

Korean BBQ-To-Go truck, a concept that combines the flavors of Mexico and South Korea in a single tortilla shell. These spicy soft tacos, the creation of two out of work chefs, are the talk of the town lately, and it probably won't be long before Korean eateries start popping up all over the city.

Translation 고국의 요리, 새로운 나라의 발상

미국 도시의 풍경은 일본 식당으로 점재되어 있습니다. 수 년간 미국인들은 일본 식당의 꼼꼼한 간결함과 정교함을 높이 평가해 왔습니다. 과거에 몇 개의 개별적인 한국 식당들이 찬사를 받아왔으나 그 경향은 느리게 인기를 얻고 있고 대개 한국 민족으로 이루어진 이웃에 한정되어 왔습니다. 지금까지는 그렇습니다. 최근 재미교포 2세와 새 이주민들이 한국의 전통 요리법을 주류에 포함시키려고 많은 노력을 하고 있습니다. 한국인과 재미교포 주방장들은 전통 요리법에 새로운 변형을 첨가하거나 영감을 얻기 위해 다른 뛰어난 전통 요리법을 접목시킵니다. 나이든 세대는 동포인 한국인을 대상으로 하는 경향이 있었으나 젊은 세대는 미국 문화에 친숙한 것을 잘 이용하여 완전히 새로운 고객에게 다가 갑니다.
뉴욕의 Orchid 레스토랑은 독특하게 18,000곡 이상이 들어있는 한국의 노래방 체험을 제공하기도 하지만, 아마 캘리포니아와 한국 음식의 전통을 혼합한 것으로 가장 잘 알려져 있을 겁니다. 반대편에 있는 LA에서는 사람들이 Kogi Korean BBQ-To-Go에서 타코를 사려고 한 시간 넘도록 줄을 서서 기다리는데, 이것은 멕시코와 남한의 맛을 하나의 조개모양의 또르띠야 안에 혼합한 것입니다. 이 매콤하면서도 부드러운 타코는 두 실직 요리사가 만들어낸 것으로 최근 그 도시에서 화제가 되고 있으며, 아마도 머지않아 그 도시 전체에 한국식당들이 여기저기 생겨나게 될 것입니다.

Comprehension Check-up

True/False

1. First generation Korean American restaurateurs mainly served the Korean community. (T/F)
2. Most contemporary Korean American chefs tend to stick to strict, traditional cooking. (T/F)
3. Second generation Korean Americans are pioneering new food concepts. (T/F)

Vocabulary Matching

1. culinary	a. customers or followers
2. entrepreneur	b. of or related to cooking
3. heritage	c. an independent business owner
4. clientele	d. something inherited

Word Challenge

Quiz

Check Your Understanding: Use the words in the box to complete each of the following sentences.

assure	ensure	insure

1. When shipping valuable items, it is a good idea to __________ them against damage or loss.
2. I'd like to __________ you that this situation will be handled in a timely manner.
3. A life insurance policy is one way to __________ your children's future.

Word Challenge

assure	Usage: "Assure," "ensure," and "insure" all have their roots in the Latin word for "safe" or "secure." In English, "assure" is to pledge or promise, to ensure, or to instill confidence. It is used with reference to people. Examples: 1. The mayor assured us that the school could be built without raising local taxes. (inform or tell positively) (시장은 지방세 없이 학교를 지을 수 있을 것이라며 우리를 안심시켰습니다.) 2. My boss assured me that my position will still be available when I return from maternity leave. (to pledge or promise) (나의 상사는 내가 출산휴가를 다녀와도 내 자리는 여전히 유효하게 해 준다고 약속을 하였습니다.) 3. That last goal helped to assure their victory over Liverpool. (to make sure; ensure) (저 마지막 골이 리버풀과의 경기에서 그들이 승리할 것이라고 확신하는데 도움을 주었습니다.)
ensure	Usage: In most cases, "ensure" and "insure" are interchangeable. Both words mean "to make sure or certain." Examples: 1. Many analysts argue that nuclear weapons do little to ensure security. (to secure or guarantee) (많은 분석가들이 핵무기는 안전을 보장하는데 거의 아무런 역할을 하지 않는다고 확신합니다.) 2. The new guidelines will ensure ethical standards are observed at all times. (to make sure) (새 지침은 윤리적인 기준이 항상 준수되어야 한다는 것을 확실히 해 줄 겁니다.) 3. Free and fair elections are the only way to ensure democracy. (to make secure or safe) (자유롭고 공정한 선거가 민주주의를 지키는 유일한 방법입니다.)
insure	Usage: While in most cases, "ensure" and "insure" are interchangeable, there is one notable difference. In American English, "insure" is the only one of the two that can be used in the commercial sense, meaning "to take out or issue an insurance policy." Examples: 1. The federal government insures deposits of up to $100,000. (to guarantee against loss) (연방정부는 최대10만 달러까지 예금액까지 보장해 줍니다.) 2. If you live in a big city, it's a good idea to insure your car against theft. (to secure in case of damage) (만약 당신이 대도시에 산다면 절도에 대비해 자동차 보험을 드는게 좋습니다.) 3. Many companies charge more to insure smokers. (to issue an insurance policy for) (많은 회사들은 보험에서 흡연자에게 더 많은 금액을 요구합니다.)

Practice

Task 4

Choose the best expression to complete each of the following sentences.

1. David resigned _______ his health problem.

   (a) because of (b) because

   (c) in spite of (d) although

2. The buildings in London are small ______ comparison with the skyscrapers of N.Y.

   (a) on (b) to

   (c) in (d) with

3. Pleasehelp yourself ______ anything you like.

   (a) with (b) for

   (c) in (d) to

4. He bought a used bicycle _______ a good price.

   (a) at (b) by

   (c) in (d) from

5. It is a two- story house composed _______ three bedrooms, a kitchen and two living rooms.

   (a) with (b) on

   (c) to (d) of

Task 5

Read each sentence carefully. If it is incorrect, correct it. If the sentence is correct, leave it alone.

	correct	incorrect
1. The peach was known as the Persian apple since many years.		
______________________________	( )	( )
2. I'm going to overseas during the next vacation.	( )	( )
______________________________		
3. Debby will come on Saturday.	( )	( )
______________________________		
4. In general, people start school at the age of eight.	( )	( )
______________________________		
5. He is suffering of a sore throat.	( )	( )
______________________________		

Culture Corner

Superbowl

Superbowl은 NFC(National Football Conference)와 AFC(American Football Conference)의 우승팀이 해마다 1월에 벌이는 NFL(National Football League 북아메리카프로미식축구리그)의 챔피언 결정전으로 미국에서 가장 큰 스포츠 행사입니다. NFC와 AFC는 NFL의 산하에 있고 NFL은 1967년 AFL(American Football League: 아메리칸풋볼리그)과 통합하여 그때부터 Superbowl이 시작되었습니다. 주요 football team으로는 Kansas City Chiefs, Dallas Cowboys, Saint Louis Lambs 등이 있습니다.

Superbowl이 열리는 매년 1월 마지막 일요일은 Superbowl Sunday라고 부르고 이날은 사람들이 경기를 함께 보기 위해 서로의 집에서 Super bowl party를 열기도 합니다. 매년 70%를 상회하는 시청률을 기록할 정도로 미국 국민들은 football에 대해 열광합니다. Superbowl이 열리는 날은 한해 중 가장 많은 음주운전 관련 교통사고를 기록하는 날이며 가장 많은 양의 피자, 아보카도, 칩 스낵들이 소비되는 날이기도 합니다. Superbowl에서 NFC 소속이 이기면 그 해 증권시장이 호황이고, AFC 소속이 이기면 약세장이 된다는 Superbowl 징크스까지 거론될 정도로 큰 관심을 모으는 스포츠입니다.

또한 1억 3천만 명의 시청자를 TV앞에 묶어두는 미국 최대의 이벤트인 Superbowl은 단순히 스포츠 게임이 아닙니다. 광고주들이 130만 달러에 달하는 30초짜리 광고 시간대를 얻고자 노력하는 광고의 전쟁터가 됩니다. 이러한 거액을 들여 광고를 하는 것은 그 효과가 매우 크기 때문입니다. 우리가 잘 알고 있는 Olympus, Pepsi Cola, Apple Computer (Apple, Inc.), 그리고 Budweiser 맥주로 유명한 Anheuser-Busch 등 여러 기업체들이 Superbowl 기간 광고를 통해 이득을 본 것으로 알려졌습니다.

Superbowl이 이토록 미국인들에게 사랑을 받는 이유 중 하나는 미국인들의 문화적 습성과 football 경기의 연관성이라고 여러 문화연구가들이말하는데 후퇴 없는 계속적 전진, 비록 단체경기이긴 하지만 개인의 역할을 최대한 인정하는 역할의 전문성과 집단 속의 개인적 특성 인정, 수비보다 공격을 중시하는 진취성, 미국사회 구조와 흡사한 개인별 경쟁 등으로 볼 수 있습니다.

- The Superbowl is always held on the last Sunday in January.
- Many companies create advertisements just for the Superbowl, which often cost millions of dollars to run.

Wrap-up

Key sentences

1. I'd rather be at home.
2. I want to talk about the argument we had.
3. I don't think good friends should ever fight over a girl.
4. She left for Europe yesterday.
5. She's the centerpiece of a huge modeling campaign.
6. The next time I see her will probably be on a billboard or in a magazine.
7. Feel free to show how sorry you are by buying dinner.
8. Despite your troubles, I'm glad we got to talk things over.

REVIEW TEST

Choose the correct words in the parentheses. (1-10)

1. The little boy is walking next (to, from, by) his mother.

2. The cup of coffee is (on, over, up) the table.

3. He works hard (through, at, from) nine to five.

4. I want to eat ice-cream, but I'm (in, on, for) a diet.

5. His success was due (from, to, of) his family.

6. My grandparents live (at, in, on) the countryside.

7. Some people choose name-brand products, regardless (of, to, with) their price.

8. The vacation house is painted (over, by, in) a fresh white color.

9. They will leave (to, for, on) Africa next week.

10. Tell me (until, by, in) Thursday whether or not you can come to the meeting.

Supplementary Reading (보충 독해)

다음 글을 읽고 문제를 풀어 보세요.

The Vitamin Myth

It is said that more than 20 percent of Koreans take vitamins. Also, several kinds of vitamin drinks sell like hot cakes, edging out traditional tonics like Bacchus. Listening to sales people, one might conclude that anyone who does not take vitamin supplements is placing himself or herself in significant jeopardy. So, should everyone take vitamin supplements even if they eat well?

Doctors point out that people who can afford vitamin supplements are usually well nourished. Specific individuals, however, may need supplements. For example, vegetarians, people with food allergies, people who live on canned or frozen foods, and people recovering from surgery are in need of vitamin supplements. For others, taking in more nutrients than the body needs does not provide added energy, more brain power, or protection against disease. In fact, taking an excess of vitamins can negatively affect a person's health.

In addition, vitamin supplements alone cannot provide people with everything they need. Eating healthy food nourishes the body with fiber, protein, energy, and lots of very important nutrients that vitamin supplements do not provide. Doctors recommend that people should increase their intake of fruits and vegetables if their body needs more vitamins. No manufactured vitamin can substitute for a salad of fresh fruits and vegetables.

Translation 비타민에 대한 통념

한국인들의 20% 이상이 비타민 영양제를 복용한다고 합니다. 또한 바카스 같은 전통 토닉 음료를 제치고 여러 종류의 비타민 음료가 날개 돋친 듯이 팔리고 있습니다. 판매하는 사람들의 이야기를 들으면 비타민제를 복용하지 않으면 자신을 큰 위험에라도 빠지게 하는 거라 생각될 수 있습니다. 그렇다면, 식사를 제대로 하고 있음에도 불구하고 모든 사람들은 비타민 보충제를 복용해야 하는 걸까요?

의사들은 비타민 보충제를 살 수 있는 사람들은 영양이 부족하지 않다고 말합니다. 그러나 특정 사람들은 보충제가 필요 할 수도있습니다. 예를 들어 채식주의자들, 음식 알레르기가 있는 사람들, 통조림이나 냉동식품만 먹는 사람들 또는 수술 후 회복 중인 사람들입니다. 그러나 다른 사람들에게는 몸에 필요한 것보다 더 많은 영양을 섭취하는 것이 에너지를 더해주거나 뇌 운동을 더 활발하게 한다거나 질병을 예방하지 않습니다. 오히려 비타민을 과다 복용하면 인체에 좋지 않은 영향을 끼칠 수도 있습니다.

또한 비타민 보충제 하나가 사람들이 필요한 모든 것을 줄 수 없습니다. 몸에 좋은 음식을 먹음으로써 섬유질, 단백질, 에너지 그리고 비타민 보충제가 줄 수 없는 여러 가지의 중요한 것을 얻게 됩니다. 의사들은 사람들에게 자신의 몸에 비타민이 더 필요하다 생각되면 과일과 야채의 섭취량을 늘리라고 권장합니다. 어느 제조 비타민도 신선한 과일과 야채로 만든 샐러드를 대신할 수 없습니다.

Explanation

1. Also, several kinds of vitamin drinks sell like hot cakes, edging out traditional tonics like Bacchus.

like 는 '~처럼' 이란 의미의 전치사로서, sell like hot cakes는 '날개 돋친 듯이 팔린다.' 라는 뜻입니다. edge out 은 '근소한 차로 ~을 밀어내다/이기다' 란 뜻이며 이 문장에서는 부대상황을 나타내는 분사구문으로 사용되었습니다.

Ex) The new novel sold like hot cakes.
(새로운 소설책은 날개 돋친 듯이 팔렸습니다.)
Seo Taiji and the Boys edged out nominees from other Asian nations to win the award.
(서태지와 아이들이 다른 아시아 국가들로 온 후보들을 근소한 차이로 제치고 그 상을 받았습니다.)

2. Listening to sales people, one might conclude that anyone who does not take vitamin supplements is placing himself or herself in significant jeopardy.

① 이 문장에서 listening to~ 는 때를 나타내는 분사구문으로써, When one listens to~ 의 뜻입니다.
② place + 목적어 + in 의 표현은 '(사람이나 물건을) ~한 위치나 상태에 두다' 라는 표현으로써 placing himself or herself in significant jeopardy은 '그 자신 또는 그녀 자신을 심각한 위험에 빠뜨리다/놓다' 라고 해석할 수 있습니다.

Ex) Listening to literature lectures, she became interested in Shakespeare.
(문학 강의를 듣고 난 후 그녀는 셰익스피어에 관심을 가지게 되었습니다.)
I placed myself in danger by walking home at night alone.
(나는 밤에 혼자 집에 걸어감으로써 내 자신을 위험한 상황에 처하게 했습니다.)

3. Should everyone take vitamin supplements even if they eat well?

everyone을 받는 대명사로는 주로 he/she와 같은 단수형이 쓰이는 데, 일상체에서는 복수형 they가 쓰이기도 합니다.

Ex) Does everyone have their tickets with them?
(모두 자신들의 티켓을 가지고 있나요?)

4. For example, vegetarians, people with food allergies, people who live on canned or frozen foods, and people recovering from surgery, are in need of vitamin supplements.

vegetarian은 채식주의자란 뜻의 단어이며, live on은 '~으로 생계를 유지하다, ~을 먹다' 란 표현입니다. recover from은 '~으로부터 회복하다', be in need of 는 '~을 필요로 하다' 란 의미를 가지고 있습니다.

Ex) He lived on alcohol after his wife passed away.
(그는 그의 아내와 사별한 후 술만 마시고 살았습니다.)
We are in need of food and shelter.
(우리는 음식과 은신처를 필요로 합니다.)

5. In fact, taking an excess of vitamins can negatively affect a person's health.

excess 는 '과잉, 과다' 란 의미의 명사이며, negatively affect는 '부정적으로 영향을 끼치다' 란 뜻입니다.

Ex) An excess of fat in one's diet can lead to heart disease. (지나친 지방 섭취는 심장병을 초래할 수 있습니다.)

6. No manufactured vitamin can substitute for a salad of fresh fruit and vegetables.

substitute for~는 '~을 대신하다' 라는 의미의 표현입니다. substitute A for B 의 형태로 'A가 B를 대신하다' 라는 의미로 쓰이기도 합니다.

Ex) He substituted for the principal who was in hospital.

(그는 입원 중인 교장 선생님을 대신해서 일했습니다.)

Q. 1 Choose the one that best describes the meaning of each underlined word.

1. Let's conclude the argument.
   a) to start
   b) to separate a person from the other
   c) to prevent or hinder
   d) to decide or settle finally

2. Taking an excess of vitamins can negatively affect a person's health.
   a) an amount of exceeding what is normal or sufficient
   b) right to see something
   c) a series of actions which are carried out
   d) the amount by which something is less than what is required or expected

3. Our lives were in jeopardy.
   a) happiness
   b) peace
   c) danger
   d) sadness

4. Manufactured shoes will be sent to retailers soon.
   a) provided with clear and detailed information
   b) processed or made, especially by machinery
   c) imported from other countries
   d) found as a defective product

5. Jane is working as a <u>substitute</u> for Samantha.
   a) something or someone that takes the place of another
   b) someone that is told to monitor workers
   c) someone who gives private lessons to students
   d) someone who makes all the decisions

6. The freelance work provides a useful <u>supplement</u> to my income.
   a) the most important one of all
   b) something spent to make use of money
   c) something added to complete a thing
   d) something that replaces one's main job for a short time

Q. 2 Choose the best answer for each of the following questions.

1. According to the article, which of the following is not true?
   a) More than 20 percent of Koreans take vitamin pills.
   b) The more nutrients people take, the more brain power they have.
   c) Vitamin supplements are good for people who are recovering from surgery.
   d) Taking an excess of vitamins can be harmful to one's health.

2. Who is not in need of vitamin supplements?
   a) vegetarians
   b) people with food allergies
   c) people who are well-nourished
   d) people recovering from surgery

3. What do doctors recommend for a person who needs more vitamins in their diet?
   a) vitamin drinks
   b) fruit and vegetables
   c) vitamin supplements
   d) canned or frozen foods

4. Which of the underlined prepositions is correct?

   a) He is recovering <u>from</u> his illness.

   b) We can substitute margarine <u>to</u> butter.

   c) A sick person is in need <u>over</u> care.

   d) Many Asian people live <u>in</u> rice.

5. Choose the ungrammatical sentence.

   a) Seeing her, he jumped with joy.

   b) Opening the bottle, Tom poured the drinks.

   c) Jim hurt his arm playing tennis.

   d) Running down the street, the envelope fell out of my hand.

Unit

12 Conjunctions

Introduction

Topic: Table Talk (식탁에서의 대화)

Lesson objectives:

Conjunctions (접속사)

- Coordinate conjunctions – and, but, or, for, so (등위 접속사)
- Subordinate conjunctions I – that, whether, if, when, while, as, before, after, etc. (종속 접속사)
- Subordinate conjunctions II – because, since, if, unless, although, as, etc. (종속 접속사)

WARM-UP

In this scene, Brett and Carrie meet for dinner. It's their first official date since they met at the bookstore. Will their interest in one another extend beyond the books they like to read? Continue on to find out.

Brett : Wow. This menu is complicated.

Carrie : How about getting a few different things, and we can share them?

Brett : Okay. That sounds good. Would you prefer salmon or chicken? (coordinate conjunction)

Carrie : Not that I don't like salmon, but I'd rather have chicken. (coordinate conjunction)

Carrie : Would you prefer red wine or white wine? (coordinate conjunction)

Brett : I'd rather have white wine.

Brett : I think that we're ready then. (subordinate conjunction)

Carrie : I don't see our waiter anywhere in sight.

Brett : So, tell me more about yourself.

Carrie : Well, I'm obsessed with golf.

Brett : Golf? So you're not only a lover of great literature, but also an athlete. (coordinate conjunction)

Carrie : Well, I don't know about that. But I've been playing golf since I was in grade school. (subordinate conjunction)

Carrie : Enough about me. How did your big presentation turn out?

Brett : It turned out great, actually. So good, in fact, that I got promoted to vice-president of marketing for the Asia division. (subordinate conjunction)

Carrie : So you're not only a fan of Philip Roth, but also a high-powered executive. (coordinate conjunction)

Brett : Well, I don't know if I would put it that way. (subordinate conjunction)

Carrie : I wonder if the waiter is ever going to take our order. (subordinate conjunction)

Brett : Right, the waiter.

Translation

이번 장면에서 Brett와 Carrie는 저녁식사를 하기 위해 만납니다. 그들이 서점에서 만난 이후 이번이 공식적인 첫 번째 데이트입니다. 그들이 좋아하는 책을 넘어 서로에 대한 관심이 더욱 확장될 수 있을까요? 계속 살펴보며 알아봅시다.

Brett : 와, 메뉴가 복잡하네요.

Carrie : 다른 종류의 음식을 조금씩 시켜서 나누어 먹는 건 어때요?

Brett : 좋아요. 연어랑 닭고기 중무엇을 더 좋아하세요?

Carrie : 연어를 좋아하지 않아서가 아니라, 왠지 닭고기가 더 끌리네요.

Carrie : 적포도주와 백포도주 중 어떤 것을 더 좋아하세요?

Brett : 백포도주가 좋겠어요.

Brett : 그럼 준비가 된 것 같은데요.

Carrie : 웨이터가 안 보여요.

Brett : 저, 본인 소개를 좀더 해 주시겠어요?

Carrie : 글쎄요, 전 골프를 굉장히 좋아해요.

Brett : 골프요? 그러니까 당신은 좋은 문학작품을 사랑할 뿐만 아니라 운동도 즐기시는 군요.
Carrie : 그건 잘모르겠어요. 하지만 초등학생 때부터 골프를 쳐 왔죠.
Carrie : 저에 대해서는 충분한 것 같고. 중요한 프레젠테이션은 어떻게 됐어요?
Brett : 결과가 정말 좋았어요. 사실 매우 좋아서 아시아 지역마케팅팀의 부사장으로 승진하게 되었습니다.
Carrie : 그러니까 당신은 Philip Roth의 팬일 뿐만 아니라 높은 지위의 기업 임원이시군요.
Brett : 그렇게 말해도 될 지 모르겠습니다.
Carrie : 웨이터가 우리 주문을 받기는 할는지 궁금하네요.
Brett : 그러게요, 웨이터.

Comprehension Check

1. This conversation takes place while:
   (a) Brett and Carrie are eating dinner
   (b) Brett and Carrie are finishing dinner
   (c) Brett and Carrie are paying for dinner
   (d) Brett and Carrie are waiting to place an order for dinner

2. Brett is __________ when he learns that Carrie is an avid golfer.
   (a) surprised
   (b) annoyed
   (c) unimpressed
   (d) exasperated

3. Which of the following could NOT be used to describe this conversation?
   (a) chatting
   (b) making small talk
   (c) flirting
   (d) bickering

Useful Expressions

In this dialogue	Explanation
1. Not that I don't like salmon, but I'd rather have chicken.	1.Use this construction when you want to gently turn down one option and state a preference for another. Let's take a look at a few additional examples. a. Not that I don't like the red dress, but I think the blue one really brings out your eyes. (=I like the red dress, but I like the blue one more.) b. Not that I wouldn't like to go along, but I've got a ton of work to do. (=I'd like to go, but I have a lot of work to do.)
2. I'm obsessed with golf.	2. Are all of your efforts directed toward one goal? Do you eat, sleep, and breathe for one reason alone? You can use this expression to talk about something that preoccupies your thoughts, whether it's a sport, a hobby, or a band.
3. Enough about me.	3. Conversations should be two-sided. The next time a date starts to feel like an interrogation, you can use this expression to direct the focus of attention away from your self. "Enough about me; I'd like to hear more about you," you could say.
4. I don't know if I would put it that way.	4. There's always morethan one way to say something. So, when you feel that certain language is too strong, too direct, or perhaps just plain inaccurate, this expression might prove a useful response. In today's dialogue, Brett doesn't seem comfortable being called a high-powered executive and hints that he might describe himself differently given the opportunity.

Grammar

Focus 1 Kinds of Conjunctions and Coordinate Conjunction (접속사 종류와 등위 접속사)

01 접속사 종류

(1) 의미상 종류

A. 등위 접속사: 단어와 단어, 구와 구, 절과 절을 대등하게 연결하는 접속사 (and, but, or, for 등)

B. 종속 접속사: 주절과 종속절을 연결하는 접속사 (if, whether, that, because 등)

(2) 형태상 종류

A. 단순 접속사: and, when, for, if 등

B. 상관 접속사: either ~ or, both ~ and, not only ~ but also 등

C. 접속사구: as long as, as soon as, in case 등

(3) 접속사와 전치사

대부분의 종속 접속사는 전치사로도 쓰이는 데, 절의 요소(주어+동사)가 나오면 접속사이고, 명사상당어구가 나오면 전치사입니다.

- You should wash your hands after you get home. (접속사)
  (당신은 집에 도착하면 손을 씻어야 합니다.)
- We'll leave after lunch. (전치사)
  (우리는 점심 후에 출발할 것입니다.)

02 등위 접속사

(1) and

단어, 구, 절 등을 의미상 순접 관계로 연결합니다. '~와', '~그리고' 의 의미입니다.

- John, you're a gentleman and a scholar.
  (John, 당신은 신사이자 학자입니다.)

- The boy was sick and took some medicine.
  (그 소년은 아파서 약을 먹었습니다.)

cf) The poet and statesman is famous.
  (시인이자 정치가는 유명합니다. (한 사람))
  – The poet and the statesman are famous.
  (시인과 정치가는 유명합니다. (두 사람))

명령문 다음에 and가 오면, '~해라, 그러면' 의 의미입니다.

- Study hard and you will pass the entrance examination.
  (열심히 공부하세요. 그러면 입학 시험에 합격할 것입니다.)
- Stick with me and everything will be all right.
  (내 곁에 있으세요. 그러면 모든 것이 잘 될 겁니다.)
- Take two tablets, three times per day and you should start feeling better in about a week.
  (하루에 세 번 알약 두 개를 복용하세요. 그러면 일주일정도 후에 나아지기 시작할 겁니다.)

(2) or

두 개 이상의 요소 가운데 하나를 선택하는 의미를 갖는 것으로, '혹은', '또는' 의 뜻입니다.

- Would you prefer salmon or chicken?
  (연어가 좋으세요, 아니면 닭고기가 좋으세요?)
- Would you prefer red wine or white wine?
  (적포도주와 백포도주 중 어떤 것을 더 좋아하세요?)
- Facebook allows you to keep in touch with close friends or relatives.
  (페이스북은 여러분이 가까운 친구나 친척들과 연락을 주고받을 수 있게 해 줍니다.)
- I'm from New York, but I don't like the Yankees or the Mets.
  (저는 뉴욕에서 왔지만 양키스팀이나 메츠팀을 좋아하지 않습니다.)

명령문 다음에 or가 오면, '~해라, 그렇지 않으면' 의 의미입니다.

- Hurry up, or we're going to miss the bus.
  (서두르세요. 그렇지 않으면 버스를 놓칠 겁니다.)
- Finish your vegetables, or you're not going to get dessert.
  (당신 채소를 다 드세요. 그렇지 않으면 디저트를 먹을 수 없을 겁니다.)
- Be careful with your credit cards, or you'll be in a lot of debt before you know it.
  (신용카드를 조심하세요. 그렇지 않으면 알아차리기도 전에 엄청난 빚을 질 것입니다.)

(3) but

역접, 즉 의미상의 반대 또는 대조를 나타낼 때 쓰이며, '그러나~', '~지만'의 의미입니다.

- He did not come on Sunday but on Monday.
  (그는 일요일에 오지 않고 월요일에 왔습니다.)
- The new laws against drunk driving are strict, but they're not very effective.
  (음주운전을 금하는 새로운 법은 엄정하지만 매우 효과적이지는 않습니다.)
- Money is important, but it can't guarantee happiness.
  (돈은 중요합니다. 하지만 그것이 행복을 보장할 수는 없습니다.)

'not that A but (that) B'는 'A 때문이 아니라 B 때문이다' 라는 뜻입니다. but(that)에서 that은 자주 생략됩니다.

- Not that I don't like salmon, but I'd rather have chicken.
  (연어를 좋아하지 않아서가 아니라, 닭고기를 더 먹고 싶어서 입니다.)
- It's not that I don't like the game, but that I have no time.
  (내가 그 게임을 좋아하지 않는 게 아니라 시간이 없습니다.)
- Not that I don't like you, but I'm not looking for a serious relationship right now.
  (내가 당신을 좋아하지 않아서가 아니라 지금 당장은 진지한 관계를 찾고 있지 않아서 입니다.)
- Not that I've never learned anything from TV, but I sure haven't learned anything useful from it.
  (내가 TV에서 아무 것도 배우지 않아서가 아니라 TV에서 유용한 것을 배운 적이 확실히 없어서 입니다.)

(4) for

이유를 나타내는 등위 접속사 for는 because와는 구분해서 사용해야 합니다. because는 종속절이 주절의 직접적인 원인이나, 이유가 될 때 사용할 수 있습니다. 이에 비해 for는 종속절이 주절에 대한 주관적 판단의 근거가 되거나 추가적 설명을 할 때 사용합니다. 또한, for는 문장 맨 앞 자리로 나오지 않습니다.

- It's morning, for birds are singing.
  (새들이 우는 걸 보니, 아침이로군요.)
- He must be ill, for he looks pale.
  (창백해 보이는 것을 보니, 그는 아픈 것이 틀림없습니다.)
- We must act quickly, for we cannot allow these atrocities to continue.
  (이 잔학한 행위가 계속되는 걸 두고 볼 수 없으니 빨리 움직여야 합니다.)

(5) yet

'그러나, 그럼에도 불구하고' 의 뜻으로 but과 비슷하게 쓰입니다.

- She quit school, yet (she) can't help regretting it.
  (그녀는 학교를 그만뒀지만 후회하지 않을 수 없습니다.)
- They broke up months ago, yet she hasn't gone on a single date since.
  (그들은 몇 달 전에 헤어졌지만 그녀는 그 이후 한 번도 데이트를 하지 않고 있습니다.)
- My cell phone bill seems to increase every year, yet the service doesn't seem to improve.
  (내 핸드폰 사용료는 매년 늘고 있는 것 같은데 서비스는 좋아지는 것 같지 않습니다.)

(6) so

'그래서' 의 뜻으로 결과를 나타냅니다.

- He couldn't find her phone number, so he sent her an email.
  (그는 그녀의 전화번호를 찾을 수 없어서 이메일을 보냈습니다.)
- There was a lot of traffic this morning, so I decided to take the subway to work.
  (오늘 아침에 길이 많이 막혔기 때문에 난 지하철을 타고 출근하기로 결심했습니다.)
- I'm married with two children, so free time isn't something that I have a lot of.
  (나는 결혼해서 두 아이가 있기 때문에 자유 시간을 많이 가질 수가 없습니다.)

(7) nor

'~도 또한 아닌' 의 뜻으로 nor 다음에 주어와 동사가 도치됩니다.

- I am not rich, nor do I wish to be.
  (나는 부자가 아니고 그렇게 되길 원하지도 않습니다.)
- Credits obtained more than 10 years ago are not valid, nor are credits obtained at foreign universities.
  (십 년 전에 받은 학점은 유효하지 않고 또한 외국대학에서 받은 것도 마찬가지입니다.)
- I don't doubt that you are telling the truth, nor do I have any reason to.
  (나는 당신이 진실을 말하고 있다는 것을 의심하지 않고 또한 그럴 이유도 없습니다.)

03 등위상관접속사

(1) either ~ or

'either A or B'는 'A 혹은 B 둘 중 하나'의 의미로 양자 택일을 나타냅니다.

- You can either go with me or stay home.
  (당신은 나와 함께 가거나 혹은 집에 있어도 됩니다.)
- Either accept my invitation or reject it, but please don't keep me wondering for days.
  (내 초대를 받아들이거나 거절하세요. 하지만 오랫동안 나를 궁금하게 만들지는 마십시오.)
- Politicians these days are either corrupt or incompetent.
  (요즘 정치인들은 부패하거나 무능력합니다.)

(2) neither ~ nor

neither A nor B는 'A도 아니고 B도 아닌' 의 의미로 양자 부정을 나타냅니다.

- He can speak neither English nor French.
  (그는 영어도 못하고 불어도 못합니다.)
- My sister is neither mature enough nor responsible enough to hold down a job.
  (내 여동생은 그 일을 계속할 만큼 성숙하지도 않고 책임감이 있지도 않습니다.)
- It seems that teenagers can talk to neither their teachers nor their parents when it comes to sex.
  (십대 청소년들은 성에 대해서 선생님이나 또는 부모님과 대화를 나눌 수 있는 것 같지 않습니다.)

(3) not only ~ but also

not only A but also B 구문은 'A뿐만 아니라, B도'의 의미로, also는 생략되기도합니다. 또한 B as well as A 와 같은 의미입니다.

- You're not only a lover of great literature, but also an athlete.
  (당신은 좋은 문학작품을 사랑할 뿐만 아니라 운동도 즐기시는군요.)
- You're not only a fan of Philip Roth, but also a high-powered executive.
  (당신은 Philip Roth의 팬일 뿐만 아니라 높은 지위의 기업 임원이시군요.)
- Not only do they need clothing, but they are also short of food.
  (그들은 옷이 필요할 뿐만 아니라, 음식도 부족합니다.)

- Newspapers not only offer insight into world events, but are also a great way to improve vocabulary.
  (신문은 세상사에 대한 통찰력을 제공할 뿐만 아니라 어휘력을 늘릴 수 있는 뛰어난 수단이기도 합니다.)

(4) not ~ but

not A but B는 'A가 아니라 B'라는 의미입니다.

- The house is not his but mine.
  (그 집은 그의 소유가 아니라, 내 것입니다.)
- Not you but I am responsible for the work.
  (당신이 아닌 내가 그 일에 책임이 있습니다. (내 책임입니다.))
- There are not eleven but twelve in a dozen.
  (한 다스에는 11개가 아니라 12개가 있습니다.)

(5) both ~ and

both A and B는 'A와 B 둘 다'의 의미입니다.

- She is both intelligent and beautiful.
  (그녀는 똑똑하기도 하고 예쁘기도 합니다.)
- He is remarkable both for his intelligence and for his skill.
  (그의 지능과 실력은 뛰어납니다.)
- This event is both tragic and regrettable.
  (이 사건은 비극적이며 유감스러운 일입니다.)

Task 1

Choose the correct word(s) from the box to complete each sentence.

and	not	but	or	nor	but also	so

1. College is not only a time of intellectual growth, __________ a time when many lifelong friendships are created.
2. Wear your coat, __________ you'll feel cold.
3. His latest film is both imaginative __________ provocative.
4. Richard has a lot of money, __________ he is not happy.
5. I like neither coffee __________ tea.

Focus 2 Subordinate conjunction I

(종속접속사 – that, whether, if when, while, as, before, after, etc.)

01 명사절을 이끄는 접속사

(1) that

명사절을 이끄는 구실을 합니다. 즉, '~이라는 것'의 의미로 문장에서 주절, 목적절, 보어절을 이끕니다. 목적절을 이끄는 that은 생략할 수 있습니다. the fact, the hope, the proof, the belief, the idea, the news 다음에 오는 that절은 동격의 역할을 합니다.

- I think (that) we're ready then.
  (이제 준비가 된 것 같습니다.)
- That they were able to make it out alive is something of a miracle.
  (= It is something of a miracle that they were able to make it out alive.)
  (그들이 살아서 도망칠 수 있었던 것은 기적입니다.)
- Earlier today, government officials said (that) education standards would be reviewed.
  (오늘 일찍 정부에서는 교육 수준을 재검토하겠다고 밝혔습니다.)
- My point is that we don't have enough time.
  (내 말의 요점은 우리에게 시간이 충분하지 않다는 것입니다.)
- They are concerned about the fact that the family is losing its traditional roles.
  (그들은 가족이 그 전통적인 역할을 잃어가고 있다는 사실을 염려합니다.)

(2) whether, if

'~인지, 아닌지'의 의미로, 문장 내에서 명사절을 이끕니다. if가 이끄는 명사절은 문장 내에서 목적어의 역할만을 합니다. whether가 이끄는 절만이 바로 뒤에 or not이 따라 올 수 있습니다.

- I don't know if I would put it that way.
  (그렇게 말해도 될지 잘 모르겠습니다.)
- I wonder if the waiter is ever going to take our order.
  (웨이터가 우리 주문을 받기는 할는지 궁금합니다.)
- Many parents have trouble deciding if private school is really worth the money.
  (사립학교가 비싼 만큼의 값어치가 있는지 결정하는데 많은 부모들이 어려움을 겪습니다.)
- An intense debate ensued about whether safety justifies a loss of privacy.
  (안전이 사생활 침해를 정당화하는가에 대해 격렬한 토론이 벌어졌습니다.)

- It is unclear whether alcohol played a role in the accident.
  (술이 그 사고에 영향을 미친 건지 확실하지 않습니다.)
- Whether it is a good plan or not is a matter for argument.
  (그것이 좋은 계획인지 아닌지는 의논할 문제입니다.)

cf) I don't know **whether or not** he will come.
I don't know if or not he will come. (x)
(나는 그가 올 지 안 올 지 궁금합니다.)

(3) 종속 의문절

의문사가 명사절을 유도할 수 있습니다. 의문사가 이끄는 종속절은 '의문사 + 주어 + 동사' 의 순이 됩니다.

- I could hardly understand what he wanted to do.
  (나는 그가 무엇을 하고 싶어 했는지 이해할 수가 없었습니다.)
- We're still trying to determine where the problem began.
  (어디에서 문제가 시작되었는지 결정하려고 아직 노력 중입니다.)
- It's still unclear which candidate will win.
  (어느 후보가 우승할 지 아직도 확실하지 않습니다.)

02 시간 부사절 접속사

(1) when

시간을 나타내는 대표적인 종속 접속사로, '~할 때' 라는 의미입니다.

- When I last heard from him, he was living in New York.
  (내가 마지막으로 그에게 소식을 들었을 때 그는 뉴욕에 살고 있었습니다.)
- When you fly across several time zones, your body's normal rhythm becomes confused.
  (여러 시간대를 날아서 지나갈 때 당신 몸의 정상적인 리듬은 혼란을 겪게됩니다.)

(2) while, as

while과 as가 이끄는 부사절은 주절과 시간이 동시적입니다. 다만, while은 부사절의 시간 폭이 상대적으로 넓어서, '~하는 동안' 의 의미이고, as는 '하는 순간, 동시에'의 의미입니다.

- She was reading a book while she was waiting for her son.
  (그녀는 그녀의 아들을 기다리는 동안, 책을 읽고 있었습니다.)
- Promise that you'll write me every day while you're away!
  (당신이 떠나있는 동안 매일 나에게 편지 쓰겠다고 약속해요!)

- He went out as I came in.
(내가 들어올 때, 그는 나갔습니다.)
- Step toward the ball as you begin your swing.
(스윙할 때 공을 향해 한 걸음 내디디세요.)

(3) before, after

- Brush your teeth before you go to bed.
(잠자기 전에 이를 닦아라.)
- The product was recalled after several consumers reported injuries.
(일부 고객들이 피해를 제보한 후 그 제품은 회수되었습니다.)

(4) till/until

'~까지'의 의미로, till과 until의 의미는 같으나, until이 더 자주 사용됩니다.

- Until she spoke, I hadn't realized she was a foreigner.
(그녀가 말하기 전까지는 그녀가 외국인이라는 것을 미처 몰랐습니다.)
- Add the cream and stir until the mixture is consistent.
(그 혼합물이 골고루 섞일 때까지 크림을 넣고 저으세요.)

(5) since

(과거의 어떤 시점부터 지금까지)란 뜻을 나타내기 때문에 since절에서 과거 시제가 쓰이는 경우 주절은 계속을 나타내는 현재 완료 진행형이 주로 쓰입니다.

- I've been playing golf since I was in grade school.
(제가 초등학교 학생일 때부터 줄곧 골프를 쳤습니다.)
- Erica has been working as a newspaper reporter since she graduated from college.
(Erica는 대학을 졸업한 이후로 줄곧 신문사 리포터로 일하고 있습니다.)
- This suitcase has been sitting in front of the door since you got home last week.
(지난 주에 당신이 귀가한 이후로 이 여행가방이 문 앞에 계속 놓여 있습니다.)

(6) by the time

'~할 때쯤'이라는 의미로 미래를 나타낼 때와 과거를 나타낼 때 모두 쓸 수 있습니다.

- It's not worth going shopping now. By the time we get to the store, it will be closed.
(지금 시장 보러 가도 소용 없습니다. 가게에 도착할 때쯤이면, 그 가게가 문을 닫을 겁니다.)

- I had a lot of work to do yesterday evening. By the time I finished, I was very tired.

  (나는 어제 저녁에 해야 할 일이 많았습니다. 다 끝났을 때쯤, 나는 정말 피곤했습니다.)

- By the time the police arrived, the suspects had already fled the scene.

  (경찰이 도착했을 때쯤 용의자들은 이미 그 장소를 도망쳤습니다.)

(7) as soon as, hardly~when, scarcely~before, no sooner~than

'~하자마자, ~하다' 라는 뜻입니다.

- He went home as soon as he got the phone call.

  (그는 전화를 받자마자 집으로 갔습니다.)

- We had hardly had a chance to get to know one another when her parents sent her away for the summer to study French.

  (우리가 서로 알게 될 기회를 얻자마자 그녀의 부모님은 여름 동안 불어를 공부시키기 위해 그녀를 멀리 보냈습니다.)

- Many convicted criminals scarcely get a taste of freedom before they end up back in prison.

  (유죄를 선고받은 많은 범죄자들이 자유를 맛보기도 전에 다시 수감됩니다.)

- We had no sooner sat down than the curtain rose.

  (우리가 자리에 앉자마자 막이 올랐습니다.)

Task 2

Choose the correct conjunction from the box to complete each sentence.

whether	than	which	that	since	before	as

1. __________ she didn't remember my name disappointed me.
2. I don't know __________ or not he can come to the party in time.
3. Jane has loved her husband __________ she first met him.
4. No sooner had he left home __________ he began to run for school.
5. I'm not sure __________ she prefers.

Focus 3 Subordinate conjunction II

(종속접속사 – because, since, as; if, unless; so that; so~that; though, although, even if)

01 이유, 원인

(1) because

종속절이 주절에 대한 직접적인 이유와 원인을 나타내며, 주로 종속절이 주절 뒤에 많이 쓰입니다. not because A, but because B는 'A 때문이 아니라 B 때문이다' 라는 뜻입니다. 또한 It is because ~ that~ 의 강조구문에 쓸 수 있습니다.

- The concert was canceled because the lead singer came down with the flu.
  (리드보컬이 독감에 걸렸기 때문에 그 콘서트는 취소되었습니다.)
- Many local pharmacies refuse to carry the drug because it is costly and few people request it.
  (많은 동네 약국에서는 그 약이 비싸고 그걸 원하는 사람이 거의 없기 때문에 그 약을 가져가길 거부합니다.)
- I think Apple products are so popular not because they are on the cutting edge of technology, but because they are designed so well.
  (Apple사 제품은 최첨단 기술 때문이 아니라 디자인을 무척 잘하기 때문에 매우 인기가 있는 것 같습니다.)
- It was because I had to take care of the baby that I couldn't go out.
  (내가 나갈 수 없었던 것은 아기를 돌보아야 했기 때문입니다.)

(2) since, as

because보다는 종속절과 주절의 인과관계가 약할 때 사용합니다. 즉, 종속절이 주절에 대한 간접적인 이유와 원인이 될 때 사용합니다.

- Since it's raining, I think I'll stay home.
  (비가 오고 있기 때문에 집에 머물러야 할 것 같습니다.)
- As there are only a limited number of seats available, the competition for admission will be intense.
  (이용 가능한 자리의 수는 한정되어 있기 때문에 입장 경쟁이 치열할 것입니다.)

(3) now (that)

'이제 ~했으니까'의 의미로 주절의 간접적인 이유를 나타냅니다.

- Now that he is over twenty, he can drink alcohol.
  (그는 20살이 넘었으니까 술을 마실 수 있습니다.)

- Now that we've started going to counseling, our marriage is much stronger.
  (상담을 받기 시작했으니까 우리 결혼생활은 훨씬 좋아질 겁니다.)
- Now that you are feeling better, you can clean out the garage.
  (당신 기분도 나아졌으니까 차고 청소를 할 수 있을 겁니다.)

(4) seeing/considering that

'~을 고려하면, ~을 생각하면, ~을 감안하면'의 의미입니다.

- His English is not bad, seeing that he has only studied it for a year.
  (그가 영어를 공부한지 1년 밖에 되지 않았다는 것을 감안하면, 그가 영어실력이 아주 나쁜 것만도 아닙니다.)
- Multi-million dollar executive bonuses are excessive, considering that most people won't earn that amount of money in a lifetime.
  (대부분의 사람들이 평생 동안 그만큼의 돈을 벌지 않는다는 사실을 고려하면 수백만 달러의 임원 보너스는 지나칩니다.)

02 조건

(1) if

조건을 나타내는 가장 일반적인 접속사로, '만약 ~하면'의 의미입니다.

- You can close the window if you're cold.
  (추우면 창문을 닫아도 됩니다.)
- They will be angry if I don't visit them.
  (내가 그들을 방문하지 않으면, 그들이 화를 낼 겁니다.)
- If this were true, there'd likely be evidence to support your claim.
  (이것이 사실이라면 당신 주장을 뒷받침할 만한 증거가 있을 겁니다.)

(2) unless

'~한 조건을 제외하면'의 의미이거나, 경고의 의미로 '~하지 않으면'의 의미로 쓰입니다. unless는 가정법에서는 쓰이지 않습니다.

- Don't tell Ann what I said unless she asks you.
  (내가 한 얘기를 Ann이 물어보지 않으면 하지 마십시오)
- We'll be late unless we hurry.
  (서두르지 않으면 늦겠어요.)

- Tickets to Thailand are relatively inexpensive unless you want to travel during the peak season.
  (성수기에 여행하길 원하는 것이 아니라면 태국행 표는 비교적 비싸지 않은 편입니다.)

(3) in case (that), provided/providing (that), suppose/supposing (that), given (that), on condition (that)

- Buy insurance in case you have an accident.
  (사고 당할 경우를 대비해서 보험에 가입하십시오.)

cf) Call 9-1-1 **in case of** an emergency.
(긴급상황이 발생하면 911로 전화하세요.)

- Provided your task is done, you may go home.
  (일이 다 끝나면 귀가해도 좋습니다.)
- Providing that this treatment is successful, you should be on the road to recovery in a month or two.
  (이 치료가 성공적이면 당신은 한 달이나 두 달 후 회복세에 있을 겁니다.)
- Supposing your father knew, what would he say?
  (당신의 부친께서 아신다면 뭐라고 말씀하실까요?)
- Given that only ten people attended this year's reunion, I don't think we'll be having one next year.
  (올해 친목회에 단지 열명만 참석했다고 한다면, 우리가 내년에 친목회를 할 수 있을 것 같지 않습니다.)

cf) **Given** the chance, I'd do it all over again.
(기회가 주어지면 처음부터 다시 하고 싶습니다.)
On condition that I am paid, I'll do it.
(대가(급여)가 있는 거라면 제가 하겠습니다.)

03 목적

'~하기 위해서'의 의미입니다.

(1) so that, in order that

- It's important to learn about history so that we may better understand the future.
  (미래를 더 잘 이해하기 위해 역사를 배우는 것은 중요합니다.)
- You should turn your cell phone off so that you don't disturb other people.
  (다른 사람들에게 방해가 되지 않도록 휴대폰을 꺼야 합니다.)

- A carpool lane was designated in order that high occupancy vehicles might reach their destinations more quickly.
  (다인승 차량이 좀 더 빨리 목적지에 도달하도록 합승 차선이 지정되었습니다.)

(2) lest~should, for fear that

'~하지 않도록, ~할까 봐'의 의미입니다.

- After finishing a paper, I check it twice lest I should make a mistake.
  (나는 레포트를 마친 뒤 실수하지 않도록 두 번 확인하였습니다.)
- Many employees are reluctant to speak out about harassment for fear that they will be fired.
  (많은 직원들은 해고될까 봐 고민거리에 대해 말하기를 꺼려 합니다.)

04 결과

(1) so~that

- It turned out great, actually. So good, in fact, that I got promoted to vice-president of marketing for the Asia division.
  (결과가 정말 좋았어요. 사실 매우 좋아서 아시아 부서 마케팅팀의 부회장으로 승진하게 되었습니다.)
- He spoke so fast that nobody could understand him.
  (그가 너무 빨리 말해서 아무도 그의 말을 이해할 수 없었습니다.)
- This croissant is so delicious that I actually feel like I'm in Parisian café.
  (이 크로아상은 너무 맛있어서 내가 마치 파리의 까페에 있는 듯한 느낌이 듭니다.)
- His story was so moving that it brought me to tears.
  (그의 이야기는 너무 감동적이라 나를 눈물짓게 만들었습니다.)

(2) such~ that

- The situation in Darfur has become such a disaster that many NGOs are packing up and heading home.
  (Darfur의 상황은 끔찍해서 많은 NGO들이 짐을 싸서 집으로 향하고 있습니다.)
- Traffic on the 405 freeway is such a mess that only the bravest of souls still dare to drive it during rush hour.
  (405번 고속도로 교통상황은 너무 혼잡해서 용감한 사람만이 러시아워 시간에 그곳을 운전합니다.)
- I am not such a fool as to make an enemy of him.
  (나는 그를 적으로 만들 만큼 바보는 아닙니다.)

05 양보

(1) though, although

'비록 ~하더라도, 비록 ~하지만'의 의미입니다.

- A graduate degree is a marketable asset although no one can guarantee you a job.
  (비록 아무도 일자리를 보장해 줄 수는 없지만 졸업 학위는 시장성이 높은 자산입니다.)
- Though his parents grew suspicious, they didn't know exactly what he was up to.
  (비록 그의 부모님은 의심스러워지기 시작했지만 정확히 그가 어느 정도 되는지는 알지 못했습니다.)

(2) even if/even though

if 와 though 앞에 even이 붙어서 강조의 의미를 갖게 됩니다. '심지어 ~하더라도, ~한데도'의 의미입니다. even if는 가정의 의미를 가집니다.

- Even if gas prices go down in the short term, they will eventually go back up as the oil supply diminishes.
  (휘발유 가격이 잠깐 내려 간다 해도 기름 공급이 감소하면서 결국 다시 오를 겁니다.)
- Even though he could not swim, he jumped into the water.
  (그는 수영을 못하는데도 물속으로 뛰어들었습니다.)
- Even though other countries have superior training facilities, Jamaica produces some of the finest runners in the world.
  (비록 다른 국가에 더 우수한 훈련시설이 있지만 자메이카는 세계에서 가장 뛰어난 달리기 선수를 배출해 냅니다.)

(3) while, whereas

'~그런데, ~한데, ~한데 반해서'의 의미입니다.

- While there are numerous reasons to invest in education, long term economic growth is the most important among them.
  (교육분야에 투자해야 할 수 많은 이유가 있지만 장기 경제 성장이 그 중 가장 중요합니다.)
- Many countries have signed the agreement, whereas Korea still refuses.
  (많은 국가들이 그 협정에 서명했지만 한국은 여전히 거부합니다.)

(4) as

'~이기는 하지만', '~이라고는 하나'의 의미입니다.

- Poor as he was, he had won the general respect of the neighborhood.
  (그가 가난하기는 했지만 이웃 사람들의 존경을 받았습니다.)
- Ridiculous as it sounds, it's the honest truth. (=Despite sounding ridiculous, it's true.)
  (이상하게 들리겠지만 사실입니다.)

06 양태

'~과 같이', '~처럼', '~대로'의 의미입니다.

(1) as

- As I mentioned earlier, this year's budget includes a provision for new computers.
  (내가 전에 말한 대로 올해 예산에는 새 컴퓨터 설비도 포함됩니다.)
- As you sow, so you reap. (속담)
  (뿌린 대로 거둡니다.)

cf) The project must be completed within 90 days from breaking ground, as was agreed upon at our last meeting. (관계대명사)
(그 프로젝트는 지난 회의에서 합의한 대로 착수하는 것부터 시작해 90일 내에 끝나야 합니다.)

Task 3

Choose the correct conjunction to complete each sentence.

1. Young (that, as) he is, he is a very responsible man.
2. The rain will stop (by the time, until) you get home.
3. (If, Unless) you get up early, you will be late for work.
4. He studies hard (so that, lest) he may pass the examination.
5. (Though, Since) he was angry, he listened to me patiently.

Reading Unlikely Brand

Ernesto "Che" Guevara was many things in his time: a doctor, a writer, a revolutionary, a politician, and a military leader. His ideas were shaped by his travels throughout Latin America and the extreme poverty he witnessed. He fought side by side with Fidel Castro to overthrow the Cuban government in 1959. He died at the age of 39 trying to bring revolution to Bolivia, and is remembered for his idealism as well as his brutality.

In 1960, Alberto Diaz Guitierrez snapped a photograph of Che Guevara staring off into the distance at a funeral service and it has since become one of the most widely disseminated images in the world. This timeless image, first appearing in a magazine seven years after Che's death, can be found over the world on T-shirts, key chains, and posters that line college dormitories. From Havana to Seattle to Madrid to Damascus, Che has become as much a brand as a symbol of revolution.

Today, Guitierrez's iconic image of Che is still embraced as a symbol of protest, idealism, and triumph over adversity. These days, however, that version of Che is probably less popular than the commercial, chic rendition of his likeness. One can only wonder what the anti-capitalist revolutionary himself would think of the for-profit Che Guevara.

Translation 믿기 어려운 상표

체 게바라는 그 시대에 의사, 작가, 혁명가, 정치가, 군 지도자로 많은 활동을 하였습니다. 그의 사상은 그가 라틴 아메리카를 두루 여행하고 극심한 가난을 목격함으로써 형성되었습니다. 그는 1959년 쿠바 정부를 무너뜨리기 위해 피델 카스트로와 협력하여 투쟁하였습니다. 그는 볼리비아에 혁명을 불러 일으키려다 39살의 나이로 사망하였는데, 그는 그의 무자비한 행위뿐만 아니라 이상주의로도 기억되고 있습니다. 1960년 Alberto Diaz Guitierrez는 에르네스토 체 게바라가 장례식에서 먼 곳을 응시하고 있는 스냅 사진을 찍었는데 그 후 이 사진은 전 세계에 가장 널리 유포된 사진 중 하나가 되었습니다. 시대를 초월하는 이 사진은 체 게바라가 사망한 지 7년 후에 한 잡지에 최초로 실렸는데, 전 세계의 티셔츠, 엽서, 열쇠꾸러미, 대학 기숙사에 줄지어 있는 포스터에서 발견할 수 있습니다. 아바나에서 시애틀, 마드리드, 다마스쿠스에 이르기까지 체 게바라는 혁명의 상징을 나타내는 브랜드가 되었습니다.

오늘날 Guitierrez가 찍은 체 게바라의 이미지는 여전히 저항, 이상주의, 역경을 딛고 일어난 승리의 상징으로 받아들여 집니다. 하지만 요즘 체 게바라의 그런 이미지보다는 상업적이고 세련된 연출로 만들어진 이미지가 더 인기가 있는 것 같습니다. 이윤을 추구하는 체 게바라를 반 자본주의 혁명가인 체 게바라 자신은 어떻게 생각할지 궁금해 지기도 합니다.

Comprehension Check-up

True/False

1. Che Guevera is remembered as a peaceful man. (T/F)
2. Many social movements still adopt the image of Che Guevera. (T/F)
3. Alberto Diaz Guitierrez's photograph of Ernesto "Che" Guevera has gained world-wide popularity since it was published in 1967. (T/F)

Vocabulary Matching

1. poverty	a. misfortune, distress
2. revolutionary	b. a supporter of a radical change
3. idealism	c. having little or no money
4. adversity	d. pursuit of noble principles

Word Challenge

Quiz

Check Your Understanding: Use the words in the box to complete each of the following sentences.

lay lie

1. On a clear night, I like to __________ down on the ground and stare up at the stars.
2. __________ it down here.
3. Morocco and Algeria __________ just to the west of Libya.
4. At next month's shareholder meeting, we plan to __________ out our strategy for the upcoming fiscal year.

Word Challenge

lay	Usage: "Lay" and "lie" are frequentlyconfused by native English speakers and English learners alike. As a good general rule, remember that if you mean "put" or "place," then "lay" is probably the verb you're looking for. It almost always requires an object. Examples: 1. I nervously laid my essay down on top of the others. (to place in a position of rest) (나는 초조하게 내 에세이를 다른 에세이들 위에 내려 놓았습니다.) 2. Lay the fabric flat before ironing. (to place in a particular position) (다림질 하기 전에 천을 평평하게 놓으세요.) 3. This meeting is a great opportunity to lay the foundation for an ongoing partnership. (to establish) (이 회의는 진행 중인 파트너십 토대를 마련할 엄청난 기회입니다.) 4. On Monday, prosecutors laid out the case against former Enron executives. (to present for consideration) (월요일에 검찰은 전 Enron의 임원에 불리한 경우를 제시하였습니다.)
lie	Usage: "Lie," unlike "lay," is an intransitive verb, meaning that it doesn't require an object, and often means "to recline" or "rest." What's more, its past forms are irregular, e.g., The region lies untouched by humans. The region lay untouched by humans until the 1920s. The region has lain untouched by humans for centuries. Examples: 1. I thinkl need to lie down. (to rest flat or recline) (난 누워야 할 것 같습니다.) 2. Bears lie dormant during the winter. (to remain inactive) (곰은 겨울 동안 동면합니다.) 3. The Himalayan Mountains lie to the east. (to be placed or situated) (히말라야 산맥은 동쪽에 놓여 있습니다.) 4. The solution lies in effective leadership. (to consist or be grounded in) (해결책은 효과적인 리더십에 달려 있습니다.)

Practice

Task 4

Choose the appropriate conjunction to complete each sentence.

1. The design consultants can help clients decide whether to use curtains _______ blinds when decorating their windows.
   (a) so (b) but (c) nor (d) or

2. A meeting for all department managers has been arranged _________ we can discuss the most recent personnel problems.
   (a) in order to (b) so that (c) because of (d) such

3. _________ she graduates from the university, she will apply for a job.
   (a) No sooner (b) Not sooner than (c) Hardly (d) As soon as

4. Port Stephen is both a resort town _________ an economic center where luxury goods from around the world are available duty-free.
   (a) and (b) or (c) but (d) between

5. Peter is in the hospital __________ he had an accident.
   (a) if (b) when (c) because (d) while

Task 5

Read each sentence carefully and replace the underlined conjunction with the correct one.

1. All employees should neither arrive after 9 A.M. <u>or</u> leave before 5 P.M., except under special circumstances.

   ____

2. It was raining cats and dogs <u>during</u> they arrived at the foot of the mountain.

   ____

3. <u>As</u> I have spoken on the phone with Mr. Kang several times, I have never met him in person.

   ____

4. Some research suggests <u>what</u> there is a link between the body's calcium balance and tooth decay.

   ____

5. Despite the relatively low salary, George took the job as a junior reporter for the local newspaper <u>such that</u> he could gain valuable job experience.

   ____

Culture Corner

Black and White

black and white, 검은색과 흰색은 가장 단순하면서도 확실하게 구분되는 두 가지 색깔입니다. 그리하여 우리가 흑백이 분명하다고 하는 것처럼 영어에서도 확실하게 구분되는 것 또는 아주 간단하고 명료한 것을 흔히 black and white이라고 표현합니다. He can't tell black from white. 는 '그는 흑과 백을 구분 못하는 둔한 사람이다.' 라는 뜻이 됩니다. 이 두 색깔이 완전히 상반된 만큼 이를 이용한 표현들의 의미도 서로 반대되는 것이 많은데 그러한 표현들에 대해 알아봅시다.

black은 어둡고 부정적인 이미지가 강하여, black market은 검은 시장, 즉 암 시장을 의미합니다. 가족이나 어떤 단체에서 black sheep (검은 양)이라고 표현하면, 혼자만 다르거나 말썽꾸러기, 천덕꾸러기를 의미합니다. My sister is the black sheep of the family. (나의 여동생은 가족의 말썽꾸러기 입니다.)

blacklist는 감시대상 인물이나 요주의 인물 명단, blackmail은 공갈 협박하는 행위를 의미합니다. 또한 black은 미국이나 유럽에서 죽음을 상징하기 때문에 사람들은 장례식에서 검은 옷차림을 합니다. 이에 반해 우리와 일본 중국 같은 동양국가에서는 장례식 때 흰색을 사용하지요.

그러면 이제 white를 사용하는 표현에 대해 알아봅시다. 대표적인 예는 white lie, 우리 말로는 '선의의 거짓말'이라는 표현이 있습니다. 또 whitewash는 어떠한 부정행위나 국치 같은 사건들을 국민들이 당황하거나 놀라지 않도록 완화시켜 진정시키는 어조로 공표하는 행위를 뜻합니다. 또한 white collar job은 월급을 받는 직업을 가리키는 말입니다. 하지만 검은색과 대조되는 흰색이라 하여서 꼭 긍정적인 뜻만 나타내는 것은 아닙니다. 예를 들어, wave a white flag는 '굴복하다(surrender), 포기하다(give up)'의 의미로 쓰입니다. 또한 white elephant는 원치 않는, 처치 곤란한 소유물이나 부동산 같은 것을 지칭할 때 쓰입니다.

마찬가지로, black도 어둡고 부정적인 의미를 나타내는 표현으로만 쓰이는 것은 아니며, 긍정적인 의미로 쓰일 때도 있습니다. 태권도 (Taekwondo)에서 제일 높은 수준을 검은 띠로 나타내고 있어서, 이를 영어로도 black belt라고 합니다. 이 말은 태권도뿐만 아니라 다른 분야에서도 최고 수준을 가리키는 표현으로 쓰일 수 있습니다. in the red이 '적자'라는 좋지 못한 뜻을 가진 반면, in the black은 '흑자'라는 뜻으로 쓰입니다.

- He can't tell black from white.
- My sister is the black sheep of the family.
- A little white lie now and again isn't a bad thing.

Wrap-up

Key sentences

1. Coordinate conjunctions
   - Would you prefer salmon or chicken?
   - Not that I don't like salmon, but I'd rather have chicken.
   - You're not only a lover of great literature, but also an athlete.
   - You're not only afan of Philip Roth, but also a high-powered executive.

2. Subordinate conjunctions
   - I think that we're ready then.
   - I don't know if I would put it that way.
   - I wonder if the waiter is ever going to take our order.
   - I've been playing golf since I was in grade school.
   - It turned out great, actually. So good, in fact, that I got promoted to vice-president of marketing for the Asia division.

REVIEW TEST

Choose the appropriate conjunction to complete each sentence. (1-5)

1. I don't know __________ he will be glad to get my invitation.
   (1) as (2) if (3) what (4) when

2. He resigned from his position __________ the salary was not reasonable.
   (1) but (2) because (3) if (4) what

3. Believe in yourself, __________ you can succeed.
   (1) and (2) but (3) or (4) so

4. Good writing skills will prove useful not only in your academic life __________ also later when you enter the business world.
   (1) nor (2) or (3) and (4) but

5. __________ you get up early, you will be late for school.
   (1) As (2) Because (3) If (4) Unless

Fill in the blank with the most appropriate conjunction. (6-10)

6. I have been missing you ____________ you left.

7. __________ the night was hot, they slept soundly.

8. The value of health is not known __________ it is lost.

9. It was so smoky in the room __________ I couldn't stop coughing.

10. It's up to you to decide __________ we'll take the project or not.

Supplementary Reading (보충 독해)

다음 글을 읽고 문제를 풀어 보세요.

Well-Being in Korea

"Well-being" is a popular term in Korea these days. Everyone encourages, discusses, and pursues a healthier, more peaceful lifestyle, regardless of age, income, location or social orientation. The five-day workweek gives people more time and accelerates the spread of a healthy lifestyle, emphasizing the importance of quality food and healthful routines, and boosting the growth of related industries. The "well-being" label has been used to sell health club memberships, organic produce, condominiums, air cleaners, magazines, cosmetics, and even instant noodles and burgers. However, the term "well-being" is often abused as a marketing tool.

The "well-being" lifestyle, however, is not just about eating healthy food, going to yoga classes, or getting facial treatments. The more important component of well-being is happiness and vitality in our lives. Physical health cannot be maintained without a healthy state of mind. People pursue well-being to free themselves from a materialistic, success-oriented society and to seek new ways to find inner peace. In addition, well-being is not about practicing a fixed lifestyle and people should not feel pressured into doing so. A person's well-being is what is 'good for' him or her. Some people can feel more relaxed and healthy just by eating seasonal vegetables, taking a daily walk in the neighborhood, or sitting in a bathtub for a bath.

The essence of well-being is a balance between the body and soul, work and leisure, family and society, you and your community. Well-being is also a way of life that can bring you closer to nature.

Translation 한국에서의 웰빙

웰빙이란 용어는 요즘 한국에서 인기가 많습니다. 나이, 소득수준, 지역과 사회 계층을 넘어서 모든 사람들이 좀 더 건강하고 좀 더 평안한 생활 양식을 권장하고, 그것에 관해 토론하며, 또 그것을 추구합니다. 주 5일 근무가 시행되면서 사람들은 여유 시간을 갖게 되었고, 먹거리의 품질과 건강한 일상생활의 중요성을 강조하고 관련 산업의 성장을 촉진시키며 웰빙 생활 양식을 빠르게 유행시켰습니다. '웰빙'이란 상표는 헬스 클럽 회원권, 유기농산물, 콘도, 공기 청정기, 잡지, 화장품, 심지어 라면, 버거 등의 판매를 촉진시키는 수단으로 사용되었습니다. 웰빙이란 용어가 종종 마케팅 수단으로 잘못 사용되기도 합니다.

그러나, 웰빙 생활양식이라는 것이 그저 건강식품을 먹고, 요가 강습을 받고, 피부 관리를 받는 것을 의미하지는 않습니다. 웰빙의 더 중요한 요소는 우리 인생의 행복감과 활력입니다. 육체적인 건강은 마음이 편안하지 않으면 결코 유지될 수 없습니다. 사람들은 물질주의적이고, 성공 지향적인 사회로부터 벗어나서 내면의 평안을 찾기 위한 새로운 방법으로 웰빙을 추구합니다. 또한 웰빙은 고정된 생활 양식대로 사는 것이 아니고, 그렇게 해야 한다는 부담감을 느껴서는 안됩니다. 어떤 사람의 웰빙이란 그 사람에게 '좋은 것'이어야 합니다. 어떤 사람들은 단순히 계절 과일을 먹거나 집 근처를 매일 산책하거나 혹은 반신욕을 하는 것만으로도 편안함을 느끼고 건강을 유지합니다.

웰빙의 본질은 신체와 정신, 일과 휴식, 가정과 사회, 당신과 당신이 속한 공동체간의 균형입니다. 웰빙은 또한 자연과 더 가까워 질 수 있는 삶의 방식이기도 합니다.

Explanation

1. Everyone encourages, discusses, and pursues a healthier, more peaceful lifestyle, regardless of age, income, location or social orientation.

① every는 각각의 사람, 각각의 개체에 초점을 두고 있기 때문에 every 다음에는 항상 단수 명사가 오고 따라서 동사의 단수형이 옵니다. each도 이와 마찬가지이므로 주의를 요합니다. every의 경우, 앞에 나온 every(one)을 다시 받을 때는 단수(he/she) 혹은 복수(they) 형태를 쓸 수 있습니다.

Ex) Everyone says, 'hello', to Mary.
(모든 사람이 Mary에게 안부를 전합니다.)

② regardless of ~ 는 '~와 관계 없이, 상관 없이' 라는 의미입니다.

Ex) Our club welcomes all students regardless of age or gender.
(우리 동아리는 연령과 성에 상관없이 모든 학생들을 환영합니다.)

2. The five-day workweek system gives people more time and accelerates the spread of a healthy lifestyle, emphasizing the importance of quality food and health, and boosting the growth of related industries.

emphasizing이 이끄는 분사 구문과 boosting이 이끄는 분사 구문이 동시 상황을 나타내고 있습니다. 또한 이 분사구문이 and로 대등하게 연결되어 있습니다.

Ex) Listening to music and drinking juice, she did her homework.
(음악을 듣고 주스를 마시면서, 그녀는 숙제를 하였습니다.)

3. The "well-being" label has been used to sell health club memberships, organic produce, condominiums, air cleaners, magazines, cosmetics and even instant noodles and burgers.

well-being이란 상표를 각각 열거된 상품의 판매 수단으로 사용했다는 의미입니다. 능동태 문장의 목적어인 well-being 에 focus를 두기 위해 수동태 문장으로 전환시켜 현재완료 수동태로 표현된 문장입니다.

Ex) The floor and windows have been cleaned up.
(바닥과 창문이 청소되었습니다.)

4. People pursue well-being to free themselves from a materialistic, success-oriented society and to seek ways to find inner peace.

① free A from B는 '~을 ~으로부터 자유롭게 하다 / 벗어나게 하다' 란 의미입니다.

Ex) He freed the birds from the cage.
(그는 새들을 새장에서 놓아주었습니다.)

② success-oriented는 '성공 지향적인' 이란 의미입니다. something-oriented라고 하면 '~지향의' 라는 의미입니다.

Ex) Now everything is so technology-oriented.
(지금은 모든 것이 너무나 기술 중심적입니다.)

5. People should not be pressured into doing so.

should not 는 '~해서는 안 된다'는 당위 혹은 금지의 표현입니다.
be pressured into는 수동태 표현으로 '~하도록 강요되다' 는 의미입니다.
Ex) Women should not be pressured into wearing skirts.
(여성들이 치마를 입도록 강요 받아서는 안됩니다.)

Q. 1 Choose the answer that best describes the meaning of each underlined word.

1. We need to accelerate the pace of change.
   (a) to make something appear greater or more important
   (b) to make a noise after a long period of silence
   (c) to make something faster or occur earlier than expected
   (d) to emphasize something or make it more noticeable

2. The government has to take action to boost the economy.
   (a) to increase or improve
   (b) to talk about something very proudly
   (c) to think in a very negative way
   (d) to interrupt someone who is speaking

3. John looked at the label on the bottle.
   (a) a point on a scale for example, a scale of amount or quality
   (b) a unit of measurement that is used to measure angles
   (c) a set of rules about how people should behave
   (d) a reference, usually on a product, that gives information about the product

4. People want to buy organic fruits and vegetables.
   (a) a part of your body for example, your heart or lungs
   (b) relating to the structure of an organization
   (c) an animal or plant, especially one that you cannot see without a microscope
   (d) produced without using artificial chemicals

5. We have managed to get most of our produce from other Asian countries.

(a) the rate at which goods are produced

(b) fresh fruits and vegetables grown for the market

(c) the process of manufacturing something

(d) a person whose job is to make plays or films

6. He showed the government how the rich and powerful can abuse their positions.

(a) to make bad and usually unethical use of something

(b) to take drugs regularly, especially illegal ones

(c) to develop resources and use them

(d) to use something for private reasons

7. Jerry lost his vitality after breaking up with his girlfriend.

(a) substances that you need in order to remain healthy

(b) something that is very important

(c) energy and enthusiasm

(d) things such as temperature which show that a person is alive

8. My mother purchases seasonal goods.

(a) having a lot of experience with/in something

(b) typical of, or suitable for, a particular time of year

(c) salt, pepper, or other spices added to food

(d) newly introduced

9. She tries to hold the balance of power.

(a) the sum of your assetsfor example, the value of your house

(b) a situation in which you have difficulty doing something

(c) a situation in which different things exist equally

(d) a situation in which people don't speak at all

Q. 2 Comprehension Test

1. According to the article, which of the following is true?
   a) The well-being lifestyle focuses on success in a society.
   b) Some people are pursuing a healthier and more peaceful lifestyle.
   c) Well-being means just eating healthy food, going to yoga class and getting facial treatments.
   d) Everybody should follow a setwell-being lifestyle.

2. What enables people to have more time and accelerates the spread of a healthy lifestyle?
   a) related industries
   b) the five-day workweek system
   c) the mass media
   d) magazines

3. According to the article, which of the following is not sold with the "well-being" label?
   a) health club memberships
   b) cosmetics
   c) instant noodles and burgers
   d) furniture

4. Which of the following is the essence of well-being?
   a) eating healthy food
   b) going to yoga classes or getting facial treatment
   c) Keeping the body and soul in balance
   d) practicing a fixed lifestyle

5. Choose the ungrammatical sentence.
   a) Every students want to study at the newly constructed library.
   b) People have the right to express their own opinions regardless of age, gender, or income.
   c) This machine is used to make copies.
   d) Each city has its own peculiarity.

Agreement and Narration

13 Unit

Introduction

Topic: Hello, I love you (안녕, 사랑해)

Lesson objectives:

Agreement and narration (일치와 화법)

- Agreement of subjects and verbs (주어와 동사의 일치)
- Agreement of tense (시제 일치)
- Direct and indirect narration (직접 화법과 간접 화법)

WARM-UP

Today we're going to listen in on a conversation between Brett and Carrie, who are on their way to see a flick. This is the last time we'll see them this semester, so it should be interesting to see how things end up. Let's get started.

Carrie : Wow. The number of Korean restaurants in this city is really increasing fast. (agreement: the number of)

Brett : Yeah. A number of them have opened up in the last year or two (agreement: a number of).

Carrie : Hey, can I have some of your ice cream? Cookies and cream is my favorite flavor. (agreement: A and B)

Brett : Here you go. The rest of it is yours. (agreement: the rest of)

Carrie : Thanks.

Brett : You're welcome.

Carrie : I think that we're only about ten blocks away from the theater.

Brett : Ten blocks is too far to walk. Let's take the bus. (agreement: ten blocks)

(waiting for the bus)

Carrie : So, you remember my friend Britney from work, right?

Brett : Is she the one with the blonde hair?

Carrie : Yes, that's her. Well, on Thursday, she said to me, "Listen. Can you do me a favor?" So, I said to her, "What is it?" And she says, "Can you work for me this Saturday?" I asked her why and she confessed to me that she had an appointment to see a cosmetic surgeon that day. (narration)

Brett : So, what happened?

Carrie : Well, I said, "I'm sorry. I have plans this weekend." And then she says, "You are a bad friend." Can you believe that? (narration)

(Camille enters)

Camille : Brett, is that you?

Brett : Camille, what are you doing here? Aaron said that you were in Europe. (narration)

Camille : Well, I was, but I'm back now.

Brett : Is everything all right? (agreement: everything)

Camille : Well, no, not exactly. There were a few misunderstandings over the terms of my contract. (agreement: there)

Brett : What do you mean?

Camille : Well, apparently, my agent sent the wrong photos. When I arrived in Europe, they said I was too short. The photographer said that if I were taller, I would have a real shot at modeling. (narration, agreement of tense)

Brett : Is that all?

Camille : Well, not only that but there are also some other things that I'll tell you about later. (agreement: there)

Brett : Well, okay.

Camille : I will cancel all my plans if you have some free time. (agreement of tense)

Carrie : Are you asking my boyfriend out right in front of my eyes? Maybe my glasses need to be cleaned. (agreement: glasses)

Camille : Who is this?

Carrie : I'm Brett's new girlfriend. Who are you?

Camille : I'm Brett's old girlfriend and I think I want him back.

Carrie : There is no way that's going to happen. (agreement: there)

Camille : There are plenty of other guys out there; you should go find one. (agreement: there)

Carrie : Brett, it's either her or me.

Camille : Yes, Brett, it's either her or me. Choose now!

Brett : Camille, neither you nor Carrie is going to be happy with what I have to say. I've decided to take a class at the Cyber Hankuk University of Foreign Studies and a lot of homework is required, so most of my time is going to be spent studying. (agreement: a lot of, most of)

THE END

Translation

오늘 우리는 Brett과 Carrie의 대화를 들어볼 건데, 그들은 지금 영화를 보러 가고 있습니다. 오늘이 이번 학기에 이들을 볼 수 있는 마지막 시간이므로 결말이 어떻게 날 지 지켜보는 것도 흥미로울 것입니다. 시작합시다.

Carrie : 와, 이 도시의 한국식당 수는 정말 빠르게 증가하고 있군요.

Brett : 네, 많은 한국 식당들이 최근 한두 해 사이에 문을 열었어요.

Carrie : 이봐요, 당신 아이스크림 좀 먹어봐도 될까요? 쿠키 앤 크림은 제가 매우 좋아하는 맛이거든요.

Brett : 여기 있어요. 남은 것 다 먹어요.

Carrie : 고마워요.

Brett : 뭘요.

Carrie : 제 생각에 우린 극장에서 단지 열 블록 정도 떨어져 있는 것 같아요.

Brett : 열 블록이면 걸어가기엔 너무 멀어요. 버스 탑시다.

(버스를 기다리며)

Carrie : 제 직장동료 Britney 기억하죠?

Brett : 금발머리인 여자분이요?

Carrie : 네, 맞아요. 글쎄, 목요일에 그녀가 나에게, "있잖아. 나 부탁 하나만 해도 될까?" 라고 하더라고요. 그래서 내가, "뭔데?" 라고 말했죠. 그러자 그녀가, "이번 토요일에 나 대신 일해줄 수 있어?" 라고 물었어요. 나는 왜 그러냐고 물었고, 그녀는 그 날 성형외과 의사를 만나기로 약속이 잡혀있다고 고백을 하는 거예요.

Brett : 그래서 어떻게 됐어요?

Carrie : 그래서 내가, "미안해. 이번 주말에는 일이 있어." 라고 했죠. 그러자 그녀가, "넌 나쁜 친구야." 라고 하더라고요. 이게 믿어져요?

(Camille이 들어온다)

Camille : Brett, 너 맞아?

Brett : Camille, 여기서 뭐 하는 거야? Aaron 말로는 너 유럽에 있다고 했는데.

Camille : 음, 그랬지. 하지만 돌아왔어.

Brett : 다 괜찮은 거지?

Camille : 음, 아니, 정확히 말하면 아냐. 내 계약 조항을 놓고 약간의 오해가 있었어.

Brett : 무슨 말이야?

Camille : 분명히 내 대리인이 잘못된 사진을 보냈어. 내가 유럽에 도착했을 때 그 사람들이 말하길 내가 너무 작대. 그 사진작가 말로는 내 키가 더 컸으면 모델로 정말 잘 나갔을 거래.

Brett : 그게 다야?

Camille : 그것뿐만 아니라 다른 것도 몇 개 있는데 나중에 말해줄게.

Brett : 그래.

Camille : 너 시간이 좀 있으면, 내 계획 다 취소할게.

Carrie : 바로 내 눈 앞에서 내 남자친구에게 데이트 신청을 하는 건가요? 아마 내 안경에 뭐가 묻었나 보군요.

Camille : 이 사람은 누구야?

Carrie : 전 Brett의 새 여자친구에요. 당신은 누구죠?

Camille : 난 Brett의 옛 여자친구인데 다시 그를 되찾고 싶어요.

Carrie : 그런 일이 일어나지는 않아요.

Camille : 밖에 널린 게 남자에요. 다른 곳에서 찾아 보세요.

Carrie : Brett, 저 여자와 나 중 한 명을 선택해요.

Camille : 그래, Brett, 저 여자와 나 중 누구야! 지금 선택해!

Brett : Camille, 너와 Carrie 둘 다 내 말에 기뻐하지 않을 것 같아. 난 사이버 한국외대에서 강의를 듣기로 결정했는데 숙제가 많아. 그래서 대부분의 시간을 공부하는데 쓸 계획이야.

끝

Comprehension Check

1. What was the cause of Carrie's disagreement with her friend?
   (a) Her friend asked for a favor, but she couldn't comply.
   (b) Carrie did her friend a favor, but the friend didn't thank her.
   (c) They both took an interest in Brett.
   (d) Carrie offended her friend by making a comment about her hair.

2. Which of the following topics do Brett and Carrie NOT discuss before their run-in with Camille?
   (a) restaurants
   (b) transportation options
   (c) the weather
   (d) a feud

3. Why did Camille return from Europe so suddenly?
   (a) to reunite with Brett
   (b) to reunite with Aaron
   (c) because her plans didn't work out
   (d) to get cosmetic surgery

Useful Expressions

In this dialogue	Explanation
1. Cookies and cream is my favorite flavor.	1. Cookies and cream, often associated with Oreo sandwich cookies, is a flavor you may have seen on labels of ice cream cartons, pies, or other frozen desserts. The menu at Coldstone Creamery features a shake by this name, and it's quite tasty. Though *cookies* and *cream* are *two* ingredients, they are combined to create *one* flavor. As such, it is treated as a singular noun, and this is reflected in the choice of the verb "is." You'll find more examples of this construction later on in this lesson.

In this dialogue	Explanation
2. Ten blocks is too far to walk.	2. In this example, the subject, ten blocks, is treated as a singular noun. As a general rule, when we refer to multiple objects collectively, we treat the aggregate as singular. This often happens with units of measurement such as *dollars, kilometers,* or *years*. If you're unsure whether to treat your subject as singular or plural, ask yourself whether you're talking about the sum total or each individual unit.
3. The photographer said that if I were taller, I would have a real shot at modeling.	3. At this point, you can probably identify the construction used in this example. If not, it's the subjunctive, and we covered it a few weeks ago in unit 11. Remember, when we make conditional statements that are contrary to fact, we use a special grammatical structure. This construction is easy to identify because it usually begins with "if." And if what follows is clearly untrue, you know that you're dealing with the subjunctive mood.
4. I've decided to take a class at the Cyber University of Foreign Studies, and a lot of homework is required, so most of my time is going to be spent studying.	4. When Brett says he's going to have a lot of homework, he likely means multiple assignments. Still, we use the singular construction and this is reflected in the verb "is." Though adverb phrases like "a lot of" or "most of" indicate plurality, we look to what they modify for direction. Confused? Let's take a look at a few examples: (1) Most of my friends are going abroad for the summer. *Here, "friends" is plural, so we use the plural construction.* (2) Most of the work is done. *Here, "work" is singular, so we use the singular construction.*

Grammar

Focus 1 Agreement of subjects and verbs (주어와 동사의 일치)

01 단수동사가 쓰이는 주어

(1) 부정대명사: everything, everybody, each, somebody, anything, each, nothing, no one, etc.

- Is everything all right?
  (모든 것이 잘 되어 갑니까?)
- Every boy and girl in this class is good at science.
  (이 반의 모든 남자아이와 여자아이는 과학을 잘합니다.)
- Each of us sees the world differently.
  (우리 각자는 세계를 다르게 봅니다.)
- No one is permitted to leave.
  (아무도 떠나는 것이 허용되지 않습니다.)
- Nothing seems to be working.
  (아무 것도 작동하지 않는 것 같습니다.)

cf) 구어체에서는 each of ~ 다음에 복수동사가 쓰이기도 합니다.
- Each of them has/have problems. (그들 각자의 문제가 있습니다.)
- Each of us has/have the power to make a difference. (우리 각자는 변화를 만들 힘이 있습니다.)

(2) 부정사, 동명사, 구나 절

- To know her is to love her. (= If you know her, you love her.)
  (그녀를 안다는 것은 그녀를 사랑한다는 것입니다.)
- Seeing is believing.
  (보는 것이 믿는 것입니다 /백문이 불여일견)
- That the girl is an adopted child is true.
  (그 소녀가 양녀라는 것은 사실입니다.)
- Whether he will accept the offer is doubtful.
  (그가 그 제안을 받아들일지 어쩔지는 잘 모릅니다.)

(3) 학문명, 국명, 병명 등

ethics, economics, physics, politics, statistics, linguistics, United States, Philippines, Netherlands, measles, billiards

- Linguistics is the scientific study of language.
  (언어학은 언어에 대한 과학적인 학문입니다.)
- Measles is spreading in my school.
  (홍역이 우리 학교에서 퍼지고 있습니다.)
- The United States is anxious to improve its image in Latin America.
  (미국은 라틴 아메리카에서 자국의 이미지를 향상시키기를 열망합니다.)
- The Netherlands is bordered by the North Sea.
  (네덜란드는 북해를 접하고 있습니다.)
- Billiards has been played since the 15th century.
  (사람들은 15세기 이후부터 당구를 쳐 왔습니다.)

(4) 시간, 거리, 금액

- Ten blocks is too far to walk.
  (열 블록은 걷기에 너무 먼 거리입니다.)
- I decided to quit my part-time job because 40 minutes was too long a commute every morning.
  (매일 아침 40분씩 통근하는 것은 너무 오래 걸리기 때문에 나는 아르바이트를 그만두기로 결심했습니다.)
- Three days is about the longest I've gone without a cigarette.
  (내가 담배 없이 지낸 건 사흘이 거의 가장 깁니다.)
- Sixty dollars a week is a small sum to him.
  (일주일에 60달러는 그에게 적은 액수입니다.)
- Javier Sotomayor is the world high jump record holder; 2.43 meters is his record.
  (Javier Sotomayor는 높이뛰기 세계신기록 소유자로, 그의 기록은 2.43미터입니다.)

(5) A and B 형식의 단일개념

bread and butter (빵과 버터), trial and error(시행착오), etc.

- Cookies and cream is my favorite flavor.
  (쿠키 앤 크림은 내가 가장 좋아하는 맛입니다.)
- Curry and rice is my favorite meal.
  (카레와 밥 (카레라이스) 는 내가 가장 좋아하는 식사입니다.)
- Early to bed and early to rise makes a man healthy, wealthy, and wise.
  (일찍 자고 일찍 일어나는 것이 사람을 건강하고, 부유하고, 현명하게 만듭니다.)

- This gin and tonic isn't very strong.
  (이 진토닉은 그리 독하지 않습니다.)
- Few people realize that fish and chips, a menu staple at any pub in the U.K., contains more than a thousand calories in a single serving.
  (영국 어느 술집에서든 메뉴의 주성분으로 들어가는 생선과 과자가 한 접시에 1,000 칼로리 이상을 포함하고 있다는 것을 아는 사람은 거의 없습니다.)
- Snow White and the Seven Dwarves was the first full-length animated motion picture produced by Walt Disney.
  (백설공주와 일곱 난쟁이는 월트 디즈니사에서 만든 최초의 무삭제 만화영화입니다.)

(6) more than one, one of~

- If things don't get better, more than one person is going to leave the job.
  (상황이 나아지지 않으면 한 명 이상은 직장을 그만둘 것입니다.)
- One of my friends is going to Greece next week.
  (내 친구 중 하나가 다음주에 그리스로 갑니다.)
- More than one out of every five children is obese.
  (다섯 명 당 한 명 이상의 어린이가 과체중입니다.)

(7) many a + 단수 명사

- Many a soldier was killed in the valley.
  (많은 군인이 그 골짜기에서 죽었습니다.)
- Many a man has succumbed to the temptation of alcohol.
  (많은 사람이 술의 유혹에 굴복해 왔습니다.)

02 복수동사가 쓰이는 주어

(1) 집합 명사

family(가족), class(학급), committee(위원회), nation(국민), public(대중), audience (청중) 등의 집합 명사를 하나의 집합체로 보면 단수 동사, 개개인을 전제로 한 경우는 복수 동사가 쓰입니다. American English (미국영어) 에서는 단수로 취급하는 경우가 많고, British English (영국영어)에서는 주로 복수로 취급합니다.

- The committee is firmly opposed to any building on the green belt.
  (위원회는 그린벨트 내의 어떤 건물도 단호히 반대합니다.)
- The committee were divided on the plan.
  (위원회는 그 안에 대해 의견이 갈라졌습니다.)

- The audience at the concert was enormous.
  (그 콘서트에 많은 청중이 왔습니다.)
- The audience were deeply moved by the story.
  (청중들은 그 이야기에 매우 감동했습니다.)
- Many polls suggest that the public feels alienated by the present government.
  (많은 여론 조사에 따르면 민심이 현 정부로부터 멀어지고 있습니다.)
- Many polls suggested that the public were divided on the matter.
  (많은 여론 조사에 따르면 그 문제에 대해 대중들이 분열되었습니다.)

(2) a number of + 복수명사

- A number of Korean restaurants have opened up in the last year or two.
  (많은 한국 식당들이 최근 한두 해 사이에 문을 열었습니다.)
- In recent years, a number of factors, including cuts in government spending and expensive technology upgrades, have forced universities to raise tuition prices.
  (최근 정부 지출비 삭감과 고가의 과학기술 업그레이드를 포함한 많은 요소들이 대학에서 등록금을 올리도록 강요해 왔습니다.)
- A number of European countries have passed laws mandating a shorter work week.
  (많은 유럽국가들이 주당 근무시간을 줄이는 법안을 통과시켰습니다.)

cf) the number of~ 는 '~의 수' 라는 뜻으로, 단수 동사가 옵니다.
The number of Korean restaurants in this city is really increasing fast.
(이 도시의 한국식당 수는 정말 빠르게 증가하고 있습니다.)

(3) some of~, all of~, part of~, more of~, most of~, none of~, any of~, half of~, plenty of~, a lot of~, the rest of~, 분수 of~

이러한 표현은 뒤에 오는 명사에 따라 단수 취급을 하기도 하고, 복수 취급을 하기도 합니다.

- Most of my time is going to be spent studying.
  (내 시간의 대부분을 공부하는데 쓸 것입니다.)
- Most of his books are English novels.
  (그의 책 대부분은 영어소설들입니다.)
- None of these tools are suitable.
  (이 도구들 중 어떤 것도 적합하지 않습니다.)
- Half of those surveyed agree that the government needs to do more to help senior citizens.
  (설문조사 응답자의 절반은 정부가 노인층을 돕기 위해 더욱 노력할 필요가 있다는 데에 동의합니다.)
- The rest of it is yours.
  (나머지는 당신의 것입니다.)

- All of the information was useful.
  (모든 정보가 유용합니다.)
- Two-thirds of the floor was carpeted.
  (바닥의 2/3에 카페트가 깔렸습니다.)
- I've decided to take a class at the Cyber Hankuk University of Foreign Studies and a lot of homework is required.
  (나는 사이버한국외대에서 수업을 듣기로 결심했는데, 숙제가 많습니다.)

(4) clothes, glasses, spectacles, trousers, socks

늘 복수형으로 쓰입니다.

- These trousers are too long for me.
  (이 바지는 나에게 너무 깁니다.)
- I've been walking around in the rain all day and my socks are soaked.
  (나는 하루 종일 비속을 걸어 다녀서 양말이 다 젖었습니다.)
- Maybe my glasses need to be cleaned.
  (아마 내 안경을 닦아야 할 필요가 있는 것 같습니다.)

cf) a pair of~ 가 붙으면 단수형 동사가 쓰입니다.

– A new pair of socks is needed. (새 양말 한 켤레가 필요합니다.)

03 주어, 동사 사이에 전치사구가 오거나, 주어가 수식을 받을 때 동사의 수에 영향을 주지 않습니다.

- The news of the government's negotiations was received with mixed emotions.
  (정부의 협상 소식은 상반된 정서로 받아들여졌습니다.)
- The problem concerning the newly built houses was discussed.
  (새로 지은 집들에 관한 문제가 토론되었습니다.)
- The bicycle, carried by my brothers, is a gift from my parents.
  (내 남동생들이 운반하고 있는 그 자전거는 부모님에게 받은 선물입니다.)
- The issue over whether girls should be allowed to join boys' sports teams has drawn the attention of many parents.
  (소녀들이 소년들의 스포츠에 합류하는 것을 허락해야 할지에 대한 문제는 많은 부모님의 관심을 이끌어 냈습니다.)

04 There~ 구문

There 구문에서는 그 다음에 오는 명사에 따라 동사의 수에 일치됩니다.

- There were a few misunderstandings over the terms of my contract.
  (내 계약의 조항에 몇 가지 오해가 있었습니다.)
- Well, not only that but there are also some other things that I'll tell you about later.
  (음, 그것뿐만 아니라 다른 것도 몇 개 있는데, 나중에 당신에게 말하겠습니다.)
- There are plenty of other guys out there; you should go find one.
  (밖에 다른 남자들이 많습니다. 가서 한 명 찾으십시오.)
- There is no way that's going to happen.
  (그런 일은 일어나지 않을 겁니다.)

05 도치구문

도치 구문에서 수 일치는 동사 뒤 주어에 맞추게 됩니다.

- On the sofa lies the cat.
  (소파 위에 고양이가 누워있습니다.)
- Gone are the days when people looked out for one another.
  (사람들이 서로를 충분히 보살피는 그러한 시대는 끝났습니다.)

Task 1

Choose the appropriate verb form to complete each of the following sentences.

1. The Philippines (is, are) a country in Southeast Asia.
2. Half of the videos here (is, are) either comedy or action.
3. All of the committee members (is, are) present.
4. Studying chemistry and physics (was, been, were) not easy for me.
5. Bread and butter (is, are) my favorite breakfast.

Focus 2 Agreement of tense (시제의 일치)

01 주절의 시제가 현재, 현재 완료, 미래

주절의 동사가 현재, 현재완료, 미래이면 종속절의 동사는 제한이 없이 쓰입니다.

- They know that this is their last chance.
  (그들은 이번이 그들의 마지막 기회라는 것을 알고 있습니다.)
- I don't know if Tom was sick.
  (Tom이 아팠었는지 나는 모릅니다.)
- I have often said that if you can't find it at Home Plus, you probably don't need it.
  (나는 당신이 그것을 홈플러스에서 찾을 수 없다면 아마 그것이 필요 없을 거라고 자주 말했습니다.)

02 주절의 시제가 과거

주절의 동사가 과거인경우에 종속절의 동사는 과거나 과거완료를 주로 씁니다. 그러나 종속절의 내용이 현재까지 지속되는 상황이거나 현재와 관련이 있을 때는 주절의 시제와 관계없이 종속절에 현재형을 쓸 수도 있습니다.

- Aaron said that you were in Europe.
  (Aaron 말로는 당신이 유럽에 있다고 했습니다.)
- Some customers complained that the bread was stale.
  (일부 고객들은 빵이 상했다며 불평했습니다.)
- He said that he would be all right by next week.
  (그는 다음 주까지는 몸이 좋아질 거라고 말했습니다.)
- They discovered that he had hidden a note in the book.
  (그들은 그가 책에 쪽지를 숨겨놓았다는 것을 발견했습니다.)
- The detectives inferred that the suspect had entered through the rear window.
  (형사들은 용의자가 뒤쪽 창문을 통해 들어왔을 거라고 추리했습니다.)

03 시제 일치의 예외

(1) 불변의 진리나 격언: 현재형

- We learned that light travels faster than sound.
  (우리는 빛은 소리보다 빨리 움직인다고 배웠습니다.)

- He used to preach that honesty is the best policy.
  (그는 정직이 최선의 정책이라고 설교하곤 했습니다.)
- Did you know that the 50 tallest mountains in the world are in Asia?
  (세계에서 가장 높은 산 50개가 아시아에 있다는 것을 알고 있었습니까?)

(2) 현재의 습관, 사실: 현재형

- Sam said that his work finishes at 6 p.m.
  (Sam은 그의 일이 오후 6시에 끝난다고 말하였습니다)
- She asked me when the shop opens.
  (그녀는 그 상점이 언제 문을 여는지 나에게 물었습니다.)
- The weather report mentioned that the tide comes in around 7:00 a.m.
  (기상 캐스터는 오전 7시경에 조수가 들어온다고 말했습니다.)
- My friend who lives in Sao Paolo said that the weather in Brazil is nice this time of year.
  (상파울로에 살고 있는 내 친구가 브라질의 날씨는 일년 중 이맘때가 좋다고 말했습니다.)

(3) 비교 또는 대조

종속절이 비교, 대조를 나타낼 때, 주절과는 관계없이 동사가 쓰입니다.

- She spoke English as fluently as you do.
  (그녀는 당신만큼 영어를 유창하게 말했습니다.)
- The consumer electronics industry was more viable last year than it is this year.
  (가전산업은 올해보다 작년에 더욱 성장할 만했습니다.)
- The Beatles are as popular today as they were in the 60's.
  (비틀즈는 60년대에 그랬던 것만큼 오늘날에도 인기가 있습니다.)

(4) 역사적 사실: 과거형

- He said that the Korean War ended in 1953.
  (그는 한국 전쟁이 1953년에 끝났다고 말했습니다.)
- Did you know that Columbus discovered America?
  (당신은 콜럼버스가 미국을 발견했다는 것을 알았습니까?)

(5) 가정법 시제

가정법 시제는 주절 동사의 시제에 따라 변하지 않습니다.

- The photographer said that if I were taller, I would have a real shot at modeling.
  (그 사진작가는 내 키가 더 컸다면 나는 진짜 멋진 모델 사진을 찍을 기회를 얻었을 거라고 말했습니다.)

- I think/thought that if more people had come out to vote, we would have stood a chance.

(만약 더 많은 사람들이 투표를 했다면 우리가 이길 가능성이 있었을 거라고 생각합니다/생각하였습니다.)

- She says/said that if I were to ask her to marry me, she would say yes.

(내가 그녀에게 청혼한다면 그녀는 승낙하겠다고 말합니다/말했습니다.)

(6) 조건이나 시간의부사절

조건이나 시간의 부사절에서는 미래시제 대신 현재시제가 쓰입니다.

- I'll cancel all my plans if you have some free time.

(당신 시간이 괜찮으면 나는모든 내 계획을 취소하겠습니다.)

- What do you think will happen when European aid finally reaches them?

(유럽의 원조가 마침내 그들에게 도착한다면 무슨 일이 생길 거라고 생각합니까?)

- Comments will be posted only if they are relevant and not abusive.

(논평은 관련성이 있고 독설이 아닐 때에만 발표가 될 것입니다.)

Task 2

Read each sentence carefully and decide whether the verb is used correctly or incorrectly. If it is used incorrectly, write the correct sentence in the space provided.

	correct	incorrect
1. It will make me sad if you will betray me.	( )	( )
2. They realized that he went home.	( )	( )
3. He asked when I have seen her last.	( )	( )
4. The teacher told us that turtles can live over a hundred years.	( )	( )
5. My textbook says that Russia had become a global power under Peter the Great.	( )	( )

Focus 3 Narration (화법)

01 Direct and indirect narration (직접 화법과 간접 화법)

직접 화법(direct narration)은 다른 사람의 말을 인용부호(" ")를 사용하여 말한 그대로를 전달하는 방법이고 간접 화법(indirect narration)은 말하는 사람의 말을 전달하는 사람의 입장에서 말을 바꾸어 그 내용을 전달하는 방법입니다.

(1) 직접 화법

- On Thursday, she said to me, "Listen. Can you do me a favor?"
  (목요일에 그녀가 나에게 "있잖아. 나 부탁 하나만 해도 될까?"하고 말했습니다.)
- So, I said to her, "What is it?"
  (그래서 제가 "뭔데?" 라고 말했습니다.)
- And she says, "Can you work for me this Saturday?"
  (그러자 그녀가, "이번 토요일에 나 대신 일해줄 수 있니?" 라고 말했습니다.)
- Well, I said, "I'm sorry. I have plans this weekend."
  (그래서 내가 "미안해. 이번 주말에는 일이 있어." 라고 말했습니다.)
- And then she says, "You are a bad friend."
  (그러자 그녀가 "넌 나쁜 친구야." 라고 말합니다.)

(2) 간접 화법

- I asked her why and she confessed to me that she had an appointment to see a cosmetic surgeon that day.
  (내가 그녀에게 왜 그러냐고 물으니까 그녀는 그 날 성형외과 의사를 만나기로 약속이 잡혀있다고 고백했습니다.)
- When I arrived in Europe, they said I was too short.
  (내가 유럽에 도착했을 때, 그들은 내가 너무 작다고 말했습니다.)

(3) 직접 화법과 간접 화법

- She said, "I feel tired."(직접 화법)
  She said that she felt tired. (간접 화법)
  (그녀는 "나는 피곤해요."라고 말했습니다. 그녀는 피곤하다고 말했습니다.)
- "I have an orange," he said to me.
  He told me that he had an orange.
  ("나는 오렌지를 한 개 가지고 있어요."라고 그가 나에게 말했습니다. 그는 오렌지를 한 개 가지고 있다고 내게 말했습니다.)

이처럼 간접화법은 화자의 관점에서 내용을 전하게 되므로 전달동사, 인칭 대명사, 지시 대명사, 시제, 부사 등을 바꾸어야 합니다.

02 평서문

(1) 전달동사

① 전달동사 say to는 tell로 바꾸고, to가 없으면 say를 그대로 사용합니다.

② 전달 동사의 시제가 현재일 때 피전달문의 시제는 변하지 않고, 시제가 과거일 때 피전달문의 시제는 시제 일치의 규칙에 맞게 현재→과거, 현재완료/과거→과거완료, 조동사→조동사의 과거형으로 변합니다.

- He says to me, "I was pleased to get a present."
  He tells me that he was pleased to get a present.
  (그는 나에게 "나는 선물을 받아서 기뻤어요."라고 말합니다. 그는 선물을 받아서 기뻤다고 나에게 말합니다.)
- He said, "I am sorry."
  He said that he was sorry.
  (그는 "미안합니다"라고 말했습니다. 그는 미안하다고 말했습니다.)
- She said to me, "I was busy."
  She told me that she had been busy.
  (그녀는 "나는 바빴다."라고 나에게 말했습니다. 그녀는 바빴다고 나에게 말했습니다.)
- And then she shouted, "I am leaving and never coming back."
  And then she shouted that she was leaving and never coming back.
  (그리고 나서 그녀는 "나는 떠나서 절대 돌아오지 않을 거야." 라고 외쳤습니다. 그리고 나서 그녀는 떠나서 절대 돌아오지 않을 거라고 외쳤습니다.)

(2) 인칭

피전달문(인용부호 속의 문장)의 1인칭(I, we)은 전달문의 주어로(말하는 사람), 피전달문의 2인칭(you)은 전달문의 목적어로(듣는 사람) 바꾸고, 피전달문의 3인칭(he, she, it, they)은 그대로 둡니다.

- He said to her, "I will give you a ride."
  He told her that he would give her a ride.
  (그는 그녀에게 "당신을 차로 모셔다 드리죠." 라고 말했습니다. 그는 그녀에게 차로 데려다 준다고 말했습니다.)
- She says (to me), "You are very generous to me."
  She tells me that I am very generous to her.
  (그녀는 나에게 "당신은 나에게 매우 너그럽습니다."라고 말합니다. 그녀는 내가 그녀에게 매우 너그럽다고 말합니다.)

(3) 부사, 지시대명사

부사와 지시대명사 등도 전달하는 사람의 입장에 맞게 적절하게 바꿉니다.

this → that　　these → those　　here → there　　now → then

ago → before　　today → that day

yesterday → the previous day / the day before

the day before yesterday → two days ago

tomorrow → the next day / the following day

last night → the night before / the previous night

next week → the following week

- He said, "I have a party this evening."
  He said that he had a party that evening.
  (그는 "난 오늘밤에 파티가 있어요."라고 말했습니다. 그는 그날 밤에 파티가 있었다고 말했습니다.)
- She said to me, "I will come here again tomorrow."
  이 문장은 전달하는 사람의 위치에 따라 아래 두 가지 간접화법 문장이 다 가능합니다.
  She told me that she would come here again the next day.
  She told me that she would go there again the next day.
  (그녀는 나에게 "나는 내일 다시 여기에 올 겁니다."라고 말했습니다. 그녀는 다음날 거기에 다시 온다고 나에게 말했습니다.)
- She said, "I'll see you next week."
  She said that she would see me the following week.
  (그녀는 "다음 주에 보자." 라고 말했습니다. 그녀는 그 다음 주에 보자고 말했습니다.)
- Before leaving, he turned around and said, "Wait for me right here."
  Before leaving he turned around and asked me to wait for him right there.
  (떠나기 전 그는 돌아서서 "여기서 날 기다려." 라고 말했습니다. 떠나기 전 그는 돌아서서 나에게 거기서 그를 기다리라고 말했습니다.)

03 의문문

직접 화법에서 전달동사 say / say to는 간접 화법에서 ask로 바꿉니다. 직접 화법에서도 전달동사 ask를 쓰기도 합니다.

(1) 의문사가 있는 의문문

의문사가 접속사 역할을 하여 '의문사+주어+동사' 의 순서가 됩니다.

- I said to the boy, "Where do you live?" / I asked (the boy), "Where do you live?" I asked the boy where he lived.
  (나는 그 소년에게 "어디에 사나요?"라고 말했습니다. 나는 그 소년이 어디에 사는지를 물었습니다.)
- He said to me, "What time is the flight?" / He asked (me), "What time is the flight?" He asked me what time the flight was.
  (그는 "몇 시 비행기인가요?"라고 나에게 물었습니다. 그는 나에게 몇 시 비행기였는지를 물었습니다.)
- One reporter stood up and said, "What is the city planning to do with the rest of this year's budget allocation?"
  One reporter stood up and asked what the city was planning to do with the rest of the year's budget allocation.
  (한 리포터가 일어나서 "이 도시는 올해 할당된 남은 예산으로 무엇을 할 계획입니까?" 라고 말했습니다. 한 리포터가 일어나서 그 도시는 올해 할당된 남은 예산으로 무엇을 할 계획인지 물어보았습니다.)

(2) 의문사가 없는 의문문

접속사로 if나 whether를 넣고, 의문사 뒤를 평서문 어순으로 바꿉니다. "~인지 아닌지" 로 해석합니다.

- I said to him, "Is this your key?"
  I asked him if/whether this/that was his key.
  (나는 그에게 "이것이 당신 열쇠입니까?"라고 말했습니다. 나는 그 열쇠가 그의 열쇠인지를 그에게 물었습니다.)
- She said to me, "Can you work on Saturdays?"
  She asked me if/whether I could work on Saturdays.
  (그녀는 나에게 "토요일에 일을 할 수 있나요?"라고 말했습니다. 그녀는 내가 토요일에 일을 할 수 있는지를 물었습니다.)
- I said to her, "Have you ever seen a tiger?"
  I asked her if/whether she had ever seen a tiger.
  (나는 그녀에게 "호랑이를 본 적이 있나요?"라고 말했습니다. 나는 그녀에게 호랑이를 본 적이 있는지 물었습니다.)
- "Are you lying to me?" her father replied.
  Her father asked if/whether she was lying to him.
  ("너 나한테 거짓말 하는 거니?" 라고 그녀의 아버지께서 응수하셨습니다. 그녀의 아버지는 그녀가 거짓말을 하고 있는지 물었습니다.)
- "Does this mean we can't see each other anymore?" she said.
  She asked if/whether this meant we couldn't see each other anymore.
  ("우리가 더 이상 서로 볼 수 없다는 뜻인가요?" 라고 그녀가 말했습니다. 그녀는 우리가 더 이상 서로를 볼 수 없다는 뜻인지 물었습니다.)

04 명령문

전달동사를 tell(말하다), ask(요청하다), order(명령하다), advise(충고하다), beg(간청하다) 등으로 알맞게 바꿉니다. 명령문의 동사는 to부정사로 바꾸고 부정 명령문일 때는 'not+ to 부정사'로 바꿉니다. 전달동사가 propose(건의하다), suggest(제안하다), demand(요구하다) 등의 경우는, 뒤에 '주어 + (should) 동사 원형' 이 옵니다.

- My parents said to me, "Do your best."
  My parents told me to do my best.
  (내 부모님은 내게 "최선을 다 해라."라고 말했습니다. 내 부모님은 최선을 다하라고 내게 말하였습니다.)
- The doctor said to me, "Don't drink coffee."
  The doctor told/advised me not to drink coffee.
  (의사는 내게 "커피를 마시지 마세요."라고 말했습니다. 의사는 내게 커피를 마시지 마라고 충고했습니다.)
- She said, "Let's take a break."
  She suggested that we (should) take a break.
  (그녀는 "좀 쉽시다."라고 말했습니다. 그녀는 쉬자고 제안했습니다.)

Task 3

Change the direct sentences to indirect sentences, and the indirect sentences to direct sentences.

1. Jane said, "Where did Tom buy this shirt?"
   ____
2. He asked me why I had called him.
   ____
3. Peter said, "I will not forget what my mom said to me."
   ____
4. Myroommate told me not to make a sound.
   ____
5. She said to me, "Have you been to the Opera House in Australia?"
   ____

Practice

Task 4

Choose the appropriate word to complete each sentence.

1. I called my friend in Thailand yesterday, and he said it ______ raining there.
   a) is b) should be c) to be d) was

2. I told you ______ turn off the computer, didn't I?
   a) not to b) don't c) not d) to not

3. The Statue of Liberty, which has welcomed immigrants, visitors, and travelers to the United States since 1886, ______ originally a gift from the people of France.
   a) was b) were c) be d) being

4. Someone ___ me there had been an accident on the freeway.
   a) asked b) said c) spoke d) told

5. She asked me where ________ find him.
   a) could she b) she can c) she could 4) can she

Task 5

Find the error in each sentence and correct it.

1. She said that(a) she will(b) stay home because she had(c) homework to do(d).

_____________ → _____________

2. One(a) of the most(b) important aspects(c) of an organic farm are(d) sanitation.

_____________ → _____________

3. A number(a) of people have(b) tried to find(c) the answer, but it(d) have all failed.

_____________ → _____________

4. The man said that(a) if(b) he has(c) been there, he might(d) have been injured.

_____________ → _____________

5. Each(a) of the states(b) along the Pacific coast are(c) expecting(d) a power shortage because of the drought.

_____________ → _____________

Wrap-up

Key sentences

1. 주어와 동사의 일치
   - Is everything all right?
   - Ten blocks is too far to walk.
   - Cookies and cream is my favorite flavor.
   - A number of them have opened up in the last year or two.
   - The number of Korean restaurants in this city is really increasing fast.
   - I've decided to take a class at the Cyber Hankuk University of Foreign Studies and a lot of homework is required, so most of my time is going to be spent studying.
   - The rest of it is yours.
   - Maybe my glasses need to be cleaned.
   - There is no way that's going to happen.
   - There are plenty of other guys out there; you should go find one.

2. 시제의 일치
   - Aaron said that you were in Europe.
   - The photographer said that if I were taller, I would have a real shot at modeling.
   - I will cancel all my plans if you have some free time.

3. 화법
   - On Thursday, she said to me, "Listen. Can you do me a favor?"
   - I asked her why and she confessed to me that she had an appointment to see a cosmetic surgeon that day.

Review 8-13

Unit 8

Choose the appropriate word to complete each of the following sentences.

1. The city implemented a new recycling policy __________ is part of a plan to reduce waste.

   a. which b. where
   c. whose d. when

2. We're free all next week. You'll be welcome __________ day you come.

   a. however b. whenever
   c. whoever d. whichever

3. This food should be stored in a dry place __________ temperature extremes are minimal.

   a. where b. which
   c. how d. what

4. That is not __________ I meant to say.

   a. which b. whatever
   c. what d. that

5. She is the person __________ most students turn to for advice.

   a. whomever b. which
   c. whoever d. whom

6. "The plan is perfect," said Mrs. Smith, _________ company drafted the plan.

a. who
b. whose
c. whom
d. which

7. The film is completely different from the book _________ it is based.

a. which
b. on which
c. whichever
d. that

8. The museum, _________ collection had started to grow stale, decided to acquire a new piece.

a. whose
b. which
c. that
d. whatever

9. The plantain, _________ is sometimes confused with the banana, is widely eaten in tropical regions.

a. what
b. who
c. that
d. which

10. I totally forgot the day _________ I made an appointment with my friends.

a. what
b. where
c. when
d. which

Unit 9

Read each active voice sentence. Then choose the best option to complete each equivalent passive voice sentence.

1. Our team won the regional championship.

→ The regional championship _________ by our team.

a. is won
b. have been won
c. was won
d. winning

2. Snow covers the mountains.

→ The mountains __________ by snow.

a. covered

b. are covering

c. are covered

d. has been covered

3. He's writing a book about his travels.

→ A book about his travels _________ by him.

a. is being write

b. is being written

c. are written

d. is written

4. Who invented the device?

→ ______________ the device invented?

a. Who did

b. By whom was

c. By whom did

d. Who was

5. People believe that the Chinese government is hoarding oil.

→ The Chinese government is believed _________ oil.

a. to be hoarded

b. to be hoarding

c. be hoarding

d. be hoarded

Choose the appropriate word to complete each of the following sentences.

6. Water is composed __________ hydrogen and oxygen.

a. of

b. by

c. in

d. with

7. We didn't go the party because we __________.

a. don't invite

b. didn't invited

c. are invited

d. weren't invited

8. I told him that his father _________ to the hospital.

a. was taking

b. had taken

c. had been taken

d. had been taking.

9. The meeting will ________ this afternoon.

a. be held
b. be hold
c. is held
d. is holing

10. Jim's diary had __________ to the detective.

a. be shown
b. been showing
c. be showing
d. been shown

Unit 10

Choose the appropriate answer to create a grammatical sentence in the subjunctive mood.

1. Had I been a few centimeters taller, I __________ from the basketball team.

a. was cut
b. will be cut
c. would be cut
d. wouldn't have been cut

2. I wish I __________ taller, thinner, and better looking.

a. were
b. am
c. will be
d. will have been

3. If you were to buy a ticket to London in June, it __________ cheaper than going in July.

a. would be
b. would have been
c. was
d. is

4. If people ___________ about the dangers of smoking sooner, many lives could have been saved.

a. have known
b. knew
c. had known
d. know

5. Should you decide to cancel your subscription during the 30 day trial period, a full refund __________.

a. will be issued b. has been issued
c. is issued d. issued

6. The professor recommended that we __________ more time studying English grammar.

a. have spent b. spend
c. are spending d. spent

7. If I were you, I __________ twice before quitting.

a. am thinking b. think
c. have been thinking d. would think

8. Had you remembered to bring the map, we __________ lost right now.

a. will be b. are
c. would have been d. wouldn't be

9. The meeting will be called off if the chief executive _________ tomorrow.

a. didn't arrive b. doesn't arrive
c. is arriving d. had not arrived

10. It's about time you _________ to bed.

a. gone b. went
c. are going d. go

Unit 11

Choose the appropriate preposition to complete each of the following sentences.

1. Baristas typically place a tip jar __________ the counter for customers to toss their spare change into.

   a. above b. in
   c. on d. over

2. She watched __________ envy as her rival was awarded first prize in this year's beauty pageant.

   a. to b. with
   c. by d. for

3. I've been lonely __________ you went away.

   a. during b. up to
   c. until d. since

4. That sort of thing only happens __________ the movies.

   a. by b. in
   c. till d. on

5. I'm reading a book __________ how to get rich in 90 days or less.

   a. at b. for
   c. about d. in

6. That was quite a surprise __________ the end of the film.

   a. on b. by
   c. at d. in

7. Several celebrities were __________ those protesting in front of city hall yesterday.

a. among
b. across
c. toward
d. at

8. I'm having some trouble deciding __________ the two.

a. over
b. through
c. among
d. between

9. The height of Mt. Halla is 1,950 meters _________ sea level.

a. below
b. above
c. in
d. on

10. They lived together peacefully __________ several years.

a. for
b. within
c. in
d. since

Unit 12

Choose the appropriate conjunction to complete each of the following sentences.

1. I don't have time to read the whole thing, __________ I'll skim through and pick out the important details.

a. but
b. nor
c. or
d. for

2. Invest in your education now, __________ your efforts will be rewarded later.

a. yet
b. and
c. but
d. or

3. No sooner had he left home _________ he began to run for school.

a. that
b. as
c. than
d. after

4. Hurry up, _________ you will miss the airplane.

a. and
b. or
c. if
d. that

5. I'm going to ask my doctor _________ he thinks acupuncture really works.

a. that
b. what
c. while
d. whether

6. _________ the earthquake occurred, I was making breakfast at home.

a. that
b. since
c. when
d. whether

7. I'm afraid we'll have to close down the store _________ business improves.

a. while
b. since
c. that
d. unless

8. This game is being closely watched _________ it involves two arch rivals.

a. because
b. while
c. when
d. till

9. _________ she didn't remember my name disappointed me.

a. What
b. Because
c. That
d. If

10. Newspapers not only offer insight into world events, _________ are also a great way to improve vocabulary.

a. and
b. neither
c. or
d. but

Unit 13

Choose the appropriate verb form to complete each of the following sentences.

1. These days, everyone __________ worried about identity theft.

   a. are　　b. am
   c. is　　d. have been

2. She asked me __________ doing.

   a. what I am　　b. what was I
   c. what I was　　d. what am I

3. Slow and steady __________ the race.

   a. winning　　b. wins
   c. win　　d. have won

4. A million dollars __________ more money than most people will earn in their lifetimes.

   a. has been　　b. will be
   c. are　　d. is

5. She said that if she were a bird she __________ across the sea.

   a. will fly　　b. could fly
   c. flew　　d. is flying

6. There __________ no clear winners and losers in this situation.

   a. am　　b. are
   c. was　　d. is

7. My roommate told me __________ a noise.

   a. not to make　　b. have not made
   c. to not make　　d. don't make

8. The number of students studying nursing __________ increasing.

a. are
b. has been
c. be
d. have been

9. Most of our clients __________ based in North America.

a. is
b. has been
c. are
d. be

10. She confessed to me that she _________ an appointment to see a cosmetic surgeon that day.

a. will have
b. have
c. has had
d. had

Culture Corner

Colloquial Expressions

미국 사람들은 공식적인 대화가 아닐 경우 colloquial expressions (일상 회화에서 쓰이는 표현)을 자주 사용합니다. 이러한 표현들은 대화할 때 유용하게 쓸 수 있으므로 몇 가지는 알아두는 것이 좋습니다.

'Are you through?' 'Are you through with that?' 이 말은 무언가를 끝냈냐고 물어 볼 때 사용하는데, 'Are you through with my book?'(내 책 다 보았니?)처럼 어떠한 행위를 마쳤냐고 물을 때 사용할 수 있고 'I'm through with her, she stood me up.' (그녀와는 다 끝났어, 날 바람 맞췄어.)처럼 사람과의 관계가 끝이 났다고도 말 할 때에도 사용할 수 있습니다. 만약 이러한 상황이 일어난다면 이 사실을 털어놓은 이에게 'Just keep it to yourself' (너 혼자만 알고 있어.) 라며 비밀 유지를 당부할 수 있겠죠.

회사에서 상사가 업무의 진행상황을 묻는다면 'Everything is under control.' 와 같은 표현이 유용할 것 같습니다. 만사가 순조롭게 진행되고 있다는 뜻입니다. 그리고 늘 아슬아슬하게 출근시간을 맞춰 직장에 오는 동료에 대해서는 'He always cuts it close.'라고 할 수 있는데 이때 그 동료는 속으로 이렇게 말할 수 있겠습니다. 'That was a close call.' 또는 'That was close.' (어휴 큰일날 뻔 했다/ 아슬아슬 했다.)

무언가에 새롭게 도전하는 사람에게는 'Give it a shot.'(한번 도전 해봐) 라고 격려해주고 성공했을 때는 'You made it!'(너 성공했어) 라고 칭찬할 수 있겠죠. 'I'll give it my best shot.'은 최선을 다하겠다고 다짐하는 말이 됩니다. 우리 모두 'Here goes nothing.'(한번 해보는 거지 뭐) 라고 마음 먹고, 과감히 무언가에 한번 도전해보는 것은 어떨까요? 어떤 경우에도 잃을 것이 없다는 뜻입니다. 처음에 두려워했던 일도 일단 도전해 보면, 'There's nothing to it. It's a piece of cake.' (별 것 아니네요. 아주 쉬운 일인데요.) 라고 말하게 될 지도 모릅니다.

이처럼 여러 가지 colloquial 표현들이 있는데, 이러한 구어체를 알아두면 외국인과의 대화를 조금 더 자연스럽고 편안하게 이끌어갈 수 있을 것입니다.

- Are you through with my book?
- I'm through with her, she stood me up.
- Just keep it to yourself.
- Everything is under control.
- He always cuts it close.
- That was a close call.
- Give it a shot.
- You made it!
- I'll give it my best shot.
- Here goes nothing.
- There's nothing to it. It's a piece of cake.

Supplementary Reading (보충 독해)

다음 글을 읽고 문제를 풀어 보세요.

The Metrosexual

Have you ever heard the term metrosexual? Since American writer Mark Simpson invented this term, it has been picked up by the media and has created a new paradigm for men. The typical metrosexual is defined as a young man with a strong aesthetic sense who spends a great deal of time and money on his appearance and lifestyle. He lives in a metropolis to be close to all the best shops, clubs, gyms, and hairdressers. It seems we are living in a time where men increasingly take an active interest in maintaining a stylish appearance while enjoying an urban lifestyle. Like soccer star David Beckham, who has been known to paint his fingernails, the metrosexual is not afraid to embrace his feminine side.

This trend is also affecting Korean society. A man's appearance is more important than ever for getting a job and furthermore to be successful. Jung Soon-won, the author of the book titled, "Cut Off Your Necktie Right Now", said that Korean men have been stuck in the stereotype of the strong man image associated with their classic suit and tie. They have given up the freedom and creativity to express themselves. Jung points out that metrosexuality could be a good starting point to break the Korean male stereotype, which is greatly influenced by Confucianism. Men shouldn't be ashamed of attempts to look different when they choose clothing and accessories that express their fashion preferences. Do you agree that Korean men need to become more fashionable?

Translation 메트로섹슈얼

메트로섹슈얼 이란 말을 들어보셨나요? 미국의 작가 Mark Simpson이 이 말을 탄생시킨 이후로 미디어를 통해 이 단어는 퍼져나갔고, 남자들에게 새로운 패러다임을 선사하였습니다. 전형적인 메트로섹슈얼이란 빼어난 미적감각을 가졌고 자신의 외모와 생활에 많은 돈을 투자하는 젊은 남자를 지칭합니다. 그는 가장 좋은 가게, 클럽, 헬스장과 미용실에 가까이 있기 위해 대도시에 삽니다. 우리는 이제 더 많은 남자들이 도시 생활을 즐기면서 멋진 외모를 유지하는 것에 적극적으로 관심을 갖는 시대에 우리는 살고 있는 듯 합니다. David Beckham과 같은 축구 스타가 손톱 칠을 하는 것처럼 메트로섹슈얼은 자신의 여성적인 면을 받아들이는 것에 대해 두려워하지 않습니다.

이러한 유행은 한국 사회에서도 그 영향을 미치고 있습니다. 남자의 외모는 취직하는데, 더 나가서는 성공하는데 있어 어느 때보다 중요합니다. "지금 당장 넥타이를 잘라라" 의 저자인 정 순원 은 한국 남자들이 정장 양복과 넥타이로 연상되는 강한 남자 이미지의 틀에 박혀있었다고 말합니다. 그들은 자기 자신을 표현 하는 창조성과 자유를 포기하였습니다. 그는 메트로섹슈엘리티는 유교의 영향을 많이 받은 한국 남자들의 정형화된 틀을 깰 수 있는 좋은 출발점이 될 수 있다고 지적합니다. 남자들이 자신의 패션 취향을 표현하는 옷과 악세서리를 고를 때, 자신들의 외모를 차별화하기 위해 노력하는 것을 부끄러워하지 말아야 합니다. 당신도 한국 남자들이 조금 더 패션에 관심을 가질 필요가 있다는 것에 동의합니까?

Explanation

1. Since American writer Mark Simpson invented this term, it has been picked up by the media and has created a new paradigm for men.

since는 전치사로써 '~부터' 라는 의미를 가졌고 has been picked up 은 현재완료시제의 수동태로써 '선택되었다, 사용되었다' 라는 의미를 가지고 있습니다. has created는 현재완료시제이며 능동태입니다.

Ex) My walkman has been used by my friend. (내 워크맨은 내 친구에 의해 사용되었습니다.)

2. The typical metrosexual is defined as a young man with a strong aesthetic sense who spends a great deal of time and money on his appearance and lifestyle.

define A as B 는 'A를 B로 정의하다' 란 표현인데 이 문장에서는 수동형으로 사용되었습니다. spend A on B 는 'A(돈이나 시간 따위)를 B에 쓰다, 소비하다' 의 뜻입니다.

Ex) A metropolis can be defined as a major city in a region or country.

(메트로폴리스는 어떤 지역이나 국가의 주요 도시라고 정의할 수 있습니다.)

Ex) Parents are spending a lot of money on their children's education.

(부모들은 자식들의 교육에 많은 돈을 쓰고 있습니다.)

3. Like soccer star David Beckham, who has been known to paint his fingernails, the metrosexual is not afraid to embrace his feminine side.

has been known은 현재완료수동형으로 '~으로 알려지다, ~으로 유명하다' 란 의미이며, 뒤에 to부정사가 오기도 하고, to 명사가 오기도 합니다. be afraid는 '두려워하다' 라는 뜻인 데, 뒤에 to부정사 또는 of 명사/동명사 가 오게 됩니다.

Ex) She is known to be a cold-hearted woman.

(그녀는 마음이 차가운 사람으로 알려져 있습니다.)

Ex) Her face is well known to movie fans all over the world.

(그녀는 전 세계 영화팬들에게 잘 알려져 있습니다.)

Ex) We are not afraid to confront her.

(우리는 그녀와 대면하는 것을 두려워하지 않습니다.)

Ex) He is afraid of his own shadow.

(그는 자신의 그림자도 두려워하는 겁쟁이입니다.)

4. A man's appearance is more important than ever for getting a job and furthermore to be successful.

more important than ever 는 '그 어느 때 보다 더 중요하다' 란 뜻이 됩니다.

Ex) These days, maintaining a healthy lifestyle is more important than ever.

(오늘날에는 건강한 생활을 유지하는 것이그 어느 때 보다 더 중요합니다.)

5. Korean men had been stuck in the stereotype of the strong man image associated with their classic suit and tie and had given up their freedom and creativity to express themselves.

had been stuck은 과거완료시제로써 '~에 박혀있었다' 라고 해석됩니다. be associated with는 '~와 관련지어 생각되다, 연상되다' 라는 의미의 수동형 표현으로, 위 문장에서는 associated 앞에 관계대명사와 be동사가 생략된 형태입니다.

Ex) A fish bone is stuck in my throat.

(생선가시가 목에 걸렸습니다.)

Ex) This song is associated with peace.

(이 노래는 평화를 연상하게 합니다.)

6. Men shouldn't be ashamed of attempts to look different when they choose clothing and accessories that express their fashion preferences.

be ashamed of는 '~을 부끄럽게 생각하다, 수치스럽게 생각하다' 란 뜻이며, 뒤에 명사 또는 동명사가 올 수 있습니다. that은 주격 관계대명사로 선행사는 clothes and accessories입니다.

Ex) The company was ashamed of their poor rate of actual exports.

(그 회사는 그들의 형편없는 수출실적이 수치스러웠습니다.)

Ex) They recaptured the elephants that had escaped from the circus.

(그들은 서커스에서 탈출한 코끼리를 다시 잡았습니다.)

Q. 1 Match each of the following words with its definition.

1. aesthetic	a) join or connect in mind
2. ashamed	b) oversimplified concepts or image
3. associate	c) example or model
4. define	d) feeling disgraceful or foolish
5. embrace	e) state the meaning of
6. paradigm	f) appreciating art and beauty
7. stereotype	g) accept an idea

Q. 2 Answer the following questions by choosing either (a) or (b).

1. Who or what was the word metrosexual created by?
   a) books and media
   b) an author

2. What is a metrosexual?
   a) a man who dresses up in stylish clothes
   b) a man who lives in a city

3. How is metrosexuality affecting Korean society?
   a) Men feel comfortable with suits and ties.
   b) Appearance is an important factor for success.

4. What does the author of "Cut off your necktie now" say?
   a) Korean men are free to express themselves.
   b) Metrosexuality offers a chance to break the old stereotype.

5. Which statement shows the influence of Confucianism in Korea?
   a) Men are afraid to look different from others.
   b) Men spend much time choosing clothing and accessories.

부록 〉〉〉 정답

Unit 01

Tenses

Comprehension Check

1. (c) 2. (a) 3. (d) 4. (c)

Translation

1. Brett은 왜 New York으로 돌아가는가?
   (a) 친구를 방문하기 위해
   (b) 그의 여자친구를 방문하기 위해
   (c) 그의 회사에서 그를 그곳으로 보내려 하기 때문에
   (d) 단기 출장을 위해

2. 아마도 Brett과 Aaron은:
   (a) 오랜 친구이다.
   (b) 사업상 아는 사이다.
   (c) 전혀 모르는 사이다.
   (d) 같은 운동 팀에 있다.

3. 전화의 목적을 가장 잘 설명한 것은:
   (a) 저녁 약속을 잡기 위한 것이다.
   (b) 영업 안내를 하기 위한 것이다.
   (c) 오랜 친구와 회포를 풀기 위한 것이다.
   (d) A와 C모두

4. 대화를 통해 볼 때, 아마도 Dan은:
   (a) 적일 것이다.
   (b) 유명 연예인일 것이다.
   (c) 두 사람의 친구일 것이다.
   (d) Aaron의 남자형제일 것이다.

Task 1

1. sang
2. sings
3. sing, will sing

Translation

1. 이틀 전 나는 학교 축제에서 노래를 불렀습니다.
2. Katie는 내가 기분이 좋지 않을 때 대개 노래를 불러줍니다.
3. 나는 오늘 노래를 부르지 않았지만, 다음 주 음악 축제 때 노래를 부를 것입니다.

Task 2

1. O
2. X (She left school last year.)
3. X (At 3:30 tomorrow, I will be playing football with my friends.)
4. O

Translation

1. 나의 어깨는 너무 많은 운동으로 인하여 아픕니다.
2. 그녀는 작년에 학교를 떠났습니다.
3. 내일 3시 30분에 나는 친구들과 축구를 하고 있을 것입니다.
4. 그들의 아이는 요즘 무척 일찍 잠에서 깹니다.

Task 3

1. I have known her/Carol for many years.
2. he has owned this house since 1998
3. I have been there/to Scotland twice
4. I had forgotten my keys

Translation

1. 당신은 얼마나 오랫동안 Carol을 알아왔습니까?
   나는 그녀를 수년간 알아왔습니다.
2. Peter가 이 집의 주인입니까?
   네, 그는 1998년부터 이 집을 소유하였습니다.
3. 스코틀랜드에 가본 적이 있습니까?
   네, 나는 그곳에 두 번 가보았습니다.
4. 당신은 방에 들어갔습니까?
   아니오, 들어갈 수 없었습니다. 왜냐하면 열쇠를 가져오지 않았기 때문입니다.

Comprehension Check-up

1. T 2. F 3. F

Translation

1. 오늘날, 기술기업들은 고급 인력을 채용하기 위한 경쟁에 직면했습니다.
2. Google직원들은 회사로부터 자동차를 지원받습니다.
3. Google직원들은 주말에 찾아볼 수가 없습니다.

Vocabulary Matching

1. d 2. c 3. b 4. a

Translation
1. 편의시설 – d. 편의, 여가를 위해 제공되는 시설들
2. 상류층의 – c. 고급스러운, 품위있는
3. 신입사원 – b. 조직의 새로운 구성원
4. 기업문화 – a. 기업의 전통과 가치

Quiz
1. look 2. see 3. watch

Translation
1. 취직 면접하는 동안 확신에 찬 것처럼 보이는 것은 중요합니다.
2. 나는 며칠간 떠나있을 겁니다. 그러나 돌아오면 당신을 볼 겁니다.
3. 바닷가에 앉아서 해지는 광경을 보는 것은 건강에 좋습니다.

Task 4
1. dying
2. have used/ have been using
3. will have moved

Task 5
1. incorrect (Andrew damaged his knee while he was playing football./ Andrew damaged his knee when he played football.)
2. incorrect (Who was the person standing beside you when I saw you yesterday?)
3. correct

Translation
1. Andrew는 축구를 하다가 무릎을 다쳤습니다.
2. 어제 내가 당신을 보았을 때 옆에 서 있던 사람은 누구입니까?
3. 나는 오늘 좋은 하루를 보냈습니다.

REVIEW TEST
1. (4)	2. (2)	3. (4)	4. (3)	5.(1)
6. went	7. arrives	8. has	9. seen	10. been

Translation
1. 우리는 여러 해 동안 빈 병을 모아왔습니다.
2. 요즈음 그녀는 보통 일주일에 세 번 정도 테니스를 합니다.
3. 그는 그의 아버지와 닮았습니다.
4. 경찰이 그 도둑을 붙잡았을 때는 이미 그가 돈을 다 써버린 후였습니다.
5. 내일 오후 4시에 나는 친구와 축구를 하고 있을 겁니다.

6. 우리는 작년에 그 산에 갔습니다.
7. 그들은 회장이 도착하기 전까지는 회의를 시작하지 않을 겁니다.
8. 질문이 있으면 그녀가 당신에게 알려줄 겁니다.
9. 그녀는 예전에 몇 번 Brown 씨를 본 적이 있었기 때문에 단 번에 그를 알아보았습니다.
10. 롯데월드에 몇 번 가 보았습니까?

Supplementary Reading

Q.1

1. surge	c) aheavy billowing or swelling motion like that of a great wave
2. pave the way	a) to make progress or development easier
3. spur (on)	e) to incite or stimulate
4. constantly	b) continually occurring; persistent
5. phenomenon	f) something that is observed to happen or exist
6. air	d) to broadcast on television or radio

Translation

돌진, 파도	– 큰 파도와 같은 거대한 움직임
길을 열어주다	– 발전시키다, 발달을 용이하게 하다
박차를 가하다	– 자극하다, 격려하다
계속해서	– 지속적으로, 방해 받지 않고
현상	– 발생하거나 존재하여 인지된 것
방송하다	– 텔레비전이나 라디오에서 방송하다

Q.2

1. F 2. F. 3. F 4. T

Translation

1. 한국 문화 상품은 지난 10년 이상 인기가 아주 높습니다.
2. 이 문화 현상은 일본에서 인기 드라마 "겨울 연가"가 방송되고 나서 시작되었습니다.
3. 베이비 복스, NRG와 같은 한국 가수들은 전 세계적으로 공연을 하였습니다.
4. 점점 더 많은 외국인들은 한국어를 배우고 싶어합니다.

Unit 02 Sentence Structure

Comprehension Check

1. d 2. c 3. d

Translation

1. Brett의 새로운 업무는
   (a) 비서로 일하는 것입니다.
   (b) 영업사원으로 일하는 것입니다.
   (c) 마케팅 부서 12명의 구성원 중 하나로서 일하는 것입니다.
   (d) 12명의 마케팅 부서 구성원을 관리하는 것입니다.

2. 이 대화에서, Brett와 이야기 하는 사람은
   (a) 그의 비서일 것입니다.
   (b) 친구일 것입니다.
   (c) 그의 상사일 것입니다.
   (d) 동료일 것입니다.

3. 다음 형용사 중 Brett의 상사를 묘사한 것으로 올바르지 않은 것은?
   (a) 직설적이다.
   (b) 권위적이다.
   (c) 거만하다.
   (d) 편안하다.

Task 1

1. feels 2. makes
3. brings 4. runs
5. exists

Translation

1. 옷은 촉감이 부드럽습니다.
2. Jane은 매일 아침 6시 기상을 규칙으로 합니다.
3. 당신의 질문을 듣고 보니 내가 제기하고 싶었던 미묘한 문제가 생각이 납니다.
4. 그 버스는 New York과 Washington D.C. 사이를 운행합니다.
5. 어떤 사람들은 화성에 생명체가 존재한다고 생각합니다.

Task 2

1. X (They have raised corn in Gangwondo for many years.)

2. O
3. O
4. X (Every spring the woodcock lays four multicolored eggs.)
5. X (She sits on her knees in front of her grandparents.)

Translation

1. 그들은 강원도에서 여러 해 동안 옥수수를 기르고 있습니다.
2. 그 왕이 그 나라의 토대를 마련하였습니다.
3. 주가가 오르락 내리락 합니다.
4. 봄이 되면 멧도요새는 네 가지색이 혼합된 알을 낳습니다.
5. 그녀는 조부모님 앞에서 무릎을 꿇고 앉습니다.

Task 3

1. The story sounds false.
2. We discussed the matter.
3. I suggested to him that he should go there.
4. She made coffee for all of us.

Translation

1. 그 애기는 거짓말인 것 같습니다.
2. 우리는 그 문제에 대해 토의했습니다.
3. 나는 그에게 그곳에 가도록 제안했습니다.
4. 그녀는 우리 모두에게 커피를 준비해 주었습니다.

Comprehension Check-up

1. F 2. F 3. T

Translation

1. 서번트 신드롬이라는 용어는 보통의 건강한 사람들에게 나타내는 '천재적인 징후'를 가르킵니다.
2. 서번트로 간주되는 사람이 전세계에 12,000명이상 있습니다.
3. 많은 서번트들이 보이는 천재성은 종종 심각한 장애를 동반하고 있습니다.

Vocabulary Matching

1. d 2. c 3. a 4. b

Translation

1. 장애 – d. 단점
2. 현상 – c. 인상적이거나 특이한 것

3. 약어 – a. 단어나 어구를 짤막하게 표현한 것
4. 압도적인 – b. 압도적이거나 대단한

Quiz

1. talk 2. speak 3. say

Translation

1. 수업 중에 말하지 마세요.
2. 당신이 분명하게 말하지 않는다면 그는 당신의 기분을 전혀 모를 것입니다.
3. 내 말은 아침 일찍 떠나는 것이 가장 좋은 선택이라는 것입니다.

Task 4

1. (b) 2. (d) 3. (b) 4. (c) 5. (a)

Translation

1. 그들은 2주 전에 런던을 떠났습니다.
2 그는 나에게 아시아에서의 멋진 경험에 대해 이야기했습니다.
3. 나는 그녀가 졸고 있는 것을 발견했습니다.
4. 그 소년은 아버지를 전혀 닮지 않았습니다.
5. 그 회사는 아이들에게 책을 공급할 것입니다.

Task 5

1. incorrect (I don't want you to show this document to anyone.)
2. incorrect (Tony introduced the girl to us at the party.)
3. incorrect (The food looked awful but it tasted good.)
4. correct

Translation

1. 나는 당신이 이 서류를 누구에게도 보여주지 않았으면 좋겠습니다.
2. Tony는 파티에서 그 소녀를 우리에게 소개했습니다.
3. 그 음식은 이상하게 보였지만, 맛은 좋았습니다.
4. 당신이 그 모임에 참석할 지 안 할 지 우리에게 알려주세요.

REVIEW TEST

1. (1) 2. (1) 3. (4)
4. (2) 5. (3) 6. seated
7. to behave 8. dissatisfied 9. called
10. resembles/resembled

Translation

1. 우리가 떠날 때쯤 그 젊은이는 우리가 상품을 사도록 만들었습니다.

2. 내일 그를 만나면 사실을 말해주겠습니다.
3. 그들은 아이들에게 계속 말하라고 했습니다.
4. 제게 맥주 좀 갖다 주시겠습니까?
5. 우리가 가게에 들어갔을 때 나는 무언가 달콤한 향을 맡을 수 있었습니다.
6. Susie는 잘생긴 두 명의 남자 사이에 앉았습니다.
7. 나는 우리 아이들이 그런 식으로 행동하는 것을 허락할 수 없습니다.
8. 선거 결과에 많은 사람들이 불만족스러워 했습니다.
9. 그녀는 자신의 이름이 불려지는 것을 들었습니다.
10. Robert는 많은 면에서 형제들과 닮았습니다.

Supplementary Reading

Q.1

1. property e) something owned
2. reduce a) to diminish in amount or degree
3. function g) a specific occupation or role
4. substance b) a material of a particular kind
5. legend f) an unproved story handed down from earlier times
6. blossom c) to come into flower, to develop
7. risk d) danger, possibility of loss

Translation

1. 자산 – 소유물
2. 줄이다 – 양이나 정도에서 감소하다
3. 기능 – 특정한 업무 또는 역할
4. 물질 – 특정한 종류의 재료
5. 전설 – 예부터 전해져 내려오는 입증되지 않은 이야기
6. 꽃피우다 – 꽃이 피다, 발전하다
7. 위험 – 위험, 상실 가능성

Q.2

1. F 2. T 3. F 4. T 5. F

Translation

1. 사과는 암이 발생할 위험을 줄이도록 도와주는 성분을 가지고 있는 유일한 과일입니다.
2. 사과를 먹지 않는 사람들은 하루에 사과를 한 개씩 먹는 사람들 보다 폐기능이 저하되는 경향이 있습니다.
3. 신선한 사과가 그렇지 않은 사과와 비교할 때 세포 손상을 억제하는 다량의 물질을 더 많이 가지고 있다는 보고가 있습니다.
4. 사과가 얼마나 오랫동안 존재해 왔는지 정확히 알지 못하나 적어도 750,000년은 넘었을 확률이 큽니다.
5. Johnny Appleseed는 미국에 사과씨를 가지고 온 첫 번째 정착민입니다.

Unit 03 Infinitive and Gerund

Comprehension Check

1. (d) 2. (c) 3. (c)

Translation

1. 다음 중 Camille을 가장 잘 표현한 것은 무엇입니까?
   (a) Brett의 옛 여자친구
   (b) Aaron의 데이트상대
   (c) 식당 종업원
   (d) Brett의 옛 여자친구이자 Aaron의 데이트 상대

2. 이 대화에서, Aaron은
   (a) 저널리스트일 것이다.
   (b) 마케팅 부서 관리자일 것이다.
   (c) 사진작가일 것이다.
   (d) 여행사 직원일 것이다.

3. Camille과 Brett은 왜 이전 관계를 정리했습니까?
   (a) Camille이 이사를 가서
   (b) Aaron이 남미로 이주해서
   (c) Brett이 California로 이사를 가서
   (d) Camille이 Fashion Week 행사로 바빠서

Task 1

1. to buy 2.to give 3. to vote
4. to spend 5. to turn down

Translation

1. 나는 옷을 살 돈이 없습니다.
2. 그 소녀에게 그 작품을 연주할 기회를 한번 더 주는 것은 공정하지 못합니다.
3. Mark는 선거할 수 있을 정도로 나이가 들지 않았습니다.
4. 그녀는 너무 바빠서 가족들과 함께 시간을 보내지 못했습니다.
5. 그러한 제안을 거절하다니 당신은 어리석군요.

Task 2

1. O
2. O

3. X (He is able to do it.)
4. X (We really hope to meet you again.)
5. X (Mel didn't buy anything because she wanted to save money.)

Translation

1. 당신은 이미 약속에 늦었기 때문에 택시를 타고 가도 소용이 없습니다.
2. 그녀는 친구들을 위해 케익을 굽는 것을 좋아합니다.
3. 그는 그것을 할 수 있습니다.
4. 우리는 당신을 다시 만나기를 진심으로 희망합니다.
5. Mel은 돈을 절약하기 위해서 아무것도 사지 않았습니다.

Task 3

1. We should not postpone cleaning up the oil spill. That work is urgent.
2. Bob forgot to post Nancy's birthday card, which disappointed her.
3. Can you imagine living without a cell phone?
4. I can't afford to buy a new bicycle.
5. I have to practice driving so that I can pass my driving test.

Translation

1. 우리는 누출된 석유를 제거하는 것을 더 이상 미뤄서는 안됩니다. 그 작업은 긴급한 일입니다.
2. Bob은 Nancy의 생일카드를 부칠 것을 잊었고, 그것은 그녀를 실망하게 했습니다.
3. 휴대폰 없이 살아가는 것을 상상할 수 있습니까?
4. 나는 새 자전거를 살 여유가 없습니다.
5. 나는 운전 시험에 합격 할 수 있도록 운전연습을 해야 합니다.

Comprehension Check-up

1. F　　2. T　　3. F

Translation

1. 커피섭취에 관한연구결과들은 항상 광범위하게 일치되어져 왔습니다.
2. 최근 많은 연구에 따르면, 커피를 많이 마실수록, 당신은 더 많은 이점을 얻게 될 것입니다.
3. 커피의 과다섭취와 연관된 부정적인 측면은 없습니다.

Vocabulary Matching

1. b　　2. c　　3. a　　4. d

Translation

1. 치료 – b. 치료약이나 처치
2. 손해 – c. 불리, 손실

3. 논쟁 – a. 불일치
4. 병 – d. 질병

Quiz

1. listen 2. hear 3. listen

Translation

1. 주의를 기울이지 않는 학생들은 처벌을 받을 것입니다.
2. 텔레비전 소리가 잘 안 들립니다. 소리를 높여 주시겠습니까?
3. 나는 출근 길에 매일 아침 라디오 토론을 듣습니다.

Task 4

1. My parents managed to get there in time.
2. He is not accustomed to speaking in public.
3. We haven't seen Mary for a long time, but we expect to hear from her soon.
4. No matter how hard I tried, my friend wouldn't stop crying.
5. It was stupid of you to make such a mistake.

Translation

1. 부모님께서는 용케 시간 내에 도착하셨습니다.
2. 그는 대중 앞에서 말하는 것에 익숙하지 않습니다.
3. 우리는 오랫동안 Mary를 보지 못했지만 그녀로부터 곧 소식이 오기를 기대하고 있습니다.
4. 내가 열심히 노력했음에도 불구하고, 내 친구는 울음을 그치려 하지 않았습니다.
5. 당신이 그런 실수를 하다니 어리석었군요.

Task 5

1. incorrect (Mary seems to know the answer.)
2. correct
3. incorrect (Would you mind opening the window?)
4. incorrect. (My parents persuaded me to go on a blind date.)
5. correct

Translation :

1. Mary는 답을 알고 있는 것처럼 보입니다.
2. 그들은 소설을 읽는 것을 즐깁니다.
3. 창문 좀 열어주시겠습니까?
4. 부모님께서는 맞선을 보러 나가라고 나를 설득하셨습니다.
5. 당신은 이번 토요일에 당신을 도와줄 사람을 찾았습니까?

REVIEW TEST

1. (3) 2. (4) 3. (3) 4. (2) 5. (3)

6. traveling/travelling 7. to reach 8. to buy
9. to apply 10. worrying

Translation

1. 저는 이번 여름에 휴가를 가질 여유가 없습니다.
2. Linda는 자신이 그 일을 얻지 못했다는 사실에 실망하였습니다.
3. 사장은 회사 운영을 포기하였습니다.
4. 저는 많은 사람들 앞에서 발표하는 것에 익숙하지 않습니다. 항상 긴장이 되거든요.
5. 오늘 오후에 뭐하세요? 저랑 쇼핑 가는 거 어때요?
6. 저희와 함께 즐거운 여행이 되셨기를 바랍니다.
7. 저 상자에 닿을 만큼 키가 크세요? 맨 위 선반에 있는 거요.
8. 일이 끝나고 집으로 돌아가는 길에 맥주를 사려고 가게에 들렀습니다.
9. 마침내 그는 그 일에 지원하기로 결심했습니다.
10. 저는 그녀의 상태에 대해 걱정하지 않을 수 없었습니다.

Supplementary Reading

Q.1

1. strive c) to try extremely hard
2. correspond e) to be in agreement or harmony
3. reserved f) keeping one's thoughts and emotions to oneself
4. indecisive b) exhibiting hesitation
5. critical d) inclined to judge severely
6. genetic g) relating to genes
7. straightforward a) without complication, honest

Translation

1. 얻으려고 애쓰다 – 아주 열심히 노력하다
2. 상응하다 – 화합 또는 조화를 이루다
3. 내성적인 – 자신의 생각과 감정을 밝히지 않다
4. 우유부단한 – 머뭇거림을 보이는
5. 비판적인 – 엄격하게 판단하는 경향이 있는
6. 유전의 – 유전인자와 관련 있는
7. 직선적인 – 복잡하지 않은, 정직한

Q.2

1. F 2. F 3. T 4. F 5. F 6. T

Translation

1. O형 사람들은 자신감이 있고 감수성이 예민하며 우유부단합니다.
2. 과학은 성격이 혈액형에 의해 결정된다는 이러한 믿음을 지지합니다.
3. 많은 한국인과 일본인들은 혈액형이 개인의 성격을 결정짓거나 그에 상응한다고 생각합니다.
4. 혈액형은 사람들의 직업과 파트너 선택에 영향을 줍니다.
5. 혈액형은 유전적으로 그리고 환경적으로 결정됩니다.
6. 서구에서는 사람들이 별점과 별자리에 대해 자주 얘기합니다.

Unit 04

Auxiliary Verbs

Comprehension Check

1. (d) 2. (d) 3. (b)

Translation

1. Brett의 처음 태도는:
   (a) 확신에 차있습니다.
   (b) 열정적입니다.
   (c) 자신감이 넘칩니다.
   (d) 주저함입니다.

2. Brett이 Camille에게 전화한 이유는 무엇입니까?
   (a) 과거 잘못을 시인하기 위하여
   (b) 그의 회사에서 하는 휴일 파티에 그녀를 초대하기 위하여
   (c) 저녁식사를 함께 하기 위하여
   (d) A와C 둘 다

3.Camille은 California로 이주한다는 Brett의 결정을
   (a) 이야기했을 겁니다.
   (b) 인정하지 않았을 겁니다.
   (c) 아쉬워했을 겁니다.
   (d) 인정했을 겁니다.

Task 1

1. Would you like some tea now?
2. You may as well make the best of the situation.
3. Luckily, the driver was able to stop before he crashed into the bus.
4. The story can not possibly be true.

Task 2

1. X (Joanna keeps crying. She must have a problem.)
2. O
3. X (Passengers must not smoke in the toilet.)
4. X (Let's go to the movies, shall we?)
5. O

Translation

1. Joanna 는 계속해서 웁니다. 그녀에게 어떤 문제가 있음에 틀림없습니다.
2. 그는 그녀에게 그 서류에 서명하기 전에 변호사와 만나보라고 제안하였습니다.
3. 승객들은 화장실에서 담배를 피워서는 안됩니다.
4. 영화 보러 가는 게 어때요?
5. 당신의 지원서는 너무 늦게 도착했습니다. 좀 더 일찍 지원서를 보냈어야 했습니다.

Task 3

1. used to
2. take
3. used to
4. to handle
5. to climb

Translation

1. 저기에 큰 집이 한 채 있었습니다. (지금은 없습니다)
2. 그가 어떻게 감히 내 컴퓨터를 자기 방으로 가져갈 수 있을까?
3. 그들은 일요일에 교회에 가곤 했습니다.
4. 소포를 조심스럽게 다뤄야 합니다.
5. 그들은 내게 나무 꼭대기에 올라가는 도전을 해보라고 하였습니다.

Comprehension Check-up

1. F　　2. T　　3. T

Translation

1. 몬테소리 방식은 교육계에서 논란이 전혀 없습니다.
2. 몬테소리 교실에서 선생님들은 강의자가 아닌 학습 촉진자로써 역할을 합니다.
3. Maria Montessori에 의해 발전된 철학은 각각의 학생들의 욕구에 부합하는 것에서 기원했습니다.

Vocabulary Matching

1. b　　2. c　　3. d　　4. a

Translation

1. 의사 – b. 의사
2. 양육하다 – c. 지지하고 북돋아주다.
3. 전도력 있는, 도움이 되는 – d. 호의적인, 유용한
4. 널리 퍼진 – a. 퍼뜨려진, 흩어진

Quiz

1. study　　2. learn　　3. practice

Translation

1. 다음 주 시험을 위해 공부할 시간이 있을지 잘 모르겠습니다.
2. 선생님들이 학생들의 이름을 기억하는 것은 중요합니다.
3. 나는 매일 한 시간을 피아노 연습을 하도록 해놨습니다.

Task 4

1. (b) would
2. (d) used to
3. (b) do
4. (a) may
5. (c) need

Translation

1. A: 무엇을 도와드릴까요?
   B: 물 한잔 좀 주세요.
2. A: 나는 예전에 발레리나였고, 춤추는 것을 좋아했어요.
   B: 지금은 어떤가요?
3. A: 나는 당신이 그녀를 사랑한다고 생각하지 않습니다.
   B: 난 정말 그녀를 사랑합니다. 맹세할 수 있습니다.
4. A: Matt를 본 적이 있습니까?
   B: 아뇨, 그러나 아래층에 있는지도 모르겠습니다.
5. A: 서둘러요!
   B: 서두를 필요 없습니다. 여전히 시간이 많이 남아 있습니다.

Task 5

1. incorrect (It is required that students should go to the principle's office whenever they are late for school.)
2. incorrect (We need to buy a small gift to show our appreciation.)
3. correct
4. correct
5. incorrect (There's nothing more to do today, so you can go home. / There's nothing more to do today, so you may go home.)

Translation

1. 지각을 할 때마다 학생들은 교장실에 꼭 가야만 합니다.
2. 우리는 감사의 마음을 전하기 위해 작은 선물을 사야 합니다.
3. Hannah는 피카소 미술관을 찾을 수 없었습니다. 안내소를 방문할 것 그랬어요.
4. 그는 제 시간에 그 일을 마쳤을 리가 없습니다.
5. 오늘 더 이상 할 일이 없으니 집에 가도 됩니다.

REVIEW TEST

1. (3)	2. (4)	3. (3)	4. (3)	5. (2)
6. (3)	7. (2)	8. (4)	9. (1)	10. (3)

Translation

1. A: 시험 준비하느라 밤을 샜어요.
   B: 무척 피곤하시겠네요.
2. A: Mark가 차 열쇠를 어디에 두었는지 아세요?
   B: 탁자 위에 올려놓았을 거에요.
3. 그 영화는 무척 인상적이었어요. 당신도 그것을 봤어야 해요.
4. 직원들은 새로운 조건을 받아들여야 할 것입니다. 그렇지 않으면 해고됩니다.
5. A: 왜 Barbara가 방에 있는 건가요?
   B: 모르겠어요. 숙제를 하고 있을 수도 있죠.
6. 신용카드를 찾을 수가 없어요. 어디에 있는지 모르겠네요. 카드 회사에 전화하는 게 나을 것 같아요.
7. 자신의 결정이 무엇을 의미하는 지 이해하는 것이 중요합니다.
8. 저는 땅콩을 먹곤 했습니다만 알레르기가 생겼습니다.
9. 5월 1일전까지 모든 서류를 제출해야 합니다.
10. A: 새로운 직업이 마음에 드십니까?
    B: 네, 재미있습니다.

Supplementary Reading

Q.1

1. corresponding	b) similar or equivalent
2. resource	d) means of support, especially money or property
3. incentive	e) something that motivates effort or encourages action
4. fertility	g) the ability of a living organism to produce offspring
5. subsidy	c) financial aid given by one person or government
6. bid	f) to seek to win or attain something
7. consult	a) to ask advice or information

Translation

1. 상응하는, 일치하는	– 비슷한, 동등한
2. 자원, 재능	– 돈이나 자원의 지원 수단
3. 격려, 장려	– 노력을 촉진시키거나 행위를 장려하는 것
4. 비옥, 다산, 출생률	– 자손을 이어가는 능력
5. 보조금, 장려금	– 개인이나 정부로부터의 금전적 지원
6. 노력하다, 입찰하다	– 이기거나 얻으려고 노력하다
7. 의견을 묻다, 상의하다	– 충고나 정보를 얻다

Q.2

1. F	2. T	3. F	4. F	5. T

Translation

1. 한국의 출생률은 다음 세기에는 현재의 3분의 1이 줄어들 것으로 예상됩니다.
2. 제안에 따르면, 적어도 세 명의 자녀가 있는 가정만이 새 아파트를 입찰할 때 우선권을 얻을 수 있습니다.
3. 한국의 낮은 출산율은 경제 성장을 도와줍니다.
4. 한국의 출산율이 떨어지는 현상은 일시적인 것입니다.
5. 증가하는 이혼율도 감소하는 출산율과 관련 있습니다.

Unit 05

Participle

Comprehension Check

1. (c)　　2. (c)　　3. (a)

Translation

1. 어떤 종류의 광고 캠페인을 Yuan씨는 원합니까?
   (a) 크고, 새롭고, 거칠고, 눈에 띄는
   (b) 독창적이고, 신선하고, 눈에 띄고, 새로운
   (c) 크고, 새롭고, 신선하고, 눈에 띄는
   (d) 눈에 띄고, 화려하고, 멋지고, 신선한

2. 다음 중 Yuan씨의 일반적인 어조를 가장 잘 묘사한 형용사는 무엇입니까?
   (a) 걱정하는
   (b) 화가 난
   (c) 실망한
   (d) 엄격한

3. Brett은 어떻게 Yuan씨가 그에게 또 다른 기회를 주도록 설득했습니까?
   (a) 그는 엄청난 결과를 약속했습니다.
   (b) 그는 그를 부유하고 행복하게 해주겠다고 약속했습니다.
   (c) 그는 다음 아이디어를 넌지시 비추었습니다.
   (d) 그는 간청하고 호소했습니다.

Task 1

1. shocked
2. using
3. crash
4. relax
5. displayed

Translation

1. 우리는 해일에 대한 뉴스로 인하여 매우 놀랐습니다.
2. Discover Card를 사용하고 있는 고객은 모든 구매시 10%를 할인 받을 것입니다.
3. 그녀는 차가 기둥과 충돌하는 것을 느꼈습니다.
4. 클래식 음악은 긴장을 푸는데 도움이 됩니다.
5. 나는 벽에 전시된 그림들 중 하나를 사고 싶습니다.

Task 2

1. Sitting in the sun, I felt cold.
2. Using these numbers to create an estimate, you'll find that the result is positive.
3. Some books, read carelessly, will do more harm than good.
4. Walking up the stairs, he reflected back upon the meeting.
5. Having learned to knit, I was able to make a sweater for my daughter.

Translation

1. 양지바른 곳에 앉아 있었지만, 나는 추웠습니다.
2. 이 수치를 가지고 짐작해보면 결과가 긍정적이라는 것을 알 수 있을 것입니다.
3. 어떤 책들은, 부주의하게 읽으면, 이점보다는 해로운 점이 많습니다.
4. 계단을 올라가면서 Tim은 그 모임에 대해 곰곰이 생각하였습니다.
5. 뜨개질을 배웠었기 때문에 나는 나의 딸을 위해 스웨터를 짤 수 있었습니다.

Task 3

1. Supposing that you could go overseas tomorrow, where would you go?
2. Compared with his brother, he is not a good player.
3. With night coming on, the wind began to blow.
4. It being warm inside the cinema, I fell asleep.
5. Given the current economic climate, you might want to consider going back to school.

Translation

1. 내일 해외에 나갈 수 있다면 어디를 가겠습니까?
2. 그의 형과 비교해 볼 때, 그는 훌륭한 선수가 아닙니다.
3. 밤이 다가오자 바람이 불기 시작했습니다.
4. 극장 안이 더웠기 때문에 나는 잠이 들었습니다.
5. 현재 경제 상황이라면, 당신은 학교로 돌아가는 것을 고려해 보고 싶을 겁니다.

Comprehension Check-up

1. F 2. T 3. T

Translation

1. 신문의 웹사이트는 종종 인쇄판보다 수익성이 높습니다.
2. 신문의 웹사이트에 새로운 내용을 끊임없이 실어야 하는 요구 때문에 많은 조직체들은 더 큰 비용 부담을 안게 됩니다.
3. 일부 신문사들은 인터넷 상에 그들의 기사를 올리지 않기로 결정했습니다.

Vocabulary Matching

1. b 2. c 3. d 4. a

Translation

1. 곤궁한 – b. 재정적인 어려움에 있는
2. 속도 – c. 정도, 속도
3. 무리 – d. 대중 또는 집단
4. 피하다 – a. 벗어 던지다, 피하다

Quiz

1. remember　　2. recall　　3. recognize

Translation

1. 매 수업 시간에 펜이나 연필과 함께 교과서와 가져오는 것을 기억하세요.
2. 결함을 발견하고 나서 그 회사는 물건이 상점으로 나가기 전에 회수하려고 노력하였습니다.
3. 나는 너무 오래 떨어져 있어서 그를 봤을 때 나의 아버지라는 것을 거의알아 보지 못했습니다.

Task 4

1. (b)　　2. (a)　　3. (d)　　4. (c)　　5. (d)

Translation

1. Angie는 두 번이나 거절 당했기 때문에 다시 하는걸 내켜 하지 않았습니다.
2. 일 때문에 지쳐서 그는 보통 때보다 더 일찍 잠자리에 들었습니다.
3. 그 선거의 결과에 많은 사람들이 불만을 느꼈습니다.
4. 날씨가 따뜻해서 우리는 산책을 갔습니다.
5. 무슨 말을 해야 할 지 몰라서 나는 조용히 있었습니다.

Task 5

1. irritating → irritated
2. surrounding → surrounded
3. played → playing / play
4. interested → interesting
5. surprised → surprising

Translation

1. 나는 2층으로부터 끊임없이 들리는 소음 때문에 짜증이 났습니다.
2. 표적이 된 동물은 사냥꾼들로 둘러 싸인 채 가만히 서있었습니다.
3. 우리는 오늘밤 그가 멋진 콘서트에서 전자 바이올린을 켜는 것을 보았습니다.
4. 머무는 동안 여러분 모두에게 재미있고 즐거운 시간이 되기를 바랍니다.
5. 내가 놀라운 비밀을 말하자 부모님들은 한마디도 하지 못하였습니다.

REVIEW TEST

1. (2)　　2. (3)　　3. (1)　　4. (3)　　5. (4)

6. interested 7. confusing 8. impressed 9. traveling/travelling
10. Being

Translation

1. 자세히 들여다 보면 화가가 뒷 배경에 자신의 모습을 그려 놓은 걸 볼 수 있을 겁니다.
2. 책을 다 읽은 후에 그에게 돌려주었습니다.
3. 그가 새로 낸 책은 깜짝 놀랄만한 결말을 지닌 아주 재미있고 신비로운 이야기입니다.
4. 아스피린을 과도하게 복용할 시 위험할 수 있습니다.
5. 나는 내 친구들 모두에게 그것을 알렸습니다.
6. A: Alice도 오늘 밤에 우리랑 영화 보러 갑니까?
   B: 아니오, Alice는 별 관심 없는 것 같아요.
7. 이 지침은 헷갈립니다. 이해할 수가 없어요.
8. 저는 그녀의 노래에 감탄했습니다. 그녀는 정말 뛰어난 가수입니다.
9. 해외 여행을 하는 한국 국민들은 그 지역 대사관의 전화번호와 주소를 알고 있어야 합니다.
10. 나는 맏아들이기 때문에 부모님을 보살펴 드려야 할 책임이 있습니다.

Supplementary Reading

Q.1

1. b 2. c 3. a 4. c 5. d 6. b

Translation

1. 심각한 경기 침체가 캥거루족을 배출하였습니다.
   a) 출발 b) 부진 c) 부족 d) 진행

2. 몇몇의 청년 실업자들은 자의적으로 실업 상태에 있습니다.
   a) 임시로 b) 서둘러서 c) 자진해서 d) 불행히도

3. 그들은 부유한 가정에서 성장하였습니다.
   a) 부유한 b) 영향력 있는 c) 그 이후의 d) 충분한

4. 어떤 사람들은 작은 회사에서 일하기를 꺼려합니다.
   a) 관련된 b) 실망한 c) 하기 싫은 d) 거절된

5. 젊은이들은 힘든 일을 통해 무엇인가를 성취하는 것을 피합니다.
   a) 시도하다 b) 지원하다 c) 열망하다 d) 피하다

6. 그들은 목적을 달성하기 위해 노력했습니다.
   a) 실패하다 b) 얻다 c) 오르다 d) 전진하다

Q.2

1. F 2. T 3. F 4. T 5.T 6. F

Translation

1. 캥거루족은 대학교를 졸업한 젊은이들을 칭하는 용어입니다.
2. 캥거루족에 속하는 젊은이들은 부모로부터 도움을 받습니다.
3. 캥거루족으로 분류되는 젊은이들의 수가 줄고 있습니다.
4. 독립한 사람들의 취업률은 그렇지 않은 이들보다 더 높습니다.
5. 젊은이들은 편한 환경에서 성장했기 때문에 더럽거나 힘든 직업을 싫어합니다.
6. 중장년층은 젊은이들이 야망이 부족하다고 걱정을 합니다.

Unit 06 Adjectives and Adverbs

Comprehension Check

1. (a) 2.(b) 3. (d)

Translation

1. Aaron이 Brett에게 영화관에 빈 자리가 없을 것이라고 이야기한 것은:
   (a) 핑계를 댄 것입니다.
   (b) 꾸며낸 것입니다.
   (c) 예약을 한 것입니다.
   (d) 제안을 한 것입니다.

2. 대화 중에, Brett에 대한 Camille의 태도는
   (a) 실망한 것에서 화가 나는 것으로 변합니다
   (b) 우호적인 것에서 화가 나는 것으로 변합니다.
   (c) 화가 난 것에서 용서하는 것으로 변합니다.
   (d) 기뻐한 것에서 실망하는 것으로 변합니다.

3. 다음 중 사실인 것은?
   (a) Brett은 단지 안부를 전하기 위해서 Camille의 집에 들렀습니다.
   (b) Brett은 Camille과 약속이 있었습니다.
   (c) Aaron은 Brett을 같이 가자고 초대했습니다.
   (d) Camille은 영화를 보러 가지 않기로 결정했습니다.

Task 1

1. frightened 2. former 3. well 4. fond of 5. total

Translation

1. 그 겁먹은 아이가 방 구석에서 울고 있었습니다.
2. 우리 팀의 예전 코치가 다시 왔습니다.
3. 당신이 잘 지내는 것을 보니 좋습니다.
4. 아이들은 유모를 좋아하는 것 같습니다.
5. 지난 해 크리스마스 파티는 완전히 엉망이 되었습니다.

Task 2

1. X (In my job, Friday is the busiest day of the week.)
2. X (The more nervous he gets, the faster he drives.)
3. O

4. O
5. X (Of the two candidates, I think Mr. Wilson is the better one.)

Translation

1. 일을 할 때, 금요일이 일주일 중 가장 바쁜 날입니다.
2. 그는 불안해질수록 더욱 빠르게 운전했습니다.
3. 당신의 남동생은 그 이상 귀여울 수가 없습니다.
4. 우리가 예상했던 시간의 3배가 걸렸습니다.
5. 두 명의 후보자 중에서 Mr. Wilson이 더 낫습니다.

Task 3

1. The proposal I made was very well received.
2. We were absolutely shocked by the accident.
3. You should try as hard as you can to overcome that problem.
4. It's terribly cold today.
5. He always talks about the writer, Kafka.

Translation

1. 내가 한 제안은 반응이 아주 좋았습니다.
2. 우리는 그 사고로 인해 매우 놀랐습니다.
3. 그 문제를 극복하기 위해 당신은 가능한 많은 노력을 해야 합니다.
4. 오늘은 몹시 춥습니다.
5. 그는 항상 작가 Kafka 에 대해 이야기 합니다.

Comprehension Check-up

1. F　　2. F　　3. T

Translation

1. 크로스워드 퍼즐은 고대에서부터 있었습니다.
2. 호주에서는 크로스워드 퍼즐이 완벽하게 대칭적입니다.
3. Bill Clinton은 크로스워드 퍼즐을 풀었을 뿐만 아니라 만들기도 했습니다.

Vocabulary Matching

1. c　　2. a　　3. b　　4. d

Translation

1. 첫 등장 – c. 처음으로 나타남
2. 외국으로 이주한 사람 – a. 외국에서 사는 사람
3. 대칭적인 – b. 양쪽이 똑같음
4. 충성스러운 – e. 성실한

Quiz

1. any 2. some 3. little

Translation

1. 당신은 어떤 독일인에게 물어보더라도 그들은 똑같이 당신에게 말해줄 것입니다.
2. 커피 좀 더 주십시오.
3. 그녀는 크게 여유 있는 우승을 했고, 도중에 별 어려움이 없었습니다.

Task 4

1. (b) 2. (b) 3. (a) 4. (b) 5. (a)

Translation

1. 나에게 뭔가 뜨거운 마실 것을 주세요.
2. Jack Russells은 살아있는 가장 영리한 개들입니다.
3. 새로 건설된 고속도로는 20 마일이라고 합니다.
4. 개의 사고력은 고양이의 그것보다 훨씬 뛰어납니다.
5. 가능한 한 많이 배우도록 노력할 것입니다.

Task 5

1. incorrect (Your Chinese ability is superior to mine.)
2. correct
3. incorrect (This movie is the worst one I've ever seen.)
4. incorrect (She is much/far/even/a lot faster than her friends.)
5. correct

Translation

1. 당신의 중국어 실력은 나보다 낫습니다.
2. 둘 중에서 그가 더 좋습니다.
3. 그 영화는 내가 지금까지 본 것 중 가장 형편없는 것입니다.
4. 그녀는 그녀의 친구들보다 훨씬 빠릅니다.
5. 그는 그의 누나들만큼 지적입니다.

REVIEW TEST

1. (2) 2. (3) 3. (3) 4. (2) 5. (4)
6. cheaper 7. frankly 8. more pleasant 9. best 10. widely

Translation

1. Tom은 자신의 차를 수리해 준 정비사에 대해 칭찬을 아끼지 않았습니다.
2. Susan은 사람들과 대화할 때 종종 쾌활하게 웃습니다.
   그녀는 오늘 즐거워 보입니다.

3. 전화 상태가 너무 안 좋아서 그가 하는 말을 거의 알아들을 수 없었습니다.
4. 새로운 일을 시작해서인지 Melissa는 훨씬 행복해 보입니다. 예전 직업은 이만큼 좋아하지 않았거든요.
5. Jane에게는 세 명의 딸이 있습니다. 그중 Marge가 맏딸인데 엄마를 가장 닮았습니다.
6. 그 식당이 비쌀 줄 알았는데 생각했던 것보다는 저렴했습니다.
7. 그녀는 일을 제대로 하고 있지 않았다고 솔직하게 인정했습니다.
8. 친구와 여행하는 것만큼 즐거운 일은 없습니다.
9. 이 영화는 정말 잘 만들어졌습니다. 내가 최근 본 영화 중 최고입니다.
10. 어느 서점에서든 이 잡지를 구입하는 것은 어렵지 않습니다. 이것은 널리 이용되고 있습니다.

Supplementary Reading

Q.1

1. accomplish	f) achieve
2. utilize	d) make use of
3. pave	b) form a surface with stone or brick
4. regulate	e) control, adjust
5. trait	a) characteristic, feature
6. override	c) overrule, dominate

Translation

1. 성취하다 – 이룩하다
2. 사용하다 – 사용/ 활용하다
3. 도로 따위를 포장하다/덮다 – 표면을 돌이나 벽돌로 덮다
4. 조절하다 – 조정하다, 맞추다
5. 특성 – 특징, 성질
6. ~에 보다 우위에 서다, 무시하다 – 무효로 하다, 압도하다

Q.2

1. d 2. b 3. c 4. a

Translation

1. 윗글에 비추어 다음 중 사실이 아닌 것은?
   a) 하루를 효율적으로 쓰는 것이 성공으로 가는 길입니다.
   b) 일찍 일어나는 사람은 산책하거나, 헬스장에 가거나 쉴 수도 있습니다.
   c) 과학자들은 사람들의 아침이나 저녁에 대한 선호도는 유전자와 관련이 있다는 것을 알아냈습니다.
   d) 사람 안에는 생체시계가 있는 데, 그것은 그 유전자를 지배합니다.

2. (1)에 쓰인 it과 용법이 같은 것이 쓰인 문장은?
   a) 그것은 그들의 베스트셀러 중에 하나입니다.
   b) 나는 그이 아이들을 돕는 것이 나의 의무라고 느꼈습니다.
   c) 그 캠퍼스에서 그 도시까지는 얼마나 됩니까?
   d) 그는 나에게 그것이 사실이 아니라고 말했습니다.

3. 아침형 인간이 여분의 시간에 하는 것으로 윗글에서 언급되지 않은 것은?
   a) 산책을 합니다.
   b) 쉽니다.
   c) 빨래를 합니다.
   d) 외국어를 공부합니다.

4. 윗글에 따르면 유전적 특징은
   a) 사람의 생체시계와 연관되어 있습니다.
   b) 우리의 생활 방식을 결정짓는 가장 중요한 부분입니다.
   c) 인생의 성공과 실패를 결정합니다.
   d) 조절될 수가 없습니다.

Unit 07 Pronouns & Review

Comprehension Check

1. (a) 2.(d) 3. (b)

Translation

1. Carrie는 어떤 것을 구실로 해서 대화를 시작했습니까?
   (a) 책에 대한 흥미
   (b) 서로의 친구인 Phillip
   (c) 잃어버린 지갑
   (d) 배경에 흘러나오는 노래

2. 대화를 시작할 때, Brett은:
   (a) 선물을 사기 위해 쇼핑하고 있었습니다.
   (b) 친구와 대화 중이었습니다.
   (c) 시험공부 중이었습니다.
   (d) 소설을 훑어보는 중이었습니다.

3. Brett과 Carrie는:
   (a) 사랑에 빠졌습니다.
   (b) 뭔가 공통의 관심사를 가졌습니다.
   (c) 오래된 학급 동기생입니다.
   (d) 중요한 주제에 대해 견해가 엇갈립니다.

Task 1

1. Your bag looks nicer than hers.
2. She called herself a master of negotiations, which was true.
3. It is one of her best sellers this year.
4. Joe, Robert, and she are planning a weekend trip to the mountains.
5. Joan was beside herself with joy when she heard the news.

Translation

1. 당신의 가방은 그녀의 가방보다 더 멋져 보입니다.
2. 그녀는 스스로를 협상의 대가라고 칭했는데 그것은 사실이었습니다.
3. 그것은 올해 그녀의 베스트셀러중의 하나입니다.
4. Joe, Mary, 그리고 그녀는 산으로의 주말여행을 계획하고 있습니다.
5. Joan은 그 소식을 듣고 기쁨에 넘쳐 어쩔 줄을 몰라 했습니다.

Task 2

1. incorrect (It was my uncle who took my brother to the hospital yesterday.)
2. correct
3. incorrect (Is it cold outside?)
4. correct
5. incorrect (Scientists such as Einstein are rare.)

Translation

1. 어제 내 남동생을 병원으로 데리고 갔던 사람은 우리 삼촌이었습니다.
2. John이 그 수업에 오지 않은 것이 이상합니다.
3. 밖이 추운가요?
4. 박물관이 토요일에 문을 여나요? 네, 그럴 거에요.
5. 아인슈타인 같은 과학자는 드뭅니다.

Task 3

1. everything
2. none
3. either
4. both
5. one

Translation

1. 그는 화재로 모든 것을 잃었습니다.
2. 나는 자물쇠에 모든 열쇠를 맞추어 보았지만, 그 어떤 것도 맞지 않습니다.
3. 나는 내 영어선생님 둘 다 좋아하지 않습니다.
4. 그들은 둘 다 그녀를 기다리고 있는 중이었습니다
5. 저는 펜이 없습니다. 제게 한 개 빌려주시겠습니까?

Task 4

1. (c) It
2. (d) some
3. (a) hers
4. (a) those
5. (b) who

Translation

1. Sarah가 그 파티에 오지 않은 것은 이상합니다.
2. 당신이 오렌지 주스를 원하면 그녀가 가게에서 사줄 겁니다.
3. 저것이 당신의 열쇠인가요? 아니면 그 여자의 것인가요?
4. 초청장을 가진 사람 외에는 누구도 들어올 수 없습니다.
5. 사람들은 셰익스피어가 누구였는지 그가 어떻게 살았는지를 거의 모릅니다.

Task 5

1. correct
2. incorrect (Who do you think will participate in the contest?)
3. correct
4. incorrect (Her opinion is different from his.)
5. incorrect (Would you like some coffee?)

Translation

1. 나는 두 명의 형제가 있는데 한 명은 캐나다에 한 명은 프랑스에 있습니다.
2. 당신은 누가 그 경기에 참가할 거라고 생각하십니까?
3. 천안의 인구는 부산보다 적습니다.
4. 그녀의 의견은 그의 의견과는 다릅니다.
5. 커피 좀 드실래요?

Review 1-7

Unit 1 Tenses

1. (a)	2. (b)	3. (d)	4. (c)	5. (c)
6. (d)	7. (d)	8. (b)	9. (a)	10. (c)

1. Translation

위원회는 이미 내년 예산을 승인했습니다.
해설: 문맥상 이미(already) 예산을 승인한 과거의 일(과거의 동작)이므로 과거시제를 써야 합니다.

2. Translation

그녀의 연설은 수년에 걸쳐 수백만의 사람들에게 영감을 주고 있습니다.
해설: 현재완료 계속의 용법으로 과거에 일어난 사건이 현재까지 영향을 미치고 있음을 나타냅니다.

3. Translation

다음주 목요일, 우리는 새로운 의장을 뽑을 것입니다.
해설: 미래시점의 일을 나타내므로 단순 미래형을 써야 합니다.

4. Translation

최근의 설문 결과는 대부분의 사람들이 보수주의 후보를 선호한다는 것을 나타냅니다.
해설: 현재 시제이며 주어가(The latest poll results) 복수이므로 suggest가 답이 됩니다.

5. Translation

다음주 토론에서, 후보자들은 곤란한 질문들을 받을 것입니다.
해설: 미래시점의 일을 나타내므로 단순 미래형을 써야 합니다.

6. Translation

Oliver Percovich는 2007년에 Kabul에 도착했습니다.
해설: 과거를 명확하게 나타내는 시점(2007)이 있으므로 과거시제를 씁니다.

7. Translation

하루 종일 비가 내립니다. 언제 그칠지 궁금합니다.
해설: 하루 종일(all day)이라는 표현이 있으므로 현재완료 시제를 써야 합니다. 특히 현재완료 진행시제는 과거에 시작한 동작이 현재까지 계속되고 있다는 의미를 강조할 때 씁니다. (have/has + been + -ing)

8. Translation

내가 방에 들어갔을 때 Janice와 Alice는 무언가에 관해 논쟁을 벌이고 있었습니다. 그들을 말리느라 힘들었습니다.
해설: 과거의 어느 시점에 진행 중이던 동작, 사건을 나타낼 때 과거 진행형을 씁니다. (be동사의 과거형 + -ing)

9. Translation

A: 이번 토요일에 Marge가 일하나요?
B: 확실하지는 않지만 보통 토요일에는 쉬어요.
해설: 일반적인 일, 언제나 일어나는 일, 사실 등에 대해서 말할 때 단순 현재 시제를 씁니다.

10. Translation

만약 당신이 지금 출발하면 마지막 기차를 탈 수 있을 겁니다.
해설: 시간이나 조건의 부사절에서는 미래를 표현할 때, 미래를 나타내는 동사 대신 현재형으로 씁니다.

Unit 2 Sentence Structure

1. (b)	2. (d)	3. (d)	4. (a)	5. (c)
6. (a)	7. (d)	8. (a)	9. (c)	10. (b)

1. Translation

나는 당신이 당신 차의 브레이크를 점검할 필요가 있다고 생각합니다.
해설: have는 사역동사로 have+목적어+원형부정사(~에게 ~을 시키다)를 취하지만, 여기서는 목적어인 the brakes in your car가 사람이 아닌 사물이므로 수동의 의미를 나타내기 위해 목적보어로 과거분사를 씁니다.

2. Translation

그들은 그 문제를 오랫동안 토의했으나, 그들의 노력은 결과적으로 실패하였습니다.
해설: discuss는 타동사로 뒤에 바로 목적어가 따라옵니다. result는 자동사로 result+전치사+명사(결과적으로 ~하게 되다)로 쓰입니다.

cf) 주의하여야 할 타동사: resemble, discuss, attend, marry, enter, reach, greet, mention 등은 타동사로 목적어 앞에 전치사가 오지 않습니다.

3. Translation

그들의 부모님이 그들이 선량하고 정직한 시민이 되도록 격려하였습니다.
해설: encourage는 불완전 타동사로 목적어+to부정사(~를 격려해서 ~하게 하다)가 따라 옵니다.

4. Translation

그는 몸이 아파서 그 회의에 참석하지 않았습니다.

해설: attend는 자동사로 착각하기 쉬운 완전 타동사입니다. 바로 목적어가 따라옵니다. attend to/at (X)

5. Translation

나에게 맥주를 한 병 갖다 주겠습니까?

해설: 4형식 문장을 3형식으로 고칠 때는 직접 목적어를 간접목적어 앞에 쓰며, 간접 목적어 앞에 to, for와 같은 전치사를 써서 부사구를 만듭니다.

cf) 간접목적어를 부사구로 만들 때, 사용하는 전치사

to 사용: give, bring, teach, offer, lend, send, promise, show, write, owe, hand
for 사용: make, buy, find, build, get, choose
of 사용: ask, beg, require

6. Translation

나는 간략하게 서류들을 훑어본 후 탁자 위에 올려 놓았습니다.

해설: 다음 동사들의 쓰임을 잘 기억해 두시기 바랍니다. 여기서는 '~을 놓다' 라는 의미의 타동사 lay의 과거형이 와야 합니다.

lie: ~에 놓여있다, 눕다 (vi) lie - lay - lain
lie: 거짓말하다 (vi) lie - lied - lied
lay: ~을 놓다 (vt) lay - laid - laid

7. Translation

나는 조언을 얻기 위해 그에게 내 계획안을 보여주었습니다.

해설: '~에게 ~을 보여주다' 라는 의미로 쓰일 때, 바로 간접 목적어가 따라 올 수 있는 동사는 show입니다.

cf) 주의하여야 할 동사

explain, suggest, introduce, propose, mention, say 등은 수여동사가 아니므로, 사람 앞에 전치사 to를 써야 합니다.

8. Translation

당신이 생각하고 있는 걸 그에게 알려주지 그랬어요?

해설: let은 사역동사로 목적어+목적보어를 취합니다. 목적어와 목적보어가 능동의 관계이면 목적보어 자리에 동사원형을 쓰고, 수동의 관계이면 과거분사를 씁니다.

9. Translation

나는 나의 사무실 창문으로부터 그들이 주차장을 짓고 있는 것을 볼 수 있었습니다.

해설: watch는 지각동사로 목적어+목적보어의 관계가 능동이면 목적보어 자리에 동사원형이 옵니다. 목적어가 '~하고 있는' 진행의 뜻을 강조하고자 하는 경우에는, 동사원형 대신에 현재분사(~ing)가 옵니다.

10. Translation

이 재킷이 당신한테 잘 어울리는 것 같아요. 당신은 초록색이 잘 어울려요.

해설: look+형용사(~처럼 보인다), suit+목적어+well(의복 등이 ~에게 잘 어울리다)

Unit 3 Infinitives and Gerunds

1. (a)	2. (b)	3. (d)	4. (c)	5. (c)
6. (b)	7. (a)	8. (d)	9. (a)	10. (c)

1. Translation

나의 아버지는 내가 콘서트에 가는 것을 허락하지 않으셨습니다.
해설: refuse 는 to부정사를 목적어로 취하는 동사입니다.

2. Translation

The Bill and Melinda Gates Foundation에서는 개발도상국에서 발생하는 질병들을 근절시키는 것을 목표로 하고 있습니다.
해설: aim 은 to부정사를 목적어로 취하는 동사입니다.

3. Translation

교육의 목표는 스스로 생각하도록 장려하는 것입니다.
해설: to 부정사의 명사적 용법으로, <to + 동사원형>의 형태로 주어에 대해 보충 설명하는 역할을 하는 주격보어로 쓰였습니다.

4. Translation

무엇이 중요한지 못보고 놓치기 쉽습니다.
해설: to 부정사의 명사적 용법으로, it은 가주어, to부정사 이하는 진주어입니다. lose sight of~는 '못 보고 놓치다, 잊어버리다'는 의미를 갖습니다.

5. Translation

저는 일기를 쓰지 않습니다.
해설: 전치사(of)의 목적어로 ~ing 형태의 동명사가 쓰여야 합니다. be in the habit of~는 '~하는 버릇이 있다' 라는 의미입니다.

6. Translation

저도 가고 싶었지만 늦게까지 일해야만 했습니다.
해설: want 는 to부정사를 목적어로 취하는 동사입니다.

7. Translation

해외여행을 가기 위해 항상 돈을 많이 쓸 필요는 없습니다.
해설: need 는 to부정사를 목적어로 취하는 동사입니다. need는 긍정문에서는 언제나 조동사가 아니라 본동사로 쓰입니다.

8. Translation

이 쓰레기를 치워주시겠어요?
해설: mind 는 동명사를 목적어로 취하는 동사입니다.

9. Translation

오늘 아침 전 당신에게 계속 전화를 걸었습니다. 하지만 통화 중이더군요.
해설: keep은 enjoy, admit, consider, finish 등과 함께 동명사를 목적어로 취하는 동사입니다. try+to부정사는 '~하려고 노력하다'라는 의미입니다.

10. Translation

제가 이 책을 다 읽을 수 있을 것 같지 않습니다. 지루하기도 하고 헷갈리거든요.
해설: finish 는 동명사를 목적어로 취하는 동사입니다.

Unit 4 Auxiliary Verbs

1. (a)	2. (b)	3. (c)	4. (b)	5. (b)
6. (a)	7. (d)	8. (a)	9. (d)	10. (d)

1. Translation

A: 불어를 할 줄 아세요?

B: 조금 할 수 있습니다.

해설: can '~을 할 수 있다' 라는 뜻으로, 능력, 허락, 요청, 가능성을 표현할 때 쓰이는데, 이 문장에서는 능력을 나타냅니다.

2. Translation

A: 이 일에 대해 우리가 무엇을 할 수 있을까요?

B: 제 생각에는 사람들의 의견을 듣기 위해 회의를 열어야 할 것 같습니다.

해설: should는 의무, 추측, 목적 등으로 '~해야 한다, ~일 것이다, ~하지 않도록/ ~할까 봐(lest~should)' 이라는 뜻을 가지고 있습니다. 또한 '~일 리가 있겠는가' 라는 뜻으로 뜻밖의 상황이나 의아스러움을 나타낼 때 사용하기도 합니다. 이 문장에서는 의무를 나타냅니다.

3. Translation

A: 내일 수업 가세요?

B: 아마 빠질 것 같아요.

해설: 불확실한 추측으로 might가 쓰입니다.

4. Translation

A: 저는 네 살 때 큰 수로 나누는 나눗셈을 할 수 있었습니다.

B: 저는 다섯 살 때 대수학을 할 수 있었습니다.

해설: can의 과거형으로 과거에 '~할 수 있었다'는 능력을 나타냅니다.

5. Translation

A: 제대로 작동하는 게 아무것도 없는 것 같습니다.

B: 뭔가 새로운 방법을 시도해야 합니다.

해설: need to '~해야 한다'는 의미입니다. need는 긍정문에서는 본동사로 쓰여 뒤에 to부정사가 따라 옵니다.

6. Translation

A: 여기 좀 도와주실래요?

B: 제가 할 수 있는 일이면 도와드리겠지만 그럴 수 없을 것 같네요.

해설: 가정법 과거는 현재 상황에 대한 가정을 나타내며, 조건절에서 if +주어+조동사 과거형이 나옵니다.

7. Translation

A: 전 일주일 넘게 감기에 걸려있어요.

B: 꼭 검진을 받아보세요.

해설: 의무를 나타내는 ought to가 옵니다. 참고로 must는 강제적인 명령이나 강한 권유의 의미가 있고, should나 ought to는 그보다 약한 권유나 충고의 의미가 있습니다.

8. Translation
다이어트 계획을 짜기 전에 의사와 상담을 해야 합니다.
해설: should는 의무를 나타냅니다. Need는 to부정사가 따라오기 때문에 답이 될 수 없습니다.

9. Translation
강이 오염되기 전 우리는 그 곳에서 수영이나 낚시를 하곤 했습니다. 불행하게도 거기서 더 이상 수영과 낚시를 하지 못합니다.
해설: used to + 동사원형은 ‘ ~하곤 했다’의 의미로 과거의 규칙적인 습관이나 과거의 계속적인 상태를 나타냅니다.

10. Translation
만약 당신이 거기 있었다면 그는 다르게 행동했을지도 모릅니다.
해설: 가정법 과거완료 형태로, 종속절에서는 had+p.p.가 나오고, 주절에서 may/might have ‘p.p.가 나옵니다. may/might have p.p.는 ‘ ~이었을지도 모른다’는 의미입니다.

Unit 5 Participle

1. (a)	2. (a)	3. (b)	4. (c)	5. (d)
6. (a)	7. (b)	8. (b)	9. (d)	10. (c)

1. Translation
내 사촌과 함께 살고 있는 그 여자는 Susan입니다.
해설: 현재분사(~ing)가 구를 이루어 명사 뒤에서 명사를 수식하는 경우입니다. The woman (who is) living with my cousin is Susan.

2. Translation
공원에서 캐리커처 그리는 여자 보셨어요?
해설: 지각동사(see, watch, notice, hear, smell)+목적어+목적보어(동사원형/~ing)의 구문입니다.

3. Translation
오늘의 특별 점심은 현미 위에 제공되는 얇은 조각의 연어입니다.
해설: 분사가 구를 이루어 명사를 수식 할 때는 명사의 뒤에서 명사를 수식하며, 수동의 의미 (연어가 제공되는 것)이므로 과거분사를 씁니다.

4. Translation
중국에 대해 이야기해 보자면 세계에서 가장 빠른 통근열차를 만든다는 계획에 대해 들어보셨습니까?
해설: Speaking of~는 ‘ ~에 관해서 말한다면’ 의 뜻입니다.

5. Translation
월 가의 분위기는 침체되어 있습니다.
해설: ‘~한 감정을 느끼게 하는’ 의 뜻일 때는 현재분사를 씁니다. 사물 주어(월 가의 분위기)가 침체된 감정을 사람들에게 느끼게 하므로 depressing 이 옵니다.

6. Translation

그 곳에 가본 적이 있으니 당신을 구경시켜 줄 수 있습니다.

해설: 분사를 이용하여 부사절을 부사구로 바꾼 분사구문으로, 부사절의 시제가 주절의 시제보다 앞설 때에는 <having + p.p.>를 써서 분사구문을 만듭니다.

7. Translation

일반적으로 경영자들은 경험에만 너무 치중하고 문제해결 능력에는 충분한 관심을 기울이지 않는 경향이 있습니다.

해설: 주어가 막연한 일반인인 경우, 일반인 주어를 생략하여 관용적으로 사용되는 분사구문입니다. generally speaking(일반적으로 말하자면)

8. Translation

수술을 기다리는 동안 나는 매우 긴장되고 떨렸습니다.

해설: 동시 동작을 나타내는 분사구문 입니다.

9. Translation

그의 새 책은 상당히 재미있습니다. 비록 그의 최고 작품은 아니라 하더라도.

해설: 사물이 주어로 와서 '~을 느끼게 하는'의 의미로 쓰일 때는 현재분사인 ~ing가 옵니다. 반대로 주어가 '~한 감정을 느끼는' 의 뜻일 때는 과거분사를 씁니다.

10. Translation

주변의 다른 곳들과 비교해 봤을 때 그 호텔은 다소 비싸지만 조용하고 안락합니다.

해설: 분사를 이용하여 부사절을 부사구로 바꾼 분사구문으로, being 이 생략되고 과거분사로 시작된 문장입니다. Compared with~(~와 비교하면)

Unit 6 Adjectives and Adverbs

1. (a)	2. (b)	3. (d)	4. (a)	5. (c)
6. (b)	7. (b)	8. (c)	9. (d)	10. (a)

1. Translation

당신의 안전만큼 중요한 것은 아무것도 없습니다.

해설: no~ as + 원급 + as 는 '~ 만큼 ~한 것은 없다' 는 최상급의 의미입니다.

2. Translation

해마다 이 맘 때쯤이 가장 춥습니다.

해설: 동일사물 혹은 동일개념 자체의 속성을 비교할 때는 최상급이라도 the를 쓰지 않습니다.

3. Translation

도쿄보다 서울의 부동산 가격이 더 비쌉니다.

해설: 형용사 expensive의 경우는 more를 써서 비교급을 나타냅니다.

4. Translation

많은 주민들이 동네에 공장을 건설하는 데 강하게 반대합니다.

해설: '~에 반대하다'는 be against를 수식하므로 부사를 써주셔야 합니다.

5. Translation
최근에 영화 본 적 있으세요?
해설: '최근에'라는 부사는 lately입니다. 참고로 late는 형용사, 부사로 다 쓰여서 '늦은, 늦게' 라는 의미를 갖습니다.

6. Translation
Edna는 자신의 일에 익숙해진 것 같습니다. 요즘 그녀의 실수가 줄어들었습니다.
해설: 셀 수 있는 명사(mistake)를 수식하는 few의 비교급으로 fewer를 씁니다.

7. Translation
우리가 극장에 도착했을 때 비가 오기 시작했습니다. 영화가 끝났을 때도 여전히 비가 내리고 있었습니다.
해설: still '아직도, 여전히' 의 의미로 쓰입니다.

8. Translation
그 수프가 너무 뜨거워서 조심스럽게 맛을 보았습니다. 수프 맛이 나한테는 조금 짰습니다.
해설: '~음식을 맛보다'라는 의미의 타동사로 쓰인taste를 수식하는 것은 부사형태인 carefully 입니다. taste가 '~한 맛이 나다' 라는 의미의 자동사로 쓰일 때는 형용사salty가 따라와야 합니다.

9. Translation
Jake는 정말 유머가 넘칩니다. 그는 내가 아는 가장 재미있는 사람 중 한 명입니다.
해설: one of the+최상급은 '가장 ~한 것 중의 하나'라는 의미로 쓰입니다. 형용사 funny의 최상급은 funniest입니다.

10. Translation
그가 말을 할수록 나는 더 지루해졌습니다.
해설: the+비교급, the+비교급은 '~하면 할수록 더 ~한'의 의미입니다.

Unit 7 Pronouns

1. (a)	2. (c)	3. (a)	4. (b)	5. (d)
6. (b)	7. (c)	8. (d)	9. (a)	10. (c)

1. Translation
우리가 도착했을 때는 남아있는 사람이 아무도 없었습니다.
해설: none 은 독립적으로 쓰이는 경우 주로 복수동사와 함께 쓰입니다. 위 문장에서는 복수동사 (were)와 쓰이며 '아무도 없었다'라는 뜻을 나타내는 것은 none 뿐입니다.

2. Translation
나는 그것들 중 어느 쪽도 즐기지 않습니다.
해설: 부정어(not) 다음에 either of~가 쓰이면 '어느 쪽도 ~아니다'라는 의미를 갖습니다.

3. Translation
희생자의 피는 부엌 바닥에서 발견된 것과 달랐습니다.
해설: that 은 이미 언급된 단수 명사의 반복을 피하기 위해 쓰입니다.
cf) 복수 명사를 대신하거나 나타내고자 할 때에는 that 대신 those를 이용합니다.

4. Translation

다음주 화요일까지 우리가 모든 계약 수정안 검토를 끝낼 것을 건의합니다.
해설: '전부, 모든'의 의미로 쓰이는 대명사 all이 와야 합니다.

5. Translation

경찰에서는 누가 그 일을 했는지 아직 조사 중입니다.
해설: 의문대명사 who 는 '누구' 의 뜻으로 명사절을 이끕니다. who did it이 동사 investigate의 목적어로 쓰인 것입니다.

6. Translation

어느 쪽이 적절한 행동 방침인지 확실하지 않습니다.
해설: 의문대명사로서which 는 '어느 쪽'으로 해석됩니다. It은 가주어이고, which is the proper course of action이 진주어입니다.

7. Translation

중국 지점에서는 벌써 총 판매액 계산까지 끝났는데 당신들은 아직 자신들 것도 끝내지 못했습니다.
해설: '당신들의 것' 이라고 해석되는 소유대명사 yours (= your sales totals)가 와야 합니다.

8. Translation

멕시코행 비행기표 가격이 요즘 얼마죠?
해설: 위 문장의 what 은 의문대명사로서 '무엇' 또는 '얼마나(how much)'의 뜻으로 쓰입니다. What does it cost~/ What will it cost~는 '돈이 얼마나 들다'의 의미입니다.

9. Translation

이것은 내 동생이 잃어버린 핸드폰과 똑같은 것입니다.
해설: the same ~that~은 '~와 동일한 것' 이라는 의미입니다. 관사 the와 함께 쓰일 수 있는 것은 same입니다.

10. Translation

아이들은 게임을 하며 즐겁게 놀았습니다.
해설: 주어와 목적어의 대상이 같을 때에는 목적어 자리에 인칭대명사의 목적격대신 '재귀대명사'를 씁니다. amuse oneself는 '즐기다'라는 의미입니다.

Supplementary Reading

Q.1

1. violation — c) the breaking of a law or a promise
2. estimate — a) to guess
3. undergo — f) to experience
4. enhance — b) to make greater
5. prospect — g) a possibility, chances
6. exact — h) to force or demand
7. retribution — e) something given or demanded in repayment
8. filial — d) relating to a son or a daughter

Translation

1. 위반 – 법 또는 약속을 어기는 행위
2. 추정하다 – 어림짐작하다, 추측하다
3. 겪다, 당하다 – 경험하다
4. 올리다, 늘리다 – 강화하다, 늘리다
5. 전망, 기대 – 가능성, 기회
6. 무리하게 요구하다 – 강요하다, 요구하다
7. 보복, 갚음 – 상환으로 주어지거나 요구되는 것
8. 자식으로서 – 아들이나 딸과 관련된

Q.2

1. T 2. F 3. F 4. F 5. T

Translation

1. 한국인들은 신체를 상하게 하는 것이 부모에게 불복종하는 것이라고 생각했습니다.
2. 유교의 영향으로 인해 대부분의 아시아인들은 여전히 성형수술에 반대 합니다.
3. 한국과 일본에서는 오직 여성들만이 성형수술에 관심이 있습니다.
4. 수술 비용이 오름에도 불구하고 더 많은 남성들이 성형수술을 받습니다.
5. 서양에서보다 아시아에서 의료과실 사건의 경우 법적인 보상을 받는 것이 더 어렵습니다.

Unit 08

Relatives

Comprehension Check

1. (b) 2. (c)

Translation

1. Brett이 제시한 캐릭터는 고객들이 아마
   (a) 싫어할 것입니다.
   (b) 부러워할 것입니다.
   (c) 신기하다고 생각할 것입니다.
   (d) 무시할 것입니다.

2. Brett이 제시한 광고 캠페인이 암시하는 것은
   (a) VERVE 3000은 진정한 사랑을 찾도록 도와줄 것입니다.
   (b) VERVE 3000은 당신을 더욱 매력적으로 만들어줄 것입니다.
   (c) VERVE 3000은 당신이 성공하도록 도와줄 것입니다.
   (d) 위의 것이 모두 해당되지 않습니다.

Task 1

1. He has written a book whose name I forgot.
2. The girl who was injured in the accident is now in the hospital.
3. She is married to an actor of whom you may have heard.
4. The building which was destroyed in the fire has now been rebuilt.
5. What she did is inexcusable.

Translation

1. 그는 제목이 생각이 나지 않는 어떤 책을 썼습니다.
2. 사고로 부상당한 소녀는 지금 병원에 있습니다.
3. 그녀는 당신이 이름을 들어보았을 법한 배우와 결혼하였습니다.
4. 화재로 무너진 건물이 이제 다시 세워졌습니다.
5. 그녀가 한 행동은 용서할 수 없습니다.

Task 2

1. incorrect (This is the town (which) I was born in. / This is the town in which I was born. / This is the town where I was born.)
2. incorrect My brother, who(m) you once met, is visiting us tomorrow.
3. correct
4. correct
5. correct

Translation

1. 여기는 내가 태어난 마을입니다.
2. 내 남동생은 당신이 한 번 만난 적이 있는데, 내일 우리를 방문할 것입니다.
3. 파티에 초대 받았던 사람들 중 반은 나타나지 않았습니다.
4. 내가 이야기를 나누었던 남자는 매우 다정했습니다.
5. 그 계약은 취소 되었는데, 그것은 그가 바라던 바였습니다.

Task 3

1. The hotel where we stayed wasn't very clean.
2. This is why I refuse to go.
3. Do you know the day when exams begin?
4. They should have called him, however busy they were.
5. He helps me whenever I'm in trouble.

Translation

1. 우리가 묵었던 호텔은 아주 깨끗하지는 않았습니다.
2. 이래서 나는 가지 않으려는 겁니다.
3. 시험이 시작되는 날이 언제인지 아세요?
4. 그들이 아무리 바빴어도 그에게 전화를 걸었어야 했습니다.
5. 내가 어려움에 처할 때마다 그는 나를 돕습니다.

Comprehension Check-up

1. T 2. F 3. T

Translation

1. 거짓말쟁이는 정직하게 말하는 사람이 사용하는 언어와는 다른 언어를 사용합니다.
2. Pennebaker박사는 무슨 말을 하는 지가 어떻게 말하는 지보다 더 중요하다고 생각합니다.
3. 이 기술을 정신질환 진단에 적용될 수 있을 것입니다.

Vocabulary Matching

1. b 2. c 3. d 4. a

Translation

1. 심리학자 – b. 마음과 정신적 과정을 분석하기 위한 훈련을 받은 사람
3. ~하기 쉬운 – c. 무언가에 대한 선천적인 성향을 갖는 것
4. 실용적인 – d. 쓸모 있는
5. 잊을 수 없을 만큼 정신적 충격이 큰 – a. 심리적으로 고통스러운

Quiz

1. affect 2. effect 3. affect

Translation

1. 오염은 주민들의 건강을 침해할 수 있습니다.
2. 새로운 법인세 정책은 우리의 사업방식에 변화를 초래하기 위해 계획되었습니다.
3. 감정적으로 결정하지 마세요.

Task 4

1. (d) 2. (c) 3. (a) 4. (d) 5. (d)

Translation

1. 이 음식은 온도의 차이가 최소인 건조한 곳에 저장되어야 합니다.
2. 어떤 책을 읽건 그 책이 당신에게 도움이 될 것임을 알게 될 것입니다.
3. 필요한 것은 충분한 연료유 공급입니다.
4. Sandy는 남편이 감옥에 있는 여자입니다.
5. 우리가 이야기를 나누었던 그 비서는 매우 친절했습니다.

Task 5

1. whom → who
2. that → which
3. which → where / in which / at which
4. Whatever → However
5. where → when

Translation

1. 평화주의자는 모든 전쟁은 잘못된 것이라고 믿는 사람입니다.
2. 그는 나에게 그 일자리를 제안했지만, 난 거절했습니다.
3. 음식 맛이 정말 훌륭한 음식점을 알고 있습니까?
4. 아무리 화가 나더라도 그들에게 소리치면 안됩니다.
5. 우리가 엘리베이터에 갇혔던 그 때를 잊을 수가 없습니다.

REVIEW TEST

1. (4) 2. (2) 3. (3) 4. (2) 5. (1)
6. (3) 7. (1) 8. (1) 9. (2) 10. (4)

Translation

1. 그들은 그녀가 정말 원하는 것을 사 주었습니다.
2. 나는 아무 말도 하지 않았는데 이로 인해 그가 화났습니다.
3. 이것은 지금까지 그가 그린 그림 중 최고입니다.

4. Jane은 자신이 태어난 마을을 한 번도 떠난 적이 없습니다.
5. 내 아들은 기회가 생길 때마다 PC방에 가고 싶어 합니다.
6. 호명되지 않은 학생 있나요?
7. 당신의 신발은 제 것과 크기가 같습니다.
8. 제 월급은 인상되지 않았습니다. 하지만 이것 때문에 일을 그만둔 것은 아닙니다.
9. 우리가 Delta 항공사를 이용해야 한다고 제안한 사람이 누구든지 간에 여행을 많이 안 한 사람입니다.
10. 상식이 있는 사람이라면 누가 그런 바보 같은 짓을 하겠습니까?

Supplementary Reading

Q.1

1. companionship — d) fellowship
2. liberating — g) freeing from the restrictions
3. handicapped — b) suffering from a mental or physical disability
4. scam — c) a dishonest plan for making money
5 .confident — a) being certain in one's abilities
6. nightmare — e) an experience that is very frightening or unpleasant
7. immune — f) exempt or protected

Translation

1. 교제, 친구로 사귀기 – 동료의식
2. 자유로운 – 제약들로부터 자유롭게 되는
3. 장애가 있는 – 정신적 신체적 장애를 겪는
4. 사기, 속이는 행위 – 돈을 벌기 위한 정직하지 못한 계획
5. 자신이 있는 – 능력을 확신하는
6. 악몽, 끔찍한 경험 – 아주 두렵고 불쾌한 경험
7. 면역된 – 면제되거나 보호되는

Q.2

1. F 2. F 3. F 4. T 5. F 6. F

Translation

1. 인터넷은 새로운 직업을 찾는데 관심이 있는 사람들이 주로 씁니다.
2. 첫 번째 개인 광고는 1727년 미국에서 처음으로 나왔습니다.
3. 온라인 만남 웹사이트를 방문하는 사람들의 수가 줄어들고 있습니다.
4. 장애를 가진 사람들이 결혼할 상대를 찾기 위해 인터넷 만남 웹사이트를 이용합니다.
5. 내성적인 사람들에게는 컴퓨터 상에서 대화하는 것이 무척 어렵습니다.
6. 가상공간에서의 누군가와 처음 대화를 나눌 때 개인적인 정보를 알려주어야 합니다.

Unit 09

The Passive Voice

Comprehension Check

1. (d)　　2. (a)　　3. (a)

Translation

1. Camille은 왜 Aaron을 그렇게 급하게 만나려 합니까?
   (a) 그에게 알려줄 소식이 있습니다.
   (b) 가족일로 비상사태가 발생했습니다.
   (c) 그녀는 도시를 떠날 것입니다.
   (d) A와C 둘 다

2. Camille이 Aaron에게 말하길 이 기회는 그녀에게 있어:
   (a) 항상 꿈꿔왔던 것입니다.
   (b) 불안한 것입니다.
   (c) 예약한 것입니다.
   (d) 많이 생각하지 않았던 것입니다.

3. Aaron은 Camille이 그들의 계획을 잊어버렸다는 것에 대해 깜짝 놀랐는데 왜냐하면:
   (a) 그 날이 특별한 날이기 때문입니다.
   (b) 그가 세 번이나 그녀에게 일깨워줬기 때문입니다.
   (c) 그녀가 세운 계획이기 때문입니다.
   (d) 해당사항 없습니다.

Task 1

1. A new theory was announced by Einstein.
2. We were toldby the tour guide to have a look around.
3. The problem has already been discussedby the board of directors.
4. Alcohol is not sold in this shop.
5. This problem can be solved by Jan.

Translation

1. 새 이론은 아인슈타인에 의해서 발표되었습니다.
2. 그 여행 가이드는 우리에게 주변을 둘러보라고 말했습니다.
3. 그 문제는 이사회에 의해 이미 논의되었습니다.
4. 이 가게에서는 술을 팔지 않습니다.
5. 이 문제는 Jan에 의해서 해결될 수 있습니다.

Task 2

1. O
2. X (It is expected (that) you will get high grades. / You are expected to get high grades.)
3. O
4. O
5. X (The video must be returned on time (by you).)

Translation
1. 우리는 이 문제를 곧 처리할 겁니다.
2. 그들은 당신이 높은 점수를 받을 것으로 예상합니다.
3. 어머니는 식료품을 나르고 있습니다.
4. 나는 돈을 John에게 건네 주었습니다.
5. 비디오를 제 시간에 되돌려주어야 합니다.

Task 3

1. The room is filled with fresh air.
2. James was surprised at the test results.
3. I was sick and tired of my job.
4. He has been exposed to danger.
5. She got married to a computer programmer last fall.

Translation
1. 그 방은 신선한 공기로 가득 차 있습니다.
2. James는 그 시험 결과에 놀랐습니다.
3. 나는 내 일에 너무 싫증이 났습니다.
4. 그는 위험에 노출되어 왔습니다.
5. 그녀는 작년 가을에 컴퓨터 프로그래머와 결혼했습니다.

Comprehension Check-up

1. T 2. F 3. T

Translation
1. 전세계적인 에너지 부족 때문에 태양에너지가 각광받고 있습니다.
2. Solar Turbine Group은 태양 에너지가 경제를 발전시키기 위한 적절한 임시 해결책이라고 생각합니다.
3. 태양에너지의 잠재적인 용도는 다양하고 넓습니다.

Vocabulary Matching

1. b 2. c 3. d 4. a

Translation

1. 화석연료 – b. 석유, 석탄, 천연가스
2. 비실용적인 – c. 현명하지 못하거나 비효율적인
3. 빈곤한 – d. 가난한
4. 적용, 응용 – a. 이용

Quiz

1. deny　　2. reject　　3. refuse

Translation

1. 피고인은 자신에게 죄가 있다는 사실을 계속 거부합니다.
2. 매년 대학들은 예산의 제한 때문에 실력 있는 수백만의 지원자들을 탈락시킬 수 밖에 없습니다.
3. 난 이런 식으로 대접받는 것을 거절하겠습니다.

Task 4

1. b)　　2. c)　　3. a)　　4. d)　　5. d)

Translation

1. 그녀는 그 잡지를 위한 글을 쓰고 있었습니다.
2. 그 일은 시간에 맞춰 마무리되어야 합니다.
3. 우리 회사는 고층빌딩을 지을 것 입니다.
4. Angela는 오늘 저녁 식사에 오기로 되어 있습니다.
5. 그 아기는 그가 돌보아 왔습니다.

Task 5

1. incorrect (Children resemble their parents.)
2. correct
3. incorrect (I must have my watch repaired.)
4. incorrect (I am not satisfied with my life nowadays.)
5. correct

Translation

1. 아이들은 부모를 닮습니다.
2. 지금 들어 올 수 없습니다. 사무실 청소 중이거든요.
3. 나는 시계를 맡겨서 수리를 해야 합니다.
4. 나는 요즘 나의 생활이 만족스럽지 못합니다.
5. 그 시위에 연루된 모든 노동자들이 해고되었습니다.

REVIEW TEST

1. (4) 2. (3) 3. (2) 4. (1) 5. (2)
6. been arranged 7. was stolen 8. be embarrassed
9. is satisfied 10. be built

Translation

1. 그는 나에게 일찍 돌아오라고 요청했습니다.
2. 그는 동갑내기 여성과 결혼했습니다.
3. 각 지원자들의 이름과 주소가 양식에 쓰여 있어야 합니다.
4. 어제 그녀에게 무슨 일이 있었는지 아세요?
5. 할머니 댁에 있었을 때 난 보살핌을 받았습니다.
6. 그들이 모든 세부사항을 정리했습니다.
7. 며칠 전에 내 자전거를 도난 당했습니다.
8. 친구들 앞에서 무안해지는 것을 좋아하는 사람은 아무도 없습니다.
9. 그녀는 현재 시험 결과에 만족스러워 합니다.
10. 새로운 쇼핑 센터가 곧 시내에 지어질 겁니다.

Supplementary Reading

Q.1

1. a 2. b 3. a 4. d 5. b 6. c

Translation

1. 쓰나미는 인도양의 거대한 지진으로 인해 발생되었습니다.
2. 동물들은 아마도 거대한 물결이 오는 것을 감지했었을 수도 있습니다.
3. 그는 그 영화의 끔찍한 결말에 경악했습니다.
4. 동물은 자연적 대 재앙을 예견할 수 있습니다.
5. 동물은 지진이나 폭풍 전에 특별한 행동을 보입니다.
6. 갇힌 새들은 안절 부절하지 못합니다.

Q.2

1. b 2. d 3. c 4. a 5. a

Translation

1. 쓰나미가 발생한 원인은 무엇이었습니까?
   a) 얄라 공원의 거대한 파도
   b) 대지진
   c) 뿌리 뽑힌 나무들과 뒤집어진 차들
   d) 동물들

2. 야생 동물 관계자들이 왜 매우 놀랐습니까?
   a) 공원에 파도가 밀려와서
   b) 동물들이 이상하게 행동해서
   c) 동물원에 있는 동물들이 은신처로 뛰어가서
   d) 동물들이 한 마리도 사망하지 않아서

3. 본문에서 동물의 육감에 대한 근거로 언급되지 않은 것은 무엇입니까?
   a) 밤에 개들이 수상하게 울부짖습니다.
   b) 새장 안의 새들은 안절부절 못합니다.
   c) 닭들이 알을 낳습니다.
   d) 고양이들이 숨습니다.

4. 다음 중 본문에 대하여 옳은 것은 무엇입니까?
   a) 동물들이 가지고 있을 수 있는 육감은 다가올 위험을 감지하는 것입니다.
   b) 보고에 의하면 동물들은 재앙이 닥치기 전에 정상적인 행동을 보인다고 합니다.
   c) 쓰나미로 인해 많은 동물들이 죽었습니다.
   d) 과학자들은 동물들이 위험이 오기 전에 무엇을 감지하는 지 알아내었습니다.

5. 이 본문에 따르면 오랫동안 동물들에 관해 어떤 생각을 가지고 있습니까?
   a) 동물들은 자연 재앙을 예견할 수 있습니다.
   b) 동물들은 쓰나미를 일으킬 수 있습니다.
   c) 자연 재앙을 막기 위해 쓰일 수 있습니다.
   d) 동물들은 지구의 자기장의 미묘한 진동을 감지할 수 있습니다.

Unit 10 Subjunctive Mood

Comprehension Check

1. (c) 2. (b) 3. (d)

Translation

1. Mr. Daniels가 Brett을 부른 이유는,
   (a) 격려하기 위해서이다.
   (b) 꾸짖기 위해서이다.
   (c) 칭찬하기 위해서이다.
   (d) 무안을 주기 위해서이다.

2. Brett는 Tom을,
   (a) 해고할 것이다.
   (b) 대신할 것이다.
   (c) 승진시킬 것이다.
   (d) 생각나게 할 것이다.

3. 이 대화에서 Brett을 대하는 Mr. Daniels의 태도를 가장 잘 묘사한 것은,
   (a) 존경한다.
   (b) 중요하게 생각한다.
   (c) 높이 평가한다.
   (d) 위의 보기 모두 다 해당한다.

Task 1

1. If I had known you were coming, I would have baked a cake.
2. If I had enough money to buy a house, I would marry her.
3. If Dorothy had had time, she would have written a much more interesting essay.
4. If he had been promoted, his family would have moved to an affluent neighborhood.
5. The flower could have grown well, but I did not water it.

Translation

1. 당신이 온다는 걸 알았더라면 케이크를 구웠을 겁니다.
2. 내게 집 장만 하기에 충분한 돈이 있다면, 그녀와 결혼을 할 겁니다.
3. Dorothy에게 시간이 더 있었더라면, 훨씬 더 재미있는 에세이를 썼을 겁니다.
4. 그가 승진을 했더라면, 그의 식구들이 부유한 동네로 이사를 갔을 겁니다.
5. 물을 주었다면 꽃은 잘 자랐을 텐데, 나는 그 꽃에 물을 주지 않았습니다.

Task 2

1. correct
2. incorrect (If his father dies, what will become of him? / If his father were to die, what would become of him?)
3. incorrect (Should you be interested in this project, send me an email. / If you should be interested in this project, send me an email. / If you are interested in this project, send me an email.)
4. incorrect (If it rains tomorrow, we'll stay at home. / If it should rain tomorrow, we'll stay at home.)
5. correct

Translation

1. Sarah를 보게 되면, 안부를 전해주십시오.
2. 만약 그의 아버지가 돌아가시면, 그는 어떻게 될까요?
3. 이 프로젝트에 관심이 있다면, 나에게 이메일을 보내세요.
4. 만약 내일 비가 오면, 우리는 집에 있을 겁니다.
5. 당신이 남의 물건을 훔친다면, 그것은 큰 잘못입니다.

Task 3

1. I've eaten too much. I wish I had not eaten so much.
2. It's about time the city started recycling.
3. I don't like my brother. He sometimes behaves as if he were my father.
4. Had they preparedbetter, the team would have won the game.
5. The experts insist that the loan be reduced.

Translation

1. 너무 많이 먹었습니다. 그렇게 많이 먹지 말았어야 했습니다.
2. 그 도시는 재활용을 시작할 때가 되었습니다.
3. 나는 내 형이 마음에 들지 않습니다. 그는 때로 마치 아버지인양 행동합니다.
4. 좀 더 잘 준비했더라면, 그 팀은 경기를 이겼을 겁니다.
5. 전문가들은 부채를 줄여야 한다고 주장합니다.

Comprehension Check-up

1. F　　2. F　　3. T

Translation

1. 제임스 본드 캐릭터의 인기는 감소하고 있는 것 같습니다.
2. 제임스 본드 캐릭터는 실제 스파이의 삶에 기초를 두고 있습니다.
3. 제임스 본드와 그를 창조해낸 Ian Fleming은 비슷한 성격을 갖고 있습니다.

Vocabulary Matching

1. b 2. d 3. c 4. a

Translation

1. 독점판매권 – b. 브랜드 이름
2. 참여하다 – d. 참가하다
3. 영감 – c 동기, 영향
5. 냉혹한 – a. 무자비한, 잔인한

Quiz

1. imply 2. infer 3. imply

Translation

1. 이게 내 잘못이라고 생각하지 않길 바랍니다.
2. 당신 자신의 결론을 내려도 괜찮습니다.
3. 난 우리가 친구 이상이라는 의미를 나타낸 것 아닙니다.

Task 4

1. c
2. d
3. c
4. b
5. d

Translation

1. 라켓만 있으면, Robbie가 테니스를 칠 겁니다.
2. 우린 정말로 늦었습니다. 좀 더 일찍 출발했으면 좋았을 겁니다.
3. 돈이 좀 더 많이 있었으면, 벤츠를 샀을 겁니다.
4. 만약 당신이 .여권을 잃어버리면, 큰 일 납니다.
5. 내가 부탁 드렸다면, 이 에세이 써 주셨을까요?

Task 5

1. incorrect (If that coat were not so expensive, I would/could/might buy it.)
2. correct
3. correct
4. incorrect (If I had not been sick, I would have met you yesterday.)
5. incorrect (It's boring to live in the countryside. I wish I lived in a big city.)

Translation

1. 저 코트가 너무 비싸지 않으면 샀을 겁니다.
2. 만약 Bill과마주치면, 그에게 내 사무실에 들리라고 하세요.

3. 선생님께서는 학생들에게 책을 많이 읽으라고 요구하셨습니다.
4. 어제 내가 아프지 않았으면 당신을 만났을 겁니다.
5. 시골에서 사는 것은 지루합니다. 큰 도시에서 살았으면 좋겠습니다.

REVIEW TEST

1. (4) 2. (2) 3. (4) 4. (2) 5. (3)
6. turned 7. Were 8. could 9. changes/ is changed 10. had come

Translation

1. 당신의 도움이 없다면 사업에 실패할 겁니다.
2. 내가 만약 로또에 당첨되면 CUFS 기금에 기부할 텐데요.
3. 당신이 더 주의했더라면 가방을 잃어버리지 않았을 겁니다.
4. 나는 비밀투표로 해야 한다고 제안했습니다.
5. 어렸을 때 악기를 배웠으면 좋았을 텐데요.
6. TV를 끌 시간입니다.
7. 물이 없다면 생물은 존재하지 않을 겁니다.
8. 가족들과 지금 더 많은 시간을 보낸다면 좋을 텐데요.
9. 이용 약관이 바뀐다면 모든 구독자들은 이메일로 통보 받을 것입니다.
10. 파티는 멋졌어요! 당신도 우리와 함께 갔다면 좋은 시간을 보냈을 겁니다.

Supplementary Reading

Q.1

1. c 2. a 3. c 4. b 5. d 6. b

Translation

1. 나에게는 대안이 없습니다.
   (a) 중요하다고 생각하는 것
   (b) 다른 것들보다 중요하게 생각하는 것
   (c) 다른 어떤 것 대신에 선택할 수 있는 것
   (d) 중요하거나 가치 있다고 여겨지지 않는 것

2. 나는 중요한 시험 전에 명상하기를 좋아합니다.
   (a) 주로 조용히, 깊이 생각하다
   (b) 사람이나 그룹의 논쟁을 중재하려고 노력하다
   (c) 병을 치료하는 데 사용되는 약을 처방하다
   (d) 폭력이나 불법적인 일에 사람들을 선동하다

3. 불교 승려들은 검소한 생활을 합니다.
   (a) 여성 정치 그룹의 일원
   (b) 미래에 일어날 일을 예언하는 사람
   (c) 어떤 종교의 남자 성직자
   (d) 다른 사람들을 대신해 의사결정을 내리도록 선택된 자

4. 미니 스커트가 지금 유행입니다..
   (a) 오랫동안 유지되어 왔던 관습이나 믿음
   (b) 단기간 동안 매우 인기 있는 것
   (c) 원리나 종교적 교리
   (d) 청소하거나 보호를 위해 사용하는 것

5. Ann은 불교의 신봉자였습니다.
   (a) 가장 성공적인 사람
   (b) 다른 사람의 행동에 의해 고통 받는 사람
   (c) 회의나 선거에서 투표하는 사람
   (d) 어떤 대상을 숭배하거나 매우 열광적인 사람

6. 우리는 첫 번째 난관을 극복했습니다.
   (a) 해야 할 것을 나중으로 미루다
   (b) 어떤 어려움을 해결하는데 성공하다
   (c) 친구의 집 등에서 하룻밤 외박하다
   (d) 특정한 목표나 효과를 창출하다

Q.2

1. F 2. T 3. F 4. F 5. T 6. F 7. F

Translation

1. 요가는 역도 같은 격한 운동 보다 체중 감량에 더 효과적입니다.
2. 최근 한국에는 요가 센터들이 늘어나고 있습니다.
3. 한국인들에게 요가가 알려진 지 오래되었습니다.
4. 1960년대에 몇몇 불가의 스님들이 요가를 신도들에게 가르치기 시작했습니다.
5. 한국에는 몇몇 무자격 강사들이 헬스 클럽에서 요가를 가르치기도 합니다.
6. 요가를 마스터하려면 적어도 열 달 걸립니다.
7. 원칙적으로 요가는 체중을 감소하는 데 도움을 주고, 자세를 바로 잡아줍니다.

Unit 11

Prepositions

Comprehension Check

1. (a) 2. (c) 3. (b)

Translation

1. 대부분의 대화 내용에서 나타나는 Aaron의 말투를 가장 잘 설명한 것은 무엇입니까?
   (a) 마음이 내키지 않는
   (b) 진심이 담긴
   (c) 분노한
   (d) 따뜻한

2. Brett은 무엇을 하기로 약속했습니까?
   (a) Camille에게 전화하는 것을 그만두기로
   (b) Aaron에게 축하하는 의미로 저녁을 사기로
   (c) Aaron과 Camille 사이에 끼어들지 않기로
   (d) 좋은 사이로 남으면서 우정을 끝내기로

3. Brett이 불화를 끝내려는 이유가 아닌 것은 무엇입니까?
   (a) 그들은 전에 한 번도 싸운 적이 없습니다.
   (b) Camille은 별로 중요하지 않습니다.
   (c) 사랑보다 우정이 더 중요합니다.
   (d) 우정은 오래 지속됩니다.

Task 1

1. I plan to eat lunch at noon.
2. It has been a long time since the last meeting.
3. On a hot day like today, I like to sleep under a big tree.
4. It costs two dollars to drive through the tunnel.
5. I swam across the river to get to the other side.

Translation

1. 나는 정오 에 점심을 먹을 계획입니다.
2. 지난 번 회의 한지가 오래되었습니다.
3. 오늘처럼 더운 날엔 나는 큰 나무 밑에서 자고 싶습니다.
4. 그 터널을 통과하는데 2 달러를 내야 합니다.
5. 나는 반대편에 닿기 위해서 헤엄쳐서 강을 건넜습니다.

Task 2

1. correct
2. incorrect (There is a bridge over the lake.)
3. incorrect (In spite of my good intentions, everything went wrong./ Despite my good intentions, everything went wrong.)
4. correct
5. incorrect (I'm afraid ofbeing left by myself.)

Translation

1. 그는 환경 문제에 관해 강연을 하였습니다.
2. 호수 위에 다리가 하나 있습니다.
3. 나의 좋은 의도와는 다르게 모든 것이 잘못되었습니다.
4. 만약 문제가 생기면, 이 번호로 나에게 연락하세요.
5. 저는 혼자 남겨지는 게 두렵습니다.

Task 3

1. According to Doctor Park, I have to take this medicine for a week.
2. I cried myself to sleep because of a fight with my boyfriend.
3. Due to the storm, the plane could not land on time.
4. This letter was written in ink bymy grandfather.
5. In case of an emergency, use the stairs instead of the elevator.

Translation

1. 박 의사선생님에 의하면 나는 일주일간 이 약을 복용해야 합니다.
2. 나는 남자친구와의 싸움으로 인해 울며 잠들었습니다.
3. 폭풍으로 인하여 비행기는 제 시간에 착륙하지 못했습니다.
4. 이 편지는 나의 할아버지에 의해 잉크로 쓰여졌습니다.
5. 비상시에는 엘리베이터 대신에 층계를 이용하세요.

Comprehension Check-up

1. T 2. F 3. T

Translation

1. 1세대 재미교포 식당은 주로 한국인 지역사회에 음식을 제공하였습니다.
2. 대부분의 현재 재미교포 주방장들은 엄격하고 전통적인 요리방법을 고수하는 경향이 있습니다.
3. 2세대 재미교포들은 새로운 음식의 발상을 개척하고 있습니다.

Vocabulary Matching

1. b 2. c 3. d 4. a

Translation

1. 요리의 – b. 요리와 관련된
2. 기업가 – c. 자영업자
3. 유산 – d. 상속받은 것
4. 고객 – a. 손님 또는 추종자

Quiz

1. insure 2. assure 3. ensure

Translation

1. 귀중한 물건을 선적할 때 손상이나 분실에 대비해 보험을 드는 것이 좋습니다.
2. 이 상황은 적시에 처리될 것이라는 것을 당신에게 확신시키고 싶습니다.
3. 생명보험증권은 당신 아이들의 미래를 보장하는 한 방법입니다.

Task 4

1. (a) 2. (c) 3. (d) 4. (a) 5. (d)

Translation

1. David는 건강상의 문제로 사직했습니다.
2. 런던의 건물들은 뉴욕의 고층건물에 비하면 작습니다.
3. 원하시는 것 마음껏 드세요.
4. 그는 중고 자전거를 좋은 가격에 샀습니다.
5. 그것은 세 개의 침실, 부엌, 그리고 두 개의 거실로 이루어진 이층 짜리 집입니다.

Task 5

1. incorrect (The peach was known as the Persian apple for many years.)
2. incorrect (I'm going overseas during the next vacation.)
3. correct
4. correct
5. incorrect (He is suffering from a soar throat.)

Translation

1. 복숭아는 오랫동안 페르시아의 사과로 알려졌습니다.
2. 나는 다음 방학 동안 해외로 갈 것입니다.
3. Debby는 토요일에 올 것입니다.
4. 일반적으로 사람들은 8살에 학교를 다니기 시작합니다.
5. 그는 목이 부어서 고생하고 있습니다.

REVIEW TEST

1. to 2. on 3. from 4. on 5. to
6. in 7. of 8. in 9. for 10. by

Translation

1. 어린 소년이 엄마 옆에서 걸어 갑니다.
2. 커피잔은 탁자 위에 있습니다.
3. 그는 9시 부터 5시 까지 열심히 일합니다.
4. 아이스크림을 먹고 싶지만 다이어트 중입니다.
5. 그의 성공은 가족 덕분입니다.
6. 우리 조부모님은 시골에 살고 계십니다.
7. 어떤 사람들은 가격과는 상관없이 명품을 선택합니다.
8. 산뜻한 흰색으로 별장을 칠했습니다.
9. 그들은 다음주에 아프리카로 떠날 것입니다.
10. 회의 참석 여부에 관해 목요일까지 저에게 알려 주세요.

Supplementary Reading

Q.1

1. d　　2. a　　3. c　　4. b　　5. a　　6. c

Translation

1. 논쟁의 결말을 지읍시다.
   a) 부분으로서 포함하다
   b) 격리시키다
   c) 들어가는 것을 막다
   d) 결정하거나 최종적으로 정하다

2. 비타민을 과다로 섭취하면 인체에 해로운 영향을 미칠 수 있습니다.
   a) 적당하거나 충분한 것을 지나친 분량
   b) 볼 수 있는 권리
   c) 실행되고 있는 일련의 행동들
   d) 요구량이나 기대치보다 부족한 양

3. 우리의 생명이 위험에 처해있었습니다
   a) 행복
   b) 평화
   c) 위험
   d) 슬픔

4. 제조된 신발은 곧 소매상들에게 보내질 것입니다.
   a) 자세한 정보가 제공된
   b) 특히 기계로 인하여 만들어지거나 가공 처리된 것
   c) 해외로부터 수입된
   d) 하자가 있는 것으로 판명된

5. Jane은 Samantha 대리인으로 일하고 있습니다
   a) 다른 것을 대신하는 사람이나 사물
   b) 직원들을 감시하는 사람

c) 학생들에게 개별적으로 지도하는 사람
d) 모든 결정을 내리는 사람

6. 프리랜서로 번역하는 것은 내 소득에 유용한 보충이 됩니다.
a) 모든 것 중에서 가장 중요한 것
b) 금전을 활용하기 위해 소비된 것
c) 무엇을 완성하기 위해 추가되는 것
d) 잠시 동안 본 직업을 대신하는 것

Q.2

1. b) 2. c) 3. b) 4. a) 5. d)

Translation

1. 윗글의 내용과 맞지 않는 것은 무엇입니까?
a) 한국인 중 20퍼센트 이상이 비타민제나 음료를 복용합니다.
b) 더 많은 비타민을 섭취할수록 뇌 운동이 더 활발해 집니다.
c) 비타민은 수술 후 회복 중인 사람에게 좋습니다.
d) 비타민을 과도하게 섭취하는 것은 건강에 해로울 수 있습니다.

2. 비타민 보충제를 필요로 하지 않는 사람은 누구입니까?
a) 채식주의자들
b) 알레르기가 있는 사람들
c) 영양 섭취를 잘하는 사람들
d) 수술 후 회복 중인 사람들

3. 그들의식이요법에 비타민이 더 필요한 사람에게 의사들은 무엇을 권고합니까?
a) 비타민 음료
b) 과일과 야채
c) 비타민 보충제
d) 통조림이나 냉동식품

4. 밑줄 친 전치사의 쓰임이 맞는 것을 고르시오.
a) 그는 질병에서 회복되고 있습니다.
b) 우리는 버터 대신에 마아가린을 쓸 수 있습니다. (to → for)
c) 환자는 간호가 필요합니다. (over → of)
d) 많은 아시아인들은 쌀을 주식으로 합니다. (in → on)

5. 비문법적인 문장을 고르시오.
a) 그녀를 보자 그는 기뻐서 뛰었습니다.
b) 병을 딴 후 Tom은 음료를 들이켰습니다.
c) 테니스를 치는 동안 Jim은 팔을다쳤습니다.
d) 도로를 뛰어내려가다가 봉투를 떨어뜨렸습니다.
(Running down → While I was running down)

Unit 12 Conjunctions

Comprehension Check

1. (d)　　2. (a)　　3. (d)

Translation

1. 이 대화가 일어나는 동안
   (a) Brett과 Carrie는 저녁식사를 하고 있습니다.
   (b) Brett과 Carrie는 저녁식사를 끝내고 있습니다.
   (c) Brett과 Carrie는 저녁식사 비용을 지불하고 있습니다.
   (d) Brett과 Carrie는 식사 주문을 하려고 기다리고 있습니다.

2. Carrie가 골프를 무척 좋아한다는 사실을 알았을 때 Brett는
   (a) 놀랐습니다
   (b) 불쾌했습니다
   (c) 감동을 받지 않았습니다
   (d) 분노했습니다

3. 다음 중 이 대화를 묘사하는 데 사용되지 않은 것은 무엇입니까?
   (a) 수다
   (b) 잡담
   (c) 시시덕거림
   (d) 말다툼

Task 1

1. College is not only a time of intellectual growth, but also a time when many lifelong friendships are created.
2. Wear your coat, or you'll feel cold.
3. His latest film is both imaginative and provocative.
4. Richard has a lot of money, but he is not happy.
5. I like neither coffee nor tea.

Translation

1. 대학은 지적 성장을 위한 시기일 뿐만 아니라 평생지기 친구를 많이 사귈 수 있는 시기이기도 합니다.
2. 외투를 입어라, 그렇지 않으면 추울 꺼야.
3. 그의 최근 영화는 독창적이고 도발적입니다.
4. Richard는 돈은 많지만 행복하지는 않습니다.
5. 나는 커피도 싫고 차도 싫습니다.

Task 2

1. That she didn't remember my name disappointed me.
2. I don't know whether or not he can come to the party in time.
3. Jane has loved her husband since she first met him.
4. No sooner had he left home than he began to run for school.
5. I'm not sure which she prefers.

Translation

1. 그녀가 내 이름을 기억하지 못해서 나는 실망했습니다.
2. 나는 그가 그 파티에 제시간에 올 수 있을지 모르겠습니다.
3. Jane은 그녀의 남편을 처음 만난 이후로 줄곧 사랑해 왔습니다.
4. 그는 집을 나서자 마자 학교를 향해 뛰어갔습니다.
5. 나는 그녀가 무엇을 선호하는지 확실히 알지 못합니다.

Task 3

1. Young as he is, he is a very responsible man.
2. The rain will stop by the time you get home.
3. Unless you get up early, you will be late for work.
4. He studies hard so that he may pass the examination.
5. Though he was angry, he listened to me patiently.

Translation

1. 비록 어리지만 그는 책임감이 매우 강한 사람입니다.
2. 당신이 집에 도착할 때쯤 비가 멎을 겁입니다.
3. 일찍 일어나지 않으면 직장에 늦을 겁니다.
4. 그는 시험에 합격하기 위해 열심히 공부합니다.
5. 비록 그가 화는 났지만, 내 말을 참을성 있게 들었습니다.

Comprehension Check-up

1. F 2. T 3. T

Translation

1. 체 게바라는 온화한 사람으로 기억됩니다.
2. 많은 사회운동에서는 아직도 체 게바라의 이미지를 채택합니다.
3. Alberto Diaz Guitierrez가 찍은 에네스토 "체" 게바라의 사진은 1967년 발간된 이후 전세계적으로 인기를 얻고 있습니다.

Vocabulary Matching

1. c 2. b 3. d 4. a

Translation

1. 빈곤 – c. 돈이 거의 없거나 아예 없음
2. 혁명가 – b. 급진적 변화를 지지하는 사람
3. 이상주의 – d. 숭고한 신념 추구
4. 역경 – a. 불운, 고생

Quiz

1. lie 2. Lay 3. lie 4. lay

Translation

1. 나는 날씨 좋은 밤에 땅위에 누워 별을 쳐다보는 걸 좋아합니다.
2. 그것을 여기 내려 놓으십시오.
3. 모로코와 알제리는 리비아 바로 서쪽에 놓여 있습니다.
4. 다음달 주주총회 때우리는 다가올 회계연도를 위한 전략을 보여줄 계획입니다.

Task 4

1. (d) 2. (b) 3. (d) 4. (a) 5. (c)

Translation

1. 그 디자인사의 컨설턴트들은 고객이 창문 장식을 원할 때 커튼을 사용할지 블라인드를 사용할지 고객의 결정을 도와줄 수 있습니다.
2. 가장 최근의 인사 문제들을 토의할 수 있도록 모든 부서 책임자 회의가 주선되었습니다.
3. 그 대학을 졸업하자마자, 그녀는 직업을 구할 것입니다.
4. Port Stephen은 평온한 휴양지인 동시에 전 세계의 호화품들을 면세로 살 수 있는 경제의 중심지입니다.
5. Peter는 사고를 당해서 병원에 입원해 있습니다.

Task 5

1. All employees should neither arrive after 9 A.M. nor leave before 5 P.M., except under special circumstances.
2. It was raining cats and dogs when they arrived at the foot of the mountain.
3. Although/Though/Even though I have spoken on the phone with Mr. Kang several times, I have never met him in person.
4. Some research suggests that there is a link between the body's calcium balance and tooth decay.
5. Despite the relatively low salary, George took the job as a junior reporter on the local newspaper so that he could gain valuable job experience.

Translation

1. 모든 회사 직원들은 특별한 상황이 아니면 오전 9시 이후에 출근하거나 오후 5시 이전에 퇴근해서도 안 됩니다.
2. 그들이 산 기슭에 도착했을 때, 비가 억수로 쏟아지고 있었습니다.
3. 나는 전화로 강씨와 여러 번 통화를 했지만 그를 직접 만난 적은 없습니다.
4. 어떤 연구 결과에 따르면, 신체의 칼슘 균형과 충치 사이에 관련이 있다고 합니다.

5. 비교적 낮은 급료에도 불구하고 George는 귀중한 업무경력을 쌓기 위해 지방 신문사의 수습 기자 일을 선택했습니다.

REVIEW TEST

1. (2)　2. (2)　3. (1)　4. (4)　5. (4)
6. since　7. Though / Although / Even though　8. until
9. that　10. whether/if

Translation

1. 내 초대장을 받으면 그가 기뻐할지 기뻐하지 않을지에 대해 저도 모르겠습니다.
2. 급여가 합당하지 않았기 때문에 그는 자신의 직위에서 사임했습니다.
3. 자신을 믿으세요. 그러면 성공할 수 있습니다.
4. 글을 잘 쓰면 학교 생활에서뿐만 아니라 나중에 사회에 나가서도 유용할 것입니다.
5. 일찍 일어나지 않으면 학교에 지각할 겁니다.
6. 당신이 떠난 이후로 전 당신을 그리워해 왔습니다.
7. 열대야였지만 그들은 곤히 잠들었습니다.
8. 건강의 소중함은 잃어버린 후에야 비로소 알게 됩니다.
9. 방안에 연기가 자욱해서 기침을 멈출 수가 없었습니다.
10. 우리가 그 프로젝트를 맡을 건지 안 맡을 건지의 결정은 당신에게 달려 있습니다.

Supplementary Reading

Q.1

1. c　2. a　3. d　4. d　5. b
6. a　7. c　8. b　9. c

Translation

1. 우리는 변화를 가속화 시킬 필요가 있습니다.
   (a) 더 위대하고 중요한 것으로 보이도록 하다
   (b) 긴 침묵 후에 소리 내다
   (c) 예상보다 더 빠르거나 이르게 하다
   (d) 강조하거나 더욱 눈에 띄게 만들다

2. 정부는 경제 활성화 시키기 위해 조치를 취해야만 합니다.
   (a) 어떤 것을 늘리거나 향상시키다
   (b) 매우 자랑스럽게 이야기하다
   (c) 매우 부정적인 방식으로 생각하다
   (d) 말하고 있는 사람을 방해하다

3. John은 병에 있는 상표를 보았습니다.
   (a) 저울의 눈금, 예를 들어 양이나 질
   (b) 각을 재는 데 사용되는 단위

(c) 사람들이 어떻게 행동해야 하는지에 관한 규정
(d) 정보를 주기 위해 상품에 붙어 있는 참조

4. 사람들은 유기농 과일과 야채를 사고 싶어합니다.
(a) 신체의 부분, 예를 들어 심장이나 폐
(b) 조직의 구조에 관한
(c) 너무 작아서 현미경 없이는 미관으로 볼 수 없는 동물이나 식물
(d) 인공 화학 물질을 사용하지 않고 생산한

5. 우리는 아시아의 다른 나라들로부터 대부분의 농산물을 얻었습니다.
(a) 제품이 생산되는 속도나 정도
(b) 팔기 위해서 재배된 신선한 과일이나 야채
(c) 생산 과정
(d) 연극이나 영화를 만들어내는 사람

6. 그는 부유층과 권력자들이 그들의 지위를 어떻게 악용하고 있는 지 정부에게 보여주었습니다.
(a) 어떤 것을 잘못 사용하다
(b) 약물, 특히 불법적인 것을 주기적으로 복용하다
(c) 자원을 개발하고 사용하다
(d) 사적인 이유로 사용하다

7. Jerry 는 여자친구와 헤어진 후 활기를 잃었습니다.
(a) 건강을 유지하기 위해 필요한 것
(b) 매우 중요한 것
(c) 활력과 열정
(d) 살아있음을 보여주는 체온과 같은 것들

8. 어머니는 계절 상품을 구입하십니다
(a) 많은 경험을 가지고 있는
(b) 특정한 계절을 대표하거나, 계절에 맞는
(c) 음식에 첨가된 소금, 후추나 다른 양념
(d) 새롭게 소개된

9. 그녀는 힘의 균형을 유지하기 위해 노력합니다.
(a) 재산의 총액, 예를 들어 주택의 가치
(b) 뭔가를 하는 데 곤란함을 겪는 상태
(c) 서로 다른 것들이 동등하게 존재하는 상태
(d) 사람들이 전혀 말을 하지 않는 상황

Q.2

1. b 2. b 3. d 4. c 5. a

Translation

1. 윗글의 내용과 일치하는 것은 무엇입니까?
a) 웰빙 생활 양식은 한 사회 안에서 성공에 초점을 둡니다.
b) 더 건강하고 평안한 생활 양식을 추구합니다.
c) 웰빙이란 건강식품을 먹고, 요가 강습을 듣고, 피부 관리를 받는 것입니다.
d) 모든 사람들은 일정한 웰빙 생활 양식을 따라야 합니다.

2. 사람들이 더 많은 시간을 가지도록 하고 웰빙 생활 양식을 촉진시킨 것은 무엇입니까?
   a) 관계 산업
   b) 주 5일 근무제
   c) 대중 매체
   d) 잡지

3. 윗글에서 "웰빙" 상표를 달고 판매되는 것이 아닌 것은 무엇입니까?
   a) 헬스 클럽 회원권
   b) 화장품
   c) 인스턴트 라면과 버거
   d) 가구

4. 다음 중 어느 것이 웰빙의 본질입니까?
   a) 건강에 좋은 음식을 먹는 것
   b) 요가 강습을 받거나 피부관리를 받는 것
   c) 신체와 정신의 균형을 유지하는 것
   d) 고정된 라이프스타일을 추구하는 것

5. 문법에 맞지 않은 문장을 고르시오.
   a) 모든 학생이 새롭게 지어진 도서관에서 공부하고 싶어합니다.
      (every students want every student wants)
   b) 사람들은 연령, 성별, 소득에 상관없이 자신의 의견을 표현할 수 있는 권리를 가집니다.
   c) 이 기계는 복사를 하는 데 사용됩니다.
   d) 각 도시마다 특이성이 있습니다.

Unit 13 Agreement and Narration

Comprehension Check

1. (a)　　2. (c)　　3. (c)

Translation

1. Carrie가 친구와 논쟁을 하게 된원인은 무엇이었습니까?
   (a) 그녀의 친구가 부탁을 했지만 Carrie는 이에 응하지 않았습니다.
   (b) Carrie는 친구의 부탁을 들어줬지만 친구가 고마워하지 않았습니다.
   (c) 그들 둘다 Brett에게 관심이 있었습니다.
   (d) Carrie가 친구 머리에 대해 언급하며 친구를 불쾌하게 만들었습니다.

2. 다음 중Camille과 싸우기 전에 Brett과 Carrie가 나누었던 주제가 아닌 것은 무엇입니까?
   (a) 식당
   (b) 교통수단 선택
   (c) 날씨
   (d) 다툼

3. 왜 Camille은 그렇게 갑작스럽게 유럽에서 돌아왔습니까?
   (a) Brett과 재결합하기 위해서
   (b) Aaron과 재결합하기 위해서
   (c) 그녀의 계획이 이루어지지 않아서
   (d) 성형수술을 하기 위해서

Task 1

1. is　　2. are　　3. are　　4. was　　5. is

Translation

1. 필리핀은 동남아에 있는 나라입니다.
2. 이 곳에 있는 비디오의 반은 코미디 또는 액션입니다.
3. 위원회의 모든 위원들이 참석하였습니다.
4. 화학과 물리를 공부하는 것은 나에게 쉬운 일이 아니었습니다.
5. 빵과 버터는 내가 좋아하는 아침식사입니다.

Task 2

1. incorrect (It will make me sad if you betray me.)
2. correct
3. incorrect (He asked when I had seen her last.)

4. correct
5. incorrect (My textbook says that Russia became a global power under Peter the Great.)

Translation

1. 당신이 나를 배신한다면 나는 슬플 것입니다.
2. 그들은 그가 집에 갔다는 것을 알게 되었습니다.
3. 그는 내가 그녀를 마지막으로 본 것이 언제인지 물었습니다.
4. 그 선생님께서는 거북이가 100년 넘게 살 수 있다고 우리에게 말하셨습니다.
5. 내 교과서에 따르면 러시아는 피터 대제 통치하에서 세계적으로 강력한 국가가 되었습니다.

Task 3

1. Jane asked where Tom had bought that shirt.
2. He said to me, "Why did you call me?" / He asked me, "Why did you call me?"
3. Peter said that he would not forget what his mom had said to him.
4. My roommate said to me, "Don't make a sound."
5. She asked me if I had been to the Opera House in Australia.

Translation

1. Jane은Tom에게 그 셔츠를 어디서 샀는지 물어봤습니다.
2. 그는 나에게 "왜 나에게 전화를 했어요?"라고 물었습니다.
3. Peter는 그의 어머니가 그에게 말한 것을 절대 잊지 않겠다고 말했습니다.
4. 내 룸메이트는 나에게 "조용히 해줘."라고 말했습니다.
5. 그녀는 나에게 호주의 오페라 하우스에 가본 적이 있는지 물었습니다.

Task 4

1. d) 2. a) 3. a) 4. d) 5. c)

Translation

1. 나는 어제 태국에 사는 친구에게 전화했는데 그는 그곳에 비가 오고 있다고 했습니다.
2. 당신에게 컴퓨터를 끄라고 했잖아요, 안 그랬나요?
3. 자유의 여신상은 1886년 이래로 미국 이민자, 방문객, 관광객들을 환영해 왔는데 이것은 원래 프랑스 국민이 보낸 선물이었습니다.
4. 누군가가 나에게 고속도로에서 사고가 있었다고 했습니다.
5. 그녀는 내게 그를 어디에서 찾을 수 있는 지 물었습니다.

Task 5

1. (b) will → would
2. (c) are → is
3. (d) it → they
4. (c) has → had
5. (c) are → is

Translation

1. 그녀는 해야 할 숙제가 있었기 때문에 집에 있겠다고 했습니다.
2. 유기농장의 가장 중요한 것 중 하나가 위생입니다.
3. 많은 사람들이 그 해답을 찾으려고 노력하였으나, 모두 실패하였습니다.
4. 그 남자는 그가 거기에 있었으면 다쳤을 것이라고 말하였습니다.
5. 태평양 연안의 각 국가들은 가뭄으로 전력 부족을 예상하고 있습니다.

Review 8-13

Unit 8

1. a	2. d	3. a	4. c	5. d
6. b	7. b	8. a	9. d	10. c

1. Translation

그 도시는 쓰레기를 줄이는 계획의 일부인 재활용 정책을 실시했습니다.
해설: 선행사가 사물인 경우에는 관계 대명사 which나 that을 씁니다.

2. Translation

우리는 다음 주에 별 일 없습니다. 당신이 어느 요일에 오든지 환영입니다.
해설: 복합 관계 대명사 형용사적 용법으로 '어느 요일이든지'라는 뜻으로 whichever가 day를 수식하고 있습니다.

3. Translation

이 음식은 온도 변화가 최소인 건조한 곳에서 보관해야 합니다.
해설: 선행사가 장소일 때 관계부사 where (=in which)를 씁니다. where는 관계사절에서 부사의 역할을 합니다.

4. Translation

그건 내가 의미한 바가 아닙니다.
해설: what은 선행사를 포함한 관계대명사로, the thing which의 뜻을 갖습니다. 이 문장에서 관계대명사 what은 명사절을 이끌며 이 명사절은 전체 문장에서 보어의 역할을 하고 있습니다.

5. Translation

그녀는 대부분의 학생들이 조언을 얻으려고 하는 사람입니다.
해설: 목적격 관계대명사 whom이 정답입니다. 이 문장에서 관계대명사는 관계사절에서 전치사(to)의 목적어 역할을 하고 있습니다. 이 문장에서는 whom대신에 who가 올 수도 있습니다.

6. Translation

"그 계획은 완벽해." 라고 Mrs. Smith가 말했고, 그녀의 회사에서는 그 계획의 초안을 마련했습니다.
해설: 뒤에 company라는 명사가 있으므로 소유격 관계대명사 whose가 정답입니다.

7. Translation

그 영화는 토대로 했던 책과 완전히 다릅니다.

해설: 관계대명사가 전치사의 목적어로 쓰일 때는 전치사를 문장의 맨 끝에 두거나 관계대명사 바로 앞에 둘 수 있습니다.

8. Translation

수집품이 진부해지기 시작한 그 박물관에서는 새 작품을 구하기로 결정했습니다.

해설: 관계대명사의 비제한적(계속적) 용법으로, 뒤에 collection이라는 명사가 있으므로 관계대명사 소유격인 whose가 정답입니다.

9. Translation

플랜테인은 때때로 바나나와 혼동되는데, 열대지역 사람들이 많이 먹습니다.

해설: 관계대명사의 비제한적(계속적) 용법으로, 관계대명사 주격 which가 정답입니다.

10. Translation

난 내 친구와 약속한 날을 완전히 잊어버렸습니다.

해설: 관계부사 when(= on which)은 선행사가 시간(the day)일 때 씁니다.

Unit 9

1. c	2. c	3.b	4.b	5. b
6. a	7. d	8. c	9. a	10. d

1. Translation

지역 선수권 대회에서 우리 팀이 우승했습니다.

해설: 수동태 문장은 be + p.p. 형태로 능동태 문장에서 동사가 won과거이므로, 수동태도 be 동사의 과거형인 was를 쓴 후 과거분사를 쓰면 됩니다.

2. Translation

산들이 눈으로 덮여 있습니다.

해설: 능동태 문장이 현재형이므로 수동태 문장은 「be + p.p. 」 에서 be동사의 현재형인 are를 쓴 후 과거분사를 쓰면 됩니다.

3. Translation

그는 그의 여행에 관해 책을 한 권 쓰고 있습니다

해설: 능동태 문장이 현재 진행형이므로 수동태도 현재 진행 수동태로 바꾸어 주면 됩니다. 진행형 수동태는 「be being + p.p.」 형태로 만들어집니다.

4. Translation

누가 그 새로운 장치를 발명했습니까?

해설: 능동태의 주어인 who를 수동태로 바꾸면 목적격이 되므로 'by+ 목적격'인 by whom으로 쓰면 됩니다.

5. Translation
사람들은 중국 정부가 석유를 몰래 축적해 놓고 있다고 믿습니다.
해설: 목적어가 that절인 문장의 수동태의 경우, 1) 가주어 it을 쓰거나, 2) that절 속의 주어를 수동태 주어로 합니다. 이때 that 절은 주어가 없으므로 구(to 부정사)로 고칩니다. that 절을 목적어로 취하는 동사에는 say, know, believe, expect, think, hope, feel, fear, consider, find, intend, suppose 등이 있습니다.
이 문장에서는 능동태에서 is hoarding이 진행형이므로 to be -ing형태로 쓰였습니다.

6. Translation
물은 수소와 산소로 구성되어 있습니다.
해설: by 이외에도 with, in, at, to, of 등 다른 전치사가 수동태에 사용되어 하나의 숙어처럼 쓰입니다. be composed of (~로 구성되다)

7. Translation
우리는 초대받지 않았기 때문에 파티에 가지 않았습니다.
해설: 초대를 받지 않은 것이므로 수동태로 씁니다. 시제가 과거이므로 「were +not+ p.p.」형태로 쓰면 됩니다.

8. Translation
나는 그에게 그의 아버지가 병원에 실려갔다고 말했습니다.
해설: 완료형 수동태는 「have/had been + p.p.」 형태입니다.

9. Translation
그 회의는 오늘 오후에 열릴 겁니다.
해설: 조동사 will이 들어가 있는 문장의 수동태는 「will be + p.p.」 형태입니다.

10. Translation
Jim의 일기는 형사에게 보여졌습니다.
해설: 완료형 수동태는 「have/had been + p.p.」 형태입니다.

Unit 10

1. d	2. a	3. a	4. c	5. a
6. b	7. d	8. d	9. b	10. b

1. Translation
내가 몇 센티미터만 더 컸다면 농구부에서 제명당하지 않았을 겁니다.
해설: 가정법 과거 완료 구문입니다. 「If + 주어+ had +동사의 p.p., 주어+ would/should/could/might + have + p.p.」 형태로 표현합니다. 이 문장은 if절에서 if가 생략되고, 동사 + 주어로 도치된 것입니다.

2. Translation
난 내가 키도 더 크고, 더 날씬하고, 더 잘 생겼으면 하고 소망합니다.
해설: 'I wish + 가정법 과거'는 바라는 시점에서, 현실과 반대의 상황을 가정하여 이루어질 가능성 없는 소망을 표현합니다.

3. Translation

당신이 6월에 런던행 표를 산다면 7월에 가는 것보다 더 저렴할 것입니다.

해설: If절에 were to가 쓰이면 미래에 실현하기 어려운 것을 나타냅니다. 즉, '그럴 리는 없겠지만, 혹시라도 ~한다면' 이라는 뜻입니다. 주절에는 will/would/should/may/might + 동사원형이 옵니다.

4. Translation

사람들이 좀 더 빨리 흡연의 위험성에 대해 알았더라면 많은 목숨을 구할 수 있었을 겁니다.

해설: 가정법 과거완료로 과거의 사실과 반대되는 상황을 가정하거나, 과거에 있었던 일을 부정하거나, 또는 없었던 일에 대한 유감 혹은 소망을 나타냅니다. 「If + 주어+ had + p.p., 주어+ would/should/could/might + have + p.p.」 형태로 쓰입니다.

5. Translation

30일 간의 체험기간 동안 구독을 취소하시면 모든 금액이 환불될 겁니다.

해설: 가정법 미래는 앞으로 일어날 가능성이 희박한 일을 나타낼 때 쓰입니다. 「If+주어+should/were to/happen to+동사원형, 주어+will/ would/should/could/might/may/must+동사원형」의 형태로 나타냅니다.

6. Translation

교수님께서는 우리가 영문법을 공부하는데 더 많은 시간을 투자하도록 충고하셨습니다.

해설: 제안, 요구의 동사, order, command, recommend 등의 다음에 오는 종속절에서는 (should) 동사원형이 옵니다.

7. Translation

내가 당신이라면 그만두기 전에 두 번 생각해 볼 겁니다.

해설: 가정법 과거 문장입니다.

8. Translation

당신이 지도를 가져오는 걸 기억했더라면 우리는 지금 길을 잃지 않을 겁니다.

해설: if 가 생략된 도치 문장으로, 과거에 일어난 사건이 현재까지 영향을 미칠 때 가정법 과거완료와 가정법 과거의 혼합가정구문을 사용합니다. 「If+ 주어+ had+ p.p., 주어+would/should/could/might+동사원형」 형태로 쓰입니다.

9. Translation

사장님이 내일 도착하지 않으면 회의는 취소될 겁니다.

해설: 직설법의 조건문입니다. if절에서 현재형 동사가 쓰이고, 실현가능성이 있는 조건을 나타냅니다.

10. Translation

잠 잘 시간입니다.

해설: It's time + 가정법 과거 구문은 '~할 시간이다, (마땅히 ~할 때가 되었는데, 안하고 있을 때) 이제 ~하여야지' 란 의미입니다.

Unit 11

1. c	2. b	3. d	4. b	5. c
6. c	7. a	8. d	9. b	10. a

1. Translation

바리스타는 대개 고객들이 잔돈을 넣도록 카운터 위에 단지를 올려 놓습니다.

해설: on: '~(위)에' 라는 뜻으로 표면에 접촉된 상태를 나타냅니다.

2. Translation

그녀는 그녀의 라이벌이 올해의 미인 선발대회에서 우승하는 모습을 부러운 눈길로 지켜보았습니다.

해설: with는 '~을 가지고, ~으로'라는 뜻입니다. with envy는 '몹시 부러운 눈길로, 질투심을 가지고'라는 뜻입니다.

3. Translation

당신이 떠난 이후로 난 줄곧 외로웠습니다.

해설: since는 '~이래로' 라는 뜻으로 전치사와 접속사로 모두 쓰입니다. 주절에 완료형이 자주 오지만, 현재형이나 과거형이 올 수도 있습니다.

4. Translation

그런 종류의 일은 영화에서만 발생합니다.

해설: '영화 안에서만'이라는 의미이므로 in이 적절합니다.

5. Translation

나는 90일 정도 안에 부자가 되는 방법에 대한 책을 읽고 있습니다.

해설: 주제: about은 '~에 관하여'라는 뜻입니다.

6. Translation

그 영화의 결말은 꽤 놀라웠습니다.

해설: at the end of는'~의 끝에'라는 뜻입니다.

7. Translation

어제 시청 앞에서 시위를 한 사람들 중에는 몇몇의 유명인사도 있었습니다.

해설: among은 '셋 이상의 사이에' 라는 뜻입니다. 그러나 구어체에서는 셋 이상의 경우에도 확연히 구분할 수 있는 것에는 between을 쓰고, 집단이나 무리를 가리킬 때는 among을 씁니다.

8. Translation

난 그 두 개 사이에서 결정하는 데 어려움을 겪고 있습니다.

해설: between는 '둘 사이'라는 뜻입니다. 따라서 둘을 뜻하는 복수형, 또는 둘을 연결하는 and가 있는 목적어가 뒤따릅니다

9. Translation

한라산의 높이는 해발 1,950m 입니다.

해설: above는 '(전체적으로, 먼 거리) ~보다 위쪽에, ~을 넘는'이라는 뜻입니다.

10. Translation

그들은 몇 년 동안 평화롭게 함께 살았습니다.

해설: for는 '~동안'이라는 뜻으로, 시간의 길이를 나타내고, 숫자가 포함된 기간에 자주 사용됩니다.

Unit 12

1. a	2. b	3. c	4. b.	5. d
6. c	7. d	8. a	9. c	10. d

1. Translation
나는 전체를 다 읽어볼 시간은 없지만 훑어 보고 중요한 세부사항만 골라 내겠습니다.
해설: 앞뒤의 내용이 반대되는 것을 연결하는 대등 접속사 but 이 정답입니다.

2. Translation
지금 교육에 투자하십시오, 그러면 당신의 노력은 후에 보상받을 것입니다.
해설: '명령문 + and'는 '~해라, 그러면...'의 뜻입니다.

3. Translation
그는 집을 나서자마자 학교를 향해 달리기 시작했습니다.
해설: 'no sooner ~ than~'은 '~하자마자 ~하다'의 뜻입니다.

4. Translation
서두르세요, 그렇지 않으면 비행기를 놓칠 겁니다.
해설: '명령문 + or'는 '~해라, 그렇지 않으면...'의 뜻입니다.

5. Translation
나는 침술이 정말로 효과가 있다고 생각하는지 아닌지를 의사 선생님한테 물어볼 겁니다.
해설: whether는 '~인지 아닌지'의 뜻으로 명사절을 이끕니다.

6. Translation
지진이 발생했을 때 나는 집에서 아침 식사를 준비 중이었습니다.
해설: 시간을 나타내는 접속사 when 은 '~할 때'의 뜻입니다.

7. Translation
장사가 나아지지 않으면 우리가 가게를 닫아야 할 것 같아서 걱정입니다.
해설: unless는 조건을 나타내는 접속사로 '~하지 않는다면'의 뜻입니다.

8. Translation
이 게임에는 두 명의 중요한 라이벌이 포함되어 있기 때문에 게임은 면밀히 관찰되고 있습니다.
해설: because는 '~때문에'라는 뜻으로 원인을 나타냅니다.

9. Translation
그녀가 내 이름을 기억하지 못했다는 사실이 나를 실망시켰습니다.
해설: 접속사 that 은 명사절을 이끌어 문장에서 주어, 목적어, 보어 자리에 올 수 있습니다.

10. Translation
신문은 세계에서 발생하는 사건들에 대한 통찰력을 제공할 뿐만 아니라 어휘력을 향상시킬 수 있는 훌륭한 방법이기도 합니다.
해설: 'not only A but also B'는 'A 뿐만 아니라 B도'의 의미입니다.

Unit 13

1. c	2. c	3. b	4. d	5. b
6. b	7. a	8. b	9. c	10. d

1. Translation
요즘 모든 사람들이 신분 도용에 대해 걱정합니다.
해설: 단수동사가 쓰이는 주어로는 everything, everybody, somebody, anything, each, nothing, no one 등이 있습니다.

2. Translation
그녀는 나에게 내가 무엇을 하고 있었는지 물었습니다.
해설: 의문사가 접속사 역할을 하여 '의문사+주어+동사'의 간접의문문이 목적보어로 쓰인 것입니다.

3. Translation
천천히 그러나 꾸준히 해야 경주에서 이깁니다.
해설: 주어가 A and B 형식의 단일개념일 경우는 단수동시를 씁니다.

4. Translation
100만 달러는 대부분의 사람들이 평생 번 것보다 더 많은 금액입니다.
해설: 시간, 거리, 금액이 단일 개념으로 쓰이면, 뒤에 단수동사가 옵니다.
예) Sixty dollars a week is a small sum to him.
(일주일에 60달러는 그에게 적은 액수입니다.)

5. Translation
그녀는 만약 그녀가 새라면 바다를 건너서 날아갈 수 있을 거라고 말했습니다.
해설: 가정법 구문은 전달 동사의 시제에 관계없이 씁니다. 목적어가 가정법 과거 문장으로 「if+주어+동사의 과거형, 주어+would/should/could/might +동사의 원형」의 형식입니다.

6. Translation
이 상황에서는 확실한 우승자와 패배자가 없습니다.
해설: There 구문에서는 그 다음에 오는 명사에 따라 동사의 수에 일치됩니다.

7. Translation
내 룸메이트가 나에게 시끄럽게 하지 말아 달라고 말했습니다.
해설: 부정 명령문일 때는 'not+ to 부정사'를 씁니다.

8. Translation
간호학을 공부하는 학생의 수가 줄곧 증가하고 있습니다.
해설: 현재완료진행형으로 'have/has been ~ing' 형식입니다.

9. Translation
우리 고객의 대부분은 북아메리카에 본거지를 두고 있습니다.
해설: most of~는 뒤에 오는 명사에 따라 단수 취급을 하기도 하고, 복수 취급을 하기도 합니다. 이 문장에서는 clients가 복수이므로 복수동사를 써야 합니다.

10. Translation

그녀는 그 날 성형외과 의사를 만나기로 한 약속이 있었다고 내게 고백했습니다.
해설: 주절과 that절의 시제 일치를 나타내는 것으로, 주절의 동사가 과거인 경우에는 종속절의 동사는 과거나 과거완료가 되어야 합니다.

Supplementary Reading

Q.1

1. aesthetic — f) appreciating art and beauty
2. ashamed — d) feeling disgraceful or foolish
3. associate — a) join or connect in mind
4. define — e) state the meaning of
5. embrace — g) accept an idea
6. paradigm — c) example or model
7. stereotype — b) oversimplified concepts or image

Translation

1. 심미적 – 예술이나 아름다움의 진가를 아는
2. 수치스럽게 생각하는 – 수치스럽거나 바보 같이 느끼는
3. 연상시키다 – 마음으로 연결하다
4. 정의하다 – 뜻을 말하다
5. 받아들이다 – 생각을 받아들이다
6. 범례 – 실례 또는 모범
7. 고정 관념 – 지나치게 단순화된 개념이나 이미지

Q.2

1. b) 2. a) 3. b) 4. b) 5. a)

Translation

1. Metrosexual이란 단어는 누구에 의해 또는 무엇에 의하여 만들어졌습니까?
   a) 책과 미디어
   b) 작가

2. Metrosexual은 무엇입니까?
   a) 옷을 멋지게 잘 입는 남자
   b) 도시에 사는 남자

3. Metrosexuality는 한국 사회에 어떠한 영향을 끼치고 있습니까?
   b) 남자들은 정장을 입고 타이를 매어야 편안하게 느낍니다.
   c) 외모는 성공하는데 있어 중요한 요소입니다.

4. '지금 당장 넥타이를 잘라라' 의 작가는 뭐라고 말하였습니까?
   a) 한국 남자들은 자신을 자유롭게 표현합니다.
   b) Metrosexuality는 옛 틀을 깰 수 있는 기회를 제공합니다.

5. 다음 중 한국에서 유교의 영향을 나타내는 것은 무엇입니까?
   a) 남자들은 다른 사람과 다르게 보이는 것을 두려워합니다.
   b) 남자들은 옷과 액세서리를 고르는 데 많은 시간을 투자합니다.

에센스 영문법

개정판 1쇄 발행 2010년 3월 30일
개정판 2쇄 발행 2013년 2월 28일

지 은 이 ▪ 성 은 경
발 행 인 ▪ 박 철
발 행 처 ▪ 한국외국어대학교 출판부
130-791 서울시 동대문구 이문로 107
전화 (02)2173-2495~7
팩스 (02)2173-3363
홈페이지 http://press.hufs.ac.kr
전자우편 press@hufs.ac.kr
출판등록 ▪ 제6-6호(1969. 4. 30)
디자인 · 편집 ▪ (주)이환디앤비 (02)2254-4301
인쇄 · 제본 ▪ (주)동화인쇄공사 02)719-7181

ISBN 978-89-7464-406-2 18740 정가 16,000원(mp3 CD포함)

* 잘못된 책은 교환하여 드립니다.